COLLOQUIA MATHEMATICA
SOCIETATIS JÁNOS BOLYAI, 12.

PROGRESS IN OPERATIONS RESEARCH

Vol. I.

Edited by

A. PRÉKOPA

 NORTH HOLLAND PUBLISHING COMPANY
AMSTERDAM-LONDON

Budapest, Hungary, 1976

ISBN *North-Holland:* 0 7204 2836 X
ISBN *Bolyai:* 963 8021 13 6 Vol. I-II
ISBN *Bolyai:* 963 8021 14 4 Vol. I

Joint edition published by

JÁNOS BOLYAI MATHEMATICAL SOCIETY

and

NORTH-HOLLAND PUBLISHING COMPANY

Amsterdam-London

Printed in Hungary

ÁFÉSZ, VÁC

Sokszorosító üzeme

PREFACE

Operations Research is one of the most developing fields of Applied Mathematics. Many important problems are solved by OR methodology. Though these problems contain local specialities, most of them occur in practically all countries. This is one of the reasons why international meetings are so important in this field.

Until now there is no Operations Research Society in Hungary but there are other scientific societies which give place for this science, one of them is the Bolyai János Mathematical Society. This, together with the von Neumann Society for Computer Science and the Hungarian Economic Society organize OR meetings in Hungary starting from 1963. Since 1970 these have been annual meetings. In this series of the Eger Conference was the sixth. Out of these two were international. The first one was held in Budapest, 1963 and the second one was the 1974 Eger Conference, the Proceedings of which is this volume. Both were organized by the Bolyai Society. On the occasion of the Eger Conference IFORS was officially represented by G. Kreweras, professor of Operations Research at the University of Paris. We were happy to be able to welcome a large number of specialists from 11 countries.

No one can deny that it is exceptionally hard and beautiful to let theory and practice live together. It seems to the organizers that the Eger Conference realized this objective and the papers submitted and accepted for publication represent both features of OR. The theoretical papers contain new results in various fields of mathematical programming: linear, non-linear, integer, stochastic programming and network flows while the papers dealing with application describe solution of economic, water resources, urban, forestry, chemical engineering and maintenance problems.

As it is customary in the Colloquia Mathematica series of the Bolyai János Mathematical Society the papers are arranged according to alphabetic ordering of the names of the authors.

The Editor

CONTENTS
Volume I

Volume II

August 26. Monday
Afternoon

OPENING SESSION in the Theatre of Eger 3.00 − 4.15 p.m.
Welcoming remarks
The life and work of J. Farkas

PARALLEL SESSIONS A, B, C 4.30 − 6.00 p.m.

Session A
Chairman: H. Tuy

W. Oettli: The theorem of alternative, the key theorem and the vec-
tor-maximum problem
K. Daniel: A constructive approach to some results of Miller and
Veinott
G. Donath − K.H. Elster: Generalizations of unimodal functions

Session B
Chairman: W. Ahrens

G. Kreweras: Game theoretical aspects of survival theory
S. Benedikt: A new optimization criterion for games against nature

Session C
Chairman: G. Mitra

Y. Seppälä: A stochastic multigoal investment model for public sector
J. Buga − W. Grabowski: Coordination plans in two-level planning
system by means of goal programming
Gy. Bánkövi − J. Veliczky − M. Ziermann: Prediction of macroeconomic systems under consideration of delayed variables

August 27. Tuesday
Morning

PARALLEL SESSIONS A, C, D 9.00 – 12.00 a.m.

Session A
Chairman: F. Glover

A. Prékopa: On multistage stochastic programming
J. Dupačová: Minimax stochastic programs with non-convex, non-separable penalty functions
L.V. Kantorovich: Some dynamic models of economic progress
S. Halász: On a stochastic programming problem with random coefficients
K. Tammer: About the solution of distribution problems of stochastic programming

Session C
Chairman: J. Buga

Z. Czerwiński: A mathematical model of optimum price system in the centrally planned economy
A. Móritz: Medium-term planning model for commercial enterprises
Sz. Koós – J. Szép: Modelling of the public administration

PAUSE

M. Hegedüs: Equilibrium systems
P. Futó: Computer aided management of industrial research

Session D
Chairman: J. Goffin

J. Wallenius — S. Zionts: An interactive programming method for
solving the multiple criteria problem

L.B. Kovács — M. Rupp: Graph partitioning for matrix inversion by
integer programming

G.R. Jahanshahlou — G. Mitra: Two algorithms for finding all the
vertices of a convex polyhedron

D. Richter: An algorithm for solving mixed integer convex programming problems

I. Dékány: Numerical solution of a stochastic control problem derived
from Bensoussan — Lions. Inventory model

Afternoon

PARALLEL SESSIONS A, B, C, D 3.00 — 6.00 p.m.

Session A
Chairman: W. Oettli

F. Glover — D. Klingman: Finding minimum spanning trees with a
fixed number of links and node

F. Glover — D. Klingman: Real word applications of network related
problems and break-throughs in solving them efficiently

I. Dragan: A network flow model for solving a cooperative game

PAUSE

W. Domschke: Two new algorithms for minimal cost flow problems
and their applications

G. Dehnert: A branch-and-bound method for solving fixed charge
network flow problems

A. Bakó: The solution of the multiterminal minimal path problem in
a network with gains

Session B
Chairman: G. Kreweras

T. Annaiev – T. Gergely – I. Yezhov: On the stationary regime of a mass service with variable channel

T. Gergely – T.L. Török: A stochastic process to describe the virtual waiting time in a queueing system

G. Gosztony: A stochastic service system with repeated calls and set up times in one direction

J. Pintér: An optimal solution of a control problem of stochastic objective function, obtained by simulation

L.N. Kiss: Waiting lines in the stochastic network of a car service

Session C
Chairman: Y. Seppälä

M. Sääksjärvi: Application of linear programming overtime to optimize the row wood procurement programs

G. Hegedüs: Calculation of the planning incides of the building industry

L. Domokos – G. Veress: Chemical industrial production planning by dynamic programming

A. Chulek – M. Galbavy – J. Gazda – K. Mosoni – G. Veress: Enterprise input-output model for the computation of production plan variables of a chemical combine

Z. Farkas – J. Gazda – G. Veress: Allocation of the profit of the enterprise

Session D
Chairman: J. Wessels

P.M. Camerini — L. Fratta — F. Maffioli: Relaxation methods improved by modified gradient techniques

J.L. Goffin: On convergence rates of subgradient optimization methods

C. Lamarechal: Non differentiable minimization by descent methods

PAUSE

J. Mayer: Some computational experiences with the reduced gradient method

C. Richter: Cuttingplane methods for convex optimization

August 28. Wendesday
Excursion

August 29. Thursday
Morning

Session A
Chairman: J. Guddat

P. Lindberg: On local minima in nonlinear optimization in integers

L.B. Kovács: A complex enumeration algorithm for solving pure integer linear programming problems

PAUSE

V.A. Gorelik: The method of penalty functions in minimax problems

F. Forgó: Some transformations of integer programming

Session B
Chairman: A. Heppes

J.E. Beyer – O.B.G. Madsen: A simulation model for analysing the effects of different waste water treatment plans

A. Salamin: Optimization of dam controlling with a given stochastic forecast

PAUSE

L. Dávid – F. Szidarovszky: Dynamic model for long-term water resources development
J. Varga: On a growth model of water economy
L. Dávid – J. Mócsi – Mrs. P. Nagy: A water passing model for the Tiszalök irrigation system in bounded state

Session C
Chairman: J.B. Ljubimov

Gy. Erdősi – P.L. Timár: Some questions of the modelling by the research and development institutes from the point of view of system engineering
Á. Kovács: On the normative behaviour of the firm in the Hungarian profit system

PAUSE

A.J. Radzievsky: Dantzig – Wolfe algorithm and centralization – decentralization problem in the economics control.
K. Kelemen – A. Vári: Some methodological problems of simulation in connection with a model of the oil industry
W. Welfe: On a class of econometric industrial models

Session D
Chairman: G.Sh. Rubinstein

J.A.E.E. van Nunen: Successive approximation methods for discounted Markov decision process

J. Wessels: A principle for generating successive approximation methods

O.H. Vaarmann: About the methods of successive approximation by pseudoinverse operators

PAUSE

A. Sacharin: Some questions on the control of processes with discrete components

Gy. Gyimesi – O. Papp: The solution of the transportation problem under several optimum criteria

C. Saguez: Integer programming applied to optimal control

Afternoon

PARALLEL SESSION A, C, D 3.00 – 6.00 p.m.

Session A
Chairman: P. Lindberg

H. Tuy: On necessary conditions for extremal problems

J. Guddat: Stability in convex quadratic programming

PAUSE

L. Gerencsér: An application of OR decomposition in nonlinear programming

J. Stahl: On a linear programming decomposition procedure

Session C
Chairman: K. Daniel

   L.F. Gelders: Solving an overall production planning problem in a
         simple job-shop
   S. Povilaitis – L. Zeöld: Computer technical aspects of an optimal
         control in economic modelling
   A. Heppes – G. Lugosi: Scheduling for the minimization of setup
         time in case of alternative machine choice

PAUSE

   A.P. Cherenkov: On some models of the resources allocation with
         saturation
   J.B. Ljubimov: A job-shop scheduling problem

   K. Jakob: Application of a matrix generator program for production
         planning of independent and integrated companies

Session D
Chairman: P.M. Camerini

   A. Orden: Computational investigation and analysis of probabilistic
         parameters of simplex method convergence
   L. Király: Deductive information systems
   Gy. Sonnevend: On optimization of numerical algorithms
   J. Fichefet: GPSTEM: An interactive multiobjective optimization
         method

Morning

PARALLEL SESSION A, C 9.00 – 12.00 a.m.

Session A
Chairman: A. Orden

M. Kovács: A modification of conjugate gradient method by the aid
of the maximum principle for discrete optimal control
G.Sh. Rubinstein: Characteristics of saturation of the class of convex
functions

PAUSE

A.B. Yadykin: An algorithm for dynamic linear programming using
modified Lagrange functions
L. Mihályffy: The method of characteristic matrices in linear programming

Session C
Chairman: A.J. Radzievski

Gy. Janik – I. Papanek – N. Remsei – G.E. Veress: Problems arising
in the application of mathematical models for agricultural
machinery maintenance control
I. Szarvas: Application of reliability when fixing the time of
maintenance

COLLOQUIA MATHEMATICA SOCIETATIS JÁNOS BOLYAI

12. PROGRESS IN OPERATIONS RESEARCH, EGER (HUNGARY), 1974.

NUMERICAL EXPERIENCE WITH HEURISTIC RULES IN SPECIFIC BINARY OPTIMIZATION ALGORITHMS

W. AHRENS

SUMMARY

Concerning the planning of regional waste water disposal systems there is a trend from the traditional comparison of alternatives to the formulation and solution of mathematical optimization problems.

The problem definition shows nonlinear and, in general, a concave structure of the problem which has the format of the Transshipment Problem.

It is well-known that concave optimization problems are more difficult to solve than the convex ones because local minima can be generated at the vertices of the constraint polyhedron.

Branch-and-Bound methods are commonly used as solution algorithms. Another possibility is the transformation of the concave problem containing continuous variables into a linear optimization problem with binary variables. This is possible if there are no capacity constraints. In this case there is no branching of network flows (single assignment property) and every continuous variable belongs to a finite set. This set of discrete numbers allows the discretization i.e. the transformation into the binary form.

The numerical experience with binary algorithms (algorithm of Land and Doig, additive algorithm of Balas, permanent-additive algorithm of Brauer, the Filter-method of Balas, the Pseudo-Boolean Programming of Hammer and Rudeanu) indicate for the given problem structure and the great number of variables resulting from the transformation that problems of a practical size cannot be solved.

Hence the Balas-algorithm will be adjusted to the given special problem structure. The numerous heuristic rules, in particular the augmentation rules, will be compared with respect to the computing time and suggestions concerning their application will be made.

INTRODUCTION

In the planning process involving capital intensive investments of public utilities for water supply, waste water disposal, solid waste management systems analysis techniques are increasingly utilized. This trend for thorough analysis is caused by factors like rising costs and environmental concern. Despite of the progress made in applying operations research methods bottlenecks of numerical solutions appear with regard to computation time and storage requirements. The problem of regional planning which will be discussed in this paper concerns the cost minimization of waste water treatment plants and long distance canal connections, and their optimal allocation.

A mathematical model as a Transshipment Problem can be constructed given a set E of waste water generating communities, a set V of optional plant locations, a set W of canal lines. The variables are the capacities of the treatment plants and of the canals. Economies of scale for construction and OMR costs are assumed

(1) $c(x) = \alpha x^{\beta}$

$0 \leqslant \beta \leqslant 1$

$\alpha \geqslant 0$.

A nonlinear treatment is avoided by the transformation to a binary optimization problem though the binary variables require specific consideration.

1. MODELS FOR THE REGIONALIZATION PROBLEM

The following optimization problem

$$(2) \qquad \Phi(x_i, x_{ij}) = \sum_{i \in V} \alpha_i x_i^{\beta_i} + \sum_{(i,j) \in W} \alpha_{ij} x_{ij}^{\beta_{ij}} \rightarrow \min$$

$$(3) \qquad x_i + \sum_{(i,j) \in W} x_{ij} - \sum_{(j,i) \in W} x_{ji} = q_i \qquad (i = 1(1)m, \ j = 1(1)m)$$
$$\qquad i \in V \qquad \qquad \qquad \qquad i \in E$$

$$(4) \qquad \begin{aligned} & x_i \geqslant 0, \quad i \in V \\ & x_{ij} \geqslant 0, \quad (i, j) \in W \end{aligned}$$

$$(5) \qquad \begin{aligned} & \alpha_i, \alpha_{ij} \geqslant 0 \\ & 0 \leqslant \beta_i, \ \beta_{ij} \leqslant 1 \end{aligned} \qquad (i = 1(1)m, j = 1(1)m)$$

is called the regionalization problem which is characterized as a concave, uncapacitated transshipment problem.

It means

E = set of pollutants, flows q_i, (sources)

V = set of treatment facilities (sinks)

W = set of transport lines

X_i = unknown flow quantity treated at node i

X_{ij} = unknown flow between node i and node j

m = number of nodes.

Theorem 1. *Let $\Phi(X)$ be a concave objective function of the regionalization problem which is defined over the closed convex set (3)-(4),* *then the global minimum of* $\Phi(X)$ *occurs at one or more local minima that are feasible basic solutions of* (3)-(4).

Theorem 2. *Every feasible basic solution of the regionalization problem represents a set of trees of the initial graph.*

Optimization algorithms to solve problem (2)-(5) have to take these theorems into consideration. Gradient methods for instance are not helpful, they would terminate at a local optimum.

An explicit enumeration of the basic solutions as the algorithm of M a n a s and N e d o m a is applicable only for small problems. (See computation time in Figure 1).

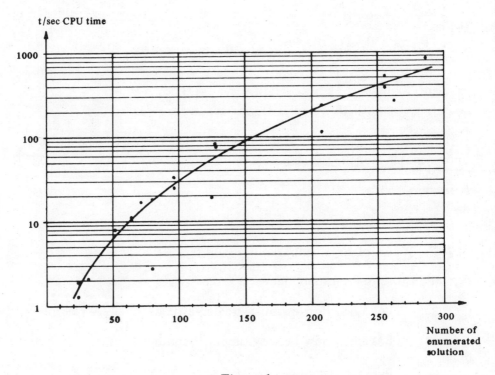

Figure 1

Computation times of explicit enumeration by Manas and Nedoma dependent on the number of feasible basic solutions

An estimation of the computation time given the problem size is not possible. Upper and lower bounds for the number of solutions are not binding i.e. the theoretical number of maximum and minimum solutions do not apply (see Saaty [62], Bartels [8]). Only in the case of *complete* regionalization problems the number of solutions ξ is

$$(6) \qquad \xi(m) = \sum_{i=1}^{m-1} \left\{ \prod_{j=0}^{i-2} (m-j) \right\} (m-i+1)^{m-1} + 1 \ .$$

In practice, complete regionalization problems hardly exist. Hence, formula (6) is a too large upper bound.

Implicit enumeration of local minima is another possibility for the solution of concave optimization problems. The respective procedures use different cost functions, but are similar, e.g. the algorithms by Murty [57] for the fixed cost problem, by Cabot and Francis [19] for the quadratic form and by Deininger and Su [25] for the regionalization problem. Experience shows that for practical date the enumeration limiting bounding rule is hardly active. Hence, almost a total enumeration is required. Algorithms that use the analogous network flow formulation prove to be more effective by amploying algorithms from graph theory to solve relaxed embedded subproblems. Theorems 1 and 2 describe implicitly a property which is called the Single Assignment Property, i.e. there is no flow splitting in a feasible basic solution (tree property).

With this property, to any variable x_i resp. x_{ij} of the regionalization problem is a finite, discrete set of values attached to allow the transformation to a linear binary optimization problem.

The sets of values of the variables x_i resp. x_{ij} are given as follows

$$(7) \qquad \begin{aligned} x_i &\in Q_i = \{Q_{i_1}, Q_{i_2}, \ldots, Q_{i_{k_i}}\} \\ x_{ij} &\in Q_{ij} = \{Q_{ij_1}, Q_{ij_2}, \ldots, Q_{ij_{k_{ij}}}\} \ . \end{aligned}$$

The binary regionalization problem follows from the transformation

$$(8) \quad x_i = \sum_{l=1}^{k_i} Q_{i_l} x_{i_l}^b$$

$$x_{ij} = \sum_{l=1}^{k_{ij}} Q_{ij_l} x_{ij_l}^b$$

to

$$(9) \quad \Phi(x_{i_l}^b, x_{ij_l}^b) = \sum_{i \in V} \sum_{l=1}^{k_i} c_{i_l} x_{i_l}^b + \sum_{(i,j) \in W} \sum_{l=1}^{k_{ij}} c_{ij_l} x_{ij_l}^b \to \min$$

$$(10) \quad \sum_{\substack{l=1 \\ i \in V}}^{k_i} Q_{i_l} x_{i_l}^b + \sum_{(i,j) \in W} \sum_{l=1}^{k_{ij}} Q_{ij_l} x_{ij_l}^b - \sum_{(j,i) \in W} \sum_{l=1}^{k_{ji}} Q_{ji_l} x_{ji_l}^b = q_i \quad i \in E$$

$$(11) \quad x_{i_l}^b, x_{ij_l}^b \in \{0, 1\}$$

$$(12) \quad c_{i_l} = \Phi_i(Q_{i_l}), \quad c_{ij_l} = \Phi_{ij}(Q_{ij_l}) .$$

An approximation results from (9)-(11) in the case, that not all combinations of flows are contained in (7), that is

$$(13) \quad Q_i' \subseteq Q_i, \quad Q_{ij}' \subseteq Q_{ij} .$$

Another possibility to generate an approximation is given by the discretization of a set of flows that are not necessarily the real combinations of waste water flows.

This leads to a mixed integer programming problem, because the continuity is destroyed.

With the sets of values

$$(14) \quad x_i \notin Q_i'' = \{Q_{i_1}'', Q_{i_2}'', \ldots, Q_{i k_i''}''\}$$

$$x_{ij} \notin Q_{ij}'' = \{Q_{ij_1}'', Q_{ij_2}'', \ldots, Q_{ij k_{ij}''}''\}$$

the problem is given as follows

$$(15) \quad \Phi(x_i, x_{ij}, x^b_{i_l}, x^b_{ij_l}) = \sum_{i \in V} \sum_{l=1}^{k''_i} c''_{i_l} x^b_{i_l} + \sum_{(i,j) \in W} \sum_{l=1}^{k''_{ij}} c''_{ij_l} x^b_{ij_l} \to \min$$

$$(16) \quad x_i + \sum_{(i,j) \in W} x_{ij} - \sum_{(j,i) \in W} x_{ji} \qquad\qquad = q_i \atop i \in E$$

$$(17) \quad x_i \qquad\qquad - \sum_{l=1}^{k''_i} Q''_{i_l} x^b_{i_l} \qquad\qquad \leqslant 0, \ i \in V$$

$$(18) \qquad\qquad x_{ij} \qquad\qquad - \sum_{l=1}^{k''_{ij}} Q''_{ij_l} x^b_{ij_l} \leqslant 0, \ (i,j) \in W$$

$$(19) \quad \begin{aligned} &x_i, x_{ij} \geqslant 0 \\ &x^b_{i_l}, x^b_{ij_l} \in \{0, 1\} \end{aligned}$$

$$(20) \quad c''_{i_l} = \Phi_i(Q''_{i_l}), \quad c''_{ij_l} = \Phi_{ij}(Q''_{ij_l}) \ .$$

In the formulation of a binary or mixed binary model care has to be taken that no capacity constraint is introduced which does not observe the discretization.

Finally, an algorithm based on Balas' additive algorithm (see B a l a s [5]) is described to solve the problems (9)-(11) or (14).

2. AN ALGORITHM TO SOLVE THE BINARY REGIONALIZATION PROBLEM

In a single form the problem (9)-(11) is as follows

$$(21) \quad \Phi(x_j) = \sum_{j=1}^{n} c_j x_j \to \min$$

$$(22) \qquad \sum_{j=1}^{n} a_{ij} x_j = b_i, \quad i = 1(1)m$$

$$(23) \quad x_j \in \{0, 1\}, \ c_j \geqslant 0, \quad j = 1(1)n \ .$$

The c_j are generated by the previous concave functions.

To understand the following outline of the algorithm see especially
G e o f f r i o n [30].

The following sets of indices are introduced

(a) $N = \{1, \ldots, n\}$ set of variables

(b) $M = \{1, \ldots, m\}$ set of constraints

(c) S^k partial solution set of fixed variables at iteration stage k

(d) F^k set of variables which are free at iteration stage k

(e) $P_i = \{j \mid j \in N, \ a_{ij} > 0\}$ set of variables with positive coefficient at line i, $\forall i \in M$

(f) $Q_i = \{j \mid j \in N, \ a_{ij} < 0\}$ set of variables with negative coefficient at line i, $\forall i \in M$.

Outline of the algorithm

$$\S 1: \ k \leftarrow 0, \ S^0 \leftarrow \phi, \ F^0 \leftarrow N, \ \Phi^P = 1 + \sum_{j \in N} c_j$$

$\S 2$: Is S^k to fathom?

(i) thereby, that the *best* completion of S^k is feasible?

yes: S^k is fathomed, go to $\S 4$

no: go to (ii)

(ii) by applying the *Infeasibility Test?*

yes: all free variables with negative/positive coefficients together are not able to remove infeasibility of the partial solution S^k

S^k is fathomed, go to $\S 5$

no: go to (iii)

(iii) by applying the *Optimality Test?*

yes: if possible a feasible completion of S^k is not better than the incubent

S^k is fathomed, go to §5

no: S^k is not fathomed, go to §3.

§3: Augmentation of the partial solution S^k

§4: Store or print out the current solution. The best computed solution gives a new incubent with a value Φ^p

Go to §5

§5: All indices of S^k negative, i.e. all subproblems with $x_j = 0$ and $x_j = 1$ examined?

yes: ready

Last solution stored resp. printed is the optimal one

If no solution found, the problem is inconsistent

Terminate

no: make last positive element of S^k negative, forget all indices on the right hand side of this element

$k \Leftarrow k + 1$, go to §2

End of the algorithm.

2.1. *The Infeasibility Test*

A constraint (19) is not satisfied, if $z_i \neq 0$ for any a $i \in M$ is valid, with

$$(24) \qquad z_i = b_i - \sum_{\substack{j \in S^k \\ j > 0}} a_{ij} .$$

It follows

A partial solution S^k is called fathomed, if

(i) for any a $i \in M$ with $z_i < 0$ is valid

(25) $$z_i - \sum_{j \in F^k \cap Q_i} a_{ij} < 0$$

(ii) for any a $i \subset M$ with $z_i < 0$ is valid

(26) $$z_i - \sum_{j \in F^k \cap P_i} a_{ij} > 0 .$$

2.2. *The Optimality Test*

The Optimality Test is also enlarged to a two-side test

A partial solution S^k is called fathomed, if

(i) for any a $i \in M$ with $z_i < 0$ is valid

(27) $$T_i^k = \{j \mid j \in F^k \cap Q_i, \ c_j < \Phi^p - \Phi(S^k)\} = \phi$$

(ii) for any a $i \in M$ with $z_i > 0$ is valid

(28) $$T_i^k = \{j \mid j \in F^k \cap P_i, \ c_j < \Phi^p - \Phi(S^k)\} = \phi .$$

2.3. *Augmentation rules*

Augmentation rules give answers about variables to select. They are only heuristic rules. No mathematical criterion about computation time is given.

(a) Augmentation rule No. 1

For every not satisfied row i a variable $j^*(i)$, element of T_i^k, is selected in a manner which minimizes infeasibility

(29) $$S^{k+1} = S^k \cup \left\{ \bigcup_{i \in M} j^*(i) \right\}$$

with $j^*(i)$ from

(30) $$d_{j^*(i)} = \min_{j(i) \in T_i^k} \{d_{j(i)}\}, \quad i \in M$$

and

(31) $d_{j(i)} = \sum_{i \in M} \text{abs}(z_i - a_{ij}),\quad j \in T_i^k,\ z_i \neq 0,\ i \in M.$

(b) (b) Augmentation rule No. 2.

For every not satisfied row i a variable $j^*(i)$ is selected in a manner, which minimizes infeasibility of all binary variables assigned to transportation variables and which minimizes costs of all binary variables assigned to treatment variables

(32) $S^{k-1} = S^k \cup \left\{ \bigcup_{i \in M} j^*(i) \right\}$

with $j^*(i)$ from

(33) $j^*(i) = \begin{cases} T_{i_1}^k \mid T_{i_1}^k \leqslant n_1, & z_i \neq 0,\ i \in M \\ j^*(i) \mid d_{j^*(i)} = \min\limits_{j(i) \in T_i^k} \{d_{j(i)}\}, & i \in M \end{cases}$

$d_{j(i)} = \sum_{i \in M} \text{abs}(z_i - a_{ij}),\quad j \in T_i^k,\ j > n_1,\ z_i \neq 0,\ i \in M.$

(c) Augmentation rule No. 3.

For every not satisfied row i a variable $j^*(i)$ is selected in a manner, which minimizes the costs of all variables and infeasibility simultaneous.

(34) $S^{k+1} = S^k \cup \left\{ \bigcup_{i \in M} j^*(i) \right\}$

with $j^*(i)$ from

(35) $d_{j^*(i)} = \min\limits_{j(i) \in T_i^k} \{d_{j(i)} c_{j(i)}\}$

(36) $d_{j(i)} = \sum_{i \in M} \text{abs}(z_i - a_{ij}),\quad j \in T_i^k,\ z_i \neq 0,\ i \in M.$

3. NUMERICAL EXPERIENCE

To use general computation time as a quality criterion and a tool for comparison is difficult. They depend in part upon the hardware facilities as well as on the operating system. Also, it seems impossible to define a single parameter to describe the computation time for this given problem.

Figure 2 displays the computation time with respect to the number of variables for the algorithm presented in this paper.

This picture is only partially true since the computation time differs substantially for the same problem size and various objective functions. The

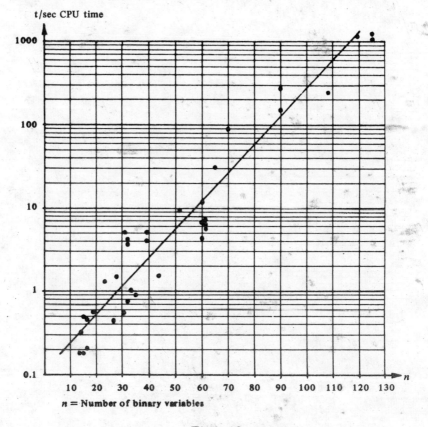

Figure 2

Computation time in sec versus the number of binary variables
(UNIVAC 1108, Computation Center, University of Karlsruhe)

choice of the augmentation rule also influences the computation time. To specify the objective function a number was introduced which ranks optimal solutions according to their degree of regionalization. This is based on Theorem 2 which states that any solution represents one or more spanning trees, components.

If $\tilde{m} \leqslant m$ is the number of sources and p the number of components let the degree of regionalization be

$$(37) \qquad \eta = \frac{\tilde{m} - p}{\tilde{m} - 1} .$$

Figure 3 shows the variation of computation time for the same problem of 8 constraints and 70 binary variables and various degrees of regionalization.

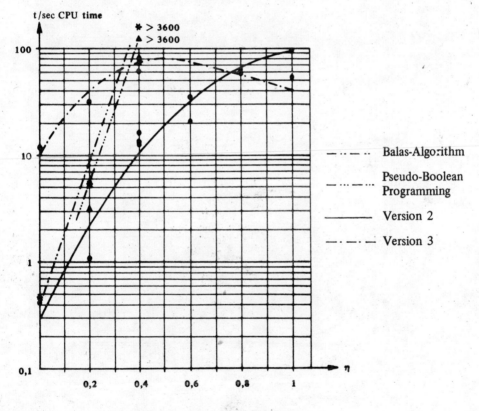

Figure 3

Computation time versus the degree of regionalization

Nevertheless, the following experiment shows that the description using the degree of regionalization is not sufficiently exact. For the same problem of 70 variables and degree of regionalization η but for different coefficients c_j, the computation time is now expressed with respect to a parameter of standard deviation

$$(3.8) \qquad \sigma = \left\{ \frac{1}{n-1} \sum_{j=1}^{n} (c_{j.} - \bar{c}) \right\}^{\frac{1}{2}}$$

$$(3.9) \qquad \bar{c} = \frac{1}{n} \sum_{j=1}^{n} c_j .$$

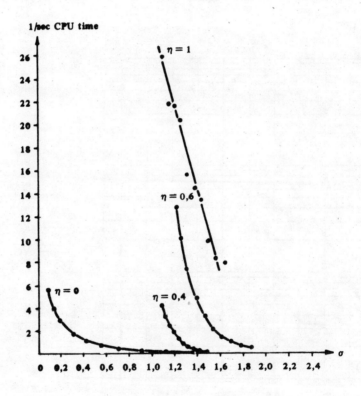

Figure 4

Computation time versus standard deviation

These explanations show that general declarations about computation times are not very helpful if there is no further information about parameters especially about the influence of the objective function.

4. EXAMPLES

First a simple example is given to show the transformation and the enumeration steps. A second example shows the application of the technique to Greater Abidjan.

Given the following regionalization problem

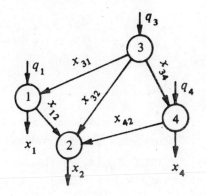

Figure 5

Graph of a simple example

It follows

$$E = \{1, 3, 4\}$$
$$V = \{1, 2, 4\}$$
$$Z = \phi$$
$$W = \{(1, 2), (3, 1), (3, 2), (4, 2), (3, 4)\} .$$

The constraints are

$$x_1 \quad\;\; - x_{31} + x_{12} \qquad\qquad\qquad\quad = q_1$$

$$x_2 \;\; + x_{31} - x_{12} - x_{32} - x_{42} \qquad\quad = 0$$

$$+ x_{32} \qquad\quad + x_{34} = q_3$$

$$x_4 \qquad\qquad\qquad\quad + x_{42} - x_{34} = q_4$$

$$x_{ij} \geqslant 0, \quad (i,j) \in W$$

$$x_i \geqslant 0, \quad i \in V.$$

The objective function is

$$\Phi(x) = \alpha_1 x_1^{\beta_1} + \alpha_2 x_2^{\beta_2} + \alpha_4 x_4^{\beta_4} + \alpha_{31} x_{31}^{\beta_{31}} + \alpha_{12} x_{12}^{\beta_{12}} +$$

$$+ \alpha_{32} x_{32}^{\beta_{32}} + \alpha_{42} x_{42}^{\beta_{42}} + \alpha_{34} x_{34}^{x_{34}} \to \min.$$

With $q_1 = q_3 = q_4 = 1 (\mathrm{m}^3/\mathrm{sec})$ the sets of values of the variables are

variables x_j resp. x_{ij}	sets of values k_i, k_{ij}	Q_i, Q_{ij}
x_1	2	1, 2
x_2	3	1, 2, 3
x_4	2	1, 2
x_{31}	1	1
x_{12}	2	1, 2
x_{32}	1	1
x_{42}	2	1, 2
x_{34}	1	1

Table 1

Sets of values of the variables x_j resp. x_{ij}

$$\rightarrow n = \sum_i k_i + \sum k_{ij} = 14.$$

The matrix of the binary constraints is

$$A = \begin{pmatrix} 1 & 2 & 0 & 0 & 0 & 0 & 0 & -1 & 1 & 2 & 0 & 0 & 0 & 0 \\ 0 & 0 & 1 & 2 & 3 & 0 & 0 & 0 & -1 & -2 & -1 & -1 & -2 & 0 \\ 0 & 0 & 0 & 0 & 0 & 0 & 0 & 1 & 0 & 0 & 1 & 0 & 0 & 1 \\ 0 & 0 & 0 & 0 & 0 & 1 & 2 & 0 & 0 & 0 & 0 & 1 & 2 & -1 \end{pmatrix}.$$

The optimization algorithm requires the following sets of numbers

$$N = \{1, 2, \ldots, 14\}, \quad M = \{1, 2, 3, 4\} \quad n_1 = 7$$

$$P_1 = \{1, 2, 9, 10\} \qquad Q_1 = \{8\}$$
$$P_2 = \{3, 4, 5\} \qquad Q_2 = \{9, 10, 11, 12, 13\}$$
$$P_3 = \{8, 11, 14\} \qquad Q_3 = \phi$$
$$P_4 = \{6, 7, 12, 13\} \qquad Q_4 = \{14\}.$$

With cost coefficients c_j Table 2 shows the enumeration steps by applying augmentation rule No.2.

$$c_j = (1; 1.5; 0.5; 1; 1.2; 1; 1.2; 0.5; 0.7; 1; 0.6; 1; 1.3; 0.7).$$

Another realistic example is given by a study concerning the economic feasibility of the urban drainage and sewage system of the city of Abidjan — Ivory Coast.*

Figure 6 shows the map of Abidjan and a graph of possible treatment plants and possible sewer lines.

The following figures (Fig. 7, 8, 9) show an abstract graph like Figure 5, the partitioning of the network into four parts by restrictive conditions (exclusive decomposition) and the separation of each of the four parts into four stages (dynamic decomposition) to allow dynamic programming.

---

*In cooperation with Dr. G. Holfelder, Freiburg (GER) and SCET INTERNATIONAL, Paris (FRA), two consulting engeneers.

Figure 8 and 9 show solutions of the given problem with respect to certain assumption.

The whole problem was solved in 28 minutes on a UNIVAC 1108.

4 × 14 example
enumeration steps

k	S^k	$\Phi(S^k)$	Z	T_1	T_2	T_3	T_4	Φ^P	S^P
0	φ	0.0	1, 0, 1, 1	1, 2, 9, 10	—	8, 11, 14	6, 7, 12, 13	8	—
1	1, 8, 6	2.5	1, 0, 0, 0	φ!					
2	1, 8, − 6	1.5	1, 0, 0, 1	φ!					
3	1, − 8	1	0, 0, 1, 1	—	3, 4, 5	11, 14	6, 7, 12, 13	3.1	1, 11, 6, 3
4	1, − 8, 11, 6	2.6	0, 1, 0, 0	—					
5	1, − 8, 11, 6, 3	3.1	0, 0, 0, 0						
6	1, − 8, 11, 6, − 3	2.6	0, 1, 0, 0	—	3, 4, 5	—	7, 12, 13		
7	1, − 8, 11, − 6	1.6	0, 1, 0, 1	—	φ!				
8	1, − 8, 11, − 6, 3, 7	3.3⁺	—						
9	1, − 8, 11, − 6, 3, − 7	2.1	0, 0, 0, 1	—	4, 5	—	7, 12, 13		
10	1, − 8, 11, − 6, − 3	1.6	0, 1, 0, 1						
11	1, − 8, 11, − 6, − 3, 4, 7	3.8⁺	—						
12	1, − 8, 11, − 6, − 3, 4, − 7	2.6	0, 0, 0, 1	—	φ!	—	φ!		
13	1, − 8, 11, − 6, − 3, − 4	1.6	0, 1, 0, 1	—	5	—	7, 12, 13		
14	1, − 8, 11, − 6, − 3, − 4, 5, 7	4.0⁺	—						
15	1, − 8, 11, − 6, − 3, − 4, 5, − 7	2.8	0, − 2, 0, 1	—	φ!	—			
16	1, − 8, 11, − 6, − 3, − 4, − 5	1.6	0, 1, 0, 1	—	φ!	—			
17	1, − 8, − 11	1.0	0, 0, 1, 1	—	—	14	6, 7, 12, 13		
18	1, − 8, − 11, 14, 6	2.7	0, 0, 0, 1	—					
19	1, − 8, − 11, 14, − 6	1.7	0, 0, 0, 2	φ!	—	—	7, 12, 13		
20	1, − 8, − 11, 14, − 6, 7	2.9	0, 0, 0, 0	9, 10	—	—	φ!	2.9	1, 14, 7 *
21	1, − 8, − 11, 14, − 6, − 7	1.7	0, 0, 0, 2	φ!	—	φ!	12 ■		
22	1, − 8, − 11, − 14	1.0	0, 0, 1, 1	—	—	8, 11, 14	6, 7, 12, 13		
23	1	0.0	1, 0, 1, 1	2, 9, 10	—	—	φ!		
24	1, 2, 8, 6	3.0⁺	—						
25	1, 2, 8, − 6	2.0	0, 0, 0, 1	φ!	—	—			
26	1, 2, − 8	1.5	− 1, 0, 1, 1	9, 10		8, 11, 14	6, 7, 12, 13		
27	1, − 2	0.0	1, 0, 1, 1	φ!	—				
28	1, − 2, 9, 8, 6	2.2	1, 1, 0, 0	φ!					
29	1, − 2, 9, 8, − 6	1.2	1, 1, 0, 1	φ!	—	11, 14	6, 7, 12, 13		
30	1, − 2, 9, − 8	0.7	0, 1, 1, 1	—	3, 4, 5				

Table 2. Enumeration steps of the given example

Step	Partial solution	T_1				
31	$-1,-2,9,-8,3,11,6$	2.8	0,1,0,0	—	φ!		
32	$-1,-2,9,-8,3,11,-6$	1.8	0,1,0,1	—	φ!		
33	$-1,-2,9,-8,3,-11$	1.2	0,0,1,1	—	—	14	6,7,12,13
34	$-1,-2,9,-8,3,-11,14,6$	2.9+	0,0,0,2	—	—	—	
35	$-1,-2,9,-8,3,-11,14,-6$	1.9	0,0,1,1	—	4,5	—	12 ■
36	$-1,-2,9,-8,3,-11,14,-14$	1.2	0,1,1,1	—	—	—	
37	$-1,-2,9,-8,-3$	0.7	—	—	—	—	
38	$-1,-2,9,-8,-3,4,11,6$	3.3+	0,0,0,1	—	—	φ! / 11,14	6,7,12,13
39	$-1,-2,9,-8,-3,4,11,-6$	2.3	0,-1,1,1	—	10,12	—	φ!
40	$-1,-2,9,-8,-3,4,-11$	1.7	—	—	—	14	
41	$-1,-2,9,-8,-3,4,-11,12,14,6$	4.4+	0,0,1,0	—	—	—	
42	$-1,-2,9,-8,-3,4,-11,12,14,-6$	3.4+	0,-1,1,1	—	—	—	
43	$-1,-2,9,-8,-3,4,-11,12,-14$	2.7	0,1,1,1	—	—	φ!	
44	$-1,-2,9,-8,-3,-4$	1.7	—	—	φ!	—	
45	$-1,-2,9,-8,-3,-4,5,11,6$	0.7	0,-1,0,1	—	5	11,14	6,7,12,13
46	$-1,-2,9,-8,-3,-4,5,11,-6$	3.5+	0,-2,1,1	—	—	—	
47	$-1,-2,9,-8,-3,-4,5,-11$	2.5	0,1,1,1	—	φ!	—	
48	$-1,-2,9,-8,-3,-4,-5$	1.9	1,0,1,1	—	φ!	—	
49	$-1,-2,-9$	0.7	0,2,0,0	—	φ!	—	
50	$-1,-2,-9,10,8,6$	0.0	0,2,0,1	10	—	8,11,14	6,7,12,13
51	$-1,-2,-9,10,8,-6$	2.5	—	—	φ!	—	
52	$-1,-2,-9,10,8,-6,3,7$	1.5	0,1,0,1	—	3,4,5	—	7,12,13
53	$-1,-2,-9,10,8,-6,3,-7$	3.2+	0,2,0,1	—	—	—	
54	$-1,-2,-9,10,8,-6,-3$	2.0	—	—	φ!	—	
55	$-1,-2,-9,10,8,-6,-3,4,7$	1.5	0,0,0,1	—	4,5	—	7,12,13
56	$-1,-2,-9,10,8,-6,-3,4,-7$	3.7+	0,2,0,1	—	—	—	
57	$-1,-2,-9,10,8,-6,-3,-4$	2.5	0,0,0,1	—	—	—	
58	$-1,-2,-9,10,8,-6,-3,-4,5,7$	1.5	0,2,0,1	—	5	—	φ!
59	$-1,-2,-9,10,8,-6,-3,-4,5,-7$	3.9+	—	—	φ!	—	7,12,13
60	$-1,-2,-9,10,8,-6,-3,-4,-5$	2.7	0,-1,0,1	—	φ!	—	
61	$-1,-2,-9,10,-8$	1.5	0,2,0,1	—	φ!	—	
62	$-1,-2,-9,-10,-8$	1.0	-1,2,1,1	φ!	—	—	
63	$-1,-2,-9,-10$	0.0	1,0,1,1	φ!	—	—	

■ fathomed by infeasibility test   ! fathomed by $T_1 = \phi$ of infeasibility test   + fathomed by current best solution   * optimal solution

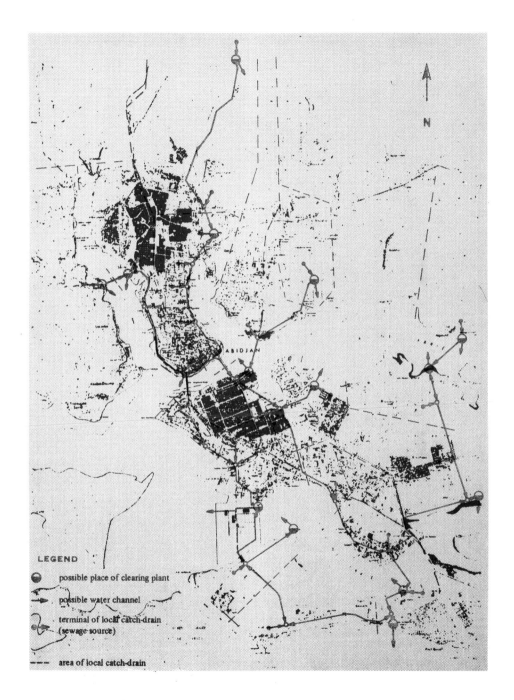

Figure 6

The map of Abidjan and a network of possible
treatment plants and possible sewer lines

SUPERPOSITION OF THE ELEMENTS OF THE BASIC SYSTEM

CONSTRAINING CONDITIONS

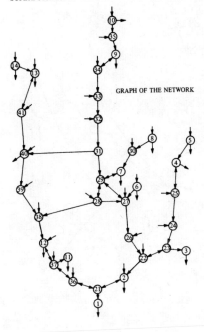

GRAPH OF THE NETWORK

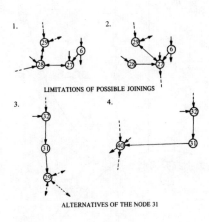

LIMITATIONS OF POSSIBLE JOININGS

ALTERNATIVES OF THE NODE 31

LEVEL OF PROTECTION	CONDITIONS OF REJECTION
LEVEL B	BIOLOGICAL CLEARING IMPOSED BEFORE REJECTION INTO THE LAGOON
LEVEL A1	MECHANICAL TREATMENT ADMITTED BEFORE REJECTION INTO THE BASION OF THE PORT (NODE 12)
LEVEL A2	MECHANICAL TREATMENT ADMITTED AT NODE 12 FOR FLOWS LESS THAN 7500 m³/h

L E G E N D

ⓘ ENTRY OF THE NETWORK (SOURCE) AT NODE i

ⓚ POSSIBLE PLACE OF A TREATMENT PLANT AND REJECTION (SINK) AT NODE 2

ⓘⓚ COLLECTOR OF POSSIBLE JOININGS FROM NODE i TO NODE k

ⓘ POINT OF DECOMPOSITION INTO PARTIAL NETWORKS

7.1

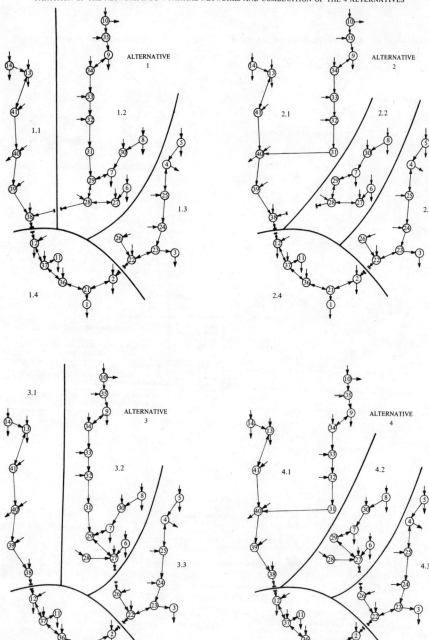

7.2

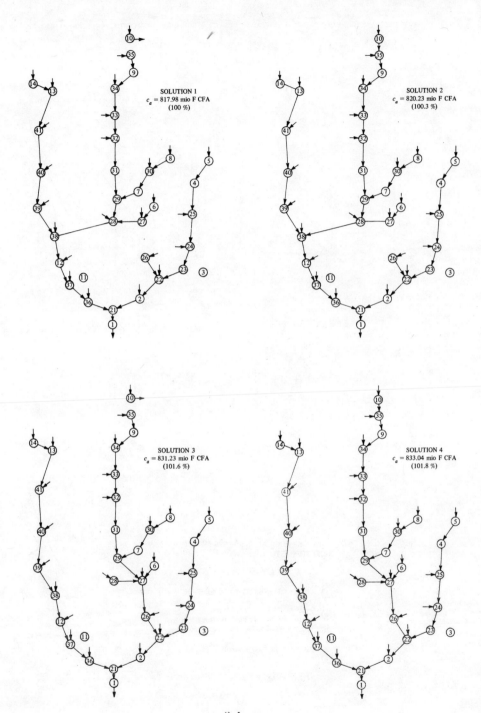

SOLUTION 1
c_a = 817.98 mio F CFA
(100 %)

SOLUTION 2
c_a = 820.23 mio F CFA
(100.3 %)

SOLUTION 3
c_a = 831.23 mio F CFA
(101.6 %)

SOLUTION 4
c_a = 833.04 mio F CFA
(101.8 %)

8.1

DECENTRALISED SOLUTION

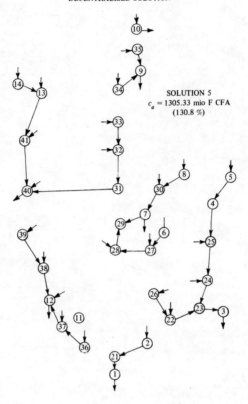

SOLUTION 5
c_a = 1305.33 mio F CFA
(130.8 %)

NOTA: BIOLOGICAL CLEARING IMOSED BEFORE
REJECTION INTO THE LAGOON

LEGEND

↓ⓘ   ENTRY OF THE NETWORK AT NODE i

ⓚ↗   CLEARING PLANT PREVISED AT NODE k

ⓘ
↓
ⓚ   COLLECTOR FROM NODE i TO NODE k

c_a TOTAL YEARLY COSTS

8.2

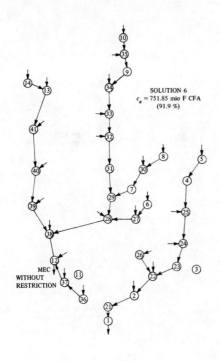

SOLUTION 6
c_a = 751.85 mio F CFA
(91.9 %)

MEC
WITHOUT
RESTRICTION

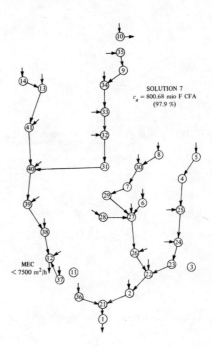

SOLUTION 7
c_a = 800.68 mio F CFA
(97.9 %)

MEC
< 7500 m²/h

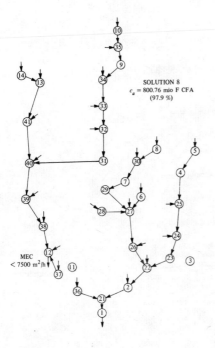

SOLUTION 8
c_a = 800.76 mio F CFA
(97.9 %)

MEC
< 7500 m²/h

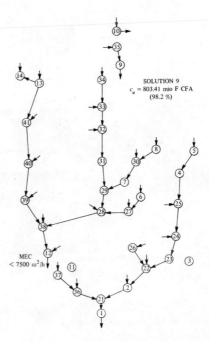

SOLUTION 9
c_a = 803.41 mio F CFA
(98.2 %)

MEC
< 7500 m²/h

9.1

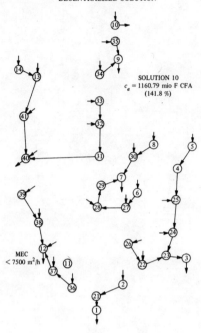

DECENTRALISED SOLUTION

SOLUTION 10
c_a = 1160.79 mio F CFA
(141.8 %)

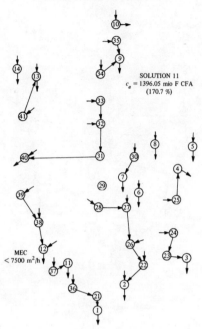

DECENTRALISED SOLUTION

SOLUTION 11
c_a = 1396.05 mio F CFA
(170.7 %)

NOTA: MECHANICAL TREATMENT BEFORE REJEC-
TION INTO THE BASIN OF THE PORT (NODE 12)

L E G E N D

i ENTRY OF THE NETWORK AT NODE i

k TREATMENT PLANT PREVISED AT NODE k

i
k COLLECTOR FROM NODE i TO NODE k

BIO BIOLOGICAL CLEARING IMPOSED BEFORE
REJECTION

MEC MECHANICAL TREATMENT ADMITTED BE-
FORE REJECTION

c_a TOTAL YEARLY COSTS

9.2

REFERENCES

[1]   W. A h r e n s, Die binäre Optimierung als Hilfsmittel bei der Planung regionaler Abwasserbeseitigungssysteme. II, *Technischer Bericht,* Nr. 8, Institut für Siedlungswasserwirtschaft, Universität Karlsruhe, (1972).

[2]   W. A h r e n s, Solving of the regionalization problem by certain branch-and-bound methods, Presented at the *ECE-Symposium on the Use of Computer Techniques and Automation for Water Resources Systems,* Washington, March-April, (1974).

[3]   W. A h r e n s, Die Lösung eines nichtlinearen Investitionsproblems mit Hile binärer Optimierungsalgorithmen — gezeigt am Beispiel der der Planung regionaler Abwasserbehandlungssysteme, *ZfOR,* 18, (1974), B131-B147.

[4]   I. A t t m a n n, Numerische Erfahrungen mit Balas-Algorithmen, Studienarbeit an Institut für Wirtschaftstheorie und Operations Research der Universität Karlsruhe, (1973).

[5]   E. B a l a s, An additive algorithm for solving linear programs with zero-one-variables, *OR,* 13 (1965), 517-546.

[6]   E. B a l a s, Discrete programming by the filter method, *OR,* 15 (1967), 915-957.

[7]   M.L. B a l i n s k i, An algorithm for finding all vertices of convex polyhedral sets, *J. of Soc. Industr. Appl. Math.,* 9 (1961), 72-88.

[8]   E.G. B a r t e l s, *A priori Informationen zur Linearen Programmierung,* Verlag Anton Hain, Meisenheim, (1973).

[9]   R.E. B e l l m a n, *Dynamic Programming,* Princeton, 1957.

[10] J.F. B e n d e r s, Partitioning procedures for solving mixed-variables programming problems, *Numerische Mathematik,* 4 (1962), 238-252.

[11] M. Benichou − J.M. Gouthier − P. Girodet −
G. Hentges − G. Ribiere − O. Vincent, Experiments
in mixed-integer linear programming, *Mathematical Programming*,
1 (1971), 76-94

[12] J. Biethahn − H.P. Liebmann, Die numerische Behandlung eines gemischt-ganzzahligen Investitionsproblems mit exakten
und heuristischen Methoden, *ZfB*, 6 (1972), 401-420.

[13] H. Bott, Anwendungsmöglichkeiten der Pseudo-Booleschen Optimierung auf Probleme der Fertigungswirtschaft und ihre rechen-
technische Realisierung, Diplomarbeit am Institut für Fertigungswirtschaft **Arbeitswissenschaft** der Universität Karlsruhe, (1974).

[14] K.M. Brauer, Optimale Produktionsplanung in Kraftwerken,
Die simultane Lösung komplexer Lastverteilungsprobleme mit Hilfe
der binären Optimierung, *ZfB*, 6 (1973), 421-443.

[15] K.M. Brauer, *Binäre Optimierung*, Carl Heymanns Verlag KG,
Köln, (1969).

[16] R.E. Burkard, *Methoden der ganzzahligen Optimierung*, Springer-Verlag, Wien, (1972).

[17] J.L. Byrne − L.G. Proll, Algorithm 341, Solution of linear
programs in 0-1 variables by implicit enumeration, *CACM*, 11
(1968), 782.

[18] J.L. Byrne − L.G. Proll, Initialising Geoffrion's implicit
enumeration algorithm to the zero-one linear programming problem,
The Computer Journal, 12 (1969), 381-384.

[19] A.V. Cabot − R.L. Francis, Solving certain nonconvex
quadratic minimization problems by ranking the extreme points,
OR, 18 (1970), 82-86.

[20] R.J. Dakin, A tree search algorithm for mixed integer programming problems, *Computer Journal*, 8, 3 (1965), 250-255.

[21]   G.B. Dantzig, *Lineare Programmierung und Erweiterungen,* Springer-Verlag, Heidelberg, (1966).

[22]   R.E. Davis, A simplex-search algorithm for solving 0-1 mixed integer programs, *Tech. Rep.,* No. 5, *Dept. of Operations Research,* Stanford University.

[23]   R.E. Davis – D.A. Kendrick – M. Weitzman, A branch-and-bound algorithm for 0-1 mixed integer programming problems, *OR,* 19 (1971), 1036-1044.

[24]   R.A. Deininger, Über die Planung von interkommunalen Systemen von Kläranlagen, *GWF-Wasser/Abwasser,* 110, 62 (1969), 1443-1445.

[25]   R.A. Deininger – S.Y. Su, Regional waste water treatment systems, *ASCE Annual and National Environmental Engineering Meeting,* Oct. (1971), St. Louis, Missouri.

[26]   F. Fiala, Algorithm 449. Solution of linear programming problems in 0-1 variables, *CACM,* 16 (1973), 445-447.

[27]   B. Fleischmann, Computational experience with the algorithm of Balas, *OR,* 5 (1967), 153-155.

[28]   R.J. Freeman, Computational experience with the Balas integer programming algorithm, P-3241, *The RAND Corporation,* Santa Monica, (1965).

[29]   R.S. Garfinkel – G.L. Nemhauser, *Integer Programming,* John Wiley & Sons, New York, (1972).

[30]   A.M. Geoffrion, Integer programming by implicit enumeration and Balas' method, RM-4783-PR, *The RAND Corporation,* Santa Monica, (1966).

[31]   A.M. Geoffrion, An improved implicit enumeration approach for integer programming, *OR,* 17 (1969), 437-454.

[32] A.M. Geoffrion – R.E. Marsten, Integer programming: a framework and state-of-the-art survey, *MS*, 18 (1972), 464-491.

[33] F. Glover – S. Zionts, A note on the additive algorithm of Balas, *OR*, 13 (1965), 546-549.

[34] F. Glover, A multiphase-dual algorithm for the zero-one integer programming problem, *OR*, 13 (1965), 879-919.

[35] J.J.H. Forrest – J.P.H. Hirst – J.A. Tomlin, Practical solution of large mixed integer programming problems with umpire, *MS*, 5 (1974), 736-773.

[36] R.E. Gomory, An algorithm for integer solutions to linear programs, IBM Mathematics Research Project, *Techn. Report*, 1 (1958).

[37] R.E. Gomory, An all-integer integer programming algorithm, in: Muth – Thompson (Ed.): *Industrial Scheduling*, Englewood Cliffs: Prentice Hall, (1963), 193-206.

[38] R.L. Gus – J.C. Liggett, Analysis of algorithms for the zero-one programming problem, *CACM*, 11 (1968), 837-844.

[39] G. Hadley, *Linear algebra*, Addison-Wesley, Reading, Mass., (1961).

[40] G. Hadley, *Linear programming*, Addison-Wesley, Reading, Mass., (1962).

[41] G. Hadley, *Nonlinear and dynamic programming*, Addison-Wesley, Reading, Mass., (1964).

[42] H. Hahn – P.M. Meier – E. Orth, Regional wastewater management systems, in: Deininger (Ed.): Models for Environmental Pollution Control, *Ann Arbor Science*, Ann Arbor, Michigan, (1973).

[43] W. Hahn, Rundungsfehler beim "all-integer integer programming algorithm" von Gomory, *Computing*, 11 (1973), 249-254.

[44] P.L. Hammer – S. Rudeanu, *Boolean methods in operations research and related areas,* Springer-Verlag, Berlin, (1968).

[45] P.L. Hammer, A B-B-B-method for linear and nonlinear bivalent programming, in: *Avi-Itzhak,* B. (Ed.): *Developments in Operations Research,* Gordon and Breach, (1971).

[46] P.L. Ivanescu – S. Rudeanu, *Pseudo-Boolean methods for bivalent programming,* Springer-Verlag, Berlin, (1966).

[47] A.H. Land – A.G. Doig, An automatic method of solving discrete programming problems, *Econometrics,* 28 (1960), 497-520.

[48] E.L. Lawler – D.E. Wood, Branch-and-bound methods, a survey, *OR,* 14 (1966), 699-719.

[49] C.E. Lemke – K. Spielberg, Direct search algorithms for zero-one and mixed-integer programming, *OR,* 15 (1967), 892-914.

[50] T.M. Liebling, On the number of iterations of the simplex method, in: *Henn* (Ed.): *Operations Research Verfahren* XVII, Verlag Anton Hain, Meisenheim, (1972).

[51] V. Klee, On the number of vertices of a convex polytrope, *Canadian Jour. of Math.,* 16 (1964), 701-720.

[52] J.C. Liebman, A branch-and-bound algorithm for minimizing the costs of waste treatment, subject to equity constraints, IBM Scientific Computing Symposium on Water and Air Resource Management, (1967), Watson Research Center, N.Y.

[53] J.C. Liebman – D.H. Marks, Balas algorithm for zoned uniform treatment, *J. San Eng. Div.,* (1968), 585-593.

[54] H.P. Liebmann – J. Biethahn, Zur Anwendung von heuristischen Methoden bei der Optimierung eines gemischt ganzzahligen und separierbaren Investitionsproblems, *ZfB,* 5 (1973), 351-372.

[55] M. Manas — J. Nedoma, Finding all vertices of a convex polyhedron, *Numerische Mathematik,* 12 (1968), 226-229.

[56] P.M. Meier, *Möglichkeiten zur technischen und wirtschaftlichen Optimierung von Zweckverbänden,* Erich Schmidt Verlag, Bielefeld, (1972).

[57] K.G. Murty, Solving the fixed charge problem by ranking the extreme points, *OR,* 16 (1968), 268-279.

[58] G.L. Nemhauser, *Einführung in die Praxis der dynamischen Programmierung,* Oldenbourg Verlag, München, (1969).

[59] H. Orth, Die binäre Optimierung als Hilfsmittel bei der Planung regionaler Abwasserbeseitigungssysteme I., *Techn. Bericht,* Nr. 7, Institut für Siedlungswasserwirtschaft, Universität Karlsruhe, (1972b).

[60] E. Orth, Dekompositionsmethoden — Ein Hilfsmittel bei der Planung regionaler Abwasserbeseitigungssysteme, *GWF-Wasser/Abwasser,* 114, 12 (1973), 576-578.

[61] H. Orth — H. Hahn, Die mathematische Optimierung als Hilfsmittel bei der Planung regionaler Abwasserbeseitigungssysteme, *GWF-Wasser/Abwasser,* 115, 1 (1974), 24-27.

[62] T.L. Saaty, The number of vertices of a polyhedron, *The American Math. Monthly,* 62 (1955), 326-331.

[63] S. Woiler,. Implicit enumeration algorithms for discrete optimization problems, Stanford University, Ph. D. Thesis (1967).

W. Ahrens

Institute of Siedlungswasserwirtschaft, University of Karlsruhe, D75 Karlsruhe, GFR.

COLLOQUIA MATHEMATICA SOCIETATIS JÁNOS BOLYAI

12. PROGRESS IN OPERATIONS RESEARCH, EGER (HUNGARY), 1974.

ON THE STATIONARY REGIME OF A MASS SERVICE SYSTEM WITH VARIABLE CHANNEL NUMBER

T. ANNAIEV — T. GERGELY — I.I. YEZHOV

1. A stationary non-ordinary Poisson flow of demands comes into a queueing system for which

$$\lambda_m \Delta + o(\Delta) \qquad (m = 1, 2, \ldots)$$

is the probability of m demands coming in during a short time interval Δ. Put as usual

$$\lambda = \sum_{m=1}^{\infty} \lambda_m .$$

The queueing system consists of an infinite number of channels all of all same type, which are put in for service by a rule as follows: if there are k demands in the system, then $\left[\dfrac{k}{r_0}\right]$ channels are taking part in the service. Here r_0 is a fixed natural number and $[x]$ is the integer part of x i.e. the greatest integer less than x. Suppose that the service time of one demand by each channel is an exponentially distributed random value with the parameter 1.

It follows from the former that, if $\xi(t)$ is the number of demands being in the queueing system at the moment t, then $\xi(t)$ is a homogeneous Markov chain with the transition probabilities in a short time Δ as follow

$$
(1) \qquad k \xrightarrow{\Delta}
\begin{cases}
k & : 1 - \left(\lambda + \left[\frac{k}{r_0}\right]\right)\Delta + o(\Delta) \\[2mm]
k + m: & \lambda_m \Delta + o(\Delta), \; m \geqslant 1 \\[2mm]
k - 1 : & \left[\frac{k}{r_0}\right]\Delta + o(\Delta) .
\end{cases}
$$

All the states of the chain $\xi(t)$ are divided into two classes. The states $\{0, 1, \ldots, r_0 - 2\}$ form the class of non-essential states. It follows, that a process $\xi(t)$ onece entered into a set $\{r_0 - 1, r_0, r_0 + 1, \ldots\}$, never returns into a set $\{0, 1, \ldots, r_0 - 2\}$ as we get it easily from (1). The rest of the states $\{r_0 - 1, r_0, r_0 + 1, \ldots\}$ forms a closed class of communicating states for it follows from (1) that the negative jumps of the process $\xi(t)$ may only be equal to unity. It follows from this that, if

$$
P\{\xi(t) = k\} = p_k(t) ,
$$

then irrespective to the distribution $\xi(0)$ the limits

$$
\lim p_k(t) = p_k \qquad (k = 0, 1, \ldots)
$$

always exist (and are independent of $\xi(0)$). It is clear that $p_0 = p_1 = \ldots$
$\ldots = p_{r_0 - 2} = 0$.

We shall now show that, if $\xi(0) \in \{r_0 - 1, r_0, r_0 + 1, \ldots\}$, then Markov chain $\xi(t)$ has the stationary distribution and hence all its states $\{r_0 - 1, r_0, r_0 + 1, \ldots\}$ form an ergodic class of states.

The stationary probabilities $\{p_k\}$ satisfy the following equations as it follows from (1) and the theorem of total probability

$$
\lambda p_{r_0 - 1} = p_{r_0}
$$

$$
(2) \qquad \left(\lambda + \left[\frac{k}{r_0}\right]\right) p_k = \left[\frac{k+1}{r_0}\right] p_{k+1} + \sum_{j=r-1}^{k-1} p_j \lambda_{k-j}, \qquad k \geqslant r_0 .
$$

Introducing the substitutions $p_k = q_{k+1-r_0}$ $(k \geqslant r_0 - 1)$ the equations (2) take the form

$$\lambda q_0 = q_1$$

(2') $$\left(\lambda + \left[\frac{m + r_0 - 1}{r_0}\right]\right) q_m = \left[\frac{m + r_0}{r_0}\right] q_{m+1} + \sum_{t=0}^{m-1} q_t \lambda_{m-t},$$

$m \geqslant 1$.

Introducting now the generating functions

$$L(z) = \sum_{m=1}^{\infty} \lambda_m z^m, \qquad Q(z) = \sum_{m=0}^{\infty} q_m z^m \qquad (|z| \leqslant 1)$$

from (2') we get

$$\frac{\lambda - L(z)}{1 - z} Q(z) = \sum_{m=0}^{\infty} \left[\frac{m + r_0}{r_0}\right] q_{m+1} z^m,$$

or

(3) $$Q'_{\frac{1}{r_0}}(z) = \frac{\lambda - L(z)}{1 - z} Q(z),$$

where

$$Q'_{\frac{1}{r_0}}(z) = \sum_{m=0}^{\infty} \left[\frac{m + r_0}{r_0}\right] q_{m+1} z^m.$$

Let us transform $Q'_{\frac{1}{r_0}}(z)$

(4) $$Q'_{\frac{1}{r_0}}(z) = \sum_{m=0}^{\infty} \left[\frac{m + r_0}{r_0}\right] q_{m+1} z^m =$$

$$= \sum_{k=0}^{r_0 - 1} \sum_{n=0}^{\infty} \left[\frac{n r_0 + k + r_0}{r_0}\right] q_{n r_0 + k + 1} z^{n r_0 + k} =$$

$$= \sum_{k=0}^{r_0-1} \sum_{n=0}^{\infty} (n+1) q_{nr_0+k+1} z^{nr_0+k} =$$

$$= \frac{1}{r_0} \left\{ Q'(z) + \sum_{k=0}^{r_0-1} (r_0 - k - 1) \sum_{n=0}^{\infty} q_{nr_0+k+1} z^{nr_0+k} \right\} =$$

$$= \frac{1}{r_0} Q'(z) + \frac{1}{r_0 z} \sum_{k=1}^{r_0} (r_0 - k) \sum_{n=0}^{\infty} q_{nr_0+k} z^{nr_0+k} .$$

Now let $1 = \epsilon_0, \epsilon_1, \ldots, \epsilon_{r_0-1}$ be the r_0 unit-roots of 1. As it is known

$$\epsilon_k = \cos \frac{2\pi k}{r_0} + i \sin \frac{2\pi k}{r_0} \qquad (k = 0, 1, \ldots, r_0 - 1)$$

Using the following

$$\epsilon_0^k + \epsilon_1^k + \ldots + \epsilon_{r_0-1}^k = \begin{cases} r_0, & \text{if } k \text{ is divisible by } r_0 \\ \\ 0, & \text{if } k \text{ isn't divisible by } r_0 , \end{cases}$$

we get

(5)
$$\sum_{j=0}^{r_0-1} \epsilon_j^{-k} Q(\epsilon_j z) = \sum_{j=0}^{r_0-1} \epsilon_j^{-k} \sum_{m=0}^{\infty} q_m \epsilon_j^m z^m =$$

$$= \sum_{m=0}^{\infty} q_m z^m \sum_{j=0}^{r_0-1} \epsilon_j^{m-k} = r_0 \sum_{n=0}^{\infty} q_{nr_0+k} z^{nr_0+k} .$$

Using (3)-(5), we obtain

$$\frac{\lambda - L(z)}{1-z} Q(z) = \frac{1}{r_0} Q'(z) + \frac{1}{zr_0^2} \sum_{k=1}^{r_0-1} (r_0 - k) \sum_{j=0}^{r_0-1} \epsilon_j^{-k} Q(\epsilon_j z)$$

or

(6)
$$Q'(z) = r_0 \frac{\lambda - L(z)}{1-z} Q(z) - \frac{1}{r_0 z} \sum_{t=1}^{r_0-1} t \sum_{\delta=0}^{r_0-1} \epsilon_j^t Q(\epsilon_j z) .$$

Since for $j \in \{1, 2, \ldots, r_0 - 1\}$

$$\sum_{t=1}^{r_0-1} t\epsilon_j^t = \frac{\epsilon_j}{(\epsilon_j - 1)^2} [(r_0 - 1)\epsilon_j^{r_0} - r_0 \epsilon_j^{r_0-1} + 1]^*$$

and $\epsilon_j^{r_0} = 1$, then

(7) $$\sum_{t=1}^{r_0-1} t\epsilon_j^t = \frac{r_0}{\epsilon_j - 1} \qquad (j = 1, 2, \ldots, r_0 - 1),$$

which together with (6) leads to

(8) $$Q'(z) = \left(r_0 \frac{\lambda - L(z)}{1 - z} - \frac{r_0 - 1}{2z}\right) Q(z) + \frac{1}{z} \sum_{j=1}^{r_0-1} \frac{Q(\epsilon_j z)}{1 - \epsilon_j}.$$

Note that in the particular case $r_0 = 1$ (8) is as follows

$$Q'(z) = \frac{\lambda - L(z)}{1 - z} Q(z).$$

This by the condition $Q(1) = 1$ leads to

(9) $$Q(z) = \exp\left\{-\int_z^1 \frac{\lambda - L(u)}{1 - u} du\right\}.$$

This is the well known result for a system with infinite channel number. If $L(z) = \lambda z$, i.e. this is the case of an ordinary flow, then

$$Q(z) = e^{\lambda(z-1)}$$

and

$$p_k = q_k = e^{-\lambda} \frac{\lambda^k}{k!} \qquad (k \geqslant 0)$$

(see e.g. [1], p. 89).

2. Let us see the solution of the functional differential equation (8). We introduce the notation

$$Q_j(z) = Q(\epsilon_j z) \qquad (j = 0, 1, \ldots, r_0 - 1).$$

*We have used here the following identity

$$\sum_1^{N-1} nx^n = \frac{x}{(1-x)^2}[(N-1)x^N - Nx^{N-1} + 1] \qquad (x \neq 1).$$

Substituting $\epsilon_l z$ in (8) into z, we get

$$Q'_l(z) = \left[\epsilon_l r_0 \frac{\lambda - L(\epsilon_l z)}{1 - \epsilon_l z} - \frac{r_0 - 1}{2z} \right] Q_l(z) +$$

(10)

$$+ \frac{1}{z} \sum_{j=1}^{r_0 - 1} (1 - \epsilon_j)^{-1} Q_{j + l \,(\mathrm{mod}\, r_0)}(z)$$

$$(l = 0, 1, \ldots, r_0 - 1).$$

Introducing the column vector

$$Q(z) = \{Q_0(z), \ldots, Q_{r_0 - 1}(z)\}$$

and the matrix

$$P(z) = \left\| \begin{array}{ccc} p_{00}(z) & \cdots & p_{0, r_0 - 1}(z) \\ \cdots\cdots\cdots\cdots\cdots\cdots\cdots \\ \cdots\cdots\cdots\cdots\cdots\cdots\cdots \\ p_{r_0 - 1, 0}(z) & \cdots & p_{r_0 - 1, r_0 - 1}(z) \end{array} \right\| .$$

where

$$p_{ll}(z) = \epsilon_l r_0 \frac{\lambda - L(\epsilon_l z)}{1 - \epsilon_l z} - \frac{r_0 - 1}{2z} ,$$

$$p_{lk}(z) = z^{-1}(1 - \epsilon_{k - l})^{-1*} \qquad (k \neq l).$$

We rewrite the linear differential equation system (10) into matrix form

(11) $$\frac{dQ(z)}{dz} = P(z)Q(z).$$

Since $Q_l(0) = q_0$ for every l, thus the system (10) is to be solved with the initial condition

(12) $$Q(0) = q_0 e,$$

where

*We mean
$$\epsilon_{-k} = \epsilon_k^{-1}.$$

$$e = \begin{pmatrix} 1 \\ 1 \\ \cdot \\ \cdot \\ \cdot \\ 1 \end{pmatrix} .$$

The solution of the system (11)-(12) (see [2], p. 433) can be written in the form

(13) $Q(z) = q_0 \Omega_0^z(P)e$,

where the matrix $\Omega_0^z(P)$ is a matricant corresponding to the matrix $P(z)$ in the interval $(0, z)$. According to [2] (pp. 430, 433-434) $\Omega_0^z(P)$ can be computed by any of the following rules

$$\Omega_0^z(P) = \sum_{k=0}^{\infty} \left[\int_0^z P(u)\, du \right]^k ,$$

$$\Omega_0^z(P) = \lim_{n \to \infty} \left[e^{\frac{z}{n} P(z)} e^{\frac{z}{n} P\left(\frac{(n-1)z}{n}\right)} \cdots e^{\frac{z}{n} P\left(\frac{z}{n}\right)} \right] ,$$

$$\Omega_0^z(P) = \int_0^{\widehat{z}} [E + P)]\, du =$$

$$= \lim_{n \to \infty} \left[E + P(z)\frac{z}{n} \right]\left[E + P\left(\frac{(n-1)z}{n}\right) \frac{z}{n} \right] \cdots$$

$$\cdots \left[E + P\left(\frac{z}{n}\right) \frac{z}{n} \right] ,$$

where E is a unity matrix.

We note about (13) the following: in reality $\Omega_0^z(P)$ does not exist since the elements of the matrix $P(z)$ are not only non-limited in the environment of 0, but also non-integrable in consequence of presence of $\frac{c}{z}$. However the limit

$$\lim_{\epsilon \to +0} \Omega_\epsilon^z(P)e$$

exists, since (a) when multiplying the elements of the matrix by e resulting column vectors are sums of the rows of the matrix; (b) in the matrix

$P(z)$ the sums of the rows don't contain any more the "unpleasant" $\dfrac{c}{z}$ values, as

(14) $\qquad \displaystyle\sum_{\substack{k=0 \\ k \neq l}}^{r_0-1} \frac{1}{1-\epsilon_{k-l}} - \frac{r_0-1}{2} = 0 \;.^{*}$

Hence it follows that we have to consider (13) in the following way

$$Q(z) = q_0 \lim_{\epsilon \to +0} \Omega_{\epsilon}^{z}(P)e \;.$$

Let

$$\Omega_{\epsilon}^{z}(P) = \| \omega_{lk}^{(\epsilon)}(z) \| \qquad (l, k = 0, 1, \ldots, r_0 - 1) \;,$$

and

$$\lim_{\epsilon \to +0} \sum_{k=0}^{r_0-1} \omega_{lk}^{(\epsilon)}(z) = \omega_l(z) \qquad (l = 0, 1, \ldots, r_0 - 1) \;.$$

Then

$$Q(z) = Q_0(z) = q_0 \omega_0(z) \;,$$

or with the normalizing condition $Q(1) = 1$,

(15) $\qquad Q(z) = \dfrac{\omega_0(z)}{\omega_0(1)} \;.$

Such a stationary distribution of the Markov chain $\xi(t)$ does exist. Its generating function coincides with the right part of the equation (15). This proves that all the states $\{r_0 - 1, r_0, r_0 + 1, \ldots\}$ form an ergodic class.

*Really according to (7)

$$r_0 \sum_{\substack{k=0 \\ k \neq l}}^{r_0-1} \frac{1}{1-\epsilon_{k-l}} = r_0 \sum_{k=1}^{r_0-1} \frac{1}{1-\epsilon_k} = -\sum_{t=1}^{r_0-1} t \sum_{k=1}^{r_0-1} \epsilon_k^t = -\sum_{t=1}^{r_0-1} t \sum_{k=1}^{r_0-1} \epsilon_1^{tk} =$$

$$= -\sum_{t=1}^{r_0-1} t \sum_{k=1}^{r_0-1} (\epsilon_t)^k = -\sum_{k=1}^{r_0-1} t \frac{\epsilon_t^{r_0} - \epsilon_t}{\epsilon_t - 1} = \sum_{t=1}^{r_0-1} t = \frac{r_0(r_0-1)}{2} \;,$$

which is the same as (14).

3. If the flow of demands in ordinary $(L(z) = \lambda z)$ then the stationary distribution can be found in clear form as in this case $\xi(t)$ is a particular case of birth and death processes. Really in the investigated case

$$p_k\left(\lambda + \left[\frac{k}{r_0}\right]\right) = \lambda p_{k-1} + \left[\frac{k+1}{r_0}\right]p_{k+1} \qquad (k \geqslant r_0 - 1),$$

or

$$(16) \qquad \lambda p_k - \left[\frac{k+1}{r_0}\right]p_{k+1} = \lambda p_{k-1} - \left[\frac{k}{r_0}\right]p_k \qquad (k \geqslant r_0 - 1).$$

Since $\lambda p_{r_0-1} = p_{r_0}$ then it follows from (16), that

$$p_k = \frac{\lambda}{\left[\frac{k}{r_0}\right]}\, p_{k-1} \qquad (k \geqslant r_0),$$

or

$$(17) \qquad p_k = \frac{\lambda^{k+1-r_0}}{\left[\frac{k}{r_0}\right]\left[\frac{k-1}{r_0}\right]\dots\left[\frac{r_0}{r_0}\right]}\, p_{r_0-1} \qquad (k \geqslant r_0).$$

Using the equation $\displaystyle\sum_{k=r_0-1}^{\infty} p_k = 1$, we get from (17)

$$(18) \qquad p_k = \left(\sum_{l=r_0}^{\infty} \frac{\lambda^l}{\prod\limits_{j=r_0}^{l-1}\left[\frac{j}{r_0}\right]}\right)^{-1} \frac{\lambda^{k+1}}{\prod\limits_{j=r_0}^{k}\left[\frac{j}{r_0}\right]} \qquad (k \geqslant r_0 - 1).$$

We investigate the case of $r_0 = 2$ in detail. It will be shown that in this case p_k's are the coefficients of the geometrical sequence of Bessel functions with fully imaginary argument. We have got

$$p_{2k} = c\,\frac{\lambda^{2k+1}}{\left[\frac{2}{2}\right]\left[\frac{3}{2}\right]\dots\left[\frac{2k-1}{2}\right]\left[\frac{2k}{2}\right]} = c\,\frac{\lambda^{2k+1}}{k!(k-1)!}$$

$$p_{2k-1} = c \frac{\lambda^{2k}}{[\frac{2}{2}][\frac{3}{2}] \cdots [\frac{2k-2}{2}][\frac{2k-1}{2}]} = c \frac{\lambda^{2k}}{(k-1)!(k-1)!}$$

$$(k = 1, 2, \ldots).$$

As (see e.g. [3], p. 213)

$$\sum_{k=1}^{\infty} p_{2k} z^{2k} = \lambda c \sum_{k=1}^{\infty} \frac{(\lambda z)^{2k}}{k!(k-1)!} =$$

$$= \lambda^2 cz \sum_{r=0}^{\infty} \frac{\left(\frac{1}{2} 2\lambda z\right)^{1+2r}}{r!(r+1)!} = \lambda^2 cz I_1(2\lambda z),$$

and

$$\sum_{k=1}^{\infty} p_{2k-1} z^{2k-1} = \lambda c \sum_{k=1}^{\infty} \frac{(\lambda z)^{2k-1}}{(k-1)!(k-1)!} =$$

$$= \lambda^2 cz \sum_{r=0}^{\infty} \frac{\left(\frac{1}{2} 2\lambda z\right)^{2r}}{r! r!} = \lambda^2 cz I_0(2\lambda z),$$

$$P(z) = \sum_{k=1}^{\infty} p_k z^k = z \frac{I_0(2\lambda z) + I_1(2\lambda z)}{I_0(2\lambda) + I_1(2\lambda)},$$

hence particularly

$$p_1 = \frac{1}{I_0(2\lambda) + I_1(2\lambda)}.$$

REFERENCES

[1] A.Ja. Khintchine, *Papers about queuing theory*, Fizmathguiz, Moscow, 1963.

[2] F.R. Gantmacher, *Theory of Matrices*, Nauka 1967.

[3] E.T. Whittaker – J.N. Watson, *Modern Analysis*, Vol. 2, Fizmathguiz, Moscow, 1963.

T. Annaiev
Turkmenian University,
T. Gergely
Central Research Institute for Physics, 1121 Budapest, Konkoly Thege M. u.
I.I. Yezhov
University of Kiev.

COLLOQUIA MATHEMATICA SOCIETATIS JÁNOS BOLYAI

12. PROGRESS IN OPERATIONS RESEARCH, EGER (HUNGARY), 1974.

SOLUTION OF THE MULTITERMINAL MINIMAL PATH PROBLEM IN A NETWORK WITH GAINS

A. BAKÓ

Several algorithms have been proposed for the solution of the multiterminal minimal path problem in case of a network having a cost (distance) function. For networks with gains the problem of finding the shortest path between two specified nodes and the maximal flow problem are also solved. The purpose of the present paper is to give an algorithm for the solution of the problem mentioned in the title.

INTRODUCTION

Let N be the set of nodes (points) and E the set of edges, further let $d(x, y) \geqslant 0$, $(x, y) \in E$ denote the travelling cost (time) from node x to node y.

We denote a path from x to y by $P = (x = x_1, x_2, x_3, \ldots, x_r = y)$. The travelling cost along the path P is

$$l(P) = \sum_{l=1}^{r-1} d(x_l, x_{l+1}).$$

The function k can be interpreted in the following way: if s units of goods are transported from x to y, then the loss of weight equals $sk(x,y)$.

The minimal path problem in a network with gains is solved by Charnes and Raike [3] and the author [1]. In this case the maximal flow problem is also solved, see e.g. Jarvis — Jezior [9] and Jewell [10].

Let $P = (x = x_0, x_1, \ldots, x_r = y)$ be a path from x to y. Let us denote by $l(x_0, x_i)$ and $m(x_0, x_i)$ the transportation cost and the weight respectively of one unit of goods along the route P leading from x_0 to x_i.

The values of l, m can easily be computed by the following recurrence formulas

(1.1)
$$l(x_0, x_0) = 0$$
$$l(x_0, x_i) = l(x_0, x_{i-1}) + m(x_0, x_{i-1})d(x_{i-1}, x_i)$$

and

(1.2)
$$m(x_0, x_0) = 1$$
$$m(x_0, x_i) = m(x_0, x_{i-1})k(x_{i-1}, x_i) .$$

The multiterminal minimal path problem is to determine the cheapest (shortest) path between every pair of nodes.

We can distinguish between two kinds of methods for the solution of the multiterminal minimal path problem. There are methods which use dynamic approach [2], [4], [5] and there are methods based on the triangle inequality valid for the shortest path [5], [7], [8], [11], [12]. Methods of the first kind use the following recurrence relations

$$d_{ij}^{(0)} = d(x_i, x_j)$$
$$d_{ij}^{(k)} = \min_{1 \leqslant l \leqslant n} (d_{il}^{(k-1)} + d_{lj}^{(k-1)}), \qquad k = 1, 2, \ldots, n .$$

Among methods using the triangle inequality Warshall's method is considered to be the best one. It gives the optimal solution in the following form

$$d_{ij}^{(0)} = d(x_i, x_j)$$

$$d_{ij}^{(k)} = \min{(d_{ij}^{(k)}, d_{ik}^{(k-1)} + d_{kj}^{(k-1)})}, \qquad k = 1, 2, \ldots, n .$$

Our algorithm works along the line of Warshall's algorithm.

1. PROBLEM FORMULATION

In a network with gains another function k is given which is the so called gain function $(0 \leqslant k(x, y) \leqslant 1)$. The multiterminal minimal path problem in a network with gains is the following: determine for every pair $x, y \in N$ the path P for which

$$(1.3) \qquad \frac{l(x, y)}{m(x, y)} = \text{minimum} .$$

The algorithm proposed for the solution of this problem is described in the next section.

2. THE ALGORITHM

The algorithm consists of subsequent steps. To every step we determine matrices $L^{(k)} = (l_{ij}^{(k)})$, $M^{(k)} = (m_{ij}^{(k)})$. Here k runs from 0 to n, where n is the number of nodes. The initial matrices belong to $k = 0$.

The initial matrix $L^{(0)} = (l_{ij}^{(0)})$ has the following entries

$$(2.1) \qquad l_{ij}^{(0)} = \begin{cases} d(x_i, x_j) & \text{if } (x_i, x_j) \in E \\ 0 & \text{if } i = j \\ K & \text{otherwise,} \end{cases}$$

where K is greater than the maximum value of $d(x_i, x_j)$ for all $(x_i, x_j) \in E$.

We also give the initial matrix $M^{(0)} = (m_{ij}^{(0)})$ by

$$(2.2) \qquad m_{ij}^{(0)} = \begin{cases} k(x_i, x_j) & \text{if } (x_i, x_j) \in E \\ c & \text{otherwise,} \end{cases}$$

where $c < \displaystyle\prod_{(x_i, x_j) \in E} k(x_i, x_j)$.

The recurrence relations at the k-th step are the following: we compute the values m_{ij} and l_{ij}

$$(2.3) \qquad m_{ij} = m_{ik}^{(k-1)} \cdot m_{kj}^{(k-1)}, \qquad i \neq k, \ j \neq k, \ i \neq j,$$

$$(2.4) \qquad l_{ij} = l_{ik}^{(k-1)} + m_{ik}^{(k-1)} l_{kj}^{(k-1)};$$

and determine the entries of $L^{(k)}$ and $M^{(k)}$ as follows

$$(2.5) \qquad l_{ij}^{(k)} = \begin{cases} l_{ij} & \text{if } \dfrac{l_{ij}}{m_{ij}} < \dfrac{l_{ij}^{(k-1)}}{m_{ij}^{(k-1)}} \\ l_{ij}^{(k-1)} & \text{otherwise,} \end{cases}$$

$$(2.6) \qquad m_{ij}^{(k)} = \begin{cases} m_{ij} & \text{if } \dfrac{l_{ij}}{m_{ij}} < \dfrac{l_{ij}^{(k-1)}}{m_{ij}^{(k-1)}} \\ m_{ij}^{(k-1)} & \text{otherwise.} \end{cases}$$

$L^{(n)}$ and $M^{(n)}$ solve the problem. The proof of this fact is presented in the next section.

3. VALIDITY OF THE ALGORITHM

First we prove two lemmas. Let $P_1 = (x_1, x_2, \ldots, x_j)$ and $P_2 = (x_j, x_{j+1}, \ldots, x_r)$ be two paths and $P = P_1 \cup P_2$.

Lemma 3.1. *For the path P we have*

$$m(x_1, x_r) = m(x_1, x_j) m(x_j, x_r).$$

Proof. The definition of the function m implies

$$m(x_1, x_r) = \prod_{l=2}^{r} k(x_{l-1}, x_l) =$$

$$= \prod_{l=2}^{j} k(x_{l-1}, x_l) \prod_{l=j+1}^{r} k(x_{l-1}, x_l) = m(x_1, x_j) m(x_j, x_r),$$

which is the required equality.

The following lemma can be proved similarly.

Lemma 3.2. *For the path P we have*

$$l(x_1, x_r) = l(x_1, x_j) + m(x_1, x_j) l(x_j, x_r).$$

The validity of our algorithm is expressed by the following theorem.

Theorem. *The elements of the matrices $L^{(n)}$ and $M^{(n)}$ belong to the minimal path leading from x_1 to x_j.*

Proof. In order to prove this theorem it is sufficient to show that in the k-th step the value $\dfrac{l_{ij}^{(k)}}{m_{ij}^{(k)}}$ belonging to the matrices $L^{(k)}, M^{(k)}$ is minimal if the optimal path leading from x_i to x_j goes through only a subset of points $x_1, x_2, \ldots, x_k$.

For $k = 1$ the theorem is obvious because $\dfrac{l_{ij}^{(1)}}{m_{ij}^{(1)}} \leqslant \dfrac{l_{ij}^{(0)}}{m_{ij}^{(0)}}$ for every i, j. Strict inequality holds if and only if x_1 enter the path.

Let us assume that the statement of the theorem is valid for $k - 1$. At the k-th step there are two cases:

(a) The optimal path going through the subset of the points $x_1, x_2, \ldots, x_k$ does not contain the point x_k. In this case $l_{ij}^{(k)} = l_{ij}^{(k-1)}$, $m_{ij}^{(k)} = m_{ij}^{(k-1)}$. Thus (2.5) and (2.6) imply the statement for k.

(b) The point x_k belongs to the path P leading from x_i to x_j. Then x_k joins two paths both of which go through certain subsets of $x_1, x_2, \ldots, x_{k-1}$. Because of the assumption these paths are optimal relative to the points $x_1, x_2, \ldots, x_{k-1}$. Considering the Lemmas (3.1) and

(3.2) we can use the recurrence formulas for these two paths. The quotient belonging to the union of these two paths is less than the former quotient because of the formulas (2.5), (2.6).

Q.E.D.

4. REMARKS

This algorithm needs $n(n-1)^2$ additions, divisions and comparisons and $2n^3$ multiplications. If we solved this problem by the simple application of the algorithm given in [1] so that we find the minimal path between each pair of points, than we should have to compute more because in this case the number of additions is $\frac{2}{3} n^3(n-1)$ and the number of comparisons, divisions and subtractions is $\frac{1}{3} n^3(n-1)$.

If we want to determine the path itself we need another matrix S. This is the so-called label matrix.

At the beginning the entries of the label matrix are

$$s_{ij}^{(0)} = j .$$

At step k the entries are the following

$$s_{ij}^{(k)} = \begin{cases} s_{ik}^{(k-1)} & \text{if } \dfrac{l_{ij}}{m_{ij}} < \dfrac{l_{ij}^{(k-1)}}{m_{ij}^{(k-1)}}, \text{ or } i = k, \text{ or } j = k, \\[2ex] s_{ij}^{(k-1)} & \text{otherwise.} \end{cases}$$

Having determined subsequently $S^{(1)}, \ldots, S^{(n)}$, from the last matrix we can find the optimal path itself in the usual way (Dreyfus [5], Ford – Fulkerson [6], Hu [8]).

REFERENCES

[1] A. Bakó, On the determination of the shortest path in a network having gains, *Math. Operationsforschung und Statistik*, 4 (1973), 63-68.

[2]   R. Bellman, On a routing problem, *Quarterly of Appl. Math.*, 16 (1958) 87-90.

[3]   A. Charnes – W.M. Raike, One-pass algorithms for some generalized network problems, *Opns. Res.*, 14 (1966), 914-923.

[4]   G.B. Dantzig, All shortest routes in a graph, *Opns. Res. House*, Stanford University, TR 66-3 1966.

[5]   S. Dreyfus, An appraisal of some shortest path algorithms, *Opns. Res.*, 17 (1969), 395-412.

[6]   L.R. Ford Jr. – D.R. Fulkerson, *Flows in networks*, Princeton University Press, Princeton, N.J. 1962.

[7]   F. Glover – D. Klingman – A. Napier, A note on finding all shortest path, *Management Science Report Series*, Univ. of Colorado, Bulder, Colorado 1972.

[8]   T.C. Hu, A decomposition algorithm for shortest path in a network, *Opns. Res.*, 16 (1968), 91-102.

[9]   J.J. Jarvis – A.M. Jezior, Maximal flow with gains through a special network, *Opns. Res.*, 19 (1971), 678-688.

[10] W.S. Jewell, Optimal flow through network with gains, *Opns. Res.*, 10 (1962), 476-499.

[11] S. Warshall, A theorem on Boolean matrices, *J. of ACM*, 9 (1962), 11-12.

[12] J.Y. Yen, On Hu's decomposition algorithm for shortest path in a network, *Opns. Res.*, 19 (1971), 983-985.

András Bakó,

Computer and Automation Institute of Hungarian Academy of Sciences, 1014 Budapest, I. Uri u. 49, Hungary.

COLLOQUIA MATHEMATICA SOCIETATIS JÁNOS BOLYAI

12. PROGRESS IN OPERATIONS RESEARCH, EGER (HUNGARY), 1974.

PREDICTION OF MACROECONOMIC TIME SERIES BY SYSTEMS OF DISTRIBUTED LAG EQUATIONS

G. BÁNKÖVI — J. VELICZKY — M. ZIERMANN

The authors briefly discuss in the paper their investigations in the field of prediction of interdependent macrocategories used for the planning of the national economy.

At first these examinations covered the contemporary static interrelationships of macrocategories (Section 1.). The experiences and theoretical considerations led the authors to the investigation of a fully recursive model (Section 2.). This dynamic model has already undergone verifications proving many interesting connections between macrocategories and lagged ones. Simulation experiments have been carried out with the recursive model (Section 3.). An a posteriori classification of the macrocategories based on a graph theoretical interpretation of the model is given (Section 6.).

Finally two new concepts are introduced: the dynamic principal components and dynamic factors which can be applied to characterize the dynamic properties of the development of economy by a lower number of variables (Section 5.).

1. MULTIVARIATE REGRESSION ANALYSIS OF CONTEMPORARY ECONOMIC CATEGORIES

The authors have been engaged since 1968 in the examination based on multivariate stochastic interrelationships of the macrocategories of economic planning. The numerical values of these categories are strongly aggregated "measuring numbers" of the economic development. These quantities are the results of partly known, partly unknown factors which are unlikely to be considered. It can be assumed that some of these "latent" factors are common to several macrocategories under examinations. In order to discover multivariate linear regression interrelationships of the time series of these categories so-called full circle computations were performed. The computations have been carried out by stepwise linear regression analysis. The regression computations were used not only for the estimation of the parameters but also for the selection of the explanatory variables to be included in the equations.*

The equation systems (macroeconomic models) contained only contemporary economic variables, i.e. they described *static systems.* These types of models are very useful for the economic analysis of static interrelationships of macrocategories involved in these regression equations; they are, however, rather problematic for prediction because, in order to predict the future values of the explained variables, the explanatory variables had to be taken "from outside". The group of exogenous variables taken from outside does by no means constitute a consistent system, so that the estimation of endogenous variables, obtained by these equations is mostly unacceptable. Difficulties increase when we are to forecast in this way for more than one period (e.g. for medium or long range planning).

The difficulties in forecasting with the above mentioned static systems (containing contemporary multivariate regression equations) convinced us that *in econometric models designed for forecasting the majority of the exogenous variables must be lagged variables.*

---

*These computations were performed together with the *Mathematical Institute and Computer Centre* of the *Lajos Kossuth University* of Debrecen.

2. FORECAST-ORIENTED RECURSIVE ECONOMETRIC MODELS

The investigation of multivariate regression interrelationships of the lagged variables of macroeconomic categories began in 1972 on the *ICL* System 4-70 computer of the *National Planning Office*. Our investigations and computations led us to the following conclusions:

(a) Economic considerations are for the application of lagged variables because the consecutive values of the macrocategories are affected by the earlier ones as it is clear also in theory;

(b) The macroeconomic variables were closely correlated partly to their own lagged time series, partly to other delayed time series;

(c) The econometric models of recursive type have many advantages from computational aspects of forecasting.

Starting from these statements we constructed the following *dynamic econometric system model*

$$(1) \qquad Y_i(t) = \sum_{h=1}^{m} a_{ih} f_h(t) + \sum_{j=1}^{n} \sum_{k=1}^{L} b_{ijk} Y_j(t-k) \quad i = 1, 2, \ldots, n,$$

where

$Y_i(t)$ is the regression estimation of the i-th time series (of the i-th "basic" variable);

f_h are functions of time (practically power functions of t);

$Y_j(t-k)$ is the j-th time series lagged by k time unit;*

m is the number of the time functions;

n is the number of the time series;

L is the maximal lag;

a_{ih}, b_{ijk} are estimated coefficients.

---

*In the domain of the "starting" data for the recursion these quantities may be equal to the original data or to any other given set of numbers.

The model described by the equation system in (1) is *fully recursive;* predicted values may be calculated step-by-step using an initial matrix of size $L \times n$ as "starting data". It does not contain contemporary relationships; this kind of equations can be, however, added to the system by introducing artificial variables in the way described in [3].

It is to be seen from the relationships (1) that $m + nL$ unknown parameters appear formally in the equation of every basic variable; on the other hand, the observations in the time series are reduced by a number L because of the consideration of the lagged variables.

In one of our special models the values were $m = 7$, $n = 15$, $L = 5$, while the data series, having originated from the period 1950-72, have shortened to a size of 18 observations. This instance, too, demonstrates the problem which has to be faced in general, except in the case of small-size models, in the course of constructing econometric models; namely that the number of parameters to be estimated possibly exceeds the number of the data available. The problem can be overcome by choosing one part (in general the greater part) of the parameters of the equation system (1) *a priori* zero. The designers of the econometric models used to do this; then the computational work consists in determining the numerical values of the parameters only, and can easily be performed by regression calculations.

Those who have already tried to verify their theoretical econometric models know well that they always had to make concessions from their ideas in the course of the calculations, replace some variables in the equations and perform further experiments. In this way it seems to be rather difficult to obtain such a goodness of fit which is indispensable for acceptable prediction.

In constructing the dynamic models we can write up a lot of relationships which "explain" the basic variables (e.g. the national income) by lagged variables. The problem is, however, by which economic criteria can (if at all) be decided which of the relationships is the best one.

If criteria of mathematical statistics are applied for the selection of the variables then the requirements can be fairly exactly defined to facilitate the decision between various alternatives. The algorithm of stepwise regression calculations* enables a multilevel decision between the *a priori m* functions and *nL* lagged variables in the equations of the basic variables. After this decision process only the statistically significant variables do remain in the equations, while the other (insignificant) ones — economically justified the same way — "fall out".

On each decision level the designer of the model has the possibility to intervene in the selection process of the explanatory variables on the basis of economic considerations and expectations.

Our procedure, however, does not guarantee us to find from among many millions of possible variants the mathematically "optimal" ones, i.e. the set of the best fitting variables. The empirical experiences are at the same time quite satisfactory ([1], [2], [3]); a close fitting is likely to be obtained by a few lagged variables.

In the *Computing Centre of the Hungarian National Planning Office* a program was prepared for the prediction procedure based on the equation system (1). This program can operate 42 time series and a lag with 6 units. The built-in $f_h(t)$ functions have the form of t^p $(-5 \leqslant p \leqslant 5)$ but also other time series can be inserted in a special way. All those time functions can be considered for which the recursive equations (equation systems) permitted in model (1) can be written up. Several examples are given in paper [3].

3. SIMULATION BY THE DYNAMIC ECONOMIC MODEL (1)

No method of forecasting the particular time series guarantees automatically that any deterministic interrelationship will remain valid for the predicted values of the basic variables. It was demonstrated in paper [3] how linear constraints of a certain type can be considered for the predicted development of the recursive economic system (1).

On the basis of various economic concepts the future development of

*In our calculations the Multiple Regression program of the ICL System 4 Statistics Scheme was used.

the basic variables in the system can be modified. We are this way enabled to create and analyse several variants of plan. It must be noted that in general the predicted values of not only the variables in the constraints will be modified but even those of all variables of the system. Several such investigations — simulation experiments — have been carried out with our verified models.

Simulation experiments are also excellent tools for obtaining numerical estimates of the prediction errors. In general, the estimation of the prediction errors of the explained variables is a rather difficult theoretical problem owing to the complicated probabilistic character of the econometric models.

4. AN A POSTERIORI CLASSIFICATION OF THE BASIC VARIABLES

In the fully recursive equation system (1) all basic variables are formally endogenous while all lagged variables are exogenous. Such a classification of variables is connected purely with the aspect of delay.*

We can classify the basic variables in a more subtle way, namely by considering the position of lagged variables in the equation system. This new *(a posteriori)* classification is based on the following two pairs of conditions

(A1): The equation of a basic variable $Y_i(t)$ $(i = 1, \ldots, n)$ contains at least one lagged variable of another time series;

(A2): The equation of $Y_i(t)$ does not contain any lagged variables of other time series.

(B1): At least one lagged variable of $Y_i(t)$ is present in the equation of some other basic variable;

(B2): No lagged variable of $Y_i(t)$ is present in the equations of the other basic variables.

*Thus all the basic variables can be predicted technically in the same manner (without making any *a priori* classification). Economic considerations may be taken into account when establishing regression equations; namely a set of variables may be excluded from entering certain equations.

We may call a basic variable $Y_i(t)$

quasi-exogenous, if (A2) and (B1) hold;

quasi-endogenous, if (A1) and (B2) hold;

mixed, if (A1) and (B1) hold;

isolated, if (A2) and (B2) hold.

The analogies between the quasi-exogenous and quasi-endogenous variables of a recursive system and the exogenous and endogenous variables of a general economic system, respectively, are quite obvious.

By using these concepts we may define several categories of sets of basic variables.

For instance, the set of variables for which (B1) holds, may be called the *kernel of the system.* It is quite natural to introduce the concepts of *an isolated subset* and of a *connected system* (containing no isolated subsets). These concepts may easily be represented by an oriented graph whose vertices are the basic variables while the edges correspond to the appearance of lagged variables in the regression equations.

The graph representation of a recursive system may be used for describing the "structure" of the system and for simulating the effects caused by an artificial change in the starting data. By our experimental calculations we might conclude that models containing "natural variables" only, could hardly describe the way of spreading of the effects in a real system; this was one of the reasons having led us to investigate "artificial variables".

An interesting paradox arises in connection with the structure of a recursive system; namely in general, by increasing the number of edges in the graph of the system, partly the flexibility of the model will be improved, partly the statistical errors will be increased (because of the decrease in the degrees of freedom).

It may be important to investigate how the structure of the system changes when we add new basic variables to the model. A model may be called *structurally stable* if the kernel of the system remains unchanged when any subset of the new variables under consideration is added to; in this case the original set of variables contains the most important informations available on the causes of economic development. We may add, however, new variables to the system with the intention of improving its structural properties; this occurs in many cases when artifical variables are constructed.

5. THE USE OF DYNAMIC PRINCIPAL COMPONENTS AN DYNAMIC FACTORS

The method of factor analysis was used by several Hungarian authors for the investigation of time series systems ([7], [8]). The factors obtainable in this way are, however, based on contemporary relations.

For that very reason we looked for such kind of artificial variables (functions of the basic variables) which can be applied to characterize the dynamic properties of a recursive system. We may consider the following aspects of the question:

(i)   If a vector process can be described by a lower number of variables it is important to find them. These variables may characterize the "dynamic invariance" of the process.

(ii)   A key to the handling of large systems is to express the basic variables as functions of a few artificial variables.

(iii)   The prediction errors can be decreased by applying "more stable" explanatory variables in the equations.

(iv)   The model may become more flexible from the point of view of the reaction to changes in starting data. In this way the paradox mentioned in §4 can be resolved.

(v)   Artifical variables can be used to measure the structural changes of the predicted paths or (as constraints) to control the forecasted process.

On the basis of aspects (i)-(v) we may easily formulate two conditions which must be imposed on "dynamic artifical variables":

(a) these artifical variables must be well predictable;

(b) the basic variables must be well expressible by the delayed artifical ones.

In general we may not be sure that both conditions (a) and (b) can be completely satisfied at the same time.

We may aim at optimizing either according to condition (a) or to condition (b); the obtained artifical variables are called *dynamic principal components* in the first case while *dynamic factors* in the second.

The mathematical problem of determining dynamic artificial variables leads to the necessity of solving non-linear equation systems. Although we have elaborated some iteration procedures and computer programs for this purpose, further investigations are planned. Below we briefly described how to determine dynamic principal components.

Determination of dynamic principal components. The dynamic principal components are to be determined one by one. As a first step a linear combination of certain basic variables is indicated. Then a recursive function is established by the investigator in an intuitive way. (In practice we consider the linear functions of certain lagged variables of the dynamic principal components.)

The task consists in maximizing the multiple correlation coefficient of the recursive regression equation in terms of the coefficients of the variables forming the component and of the parameters of the regression equation. The problem is not purely of an optimization character because we intend to consider only variables entering the linear combination in a statistically significant way and lagged variables entering the regression equation in a significant way. Therefore not only the coefficients and parameters will change their values but both the dynamic component and the recursive function may be structurally changed in the course of the investigation.

After having determined the first dynamic principal component we screen it out of all basic variables (i.e. we orthogonalize the variables with respect to the principal component). Then the second component will be determined by the same method using the orthogonalized variables instead of the original ones. After having obtained the second component we may orthogonalize the basic variables again (with respect to the first two principal components) and so on.

Experimental calculations were performed by using annual data for the period 1950-1972 of 15 important categories (characterizing production, fixed assets, investment, consumption, working power, foreign trade) of the Hungarian national economy. A recursive system of equations (with a maximal lag $L = 5$) for the variables were determined and predicted paths were calculated under several constraints. The first dynamic principal component $F_1(t)$ was constructed as such a linear combination of significantly entering variables which maximizes the correlation coefficient between $F_1(t)$ and $F_1(t - 5)$. This correlation coefficient was proved to be 0.9998. $F_1(t)$ contained five basic variables and was in the highest correlation with the gross value of fixed assets. Its curve described a nearly exponential groth with a 6% annual rate.

A second principal component $F_2(t)$ was formed as a linear combination of seven orthogonalized variables. On the basis of a preliminary analysis of the residuals this component was constructed in the way of maximizing the multiple correlation coefficient in the regression equation of $F_2(t)$ expressed as a function of $F_2(t - 1)$, $F_2(t - 2)$, $F_2(t - 3)$ and $F_2(t - 4)$. This yielded a wave shaped curve with a multiple correlation coefficient 0.991.

We may interprete the constructed dynamic principal components in the following way: the first one characterizes the *general development of the national economy* while the second one describes *fluctuations of the residual process*. We guess, however, that the construction of further dynamic principal components will be possible for the system under consideration.

REFERENCES

[1] G. Bánkövi – M. Ziermann, Estimation and prediction of macroeconomic relations by lagged variables, *Fifth Hungarian Conference on Operational Research*, Balatonfüred, 1973. A/1-4 paper. (In Hungarian).

[2] G. Bánkövi – M. Ziermann, Problems of dynamic prediction of macroeconomic relations, *Közgazdasági szemle*, 11 (1973), 1269-1286. (In Hungarian).

[3] G. Bánkövi – J. Veliczky – M. Ziermann, Prediction of time series by using recursive systems of equations, *Communications of the Computing Centre of the National Planning Office*, 1 (1973), 131-148. (In Hungarian).

[4] A.S. Goldberger, *Econometric Theory*, Wiley, New York, 1964.

[5] L.M. Koyck, *Distributed lags and investment analysis*, Amsterdam, 1954.

[6] E. Malinvaud, *Statistical Methods of Econometrics*, North-Holland Co., Amsterdam, 1970.

[7] G. Meszéna – Mrs. B. Simon, Investigations of the economic development by the application of the factor analysis, *Communications of the Research Centre for Planning of the National Planning Office*, Budapest, 1973. (In Hungarian).

[8] J. Rimler, A factoranalytical approach for the investigation of the development of the economy, *Közgazdasági Szemle*, 7-8 (1970), 913-926; No. 10. 1195-1214. (In Hungarian).

György Bánkövi

Computing Centre of the National Planning Office, 1149 Budapest, Angol u. 27,

József Veliczky

Computing Centre of the National Planning Office, 1149 Budapest, Angol u. 27,

Margit Ziermann

Hungarian National Planning Office, 1051 Budapest, Arany J. u. 6-8.

COLLOQUIA MATHEMATICA SOCIETATIS JÁNOS BOLYAI

12. PROGRESS IN OPERATIONS RESEARCH, EGER (HUNGARY), 1974.

A NEW OPTIMALIZATION CRITERION FOR GAMES AGAINST NATURE

SVETLANA BENEDIKT

Decisions must frequently be made in situations, when not all the necessary informations on the factors determining the consequences of the decision are available, for the results of the decision are also influenced by several random events, not subject of human will. The theory of games regards this situation — as known — as a game against nature. In the literature various criterions have been suggested for determining the optimum decision strategy in this case.

Such are e.g. the Bayes criterion, the principle of equal probabilities, the minimax criterion, the compromise criterion of Hurwicz, the principle of minimax risk of Savage. But the applicability of the listed criterias is strongly questionable in the case of games having the three properties given below and in certain concrete cases it is even impossible to apply them.

(A) The game occurs only once.

(B) The probability of occurence of various strategies of the nature can be estimated.

(C) Among the strategies of the nature there are strategies of small probability but grave consequences.

The games described above are mostly met with in the dispatcher control of technical systems. E.g. in preceding works of the author [1], [2], [3] it is shown that the selection of the optimum safe operation connection scheme of an electric network, — which is one of the main functions of the dispatcher control of energy systems, — may be conceived on the basis of the theory of games as the game of the dispatcher against nature. The strategies of the dispatcher are the connection schemes available for his selection, while the possible disturbances during the operation period of the schemes are the strategies of nature.

The "loss" of the dispatcher is the amount of the energy limitations appearing due to the disturbances. Fig. 1 shows the form of the possible game matrix for the case, when 3 connection schemes are available for selection and 10 various types of possible disturbances must be counted upon.

Since the combination of the possible dispatcher strategies varies from case to case, this game belongs to the category of the games played only once.

Similar situations are met with not alone with technical systems, but also in the field on human activities aimed at eliminating the failure operation of other types of systems (e.g. of the human organism).

Let us assume e.g. that a physician must decide on the most appropriate medical intervention in the case of a patient severely ill requiring fast intervention, while all the available medical interventions (e.g. drugs, surgical intervention, etc.) may involve also very dangerous complications, though of a low probability of occurrence; e.g. some drugs may have very grave secondary effects. The possible negative effects of the various medical interventions are not uniform and in addition the appearence of the negative effects of any medical intervention depends greatly on the individual peculiarities of the patient's organism, e.g. on whether the patient has an allergy against certain medicaments. As the physician is unable to know perfectly

		A_1	A_2	A_3
S_0	$p_0 = 0{,}99$	0	0	0
S_1	$p_1 = 8 \cdot 10^{-5}$	15940	0	0
S_2	$p_2 = 8 \cdot 10^{-5}$	265	250	0
S_3	$p_3 = 4 \cdot 10^{-4}$	0	0	265
S_4	$p_4 = 1 \cdot 10^{-4}$	0	2830	41000
S_5	$p_5 = 8 \cdot 10^{-5}$	0	0	340
S_6	$p_6 = 5 \cdot 10^{-4}$	6590	54	7320
S_7	$p_7 = 4 \cdot 10^{-4}$	1740	0	3700
S_8	$p_8 = 4 \cdot 10^{-4}$	4150	4150	4150
S_9	$p_9 = 4 \cdot 10^{-4}$	8300	8300	8300
S_{10}	$p_{10} = 4 \cdot 10^{-4}$	12450	12450	12450

Fig. 1

the above said peculiarities of the patient's organism at the moment of his decision, he cannot establish in advance the consequences of his decisions with a certainly of 100 percent. So the given situation may be considered as the game of the physician against nature, where his strategies are the medical interventions available for healing the actual illness, while the strategies of nature are the random factors influencing the consequences of the medical decisions. Since in this case the medical decisions may have also some very dangerous consequences, the game occurs for the patient only once.

Could the physician establish the probability of the appearance of the negative effects of all the possible medical interventions, then this game might be assigned to the category of the games to be investigated.

Let us consider now the question of the optimization criteria for the games of this type.

In the case of games having property B listed above, i.e. when the probability of the occurrence of the individual conditions of nature may be estimated, usually the Bayes principle is utilized for selecting the optimum decision.

This principle is based on the evaluation of the expected utility (loss) of the decisions, meaning that in the given case the decision A_i with the expected losses of

$$(1) \qquad \sum_{j=1, 2, \ldots, n} u_{ij} p_j$$

representing the minimum is regarded to be the optimum decision, where p_j is the probability that the nature applies strategy S_j; u_{ij} is the loss of the decisionmaker belonging to the $(A_i S_j)$ strategy pair.

The applicability of this principle is very problematic, when the conditions A and C are presented simultaneously, moreover even by the fact alonge, that the game occurs only once, as namely *the maximization, or minimization of the utility, or the expected losses permits to attain the maximum, or minimum mean value only in the case of a great number of reiterating decisions, as the law of the great numbers apply only in this case.* This is why O s k a r L a n g e [4] says that the application of the Bayes principle is meaningless in the case of a single, non-returning decision, even if the conditions of nature are reiterating and their probability may be estimated. Also P . C . F i s h b u r n [5] negates the applicability of this principle to individual decisions, but he states that this inapplicability exists in connection with *the objective, i.e. relative frequency interpretation of probability.* A . R a p o p o r t [6] presents the same view, but points out that the rationality of applying the Bayes principle for single decision may be supported in the case of the following subjective interpretation of probability: *The probability of an event is to be understood as the degree of belief in its occurrence. But the probabilities reflect in great lines the above degree only, if they are not very low,* – to this opinion.

He illustrates this statement by the following example: when our incertitude as to the occurrence of the event is highest, a probability of 0.5 may be assumed; *a 50% variation of this probability value (i.e. to 0.75, or 0.25) corresponds to approximately the same change in our estimation.* But the position is quite different, when e.g. $p = 0.0001$. In this case the degree of our belief is hardly influenced even by a 10-fold increase (to 0.001), or decrease (to 0.00001) of the value of p, while the applying the Bayes principle for the probabilities of some strategy of the nature 0,001, 0.0001, 0.00001 the decision will be influenced by the above mentioned values in a significant way (as also Rapoport illustrates it by a concrete example). Therefore he *doubts the applicability of this principle to individual decisions in the case of random events of low probability.* On the basis of the above considerations the rationality of the application of the Bayes principle cannot be sustained in the case of games against nature occuring only once and where the effects of low probability strategies of nature must also be taken into account.

Simultaneously with the possible very grave consequences of the low probability strategies of nature the application of the Bayes principle may imply high risks too.

Let us consider e.g. the following concrete situation: For a very important single application of a technical device (e.g. for an important scientific experiment) we must decide (evidently this is a single decision) on the optimum safe mode of operation of the device. Two types of disturbances are possible during the operation of the device, whose consequences depend greatly on its mode of operation. Let us assume that the game matrix shown in Fig. 2, where A_1, A_2 and A_3 are the various modes of operations, S_1 and S_2 the strategies of nature involving the disturbances of type 1 and 2 respectively, S_3 represents the absence of any disturbance corresponding to the described situation. The matrix elements represent the possible losses due to the disturbances; in addition we assume the values of $p_1 = 0{,}1$ and $p_2 = 0{,}001$.

	S_1 $p = 0{,}1$	S_2 $p = 0{,}001$	S_3 $p = 0{,}899$	$\sum u_{ij} p_j$
A_1	300	10000	0	40
A_2	500	400	0	50,4
A_3	600	300	0	60,3

Fig. 2

If the Bayes principle is going to be applied, then the strategy A_1 must be selected, implying a higher risk by far, than the other strategies, as the real possibility of the disturbance causing very grave consequences is connected to this strategy.

Let us assume now that the probabilities of the occurrence of the strategies of nature are unknown.

The principle of equal probabilities, as a specific case of the principle discussed above, cannot be applied to the given case, in principle.

The compromise principle of Hurwitz considering as optimum the decision A_i, for which the sum

$$(2) \qquad \alpha \min_{j} u_{ij} + (1 - \alpha) \max_{j} u_{ij}$$

is minimum (with the coefficients α and $1 - \alpha$ expressing the degree of optimism and pessimism respectively) is essentially closely related to the Bayes principle, it is in fact a simplified reduction of the same and as such it deserves a similar criticism [4].

Let us consider now the applicability of the minimax criterion. According to this criterion an A_i strategy with a minimum value of $\max\limits_{j} u_{ij}$ is considered as optimum. The minimax criterion may be applied to games of a given type with the advantages of a high cautiousness and the absence of risk. The criterion sets out namely from the worst possible consequences of the evaluated decisions, tries to minimize them as much as possible and offers the guarantee of the absence of losses exceeding the value $\min\limits_{i} \max\limits_{j} u_{ij}$.

The disadvantage of the minimax criterion is its unjustified pessimism in assuming, that nature applies always the strategy implying the most dangerous consequences. Hereby it disregards the probability of various strategies to be applied by nature.

So the application of the minimax criterion may easily lead to even totally irrational decisions from the aspect of common sense. Let us consider e.g. the following game matrix (Fig. 3).

	S_1 $p = 0,1$	S_2 $p = 0,0001$	S_3 $p = 0,8999$	$\max\limits_{j} u_{ij}$
A_1	1000	300	0	1000
A_2	200	1100	0	1100

Fig. 3

According to the minimax criterion the first decision is to be selected, because $\max_j u_{1j} < \max_j u_{2j}$. Yet by common sense the decision A_2 is more rational, because the value $\max_j u_{2j}$ exceeds $\max_j u_{1j}$ by a mere 10%, while the probability of the occurrence of the preceding one is 1000-times lower.

The minimax risk principle suggested by Savage as a perfection of the minimax principle fails to exclude the above disadvantage of the latter, while in the technical applications, where the absolute losses are more cardinal, than the relative ones, the application of the minimax risk criterion based on relative losses is greatly questionable.

On the basis of the above the idea of modifying the minimax criterion in a way as to preserve its cautiousness, while eliminating its wholly unjustified pessimism, offered itself. For this purpose the starting point of the criterion must be first of all modified.

The minimax criterion uses the wholly unjustified pessimistic assumption that nature selects always a strategy of maximum u_{ij} loss value, while the modified criterion suggests to consider the reasonableness of the assumptions of the occurrence of various strategies of nature and assumes that nature responds to the A_i strategies of the decision maker by a strategy of $j = m_i$ order (designated in the following by S_{mi}), for which the product of the losses by the coefficient k_j expressing the degree of before-mentioned reasonableness, is maximum, i.e. where the equality

$$(3) \qquad k_{m_i} u_{im_i} = \max_j (k_j u_{ij})$$

holds.

It means that on applying the strategy A_i the losses u_{im_i} must be counted upon.

The coefficient k_j expresses numerically how far the assumption of nature applying the strategy S_j is regarded as justified. This coefficient varies between the limits

(4) $0 \leqslant k_j \leqslant 1$.

As the value of m_i varies generally with the various i values, the justification of the basic assumption of the decisions is not identical for the various strategies A_i either. This fact is evidently not indifferent for the decision.

Let us assume namely that with the strategies A_c and A_d

(5) $u_{cm_c} = u_{dm_d}$.

At the same time

$$k_{m_c} > k_{m_d} \ .$$

So now the strategy A_c is seen to be more dangerous, than A_d, namely in proportion with $\dfrac{k_{mc}}{k_{md}}$. The position is, as if the risk incurred by applying the strategy A_i were proportional with the value of the coefficient k_{m_i} belonging to it. Therefore the modified criterion uses the value of the product $k_{m_i} \cdot u_{im_i}$ instead of u_{im_i} for evaluating the strategy A_i, which is regarded as optimum, when the value of this product is minimum. With (3) taken into account the criterion may also be formulated as follows: Optimum is the strategy A_i, to which

(4) $\min\limits_{i} \max\limits_{j} (k_j u_{ij})$

corresponds.

The coefficient k_j — whose determination is still depending — can be determined first of all on the basis of the available objective data on the probability of the occurrence of the various strategies of nature. It seems logical namely to accept that the coefficient k_j is a function of the probability p_j of the occurrence of the strategy S_j, i.e.

(5) $k_j = f(p_j)$.

At the same time in the interest of preserving the cautious character of the criterion the coefficient k_j must reflect the aspects of the cautiousness as well.

In order to account for all the above conditions the function $f(p_j)$ must satisfy the following requirements:

(1) *$f(p_j)$ must be an increasing function. This requirement reflects the fact that evidently the higher the probability of the occurrence of S_j, the more our assumption concerning the occurrence of the strategy S_j is justified.*

(2) *For the extremal values of p_j the following equalities must apply*

(a) $f(1) = 1$

(b) $f(0) = 0$.

By this requirement the following conditions are satisfied

$$k_j = 1$$
$$j = 1$$

$$k_j = 0$$
$$j = 0$$

(3) *With the p_j values tending very closely to the function $f(p_j)$ must satisfy the following condition*

$$\frac{f(p_m)}{f(p_n)} \approx \frac{p_m}{p_n}$$

meaning that at very high probabilities the coefficient k_j must very proportionally with p_j.

(4) *The ratio* $\dfrac{f(p_j)}{p_j}$ *is increasing sharply with the decrease of p_j.*
This requirement is dictated by the aspect of the cautiousness, as it serves to ensure that the strategies of nature with a relatively low probability, but implying very grave losses may also have in influence on the decision.

All our listed requirements are satisfied e.g. by the function

(5) $$f(p_j) = \frac{1}{1 - \ln p_j}$$

(1) This function is increasing in the interval $0 < p_j < 1$, as

$$f'(p_j) > 0$$

in this interval.

(2) $f(1) = 1$ and $f(0) = 0$

(3) $f'(1) = 1$. This ensures the satisfaction of 3 requirement.

(4) The function $\varphi(p_j) = \dfrac{f(p_j)}{p_j}$ decreases with the increase of p_j in the interval $0 < p_j < 1$, as here $\varphi'(p_j) < 0$, meaning that the ratio $\dfrac{f(p_j)}{(p_j)}$ is increasing with the decrease of p_j, while the logarithmic character of the function ensures a significant measure of this increase.

Let us consider now which strategy may be regarded optimum on the basis of the described criterion in the case of the game matrices shown in Figs. 2 and 3. For this purpose we evaluate the values $\max\limits_{j} [f(p_j)u_{ij}]$ and $\min\limits_{i} \max\limits_{j} [f(p_j)u_{ij}]$. These results of the evaluation are seen in Figs. 4 and 5 respectively. According to the criterion the strategy A_2 may be regarded as optimum for both cases. This evaluation complies with common sense also best, as discussed before, on the basis of the preceding considerations.

	S_1 $p = 0,1$	S_2 $p = 0,001$	S_3 $p = 0,899$	$\max_j [f(p_j)u_{ij}]$	$\min_i \max_j [f(p_j)u_{ij}]$
A_1	300	10000	0	1270	
A_2	500	400	0	152	152
A_3	600	300	0	180	

Fig. 4

	S_1 $p = 0,1$	S_2 $p = 0,0001$	S_3 $p = 0,8999$	$\max_j [f(p_j)u_{ij}]$	$\min_i \max_j [f(p_j)u_{ij}]$
A_1	1000	300	0	303	
A_2	200	1100	0	93	93

Fig. 5

REFERENCES

[1] Sz. Benedikt, *Energiarendszerek számítógépes irányításának néhány problémájáról*, Dissertation, Budapest, 1963.

[2] T. Vámos — S. Benedikt — M. Uzsoki, Some recent results in the computer control of energy systems, *Second International Congress of IFAC on Automatic Control*, 1963.

[3] S. Benedikt, A criterium for the evaluation of reliability of operative basic schemes of energy systems, (in Russian) *Electrical Engineering — Elektrotechnik*, 11, 3, Budapest, 1967.

[4] O. Lange, *Optimális döntések*, Budapest, 1966.

[5] P.C. Fishburn, *Decision and value theory*, John Wiley and Sons, New York, 1964.

[6] A. Rapoport, *Strategy and conscience*, Harper and Row, New York, 1964.

Svetlana Benedikt

Computer and Automation Institute of the Hungarian Academy of Sciences, 1502 Budapest, XI. Kende u. 13-17.

COMPUTER SIMULATIONS OF COMBINED ECOLOGICAL AND HYDRODYNAMIC PROCESSES IN A SILL FIORD

J.E. BEYER — O.B.G. MADSEN

ABSTRACT

An ecological and hydrodynamic simulation model for an estuary is described. The model makes it possible to evaluate the effects of alternative wastewater treatment plans and can thereby serve as a tool for resource planning.

The hydrodynamic model consists of a two-dimensional, 11-box model for calculation of the water movement based on data describing variations in the salinity of the water. The fiord considered is a sill fiord where practically all renewal of the bottom water, situated in the inner part of the fiord, takes place through aperiodic intrusion of ocean water, occurring during certain meteorological situations.

The ecological model consists of 11 combined DYNAMO-simulation models, one belonging to each box. Each of the simulation models has 9 levels and 21 rate-variables. The oxygen content and the transparency of the water in each box is chosen as a measure of the water quality and the model calculates these quantities from the growth of algae and mineralization of organic matter as a function of nitrogen and phosphorus amounts, the oxygen content, the temperature of the water, the intensity of the light and the material exchanges between the water and the sedimentary layer on the bottom of the estuary. Bacterial diseases and slowly decomposable toxigens are not taken into consideration.

An IBM 370/165 computer was used, and the simulation language was DYNAMO.

As a practical example a Danish sill fiord is considered. Some of the results are presented and the sensitivity of the model is tested in order to indicate how changes in uncertain data will influence the results obtained.

INTRODUCTION

In the forthcoming years the societies in industrial countries will spend considerable amounts of money for controlling the wastewater treatment. There can often be doubt about the practical effects of a planned but not constructed wastewater treatment plan, and this can cause erroneous investments.

The purpose of this paper is to present a total hydrodynamic and ecological simulation model for an estuary which may be used to estimate how a given wastewater treatment plan will determine water quality. This makes it possible to give a relation between the economic aspects of water cleaning and water quality.

The total model is based on both a hydrodynamic and an ecological model. The fiord is partitioned into a number of boxes and a total blending of the various biological components is assumed in each box. An ecological model is related to each box and the idea is then to start with some initial set of ecological conditions, then to simulate the ecological changes during one time period and then in the hydrodynamic model to calculate the water exchange between the boxes. This gives new initial concentrations in each box and it is then possible to calculate the ecological changes in the next time period and so on.

A large literature is available on qualitative behaviour of estuarine eco-systems. A recommended brief account on general estuarine ecology is Chapter 13 in (O d u m , [12]). The theory behind the box-model approach may be found in (K e e l i n g and B o l i n, [9]), and P r i t c h a r d , [11]). Not much literature is available as regards quantitative description of estu-arine ecosystems. However, single biological processes have been studied to some degree, in particular the photosynthesis production of algae (P a t t e n , [13]).

A recent preliminary investigation of the water quality in the consid-ered estuary (S m i d t h , [16]), constitutes the data source for the present study.

For a detailed description of the model and the results obtained see (B e y e r and M a d s e n, [2]) and (N i e l s e n and S a a b y e, [11]).

DESCRIPTION OF THE HYDRODYNAMIC CONDITIONS IN MARIAGER FIORD

The fiord is situated at the eastern coast of Jutland in Denmark and it has a length of 40 km. The outer half of the fiord is very shallow and has a depth of 5.7 m in a channel, while the inner part has a maximum depth of about 30 m. This means, that the volume of the inner fiord is approximately ten times larger than the volume of the outer fiord. This must be taken into consideration in the model which will be described below. The renewal of the water in the fiord takes place in two different ways

(1) The renewal of the bottom water in the inner fiord takes place almost entirely through aperiodic intrusion of ocean water, which normal-ly occurs when a strong wind has blown from west or northwest for some time. This happens, on the average, ten times a year. It is assumed that the duration of each intrusion and the time between two successive intru-sions follow exponential distributions with expectations of 3 and $(365 - 10 \times 3)/10 = 33.5$ days respectively. As it will be discussed later, the final results are not very sensitive to this assumption.

(2) The rest of the water is regularly exchanged due to the tidal water (the normal tide = 0.4 m), the wind and the fresh water runoff. There exist only a few adequate measurements of appropriate parameters. This makes it very difficult to describe in detail the total water movement in the fiord empirically.

THE HYDRODYNAMIC MODEL

The problem is to construct and solve a reasonable hydrodynamic model which can take the few existing measurements into consideration and which can describe the water movements in the fiord.

Since the purpose of the model was not to give precise predictions of such quantities as the level of the water, but to serve as a total model for both hydrodynamic and ecological relations, it was decided to construct two very simple box-models to describe the hydrodynamic conditions, one box-model for the periods without intrusion of ocean water and one for the short periods with intrusion. This decision was made because there were too few data to construct a realistic statistical model and because there was too much unknown water exchange with the sea to construct a reasonable local hydrodynamic model for Mariager Fiord based in physical equations. It had then been necessary to take the physical conditions in both North and Baltic Seas into consideration.

Fig. 2 shows a vertical picture of the box-model. The boxes are a schematic representation of the boxes shown in Fig. 1. One box represents the bottom water in the inner fiord and six boxes represent the remaining part of the fiord. The reason for choosing 6 boxes was based on a compromise between having as few boxes as possible (shorter calculation time in both the hydrodynamic and the ecological model) and needing a reasonable number of boxes in order to describe in some detail the different parts of the fiord from hydrodynamic, geographic and environmental points of view, and to verify the assumptions about the homogenity of each box. The lower boxes in the outer part of the fiord are only used in the short periods with intrusion of ocean water. The volumes of the 4 bottom boxes are from 6.5 to 50 percent of the volumes of the corresponding upper

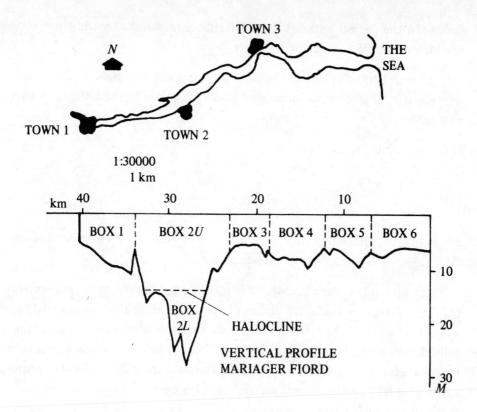

Fig. 1

Fig. 2

boxes. In the period without intrusion of ocean water the 4 bottom boxes are included in the upper boxes.

In order to calculate the water movements in the two-dimensional models, it is necessary to know one tracer and then to solve the continuity equations

(1) $$\sum_j Q_{ij} = \sum_j Q_{ji}$$

(2) $$V_i \frac{\partial c_i}{\partial t} = \sum_j Q_{ji} c_j - c_i \sum_j Q_{ij}$$

where Q_{ij} is the water flow from box i to box j, V_i is the volume of box i, c_i is the tracer concentration in box i.

If V_i and c_i are known, it is possible to find the water movements Q_{ij} by solving the linear equations (1) and (2). Here the salinity of the water is chosen as the tracer. In fact, we did not have a complete, empirically-determined, dynamic salinity profile as a function of space and time. It was therefore necessary to construct the following approximate formula for the salinity of the water, partly based on empirical measurements and partly based on a theoretical relation

(3) $$c_i(t) = A_i(1 + B_i e^{-C_i t})$$

where c is the salinity of the water in the i-th box at time t, A_i, B_i and C_i are constants.

It is necessary to use different set of constants in periods with and without intrusion of ocean water. Fig. 3 shows an example of the salinity in the i-th box as a function of time. When the constants have been determined, it is possible to find the differential change in salinity and then to solve the linear continuity equations and calculate the water movement. These can then be used as input information for the ecological model. It should be mentioned that it is not difficult to replace the above described model with any other appropriate hydrodynamic model.

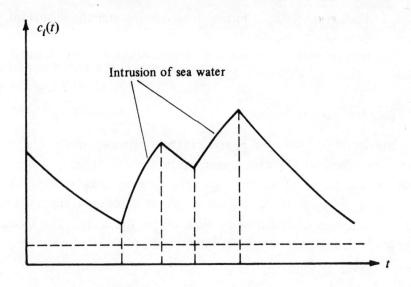

$c_i(t)$

Intrusion of sea water

Fig. 3

THE DESCRIPTIVE MODEL OF POLLUTION

The fiord under consideration represents a region with a little change of water and a high content of nutrients in the waste water. The photosynthetic production of algae, i.e. the primary production is therefore high, which reduces the transparency and makes the water unfit for bathing. At the same time a large portion of the dissolved oxygen is used for mineralization of organic matter, making the conditions unfavorable for fishes.

The first phase of the model-building process is to select the water quality parameters to be utilized. The transparency of the water and the oxygen content are the chosen parameters for water quality. The interest is, in other words, focussed on the consequence of natural and artificial eutrophication. The processes of cultural eutrophication are in principle the same as those active under natural conditions. They are however much more intensive and lead more quickly to an alternation of the character of the water region.

Cultural eutrophication is a consequence of two basic mechanisms:

1. *Primary Pollution*

The organic material in the sewage discharged decomposes and consumes the dissolved oxygen in the water.

2. *Secondary Pollution*

Nutrients, i.e. inorganic phosphorus and nitrogen, in the sewage discharge and nutrients from the mineralization of the discharged organic material give rise to an artificially great primary production of algae. This algal biomass slowly sinks to the bottom where decomposition takes place, with consumption of the oxygen dissolved in the water. The inorganic component disintegrates and goes into the water phase as nutritious material for continued growth.

Therefore the model has to include the following mechanisms and processes

1. Nutrient cycling

2. Oxygen cycling

3. Processes concerning mineralization of discharged organic material

4. Processes concerning the increase in sediment thickness

5. Sun irradiation

6. Water temperature.

The primary purpose of this section is to develop a descriptive ecological model for each box of the fiord system in such a way that it is possible to combine all the model sections into a single model which can be used to simulate the consequence of different sewage purifications. The model's time scale is less than the normal lifetime of sewage purification, say 5-30 years. This means, that the consequences due to diurnal fluctuations can be satisfactorily described by simple methods.

In the following discussion we will focus on the basic mechanism of the model using the methodology of system dynamics.

The time subscript notation applied may cause some confusion at the outset. However, the DYNAMO notation is easily illustrated. Consider for example the photosynthetic growth rate of algae, *PP*. This total growth rate may at any instant be regarded as proportional to the present amount of algal biomass, *A*, i.e.

$$A(t + \Delta t) = A(t) + \dot{\Delta}t * PP(t) + o(\Delta t)$$

with

$$PP(t) = C(t) * A(t)$$

where *t* is the time. In DYNAMO these equations read

$$A \cdot K = A \cdot J + DT * PP \cdot JK$$

and

$$PP \cdot KL = C \cdot K * A \cdot K$$

where the time step *DT* is the elapsed time between the time points *J* and *K*. Whenever used a multiplication sign is stated by a star to prevent mixing up with the time point subscription above. For further details the reader is referred to the appendix where System Dynamics and the correlated simulation language DYNAMO briefly is described.

NUTRIENT CYCLING

In the nature it is practically always phosphorus, nitrogen or light which is the limiting factor for biotic growth. Photosynthesis is therefore assumed to be satisfactorily described by a combined Michaelis — Menton expression

$$PP \cdot KL = MY * A \cdot K * PT \cdot K * DF \cdot K *$$

(4)

$$* \left(\frac{LI \cdot K}{KM + LI \cdot K}\right)\left(\frac{N \cdot K}{V * KN + N \cdot K}\right)\left(\frac{P \cdot K}{V * KP + P \cdot K}\right)$$

in which *MY, KM, KN and KP* are constants and *V* the volume of the box under consideration. It can be seen from (4) that the rate of *Primary*

Production* (PP) is limited by the availability of the *Light Intensity (LI)* and the concentration of both *Nitrogen (N)* and *Phosphorus (P)*. If the box is "saturated" by some of these factors, then the growth rate *(PP)* will be determined by the remaining factors only.

PT and *DF* temperature and daylength multipliers, respectively. The specific growth rate of phytoplankton increases approximately exponentially with increasing temperature. The maximum value, *MY*, corresponds to the maximum temperature, say 25°C. That is

$$(5) \qquad PT \cdot K = e^{-0.07 * (25 - TR \cdot K)}, \qquad TR \cdot K \leqslant 25°C$$

i.e. with a doubling temperature on 10°C. For box 2L the temperature is set constant to 5°C and for the others

$$(6) \qquad TR \cdot K = TM * \left(1 + \sin \left(\frac{2\pi}{365} (TIME \cdot K - 140) \right) \right)$$

where *TM* is the average temperature over the year. The start of the simulation, i.e. *TIME* = 0, was set to January 1. *TIME* is measured in units of 24 hours. The vernal equinox occurs at time 80. The maximum temperature occurs about 60 days after the summer solstice, resulting in a phase shift of 140.

Returning to (4) the light intensity *LI* is given as a function of depth and algal concentration by the law of Beer – Lambert (cf. C h e n, [4]). Averaging along the vertical water column gives for the upper boxes

$$(7) \qquad LI \cdot K = LO \cdot K * \frac{1 - e^{-(AL + BL * AC \cdot K) * D}}{(AL + BL * AC \cdot K) * D}$$

where *D* is the depth of the box, *AL* and *BL* are light extinction coefficients of the water alone and of algal suspension, respectively. *AC · K* is the algal concentration in the box and *LO · K* is the solar energy insolation at the water surface. The light intensity in the lower boxes is found in a similar way with the exception that *LO · K* is decreased due to the shading effect of the phytoplankton in the upper boxes.

The sinusodial expiration of the temperature results from the fact that

---

*A glossary of symbols is presented in connection with the total biological model in Fig. 5.

the total solar energy insolation per time unit to the first approximation varies sinusoidally. Also the light intensity during the day follows a sine function. This was approximated by a uniform distribution over a fictive daylength DF of $1 - 0.5 + 1/\pi$ times the real daylength, that is

$$(8) \qquad DF \cdot K = 0.5 * \left(1 + 0.5 * \sin\left(\frac{2\pi}{365}(TIME \cdot K - 80)\right)\right) * 0.82 .$$

Furthermore we have

$$(9) \qquad LO \cdot K = LM * \left(1 + 0.88 * \sin\left(\frac{2\pi}{365}(TIME \cdot K - 80)\right)\right)/DF \cdot K$$

where LM is an average value.

Finally, returning to (4), the primary production rate is proportional to the algal biomass (A) forming a positive loop. The algal biomass is represented by its total contents of N and P are present in the weight ratio 7:1 which is applied to the model. In Fig. 4 the principal causal-loop diagram for nitrogen cycling is depicted.

The corresponding causal-loop diagram for the phosphorus cycling is exactly the same.

Nitrogen is cycled by three positive feedback loops. The rate of cycling is controlled by five negative loops. The figure shows the primary cycling only, for example discharged N is omitted.

The net exchange of N and A between boxes, that is DN and DA are also omitted. These are calculated from (2) with C replaced by the concentration of the considered quantity.

The algal biomass goes either to the organic phase $(ORGS)$ or it is directly mineralized $(MINAV)$ mainly due to respiration. The amount of A which is consumed per unit time by respiration is (Anderson, [1]) proportional to the existing quantities of biomass and oxygen:

$$(10) \qquad MINAV \cdot KL = C1 * IMIDL \cdot K * A \cdot K$$

where $IMIDL$ is the average concentration of oxygen over the day. For the part which sediments we have

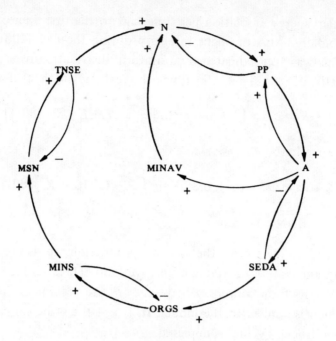

Fig. 4

A causal-loop diagram for the primary nitrogen cycle. Arrows indicate cause-and-effect relationships. For example, an increase in Nitrogen causes increases in every quantity of the big loop in the following order: Primary Production, Algal biomass, SEDimentation of Algae, ORGanic material in the Sediment, Mineralization of organic N in the sediment, aMount of inorganic N in the Sed. which finally increases the flow of N from the sed. back to N-pool.

(11) $SEDA \cdot KL = C2 * A \cdot K$

$C1$ and $C2^*$ are constants.

The mineralization of N in the sediment phase is considered to take place with rate**

---

*All quantities with prescript C are constants.

**The CLIP-function is described in the appendix.

(12) $\quad MINS \cdot KL = C8 * ORGS \cdot K * CLIP(I \cdot K, C9, I \cdot K, 10^{-7})$

similarly for Phosphorus. Finally the N-loop is closed by flow of N from SED to the water phase

(13) $\quad TNSE \cdot KL = C13 * MSN \cdot K/SEF$

where SEF is the effective thickness of the sediment layer. Notice that if the oxygen content (I) is low there will be no flow of inorganic material back to the nutrient pool even with a considerable amount of $ORGS$ in the box. This is the reason for discriminating between organic and inorganic material in the sediment.

The state variables of the sediment i.e. $ORGS, MSN$ (MSP) are of interest due to their affect on the water quality.

As the sediment layer grows the upper part of the layer will be active in the processes of material exchange only. This "effective" thickness of the layer is set constant to SEF. Denoting the real SED-thickness by STO and assuming uniform conditions within SEF gives

$$ORGS \cdot K = ORGS \cdot J + DT \cdot J *$$

(14) $\qquad * [SEDA \cdot JK - MINS \cdot JK - MIPS \cdot JK$

$\qquad CLIP(((ORGS \cdot J * TST \cdot JK)/SEF), 0, ST \cdot J, SEF)]$

where $ST = \min(STO, SEF)$ and TST is the increment in sediment thickness. In other words $ORGS$ is reduced by the fraction which exceeds SEF. Expressions analogous to (14) are used for MSN and MSP. TST is assumed to be proportional with $SEDA$ and $SEDB$, i.e. sedimentation of discharged organic material

(15) $\quad TST \cdot KL = (C14 * SEDA \cdot JK + C15 * SEDB \cdot JK)/AR$

in which AR is the bottom area of the box.

As it appears from (14) $ORGS$ represents organic material from algal sedimentation only. We have assumed that the contents of N and P in $SEDB$ can be neglected, which should be quite realistic for the fiord under consideration. Therefore we consider only the oxygen demand in the orga.ic material discharged.

The Biological Oxygen Demand* *(BOD)* is controlled by four rates. The first being

(16) $SEDB \cdot KL = C12 * BOD \cdot K$

i.e. sedimentation of nondecomposed organic material only. *SEDB* is of practical importance mainly for the increment in *TST*, see (15). The oxygen consumption of *BOD*-mineralization in the water is approximately, per unit time**

(17) $MINBV \cdot KL = C6 * BOD \cdot K$.

The net exchange of *BOD* with other boxes *(DBOD)* is calculated from (2) and finally the amount of discharged organic material *(TBSP)* is known from field measurements.

In the model discharged wastewater is controlled in time by the auxiliary *EX*,

(18) $EX \cdot K = e^{C0 * TIME \cdot K}$.

PARAMETERS OF THE WATER QUALITY

The *transparency* of the water *(SD)* is measured physically by determining the greatest depth at which it is possible to see a white disc (diameter 30 cm) when it is sinking (in the shadow of a boat). Empirical work (M a t h i e s e n, [10]) indicates that

(19) $SD \cdot K = \dfrac{5.11 * 10^{-4}}{(PP \cdot JK/V)^{\frac{1}{2}} + 5.11 * 10^{-5}}$

is a good approximation. Since the primary production *PP* is measured

---

BOD: The total consumption of oxygen when the discharged organic material in the wastewater is completely broken down under aerobic conditions.

**MINBV* is set to zero under anaerobic conditions.

in metric tons per 24 hours and the volume of the box is measured in m^3 then SD appears in m. Notice that the maximum of SD is set to 10 m.

The concentration of oxygen is the other parameter of the water quality.

OXYGEN CYCLING

The concentration of oxygen (I) varies between zero and the saturation point $(IMAX)$. A fairly good approximation of $IMAX$ in salt water is given by*

(20) $IMAX \cdot K = C_0 - C_1 * TR \cdot K + C_2 * TR \cdot K^2 - C_3 * TR \cdot K^3$.

In nature when the production of oxygen continues after the saturation level is reached, this oxygen is rapidly released into the atmosphere.

In the model the concentration of oxygen is controlled by four rates. We attempt to average over the diurnal cycle of the involved processes.

Photosynthetic production of oxygen $(IFPP)$ is proportional to the primary production

(21) $IFPP \cdot KL = C4 * PP \cdot JK/V$.

The oxygen supply from the atmosphere $(IFAT)$ is assumed to follow

(22) $IFAT \cdot KL = C3 * (IMAX \cdot K - IMIDL \cdot K) * 2/D$,

where $IMIDL$ is the average concentration of oxygen over the day. This is the opposite process to the "oxygen-relase process" mentioned above. The constant $C3$ is selected to correspond to a depth of 2 m.

The oxygen consumption due to mineralization (IFM) is

*C_0, C_1, C_2, C_3 equals respectively: $1.297 \cdot 10^{-5}$, $3.59 \cdot 10^{-7}$, $7.2 \cdot 10^{-9}$ and $8 \cdot 10^{-11}$ correspond to TR in ^0C and $IMAX$ in metric ton/m^3.

$$IFM \cdot KL = (C5 * MINAV \cdot JK + MINBV \cdot JK$$

(23)
$$+ CLIP(C5 * (MINS \cdot JK + MIPS \cdot JK)$$

$$+ SEDB \cdot JK, 0, I \cdot K, 10^{-7}))/V \,.$$

Under anaerobic conditions *IFM* is a function of *MINAV* only. Finally the net exchange of oxygen with other boxes (*DI*) is calculated from (2). From these four rates the average concentration of oxygen over the day, say *IO*, is calculated as

(24)
$$IO \cdot K = IO \cdot J + DT \cdot J$$

$$* (IFPP \cdot JK + IFAT \cdot JK + DI \cdot JK - IFM \cdot JK) \,.$$

So far the model does not take the oxygen-relase process into account. Therefore it is possible for *IO* to exceed the maximum value, *IMAX*. To prevent this, we define

(25)
$$I = \begin{cases} IMIDL & \text{if} \quad IO \leqslant IMAX \\ IMAX & \text{if} \quad IO > IMAX \end{cases}$$

where *IMIDL* = *IO*. Notice that the oxygen-relase process is modeled at the same time, indirectly.

It is necessary to find a useful expression for the average concentration of oxygen over the day (*IMIDL*) in case *I* equals *IMAX*. Introduce *IKRIT* as the lowest concentration of oxygen over the day. We then consider af 24-hour expiration of the Concentration of OXygen (*COX*) with the following approximation:

At the end of the night, i.e. at time 1, *COX* equals the present minimum value *IKRIT*. During the day *COX* increases linearly, corresponding to a constant photosynthetic production. When *COX* reaches the saturation point *IMAX*, it remains there during the rest of the day, releasing the surplus production of oxygen into the atmosphere. At time *DF* the night begins and *COX* will decrease linearly, corresponding to a constant rate of oxygen consumption (II)

(26)
$$II = IFM - IFAT - DI$$

At the end of the night, i.e. at time 1, *COX* equals the present minimum value *IKRIT*, which is assumed to be the same as the value 24 hours earlier.

In this approximation a 24-hour oxygen cycling has a trapezoid expiration. Computing the area of this trapezoid and adding *IKRIT* gives

(27)
$$IMIDL = IMAX - \frac{1}{2} II * NF^2 * IFPP/(IFPP - II * DF) ,$$
$$I = IMAX$$

where *NF* is the fictive night length, i.e. $DF + NF = 1$, the rate of oxygen consumption is given by (26) and *IFPP* is the photosynthesis production of oxygen over a day.

In the same approximation we have for the critical concentration of oxygen

(28)
$$IKRIT = \begin{cases} I - \frac{1}{2} II * NF & \text{for} \quad I = IMIDL \\ I - II * NF & \text{for} \quad I = IMAX \end{cases}$$

which is the significant quantity for the survival of the fishes.

SYMBOL GLOSSARY (in connection to Fig. 5).

Each quantity description is followed by the unit used and a formula number which refer to the text.

Abbreviation of units: m = meter $mx = m^x$
                                t = metric ton   c = t/m3
                                d = 24-hours $E \pm x = 10^{\pm x}$

A   Algal biomass represented by its total contents of *N* and *P*. *N* and *P* are present in the weight ratio 7 : 1 (t).

AR   The bottom area of the box (m2).

BOD   The total consumption of oxygen when the discharged organic material in the wastewater is completely broken down under aerobic conditions (t).

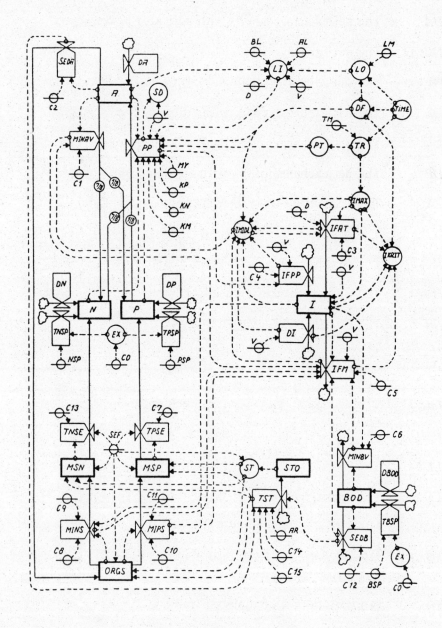

Fig. 5

Dynamo flow diagram for the total ecological box-model

D	The depth of the box (m).
DA	The net exchange of A with adjoining boxes (t/d).
DBOD	The net exchange of BOD with adjoining boxes (t/d).
DF	The fictive length of the day (1,8).
DI	The net exchange of I with adjoining boxes (c/d).
DN	The net exchange of N whit adjoining boxes (t/d).
DP	The net exchange of P with adjoining boxes (t/d).
EX	Time control of discharged wastewater (1,18).
I	The concentration of oxygen (c,25).
IFAT	The oxygen supply from the atmosphere (c/d,22).
IFM	The oxygen consumption due to mineralization (c/d,23).
IFPP	Photosynthetic production of oxygen (c/d,21).
IKRIT	The difference between the highest content of oxygen during the day and the total loss of oxygen during the night (c,28).
IMAX	The maximum content of oxygen (c,20).
IMIDL	The average concentration of oxygen over the day (c,25,27).
LI	The average value of light intensity in the box (kcal/m2 · d,7).
LO	The light intensity at the water surface (kcal/m2 · d,9).
MINAV	Mineralization of the algal biomass in the water phase (t/d,10).
MINBV	Mineralization of discharged organic material in the water phase (c/d,17).
MINS	Mineralization of organic N in the sediment layer (t/d,12).
MIPS	Mineralization of organic P in the sediment layer (t/d,12).
MSN	Inorganic N in the sediment layer (t).

MSP	Inorganic *P* in the sediment layer (t).
N	Inorganic nitrogen in the water phase (t).
NF	The fictive length of the night, i.e. $NF = 1 - DF$.
ORGS	Organic material in the sediment (t,14).
P	Inorganic phosphorus in the water phase (t).
PP	Primary production (within the box) (t/d,4).
PT	Temperature multiplies (1,5).
SD	The transparency of the water (m,19).
SEDA	Sedimentation of *A* (t/d,11).
SEDB	Sedimentation of discharged organic material (t/d,16).
SEF	The effective thickness of the sediment layer (constant) (m).
ST	The minimum of *SEF* and *STO* (m).
STO	The thickness of the sediment layer (m).
TBSP	Discharged organic material (t/d).
TNSE	Flow of *N* from the sediment to the water phase (t/d,13).
TNSP	Discharged *N* (t/d).
TPSP	Flow of *P* from the sediment to the water phase (t/d).
TPSP	Discharged *P* (t/d).
TR	The temperature (^{0}C, 6).
TST	The increment in sediment thickness (m/d,15).
V	The volume of the box (m3).

CONSTANTS

AL	$2.95E - 1$	1/m	C11	$2.00E - 6$	c
BL	$1.18E + 5$	m2/t	C12	$2.50E - 2$	1/d
C1	$1.22E + 3$	m3/t * d	C13	$1.60E - 4$	m/d
C2	$1.10E - 2$	1/d	C14	$5.31E + 2$	m3/t
C3	$6.30E - 2$	1/d	C15	$3.98E + 1$	m3/t
C4	$1.34E + 1$	1	CO	$1.28E - 5$	1/day
C5	$1.34E + 1$	1	KM	$4.32E + 2$	kcal/m2 * d
C6	$1.20E - 1$	1/d	KN	$3.00E - 7$	c
C7	$2.44E - 4$	m/d	KP	$5.00E - 8$	c
C8	$1.07E + 2$	m3/t * d	LM	$2.27E + 3$	kcal/m2 * d
C9	$2.00E - 6$	t/m3	MY	$2.00E + 0$	1/d
C10	$1.52E + 1$	m3/t * d	TM	$1.00E + 1$	^0C

The constants C6, C9, C11 and C15 are estimated while the rest of the constants are taken from (A n d e r s o n, [1]) (C1, C2, C4, C5, C8, C10 and C12), (B r o q v i s t, [3]) (TM), (C h e n, [4]) (AL, BL, KM, KN, KP and MY), (D a h l — M a d s e n and others, [5]) (C7, C13 and C14), (H a n s e n and P e d e r s e n, [7]) (LM) and (H a r r e m ö e s, [8]) (C3).

THE TOTAL MODEL

Using equation (2), the hydrodynamic and 7-11 ecological models were combined as described in the introduction. In order to reduce the errors which occur in numerical integration techniques, the step length DT was chosen to be as small as it was practical with regard to computational time required. The result was a step length of 6 hours resulting in a computation time of 5 min. on an IBM 370/165 computer for a 10-year period. The computation time is approximately proportional to the number of boxes and the planning horizon length. Fig. 6 shows an example of the DYNAMO output for a simulation over 21 years.

The output illustrates one of the water quality parameters, the oxygen content measured in 10^{-6} metric ton/m^3, as a function of time. The first

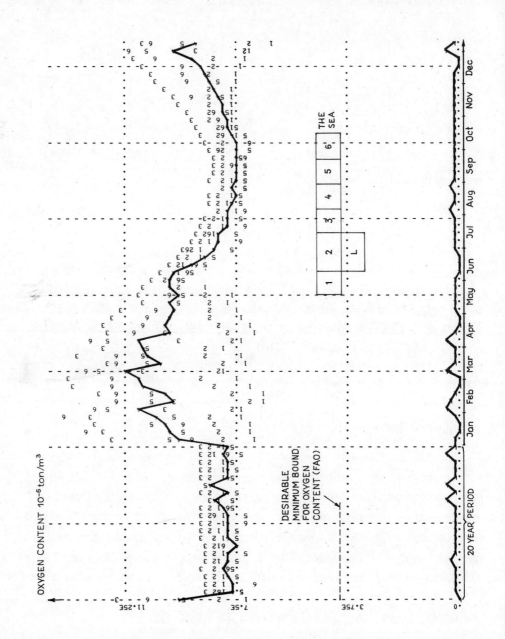

Fig. 6

20 years are represented with only one result per year. As representative time July 15-th is chosen. This is in the summer period when the oxygen content has a rather low value (normally very near the lowest value). The last year is represented by one result per week. The boxes are numbered as in Fig. 2 (except the lower box 2 which is represented by L). It is assumed that the wastewater emission is increasing by 0.5 percent every year due to population growth, but that there is no increase due to the industrial growth. It can be seen from Fig. 6 that there is a seasonal change in the oxygen content but over a longer planning horizon the situation is very stable. As the initial state, a sort of primitive state with very little pollution is arbitrarily chosen. Due to the stability of the model this initial state does not influence the results significantly.

The sensitivity of the model due to changes in the value of the constants has been analyzed and the conclusion reached is that even considerable changes in the values of the constants have no meaningful influence upon the critical oxygen content or the transparency of the water. Furthermore, an analysis has been made how different wastewater treatment plans influence the results. Several alternatives have been examined, ranging from different forms of biologic and chemical treatments to total reduction of wastewater emission. The provisional results indicate first that it is very difficult to change the critical oxygen content, second that it is possible to improve the transparency of the water if all emission of wastewater is stopped, and third that the intrusion of ocean water has only a small, short term effect on the quality parameters.

Research continues to improve and verify the model and there have been some thoughts of applying a generalization of the model to The Baltic Sea. Moreover, the model will be analyzed to evaluate its stability.

ACKNOWLEDGEMENT

We are indebted to Mr. N.H.W. Nielsen and Mr. S. Saabye, former M. Sc. students, for their cooperation. They have done a considerable part of the practical work including the preparation of the computer programs.

APPENDIX 1

A detailed description of the system dynamics approach is available in the textbooks by Forrester, e.g. (F o r r e s t e r , [6]).

System dynamics (S.D.) was developed over the last thirty years at the *Massachusetts Institute of Technology*. From a mathematical point of view S.D. is nothing more than a pictorial representation of a restricted class of deterministic models, that is, models which can be described analytically by a finite number of coupling differential equations of the first order. When we are considering complex real-world relationships such a pictorial representation is extremely important in preparation of the system analysis, because the goal of such analysis is to improve our understanding of the structure, function and development of the interacting systems. That is not to say that the "expensive" mathematics in our tool-box are unimportant. On the contrary, they are very important, but should be

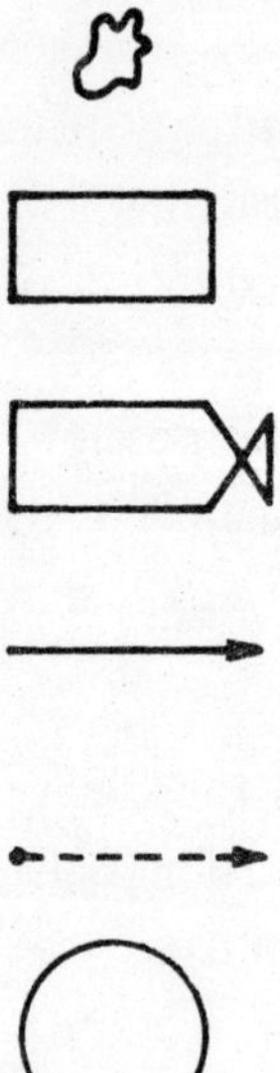

Source or sink: a level that is not of interest.

Level: the result of accumulation or depletion of flows, a state variable of the system.

Rate: the instantaneous rate of flow to or from a level, a decision or change in the state of the system.

Physical flow: a flow of some real quantity, which must be conserved.

Information flow: a functional dependence or flow of information, not necessarily conserved.

Auxiliary: a variable that is auxiliary to formulate a rate.

Constant.

Fig. A.1

DYNAMO symbols glossary

applied at a much later step in the scientific problem solving.

A basic structural element in S.D. is the "minimum" feedback loop shown in Fig. A.2.

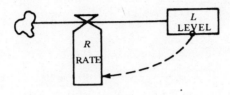

Fig. A.2

The basic feedback loop in S.D.

$$\frac{d}{dt} L(t) = R(t) \quad \text{and} \quad L(t) = \int_{t_0}^{t} R(x)\, dx .$$

As an example consider here the case where $R(t) = K * L(t)$. If the constant K is positive, there exists a positive loop, resulting in exponential growth. If K is negative the loop is negative or goal seeking.

With respect to the corresponding simulation language DYNAMO, we shall be even more brief. DYNAMO performs discrete integrations of continuous systems. By denoting the timestep by DT, the present time by subscript K, the earlier time by the subscript J, the elapsed time between J and K equals DT. Then to the first approximation

quantity $\cdot K =$ quantity $\cdot J + DT *$ rate of cange.

This is what DYNAMO does. Therefore the level equation corresponding to the simple loop above is

$$L \cdot K = L \cdot J + DT * R \cdot JK .$$

The computational sequence is level, auxiliary and rate and requires three relative time points, see Fig. A.3.

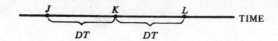

Fig. A.3

DYNAMO/TIME sequence

Once the rates have been calculated, the present time is advanced *DT* time units; all quantities that have been calculated for time *K* are now considered to be the values at time *J,* etc. As an example of a dynamo facility we can mention

$$CLIP(P, Q, R, S) = \begin{cases} P & \text{for} & R \geqslant S \\ Q & \text{for} & R < S \end{cases}$$

APPENDIX 2

```
*        MARIAGER FIORD MODEL
NOTE
NOTE
NOTE         GENERATION OF CHANGING WATER FLOW
NOTE     V – DETERMINATION OF THE WATER FLOW
NOTE     V,O AND P – DESCRIPTION OF THE BOXES IN THE OUTER FIORD
NOTE     BU AND O – DETERMINATION OF DT
NOTE
NOTE
A        K1.K=PULSE(1,0,RO.JK+BU.JK)
A        K2.K=1−K1.K
A        RTT.K=−33.5*LOGN(0.5−NOISE())
A        RTT.K=−3*LOGN(0.5−NOISE())
R        RO.KL=RO.JK*K2.K+RTT.K*K1.K
R        BU.KL=BU.JK*K2.K+BTT.K*K1.K
NOTE     BU IS THE DURATION OF THE PRESENT OR THE
NOTE         FUTURE INTRUSION OF WATER
N        RO=30
N        BU=0
R        NAT.KL=NAT.JK+(RTT.K+BU.JK)*K1.K
N        NAT=0
A        V.K=STEP(1,NAT.JK+0.01−MIN(0.01,TIME.K))
```

NOTE	V=1 MEANS THAT AN INTRUSION OF WATER TAKES PLACE
NOTE	OTHERWISE V=D
R	KAT.KL=KAT.JK*K2.K+(RTT.K+BU.JK)*K1.K
N	KAT=100
R	F.KL=V.K
A	NAK.K=KAT.JK+F.JK*1000
A	O.K=PULSE(1,NAK.K,NAK.K)
NOTE	O=1 WHEN INTRUSION OF WATER BEGINS OTHERWISE O=0
R	RC.KL=K1.K*MIN(0.01,TIME.K)/0.01
A	P.K=RC.JK
NOTE	P=1 WHEN THE INTRUSION OF WATER TERMINATES OTHERWISE P=0
NOTE	
NOTE	THE WATER FLOW
NOTE	FLOW COMING FROM A LOWER BOX IS ONLY DEFINED DURING AN INTRUSION
NOTE	OF WATER, BUT IT IS NOT NECESSARY TO PUT IT TO ZERO DURING THE
NOTE	QUIET PERIODS BECAUSE THE LEVELS IN THE THE LOWER BOXES ARE ZERO
NOTE	IN THESE PERIODS. DEFINING THESE FLOWS AS CONSTANTS A DIVISION
NOTE	BY ZERO IS AVOIDED IN THE EQUATIONS CONCERNING THE EXCHANGE OF
NOTE	MATERIAL BETWEEN THE BOXES IN THE OUTER FIORD:
NOTE	THE FLOW IS DETERMINED BY SOLVING THE LINEAR CONTINUITY EQUA-
NOTE	TIONS (1) AND (2). THIS IS DONE IN A SEPARATE PROGRAM AND THE
NOTE	RESULTING FLOW IS LISTED BELOW.
NOTE	
A	T1.K=49E5+47E5*V.K
A	T2.K=24.8E5*(1−V.K)
A	T3.K=23.6E5*(1−V.K)
A	T4.K=22.3E5*(1−V.K)
A	T5.K=31.4E5*(1−V.K)
A	T6.K=53.1E5*(1−V.K)
A	X2.K=3.0E5+6.7E5*V.K
A	X3.K=3.1E5*(1−V.K)
A	X4.K=4.22E5*(1−V.K)
A	X5.K=4.58E5*(1−V.K)
A	X6.K=2.55E5*(1−V.K)
A	Y2.K=3.0E5+28E5*V.K
C	Y3=5.5E5
C	Y4=5.8E5
C	Y5=6.6E5
C	Y6=6.4E5
A	QU12.K=0.57E5
A	QU23.K=2.4E5+21.3E5*V.K
A	QU34.K=3.25E5+23.7E5*V.K
A	QU45.K=3.46E5+25.3E5*V.K
A	QU56.K=4.02E5+27.4E5*V.K

```
A       QU6H.K=4.32E5+31.3E5*V.K
C       QL32=21.4E5
C       QL43=23.8E5
C       QL54=25.4E5
C       QL65=27.4E5
C       QLH6=31.3E5
                ..
                .
                .
                .

NOTE    *******************************
NOTE        BOX 1
NOTE    *******************************
NOTE        BOX 2 UPPER
NOTE    *******************************
NOTE        BOX 2 LOWER
NOTE    *******************************
NOTE        BOX 3 UPPER
NOTE    *******************************
NOTE        BOX 3 LOWER
NOTE    *******************************
                .
                .
                .
                .

NOTE    *******************************
NOTE    *******************************
NOTE    *******************************
NOTE        BOX 4 UPPER
NOTE    *********************
L       A4U.K=A4U.J+DT.J*(PP4U.JK+DA4U.JK-MINAV4U.JK-SEDA4U.JK)
X       -O.J*(0.075*A4U.J)+AP4U.J
A       AP4U.K=P.K*A4L.K
NOTE    0.075 IS THE VOLUME OF BOX 4 LOWER DIVIDED BY THE TOTAL VOLUME
NOTE        OF BOX 4 UPPER PLUS BOX 4 LOWER
A       SD4.K=5.11E-4/((SQRT(PP4U.JK/V4U.K))+5.11E-5)
R       DA4U.KL=(((T3.K+QU34.K)*A3U.K)/V3U.K)+((Y4*A4L.K)/V4L)+((T4.K*
X       A5U.K)/V5U.K)-(((T3.K+X4.K+T4.K+QU45.K)*A4U.K)/V4U.K)
R       MINAV4U.KL=C1*A4U.K*IMIDL4U.K
R       SEDA4U.KL=C2*A4U.K
R       PP4U.KL=MY*A4U.K*(LI4U.K/(KM+LI4U.K))*(N4U.K/((KN*V4U.K)+N4U.K))*(
X       P4U.K/((KP*V4U.K)+P4U.K))*PT.K*DF.K
A       LI4U.K=L0.K*(1-EXP(-(AL+BL*(A4U.K/V4U.K))*D4U.K))/
X       (D4U.K*(AL+BL*(A4U.K/V4U.K)))
NOTE
```

```
L       N4U.K=N4U.J+DT.J*(TNSP4.JK+(TNSE4.JK*(1 − V.J))+0.875*(MINAV4U.JK−
X       PP4U.JK)+DN4U.JK)−O.J*(0.075*N4U.J)+NL4U.J
A       NL4U.K=P.K*N4L.K
L       P4U.K=P4U.J+DT.J*(TPSP4.JK+(TPSE4.JK*(1−V.J))+0.125*(MINAV4U.JK−
X       PP4U.JK)+DP4U.JK)−O.J*(0.075*P4U.J)+PL4U.J
A       PL4U.K=P.K*P4L.K
R       DN4U.KL=(((T3.K+QU34.K)*N3U.K)/V3U.K)+((Y4*N4L.K)/V4L)+
X       ((T4.K*N5U.K)/V5U.K)−(((T3.K+X4.K+T4.K+QU45.K)*N4U.K)/V4U.K)
R       DP4U.KL=(((T3.K+QU34.K)*P3U.K)/V3U.K)+((Y4*P4L.K)/V4L)+
X       ((T4.K*P5U.K)/V5U.K)−(((T3.K+X4.K+T4.K+QU45.K)*P4U.K)/V4U.K)
NOTE
L       BOD4U.K=BOD4U.J+DT.J*(DBOD4U.JK+TBSP4.JK−MINBV4U.JK−SEDB4U.JK)
X       −O.J*(0.075*BOD4U.J)+BP4U.J
A       BP4U.K=P.K*BOD4L.K
R       DBOD4U.KL=(((T3.K+QU34.K)*BOD3U.K)/V3U.K)+((Y4*BOD4L.K)/V4L)+
X       ((T4.K*BOD5U.K)/V5U.K)−(((T3.K+X4.K+T4.K+QU45.K)*BOD4U.K)/V4U.K)
R       MINBV4U.KL=C6*BOD4U.K
R       SEDB4U.KL=C12*BOD4U.K
NOTE
R       I4U.KL=MIN(IMAX.K,MAX(0,I4U.JK+DT.K*(II4U.K+IFPP4U.JK)+IL4U.K))
A       IL4U.K=0.075*P.K*(I4L.JK−I4U.JK)
A       II4U.K=IFAT4.JK+DI4U.JK−IFM4U.JK
A       IMIDL4U.K=CLIP(IMAX.K−II4U.K*(DF.K−1)*(1−DF.K+(DF.K−1)*II4U.K/(
X       1E−15+(IFPP4U.JK/DF.K)+II4U.K))/2,I4U.JK,I4U.JK,IMAX.K)
A       IKRIT4U.K=MAX(0,I4U.JK+(1−DF.K)*II4U.K*CLIP(1,0.5,I4U.JK,IMAX.K))
R       IFPP4U.KL=(C4*PP4U.JK)/V4U.K
R       IFAT4.KL=C3*(IMAX.K−IMIDL4U.K)*2/D4L
R       IFM4U.KL=(C5*(MINAV4U.JK+(MINS4.JK+MIPS4.JK)*(1−V.K))
X       +MINBV4U.JK)/V4U.K
R       DI4U.KL=((T3.K+QU34.K)*IMIDL3U.K+Y4*IMIDL4L.K+T4.K*IMIDL5U.K
X       −(T3.K+X4.K+T4.K+QU45.K)*IMIDL4U.K)/V4U.K
A       V4U.K=149E5−11.2E5*V.K
A       D4U.K=3.34−0.25*V.K
NOTE
NOTE            DISCHARGE OF WASTEWATER
NOTE
R       TNSP4.KL=0.16*EX.K
X       *CLIP(REN,1,TIME.K,1095)
R       TPSP4.KL=0.03*EX.K
X       *CLIP(REP,1,TIME.K,1095)
R       TBSP4.KL=0.86*EX.K
X       *CLIP(REB,1,TIME.K,1095)
NOTE
```

```
NOTE            INITIAL VALUES
NOTE
N       A4U=5.9
N       N4U=6.9
N       P4U=0.57
N       BOD4U=6.4
N       I4U=0.94E-5
N       II4U=0.22E-7
NOTE            CONSTANTS
C       AR4=4.46E6
NOTE    ******************************
NOTE    ******************************
NOTE    ******************************
NOTE            BOX 4 LOWER
NOTE    ********************
L       A4L.K=(A4L.J+DT.J*(PP4L.JK+DA4L.JK-MINAV4L.JK-SEDA4L.JK))
X       *V.J+O.J*(0.075*A4U.J)
R       DA4L.KL=((QL54*A5L.K)/V5L)+((X4.K*A4U.K)/V4U.K)-
X       (((QL43+Y4)*A4L.K)/V4L)
R       MINAV4L.KL=C1*A4L.K*IMIDL4L.K
R       SEDA4L.KL=C2*A4L.K
R       PP4L.KL=MY*A4L.K*(LI4L.K/(KM+LI4L.K))*(N4L.K/((KN*V4L)+N4L.K))*(
X       P4L.K/((KP*V4L)+P4L.K))*PT.K*DF.K
A       LI4L.K=L0.K*EXP(-(AL+BL*(A4U.K/V4U.K))*D4U.K)*(
X       (1-EXP(-(AL+BL*(A4L.K/V4L))*D4L))/(D4L*(AL+BL*(A4L.K/V4L))))
NOTE
L       N4L.K=(N4L.J+DT.J*(TNSE4.JK+0.875*(MINAV4L.JK-PP4L.JK)+DN4L.JK))
X       *V.J+O.J*(0.075*N4U.J)
L       P4L.K=(P4L.J+DT.J*(TPSE4.JK+0.125*(MINAV4L.JK-PP4L.JK)+DP4L.JK))
X       *V.J+O.J*(0.075*P4U.J)
R       DN4L.KL=((X4.K*N4U.K)/V4U.K)+((QL54*N5L
X       .K)/V5L)-(((Y4+QL43)*N4L.K)/V4L)
R       DP4L.KL=((X4.K*P4U.K)/V4U.K)+((QL54*P5L
X       .K)/V5L)-(((Y4+QL43)*P4L.K)/V4L)
NOTE
L       BOD4L.K=(BOD4L.J+DT.J*(DBOD4L.JK-MINBV4L.JK-SEDB4L.JK))
X       *V.J+D.J*(0.075*BOD4U.J)
R       DBOD4L.KL=((X4.K*BOD4U.K)/V4U.K)+((QL54*BOD5L
X       .K)/V5L)-(((Y4+QL43)*BOD4L.K)/V4L)
R       MINBV4L.KL=C6*BOD4L.K
R       SEDB4L.KL=C12*BOD4L.K
NOTE
L       ORGS4.K=ORGS4.J+DT.J*(SEDA4U.JK+SEDA4L.JK
X       -MINS4.JK-MIPS4.JK-CLIP(((ORGS4.J*TST4.JK)/SEF),0,ST4.J,SEF))
```

R   MINS4.KL=C8*ORGS4.K*(I4L.JK*V.K+I4U.JK*(1−V.K))

R   MIPS4.KL=C10*ORGS4.K*(I4L.JK*V.K+I4U.JK*(1−V.K))

L   MSN4.K=MSN4.J+DT.J*(MINS4.JK−TNSE4.JK−

X   CLIP(((MSN4.J*TST4.JK)/SEF),0,ST4.J,SEF))

L   MSP4.K=MSP4.J+DT.J*(MIPS4.JK−TPSE4.JK−

X   CLIP(((MSP4.J*TST4.JK)/SEF),0,ST4.J,SEF))

R   TNSE4.KL=C13*(MSN4.K/SEF)

R   TPSE4.KL=C7*(MSP4.K/SEF)

NOTE

L   ST04.K=ST04.J+DT.J*TST4.JK

R   TST4.KL=(C14*(SEDA4U.JK+SEDA4L.JK)+C15*(SEDB4U.JK+SEDB4L.JK))/AR4

A   ST4.K=MIN(ST04.K,0.4)

NOTE

R   I4L.KL=MIN(IMAX.K,MAX(0,(14L.JK+DT.K*(II4L.K+IFPP4L.JK))*

X   V.K+O.K*I4U.JK))

A   II4L.K=DI4L.JK−IFM4L.JK

A   IMIÐL4L.K=CLIP(IMAX.K−II4L.K*(DF.K−1)*(1−DF.K+(DF.K−1)*II4L.K/(

X   1E−15+(IFPP4L.JK/DF.K)+II4L.K))/2,I4L.JK,I4L.JK,IMAX.K)

R   IFPP4L.KL=(C4*PP4L.JK)/V4L

R   IFM4L.KL=(C5*(MINAV4L.JK+MINS4.JK+MIPS4.JK)

X   +MINBV4L.JK+SEDB4U.JK+SEDB4L.JK)/V4L

R   DI4L.KL=(QL54*IMIDL5L.K+X4.K*IMIDL4U.K−(QL43+Y4)*IMIDL4L.K)/V4L

NOTE

NOTE   INITIAL VALUES

NOTE

N   A4L=0

N   N4L=0

N   P4L=0

N   BOD4L=0

N   ORGS4=76

N   MSN4=155

N   MSP4=14.8

N   ST04=0.10

N   I4L=0

N   II4L=0

NOTE   CONSTANTS

C   V4L=11.2E5

C   D4L=3.34

NOTE   *******************************
.
.
.
.

NOTE   *******************************

```
NOTE          BOX 5 UPPER
NOTE   *******************************
NOTE          BOX 5 UPPER
NOTE   *******************************
NOTE          BOX 6 UPPER
NOTE   *******************************
NOTE          BOX 6 LOWER
NOTE   *******************************
                      .
                      .
                      .
                      ,
                      ,
NOTE   *******************************
NOTE   *******************************
NOTE          FUNCTIONS COMMON TO ALL BOXES
NOTE   *******************************
A      EX.K=EXP(C0*TIME.K)
A      TR.K=TM*(1+SIN(0.0172*(TIME.K−140)))
A      PT.K=EXP(0.07*TR.K−0.175)
A      L0.K=LM*(1+(0.88*SIN(0.0172*(TIME.K−80))))/DF.K
A      DF.K=0.5*(1+0.5*SIN(0.0172*(TIME.K−80)))*0.82
A      IMAX.K=1.297E−5−TR.K*3.590E−7+(TR.K*TR.K)*
X      (7.243E−9)−(TR.K*TR.K*TR.K)*(7.777E−11)
NOTE
NOTE          CONSTANTS COMMON TO ALL BOXES
NOTE
C      ACH=1E−6
C      NCH=0
C      PCH=0
C      BODCH=0
C      C0=1.28E−5
C      SEF=04
C      MY=2.0
C      KM=4.32E2
C      KN=3.0E−7
C      KP=5.0E−8
C      AL=2.95E−1
C      BL=1.18E5
C      LM=2.27E3
C      TM=1.0E1
C      C1=1.22E3
C      C2=1.1E−2
C      C3=6.3E−2
C      C4=1.335E1
```

```
C        C5=1.335E1
C        C6=0.12
C        C7=2.44E−4
C        C8=1.07E2
C        C9=2E−6
C        C10=1.52E1
C        C11=2E−6
C        C12=2.5E−2
C        C13=1.6E−4
C        C14=5.3E2
C        C15=4.05E1
C        REN=1
C        REP=1
C        REB=1
NOTE     REN, REP OG REB GIVES THE PERCENTAGE OF N, P AND BOD WHICH
NOTE     REMAINS IN THE WASTEWATER AFTER AN EVENTUAL WASTEWATER TREAT-
NOTE     MENT HAS TAKEN PLACE. THE TREATMENT IS FIRST ACTIVE AFTER THE
NOTE     THIRD YEAR.
NOTE
NOTE          DETERMINATION OF THE VARIABLE STEPLENGTH
NOTE
R        B.KL=(TIME.K+2*BU.JK)*O.K+B.JK*(1−O.K)
N        B=O
A        S.K=1−STEP(1,B.JK+1000*O.K)
NOTE      S=1 DURING INTRUSION AND A SIMILAR AMOUNT OF TIME AFTER THE
NOTE               INTRUSION. OTHERWISE S=0
A        DT.K=DELTA*(1−0.9*S.K)
N        DT=0.1
C        DELTA=0.25
NOTE
NOTE          SPECIFICATION OF OUTPUT
NOTE
PLOT     SD1=1,SD2=2,SD3=3,SD4=4,SD5=5,SD6=6
PLOT     IKRIT1=1,IKRIT2U=2,IKRIT2L=L,IKRIT3U=3,IKRIT4U=4,
X        IKRIT5U=5,IKRIT6U=6(0,15E−6)
A        PLTPER.K=STEP(168,300)+197
SPEC     LENGTH=7665
RUN      21 YEAR WITHOUT FURTHER WASTEWATER TREATMENT
```

REFERENCES

[1]   J.M. Anderson, System simulation to test environmental policy: the eutrophication of lakes, *Environmental Letters*, 3, (3), (1972), copyright by Marcel Dekker Inc.

[2]   J.E. Beyer – O.B.G. Madsen, Concerning the dynamic models of mariager fiord (in Danish), *The Institute of Mathematical Statistics and Operations Research* (IMSOR), (1973).

[3]   S. Broqvist, A mathematical model for lake trummen (in Swedish), The research group for the theory of planning, *The Institute of Mathematics*, The technical University, Stockholm, (1970).

[4]   C.V. Chen, Concepts and utilities of ecological models, *Journal of Sanitary Engineering Division*, October 1970.

[5]   Dahl-Madsen,– Gargas,– Hansen – Heise – Nielsen – Pedersen, The pond of Haderslev 1971-1972 (in Danish), *The Institute of Waterquality*, ATV, September 1972.

[6]   J.W. Forrester, *Principles of Systems*, Wright-allen press, Cambridge, Massachusetts.

[7]   O.B. Hansen – J. Pedersen, Sun radiation (in Danish), Individual exercise, *The Laboratory of Sanitary Engineering*, The Technical University of Denmark, 1972.

[8]   P. Harremöes, Photosynthesis and oxygenbalance in streams (in Danish), *The Danish Society of Engineers*, September 1970.

[9]   C.D. Keeling – B. Bolin, The simultaneous use of chemical tracers in oceanic studies, I. General theory of reservoir models, *Tellus* XIX, 4 (1967), 566-581.

[10] H. Mathiesen, Environmental changes and biological effects in lakes (in Swedish), *Vatten*, 2 (1970).

[11]   N.H.W. Nielsen – S. Saabye, Dynamic models of mariager fiord (in Danish), *IMSOR,* 1973.

[12]   E.P. Odum, *Fundamentals of ecology,* Third edition, W.B.
Saunders Company, *Philadelphia,* 1971.

[13]   B.C. Patten, Mathematical models of plankton production,
Int. Revue ges. Hydrobiol., 53 (1968), 357-408.

[14]   D.W. Pritchard, Dispersion and flushing of pollutants in
estuaries, *ASCE,* 95, No. HY:1, January 1969.

[15]   A.L. Pugh III, *DYNAMO II user's manual,* MIT Press, 1973.

[16]   F.L. Smidth & Co, The fiord of mariager, water quality 1971
(in Danish), Copenhagen, *Dept. of Environmental Studies,* 1972.

Jan. E. Beyer and Oli. B.G. Madsen

IMSOR, The Institute of Mathematical Statistics and Operations Research, The Thechnical University
of Denmark, DK-2800 Lyngby.

COLLOQUIA MATHEMATICA SOCIETATIS JÁNOS BOLYAI

12. PROGRESS IN OPERATIONS RESEARCH, EGER (HUNGARY), 1974.

RELAXATION METHODS IMPROVED BY MODIFIED GRADIENT TECHNIQUES

P.M. CAMERINI — L. FRATTA — F. MAFFIOLI

1. INTRODUCTION

Consider the following problem

(P.1) $\max_{\pi} w(\pi)$

where

$$w(\pi) = \min_{k} \{c_k + \pi\mu_k\} = c_{k(\pi)} + \pi\mu_{k(\pi)} \, ,$$

$$k \in \{1, \ldots, K\}, \quad c_k \in R, \quad \pi \in R^n, \quad \mu_k \in R^n \, ,$$

n and K being two positive integers.

This is equivalent to

(P.2) $\max \{w: w \leqslant c_k + \pi\mu_k, \forall k\} \, ,$

which is a standard problem of linear programming. Column generation techniques [1], [2] may be used for its solution, but they may not be efficient enough, especially when the constraints are not given in explicit form, but in the form of a method to find the tightest one for each value of the variables' vector π (this happens for instance in some approaches to the travelling salesman problem [3], [5]).

In the form P.1 the problem may be solved by successive iterations following the scheme

(1) $\quad \begin{cases} \pi^0 = 0 \\ \pi^{m+1} = \pi^m + t_m s^m \end{cases}$

$\{t_m\}$ being a sequence of scalars.

An obvious choice for s^m is the gradient of $w(\pi^m)$:

(2) $\qquad s^m = \nabla w(\pi^m) = \mu_{k(\pi^m)}$.

This choice is justified in [3], where a relaxation method applied to P.2 is shown to lead to the iterative scheme (1) and (2).

Note that this iteration scheme is not applied as in conventional gradient procedures but rather, as in relaxation methods, in order to come closer and closer to the optimal region so that the objective function needs not to be improved at each step.

The computational experience made in some kind of large scale problems [3], [4], [5] has shown that the above relaxation method works much better than classical gradient techniques.

The goal of this paper is to prove that the efficiency of the previous relaxation technique is improved by selecting the modified gradient direction

(3) $\qquad s^m = \mu^m + \beta_m s^{m-1}$,

where $\mu^m = \mu_{k(\pi^m)}$ and β_m is a suitable scalar. $(s^{m-1} \overset{\text{def}}{=\!=} 0$ for $m = 0)$.

Computational results obtained by different optimization policies are reported.

2. PROPERTIES OF MODIFIED GRADIENT DIRECTIONS

The following lemmas and theorems give a basis to choose the iteration scheme (1) and (3) and lead to a policy for determining β_m and t_m at each step.

Lemma 1 [3]. *Let $\bar{\pi}$ and π^m be such that $\bar{w} = w(\bar{\pi}) \geqslant w(\pi^m) = w_m$ then*

(4) $$(\bar{\pi} - \pi^m)\mu^m \geqslant \bar{w} - w_m \geqslant 0 .$$

Lemma 2. *Let**

(5) $$0 \leqslant t_m \leqslant \frac{\bar{w} - w_m}{\| s^m \|^2}$$

and

$$\beta_m \geqslant 0 .$$

Then

(6) $$(\bar{\pi} - \pi^m)s^m \geqslant (\bar{\pi} - \pi^m)\mu^m .$$

Theorem 1. *Let*

(7) $$\beta_m = \begin{cases} - \gamma_m \dfrac{s^{m-1}\mu^m}{\| s^{m-1} \|^2} & if \quad s^{m-1}\mu^m < 0 \\ 0 & otherwise \end{cases}$$

with

(8) $$0 \leqslant \gamma_m \leqslant 2 .$$

Then

(9) $$\frac{(\bar{\pi} - \pi^m)s^m}{\| s^m \|} \geqslant \frac{(\bar{\pi} - \pi^m)\mu^m}{\| \mu^m \|}$$

---

*$\| s \|$ denotes the Euclidean norm of vector s.

Theorem 2.

(10) $\| \bar{\pi} - \pi^m \| > \| \bar{\pi} - \pi^{m+1} \|$.

Lemma 2, Theorem 1 and 2 are proved in the appendix.

Lemma 1 guarantees that the direction of μ^m forms always an acute angle with the direction leading from π^m to the optimum $\bar{\pi}$, while Lemma 2 extends this property to s^m. Theorem 1 shows that by a proper choice of β_m, s^m is always at least as good a direction as μ^m. Fig. 1 attempts to illustrate such a behaviour in a two-dimensional case. Theorem 2 guarantees that a point closer and closer to the optimum in obtained at each iteration.

A similar result was proved in [3] for the iteration scheme (1) and (2) with a condition on t_m less restrictive than (5) namely

(11) $0 < t_m < \dfrac{2(\bar{w} - w_m)}{\| \mu^m \|^2}$.

However, as it is represented in Fig. 2, the best choice for t_m would be that yielding the nearest position to $\bar{\pi}$ in both directions (H and H'). Following Lemma 1 and 2, an estimate for this step is given by letting t_m be equal either to half the upper limit of (11) or to the upper limit of (5).

3. COMPUTATIONAL RESULTS

For choosing t_m and s^m three policies have been tested.

(a) $s^m \equiv \mu^m$ and $t_m = 1$ [3]

(b) $s^m \equiv \mu^m$ and $t_m = \dfrac{w^* - w_m}{\| s^m \|^2}$

where w^* is a good estimate of the optimum $\bar{w}$.

(c) $s^m = \mu^m + \beta_m s^{m-1}$

where

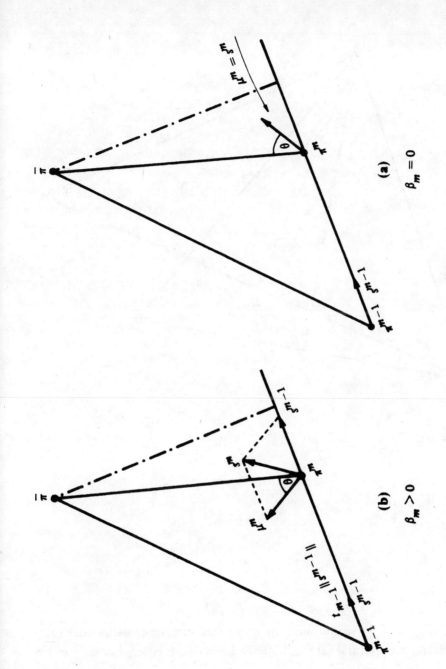

(a)

$\beta_m = 0$

(b)

$\beta_m > 0$

Fig. 1

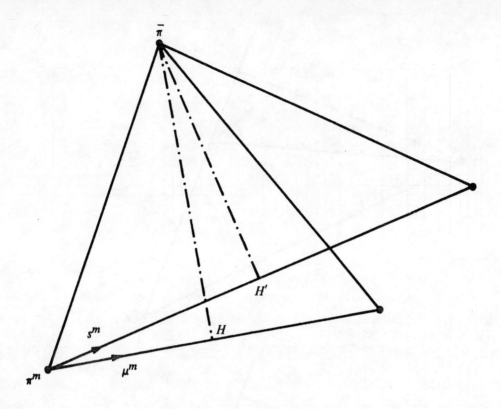

Fig. 2

$$\beta_m = \begin{cases} -\gamma \dfrac{s^{m-1}\mu^m}{\|s^{m-1}\|^2} & \text{if} \quad s^{m-1}\mu^m < 0, \\ \\ 0 & \text{otherwise} \end{cases}$$

and

$$t_m = \frac{w^* - w_m}{\|s^m\|^2}.$$

Choosing $\gamma = 1$ would amount to go in a direction orthogonal to s^{m-1}. Better computational results have been obtained choosing $\gamma = 1.5$.

Some comparative results corresponding to the above three policies are shown in Fig. 3.

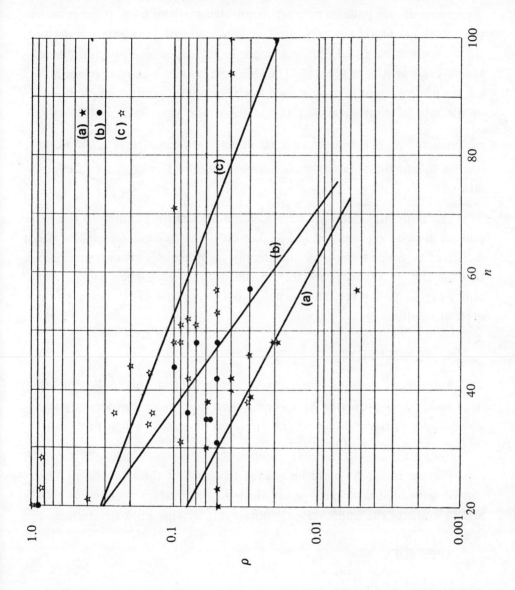

Fig. 3

Each point corresponds to the computational result obtained by applying one of the policies to a set of problems of the form P.1, for which the functions $w(\pi)$ are very similar. These sets of problems are derived from some arc weighted undirected graphs [5 ÷ 9] whose optimum hamiltonian cycle is sought [3], [5]. The abscissa, n is the number of variables, i.e. the dimension of vector π, while the ordinate ρ is a sample measure of the rate of convergence of the method, and is defined as the ratio $\frac{\delta_w}{M}$, where M is the mean number of iterations, and δ_w is the mean relative increment of $w(\pi)$ that has been obtained in each set of computations.

The minimum-mean-square regression lines corresponding to the three policies are also represented in Fig. 3, even if the number of samples is not sufficient to make these lines statistically meaningful. However one can see that for any n (except $n = 38$) ρ steadly increases when passing from policy (a), to policy (b), and to policy (c), according to the previous theoretical results.

4. CONCLUSIONS

Relaxation methods recently revisited in order to be applied to some large scale linear problems have been shown here to be considerably improved by a suitable choice of the direction of search, which turns out to be given by a modified gradient vector.

Further research would be needed to clarify if the relaxation policy can be imbedded into more sophisticated optimization techniques [10] and to evaluate the improvements obtainable by this kind of methods.

APPENDIX

Proof of Lemma 2.

The proof is by induction on m, since (6) is valid for $m = 0$, with an equality sign. Assume therefore (6) is valid for m. Hence from (5) and Lemma 1

$$t_m \| s^m \|^2 \leqslant (\bar{\pi} - \pi^m)s^m .$$

Since $\beta_{m+1} \geqslant 0,$ we may write

$$\beta_{m+1} [(\bar{\pi} - \pi^m)s^m - t_m \| s^m \|^2] \geqslant 0$$

i.e., from (1)

(12) $\beta_{m+1} (\bar{\pi} - \pi^{m+1})s^m \geqslant 0 .$

Then Lemma 2 follows from (12), Lemma 1 and (3).

Proof of Theorem 1.

The proof is trivial when $\beta_m = 0,$ When $\beta_m > 0,$

$$\| s^m \|^2 - \| \mu^m \|^2 = \beta_m^2 \| s^{m-1} \|^2 + 2\beta_m (s^{m-1} \mu^m) \leqslant 0$$

provided (8) holds.

Then

$$\| s^m \| \leqslant \| \mu^m \|$$

and from Lemma 2 the theorem follows.

Proof of Theorem 2

From (5)

$$t_m \| s^m \|^2 \leqslant \bar{w} - w_m < 2(\bar{w} - w_m) .$$

From Lemmas 1 and 2,

$$t_m \| s^m \|^2 < 2(\bar{\pi} - \pi^m)s^m .$$

This may be written, being $t_m > 0,$ as

$$\| \bar{\pi} - \pi^m \|^2 + t_m^2 \| s^m \|^2 - 2t_m (\bar{\pi} - \pi^m)s^m < \| \bar{\pi} - \pi^m \|^2$$

Q.E.D.

REFERENCES

[1]   J.F. Shapiro, A decomposition algorithm for integer programming problems with many columns, *25th Conference of ACM*, August 1972, 528-533.

[2]   G.B. Dantzig, *Linear programming and extensions*, Princeton U. Press, 1963, Ch. 23.

[3]   M. Held – R.M. Karp, The traveling salesman problem and minimum spanning trees: part II, *Mathematical Programming*, 1 (1971), 6-25.

[4]   M. Held – R.M. Karp – P. Wolfe, Large scale optimization and the relaxation methods, *25th Conference of ACM*, August 1972, 507-509.

[5]   P.M. Camerini – L. Fratta – F. Maffioli, A Heuristically guided algorithm for the traveling salesman problems, *Journal of the Inst. of Comp. Sc.*, 4 (1973), 31-35.

[6]   G.A. Croes, A method for solving traveling salesman problems, *Op. Res.*, 6 (1958), 791-812.

[7]   G.B. Dantzig – D.R. Fulkerson – S.M. Johnson, Solution of a large scale traveling salesman problem, *Op. Res.*, 2 (1954), 393-410.

[8]   M. Held – R.M. Karp, A dynamic programming approach to sequencing problems, *SIAM J. on Appl. Math.*, 10 (1962), 195-210.

[9]   L.L. Karg – G.L. Thompson, A heuristic approach to solving traveling salesman problems, *Manag. Sc.*, 10 (1964), 225-248.

[10]   M.J.D. Powell, Recent advances in unconstrained optimization, *Mathematical Programming*, 1 (1971), 26-57.

P.M. Camerini – L. Fratta – F. Maffioli

Politecnico di Milano, Instituto di Elettrotecnica ed Elettronica, 20133 Milano, Piazza Leonardo da Vinci 32, Italy.

COLLOQUIA MATHEMATICA SOCIETATIS JÁNOS BOLYAI

12. PROGRESS IN OPERATIONS RESEARCH, EGER (HUNGARY), 1974.

A MATHEMATICAL MODEL OF OPTIMAL PRICE SYSTEM IN CENTRALLY PLANNED ECONOMY

Z. CZERWIŃSKI

1. INTRODUCTORY REMARKS

Different meanings may be, and actually are attached to the concept of "optimal price system". The author must, therefore, explain as clearly as he can what he had in mind providing his paper with such a multivocal title.

A very brief historical introduction seems necessary. In the famous discusssion on the economics of socialism which took place in the thirties, the critics of socialism (L. van Mises, F. Hayek) claimed that centrally planned economy *(CP-economy)* would be unable to work rationally (or even to exist), because − deprived of free market − it would be at the same time deprived of the rational price system, which is the necessary basis of economic calculation and decision-making. Although in the seventies we do not have to worry about the existence of socialism, it must be admitted that the problem of rational price formation in the CP-economy has not been solved satisfactorily yet, neither in theory nor in practice. Practicians often complain of the existing prices, pointing out that they "deform economic calculation", "do not reflect real social inputs", "do not correspond to current economic conditions", "do not favour right economic decisions", etc. Theoreticians are still far from a common opinion as to what the rational price system ought to be like.

The development of mathematical programming has risen hopes that this is just the right tool to solve the problem. The price system is a *vector* which has to satisfy some conditions imposed on it in advance. We are searching for a vector which would be "rational", or — since it became fashionable to use this word — "optimal". Mathematical programming supplies us with techniques of finding out the optimal vector in the set of feasible vectors. It seems, therefore, that finding out the optimal price system is a typical programming problem, provided

(a) we are able to describe the conditions imposed on the price vector in mathematical terms, and

(b) we agree to accept a given criterion of choice (objective function).

Unfortunately, it is not easy to satisfy both requirements (a) and (b). The reason is that price vector differs essentially from other vectors with respect to which the problem of optimal choice is being considered in economic literature. The components of the vector of prices (i.e. quantities of monetary units paid in exchange for some fixed units of commodities) themselves are neither "desirable" quantities as, e.g., the components of the vector of outputs, nor are they "undesirable" as the components of the vector of inputs. In many problems of optimal choice considered by economists by means of mathematical programming techniques prices are assumed given, and are used in evaluating the results of feasible activities. Prices decide to what extent a given activity (production, transportation) is "desirable" or "undesirable". Whatever the model serving as the basis to find out the optimal price system may be, we must not assume in advance any system of prices, and the criterion of choice must allow for the manifold role prices play in the economic activity of producers, consumers and the state, which is particularly important in the CP-economy. No problem of finding out the optimum price system, nor even any concept of such a system may be defined, unless we assume explicitly some model of working of the economy for which we want to find such a system.

Needless to add that no mathematical model of that type may simply *describe* how the CP-economy actually works. Not only have we to simplify the picture of the real economy to a great extent. The author of any concept of the optimal price system has to impose somehow his own view as to how the CP-economy *ought to work,* taking part in the debate on functioning of the centralized economic systems.

As so much has been written on the subject discussed in the paper the reader should not expect to find much news here. The author aimed, first of all, at the systematic exposition of the subject debated longly in socialist countries. The influence of the outstanding participants of the debate — O. Lange, L. Kantorovich, J. Kornai and many others — on what has been written below, is obvious and needs not to be confirmed by special references. The author, however, would claim that his concept of optimal price vector of consumption commodities from which the whole system of prices is derived brings a new element to the debate. He would also like to draw the reader's attention to his opinion concerning the possibility of decentralization of decisions in the CP-economy, because in this field too optimistic views seem to prevail among economists.

2. "MINIMUM COMPLEXITY" MODEL OF WORKING OF THE CP-ECONOMY

2.1. *Verbal description*

To put forward the problem of the optimal price system we need a model. Many models of working of CP-economy have been considered. The choice of the model presented below is a compromise between the anxiety to construct the model allowing for all essential interrelationships between economic variables and the tendency to present the basic problem in a simple way. A too complicated model would not lead us to concrete conclusions. An oversimplified model would not make us possible even to discuss the problem in the way which might be recognized by economists as meaningful*. I have called the model presented below the "minimum complexity" model to stress that it allows for as few interrelated elements of the economy as it is necessary to put the meaningful problem of finding the optimal price system.

A simple graph (see figure) shows which subsystems of the CP-economy have been singled out and how they are interrelated. Notation used is explained and some necessary comments added in the next section. It must be stressed that our model is a "short-term" model. This is because prices should be adapted to the current position of the economy. Prices are not, and — in the author's opinion — should not be fixed for decades. The problem to what extent prices in the CP-economy should be flexible is highly debatable. There is no place here to discuss this point broadly. Generally speaking I assume that prices should be adapted to

(a) existing technology,

(b) consumers' behaviour,

(c) capital resources,

(d) some predetermined decisions ("preferences") of the centre (state) concerning accumulation,

(e) conditions prevailing in the foreign markets,

and should remain fixed as long as all the elements mentioned above do not show essential changes.

This not very precise statement will result in assuming constant values for some quantities considered in the model (or a given shape of some functions). "Short-term" implies anyway that capital resources which may be exploited in the period under considerations are given, although at the same time new durable capital goods are being produced.

---

*"Oversimplified" — in the author's opinion — are, e.g., all models in which only "technology" is assumed and, therefore, only the problem of adaptation of prices to technological relations may be considered.

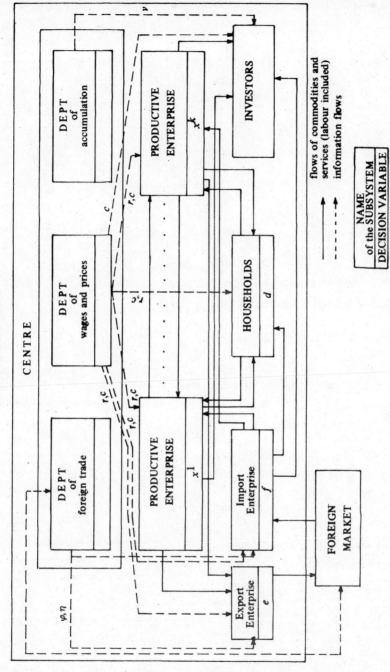

CP-ECONOMIC SYSTEM

CENTRE

DEPT of foreign trade

DEPT of wages and prices

DEPT of accumulation

PRODUCTIVE ENTERPRISE

x^1

PRODUCTIVE ENTERPRISE

x^k

Import Enterprise

f

Export Enterprise

e

HOUSEHOLDS

d

INVESTORS

FOREIGN MARKET

c

r,c

r,c

r,c

r,c

r,c

v

φ, η

⟶ flows of commodities and services (labour included)

⟶ information flows

NAME of the SUBSYSTEM

DECISION VARIABLE

2.2. *Notations and preliminary explanations*

n the number of home-producible commodities.

N the number of all commodities (home-producible or importable).

ν the number of consumption commodities.

K the number of producers (productive enterprises).

T the number of all production activities.

n_k the number of production activities which may be operated in the k-th enterprise $(k = 1, \ldots, K)$.

m_k the number of types of "capital resources" used in the k-th enterprise, $(k = 1, \ldots, K)$.

Q the set of indices of consumption commodities (those which are the object of the demand of the households).

Z_k the set of indices of production activities which may be operated in the k-th enterprise $(k = 1, \ldots, K)$.

S_j the set of indices of activities the output of which is the j-th commodity $(j = 1, \ldots, n)$. It is assumed that only *one* commodity is the output of a given activity.

1. $A^0 = [a_{jt}]$ $(n \times T)$-matrix of inputs of producible commodities per unit level of production activities. The unit level of the t-th activity is assumed to be chosen so that a unit of the j-th commodity for $t \in S_j$ is produced. If $t \in S_j$, then $a_{jt} = 0$.

2. $M = [M_{it}]$ zero-one matrix of order $(n \times T)$, such that $M_{it} = 1$ if and only if $t \in S_j$.

3. $A = M - A^0$.

4. G $((N - n) \times T)$-matrix of inputs of not home-producible commodities per unit level of production activities.

5. $B^k = [b^k_{lt}]$ $(m_k \times n_k)$-matrix of inputs of the k-th enterprise's

"capital resources" per unit level of production activities operated in the
k-th enterprise.

6. $b^k = [b_l^k]$ $(m_k \times 1)$-vector of "capital resources" being at the disposal of the k-th productive enterprise. By "capital resources" are meant
here all types of durable capital goods (machinery, means of transport etc.)
necessary to operate production activities. Their inputs may be measured
in percentage of the total productive capacity of the stock of durable capital goods of particular types per unit level of activities. Alternatively they
may be measured in terms of time of work of durable capital goods per
unit level of activities. In the latter case, "capital resources" should be
measured in terms of the feasible work time of durable capital goods. The
vector b^k will be briefly referred to as capacity of the k-th enterprise.

7. $a^0 = (a_t^0)$ $(1 \times T)$-vector of labour inputs per unit level of production activities. Labour is assumed to be homogeneous for the sake of
simplicity. No basic theoretical problems arise, if different types of labour
are allowed for. One wage rate (see below, point 21), should then be replaced by a vector of wage rates, corresponding to various types of labour
(jobs).

8. $a^e = (a_j^e)$ $(1 \times n)$-vector of additional labour inputs necessary to
export the unit of j-th home-producible commodity $(j = 1, \ldots, n)$.

9. $a^1 = (a_j^1)$ $(1 \times n)$-vector of additional labour inputs necessary to
import the unit of the j-th home-producible commodity $(j = 1, \ldots, n)$.

10. $a^2 = (a_j^2)$ $(1 \times N - n)$-vector analogous to that explained in
point 9 for not home-producible commodities $(j = n + 1, \ldots, N)$.

11. $a^f = (a^1, a^2)$.

12. $v^1 = [v_j]$ $(n \times 1)$-vector of "social accumulation" of home-producible commodities $(j = 1, \ldots, n)$.

13. $v^2 = [v_j]$ $(N - n \times 1)$-vector of "social accumulation" of not
home-producible commodities $(j = n + 1, \ldots, N)$.

The term "social accumulation" is meant to denote the amounts of all commodities the accumulation of which is considered necessary by the centre for the collective consumption, defense, and the *development of the economy*, i.e. for *investment* in all its sectors ("productive" and "non-productive").

14. R total labour force available (man-hours).

15. R_0 labour force reserved by the centre for "nonproductive" sectors: administration, education, health, etc. (man-hours).

16. H admissible by the centre balance of foreign payments, i.e. the upper limit of foreign credit in the "world currency". Only one foreign market is assumed with only one world currency.

17. $\eta = (\eta_j)$ $(1 \times n)$-vector of export prices of home-producible commodities in the world currency $(j = 1, \ldots, n)$.

18. $\varphi^1 = (\varphi_j^1)$ $(1 \times n)$-vector of import prices of home-producible commodities in the world currency $(j = 1, \ldots, n)$.

19. $\varphi^2 = (\varphi_j^2)$ $(1 \times N - n)$-vector of import prices of not home-producible commodities in the world currency $(j = n + 1, \ldots, N)$.

20. $\varphi = (\varphi^1, \varphi^2)$.

21. r the wage rate per man-hour (see point 7).

22. $x^k = [x_1^k, \ldots, x_{n_k}^k]$ vector of levels of production activities in the k-th enterprise.

23. $x = [x^1, \ldots, x^K]$. $(T \times 1)$-vector of levels of all production activities.

24. $e = [e_j]_{j=1,\ldots,n}$ vector of levels of export of home-producible commodities.

25. $f^1 = [f_j^1]_{j=1,\ldots,n}$ vector of levels of import of home-producible commodities.

26. $f^2 = (f_j^2)_{j=n+1,...,N}$ vector of levels of import of not home-pro-ducible commodities.

27. $f = [f^1, f^2]$.

The vector f^1 will be called *substitutable import*, the vector f^2 *not substitutable*. Home-producible commodities may or may not be imported. Import of not home-producible commodities is necessary, if only production activities are to be operated which make use of such commodities. e.g. of raw materials not producible in the country because of the lack of natural resources.

3. THE PROBLEM OF THE OPTIMAL PRICE SYSTEM

3.1. *The concept of admissible price vector of consumption commodities (APC-vector)*

Let U be the set of non-negative vectors $u = [x, e, f]$ satisfying the following conditions

(1) $\qquad -(M - A^0)x + e - f^1 \qquad \leqslant -v^1$.

(2) $\qquad Gx \qquad\qquad - f^2 \leqslant -v^2$.

(3) $\qquad B^k x^k \qquad\qquad\qquad \leqslant b^k \qquad (k = 1, \ldots, K)$.

(4) $\qquad a^0 x + a^e e + a^1 f^1 + a^2 f^2 \leqslant R - R_0$.

(5) $\qquad\qquad - \eta e + \varphi^1 f^1 + \varphi^2 f^2 \leqslant H$.

Let $\bar{Y}$ be the set of N-dimensional vectors $\bar{y} = [y^1, y^2]$, where

(6) $\qquad y^1 = (M - A^0)x - e + f^1 - v^1$,

(7) $\qquad y^2 = f^2 - Gx - v^2$,

and x, e, f constitute some vector u out of U. Any vector $\bar{y} \in \bar{Y}$ is then a linear transformation of some $u \in U$.

Let Y be the projection of the set $\bar{Y}$ on the ν-dimensional space, being the set of all ν-dimensional vectors $[y_j]_{j \in Q}$ generated by omitting $N - \nu$ components in vectors belonging to $\bar{Y}$ for $j \bar{\in} Q$. Y is then the set of all *producible consumption baskets.* * To any $u \in U$ corresponds only one $y \in Y$, denoted later by $\psi(u)$.

Let D be the total income of households, $c = (c_j)_{j \in Q}$ vector of prices of consumption commodities, and

(8) $d = d(c, D)$

the demand function of households, i.e. the vector-function the j-th component of which $d_j(c, D)$ for $j \in Q$ represents the effective demand of households for the j-th consumption commodity, depending on the price vector c and the total income D.

The function $d(c, D)$ may be said to exist, because consumers (households) demand some specific quantities of consumption commodities, whatever their income and the price vector c are. The following properties of the demand function will be assumed

(9) $d(c, D) \geqslant 0$,

(10) $cd(c, D) \leqslant D$,

(11)   demand function is a continuous function of c
        at any given $D > 0$.

The assumption (9) needs no justification. (10) means that households will not reduce their financial reserve (if it exists). Although one could try to justify the assumption (11) by a sort of "regularity" of consumers' behaviour, it is obvious that it has been introduced into the model for the sake of mathematical convenience.

One could ask what "total income of households" means in our model, and whether it is a given value or a variable. According to previous definitions, total labour force employed in production and foreign trade activities amounts to

(12) $R_1 = a^0 x + a^e e + a^1 f^1 + a^2 f^2$.

Producible means here such a commodity that it may be offered to households either by domestic production or by means of foreign exchange. *Home-producible* refers to the former case only.

Hence $R_0 + R_1$ is the total labour force employed, and $r(R_0 + R_1)$ is the *wage fund*. This is a variable, because R_1 depends on the levels of activities, and we do not know how those levels will be determined. If $R_0 + R_1 = R$, then both the total income of households and the wage fund will be equal to rR. What would happen if $R_0 + R_1 < R$? Unemployed labour force $(R - R_0 - R_1)$ must be somehow maintained by the state (central budget). Were the unemployment benefit equal to the wage rate, the sum of benefits would amount to $r(R - R_0 - R_1)$, and the total income of households would again be equal to rR (although the wage fund would as before amount to $r(R_0 + R_1)$).

The assumption that the wage rate equals unemployment benefit may seem too bold. Yet, if we assume that the way of choosing the levels of production and foreign trade activities (to be specified later) is such that no great excess of labour force appears (i.e., that economy does not suffer from "structural unemployment"), then the value of the wage fund plus the unemployment benefits cannot differ much from the value of rR. We will, therefore, assume further on that

(13) $D = rR > 0$,

and hence D is a given value. This assumption takes us not too far away from reality, and facilitates considerably our considerations. We shall also omit the term D in the demand function, writing $d(c)$ instead of $d(c, D)$.

A non-negative price vector c will be called *admissible price vector* of consumption commodities (APC-vector) if it satisfies the following conditions

(α) $d(c) \in Y$.

(β) $cy \leqslant D$ for any $y \in Y$.

The justification of this definition is the following. The price vector c would not be admissible, if the economic system could not meet effective demand of households induced by the prices c. Neither would it be admissible if the prices c do not make households able *to choose any* *producible consumption basket.* The postulate (α) may be called the postulate of *possible equilibrium;* the postulate (β) — the postulate of *maximum choice for households* or the postulate of *limited sovereignty of consumers.* The word "possible" is used to stress that the APC-vector itself does not ensure the equilibrium on the market of consumption commodities. It only makes the equilibrium *possible,* because the demanded basket of consumption commodities is *producible* (which does not mean that it has actually been *produced*). The word "limited" is used to underline the fact that "producible" has been defined so that it allows for some predetermined decisions of the centre related to investment plan, balance of foreign trade etc. The sovereignty of consumers is therefore limited by some constraints imposed on consumption by the centre "in the interest of the whole economic system", which seems to be an accurate characteristic of the CP-economy.*

The first problem to be put forward, once we have defined the APC-vector, is that of its existence. It turns out that the existence cannot be proved unless some additional assumptions are accepted. First we shall assume that

(14) U is a non-empty set including interior point u such that
         $y = \psi(u)$ is a positive vector.

The last assumption amounts to saying that technology of the economy, its resources and constraints imposed by the centre make it possible to supply consumers with all producible consumption commodities in some positive amounts. It excludes from the field of our considerations "very poor" economies or economies controlled by "too ambitious centre", which by its investment policy or foreign trade constraints would rule out in advance the possibility of supplying consumers with a producible commodity they might want.

---

*By this definition of the APC-vector the author avoids referring to "utility" which seems to be a rather enigmatic concept, especially with respect to the society as a whole. He also wants to avoid predetermination of the structure of consumption by the centre. As long as consumers are free to buy commodities which appear on the market in proportions chosen by themselves (as it the case in the existing CP-economies), prices of consumption commodities must sooner or later be adapted to the effective demand, unless we agree to permanent disequilibrium on the market. It seems, therefore, right to exclude from our considerations all price vectors unable to assure market equilibrium.

As the set U is a convex and bounded polyhedron (see (3), and (4)), so are the set $\bar{Y}$, being a linear mapping of U, and its projection Y. This, however, would not suffice to prove the existence of the APC-vector. We shall still assume that the set Y has the following property

(15)   if $a \in Y$ and $0 \leqslant b \leqslant a$,   then $b \in Y$,

which means that if a consumption basket a is producible, so is any basket containing no more of any commodity as is contained in a.

The last two assumptions are rather weak. It is hard to imagine an economy in which they would not be satisfied (provided the other assumptions hold).

Geometrically, the existence problem amounts to the following. Let D be a positive number and c a non-negative vector. The demand function assigns to any hyperplane P, represented by the equation $cy = D$, some point $d(c)$ lying on or below that hyperplane in the non-negative orthant of R^v. The question is: does there exist a vector $c \geqslant 0$ such that the hyperplane P leaves the whole polyhedron Y below it, and the point $d(c)$ belongs to Y?

The definition of the set Y together with the other assumptions justifies positive answer to this question, and we may state

Theorem 1. *If the economy satisfies conditions (9)-(11) and (14)-(15) then the APC-vector exists.*

The proof is given in Appendix 1. It must be noted that the APC-vector needs not to be unique. The postulates imposed on the APC-vector are rather weak and in general they may be satisfied by many price vectors of consumption goods.

3.2. *The concept of the optimal price vector of consumption commodities (OPC-vector)*

Let us denote the set of APC-vectors by C_A, and consider the following linear programming problem which will later be referred to as the *central optimization problem* (COP)

$$cy = \text{maximum}, \quad y \in Y \quad \text{for some} \quad c \in C_A.$$

Let the set of optimal solutions to the COP be $Y(c)$. By definition

(16) $\qquad cy \leqslant cz \quad$ for any $\quad y \in Y, z \in Y(c).$

Suppose that (no matter whether by the order of the centre, by chance, or by some calculation of the enterprises) the productive and foreign trade enterprises operate their activities at such levels x^k, e, f^1, f^2 that $\psi(x, e, f) = z \in Y(c)$ at prices $c \in C_A$, and that consumption commodities are sold at prices c. This itself does not guarantee the equilibrium on the market of consumption commodities, because z needs not be equal to $d(c)$. Under some more restrictive condition imposed on the demand function we may, however, expect the equality $z = d(c)$ to hold for some $z \in Y(c)$.

Let us assume that condition (10) is satisfied with equality, i.e., that

(17) $\qquad cd(c) = D,$

which means zero propensity of households to save. If condition (17) holds, we will say that the economy is *savingless*. We may state

Theorem 2a. *In the savingless economy (satisfying conditions (9)-(11) and (14)-(15)), there exists an APC vector c such that*

(18) $\qquad d(c) = z \quad$ for some $\quad z \in Y(c).$

Proof. As $c \in C_A$, so by definition of C_A

(19) $\qquad d(c) \in Y,$

and

(20) $\qquad cy \leqslant D \quad$ for any $\quad y \in Y.$

By (16) and (19)

(21) $\qquad cd(c) \leqslant cz \quad$ for any $\quad z \in Y(c).$

As, howewer, $Y(c) \subset Y$, so by (20)

(22) $cz \leqslant D$ for $z \in Y(c)$.

But by (17) we may replace D by $cd(c)$ in (22), and hence taking into account (21), we obtain

(23) $cd(c) = cz$ for any $z \in Y(c)$.

Belonging to Y by (19), the vector $d(c)$ is itself one of elements of $Y(c)$ and so the theorem is proved.

Were the optimal solution to the COP unique, the vector $d(c)$ would be its only solution. If the COP happens to have many optimal solutions, the solution chosen by chance may not coincide with the demand induced by prices used as weights in the objective function in the COP. Yet the co-incidence may be attained by selecting one of the optimal solutions.

We thus see that if prices of consumption commodities are admissible, the equilibrium on the market may be attained, and the basket of commodities demanded by households may be at the same time the basket maximizing the total value of consumption of households at those prices. The maximum effort of the economy to supply households meets in this case with the complete "market approval". This is the best situation we may expect in the conditions under consideration and, therefore, if APC-vector c is such that $d(c) = z$ for some $z \in Y(c)$, we will call it the *optimal vector of prices of consumption commodities* (OPC-vector).

The corresponding vector z out of $Y(c)$ will be called the *optimal consumption basket.*

The OPC-vector exists if the economy is savingless. Otherwise the OPC-vector may not exist. It may happen that although for some APC-vector c the effective demand of households may be met, the consumers will not be ready to buy *all* the commodities in quantities represented by components of any vector $z \in Y(c)$, whatever APC-vector has been chosen. Instead of spending all their income households may save a part of it, and a surplus of unsold consumption commodities will appear in shops. This certainly means a *relative* surplus, i.e., the surplus relative to the production possibilities of the economy (export and import activities included).

If consumers are not too poor and inexquisite to buy whatever may be bought, they may refrain from spending and save money expecting to buy commodities more suitable to their tastes in the future. In such a situation no price vector will induce them "to clear the market".*

If we do not exclude savings, instead of 2a, only a weaker theorem can be proved, i.e.,

Theorem 2b. *If the economy satisfies conditions* (9)-(11) *and* (14)-(15), *there exists an APC-vector* c *such that*

$$(24) \qquad d(c) \leqslant z \quad for\ some \quad z \in Y(c)\ .$$

3.3. *The optimal price vector of all commodities (OP-vector) and the problem of decentralization of decisions*

Until now we have said nothing about prices of commodities not entering the consumption basket, and it may be asked why we started our considerations with the prices of consumption commodities only. We did it because it seems much easier to specify the criteria of "rationality" (admissibility, optimality) for those commodities (see postulates (α) and (β)). Besides, we think that the remaining commodities — capital goods, intermediate products — serve only as means necessary to produce consumption goods, and their prices should be somehow "adapted to" or "derived from" the prices of consumption commodities.

In this section we will try show to what extent this problem may be solved.

For the sake of simplicity it will be assumed that the economy is savingless and the solution to the COP, in which components of the OPC-vector were used as weights in the objective function, is unique and non-degenerate. The unique OPC-vector and the unique solution to COP will be denoted by c^0 and y^0 respectively. With the vector y^0 (identical to $d(c^0)$) is associated some vector of *dual values* p^0. Let us see clearly what sort of vector we have in mind.

*Although considerations presented in the paper are remote from direct application, it is worth noticing that something like this may be observed at present in the Polish economy.

The set Y of producible consumption baskets has been so defined, that solving the COP amounts to the same as solving the linear programming problem of finding such a non-negative vector $u = [x, e, f]$ satisfying inequalities (1)-(5) for which the weighted sum of dummy variables, introduced to bring these inequalities to equalities, attains maximum, if the weights c_j^0 are attached to the dummy variables corresponding to the inequalities (1)-(2) for $j \in Q$, and zero weights to the remaining ones.

The vector y^0 is determined by the optimum solution $[u^0, \bar{y}^0]$ of this linear programming problem which we will also assume to be unique and non-degenerate (y^0 is a subvector of the vector $\bar{y}^0$). By the vector p^0 we mean the vector of dual values corresponding to the solution $[u^0, \bar{y}^0]$. This is a $N + \sum_{k=1}^{K} m_k + 2$-dimensional vector the components of which would be convenient to group in the following way

$$p^0 = (\pi_1, \ldots, \pi_n, \pi_{n+1}, \ldots, \pi_N, \beta_1^1, \ldots, \beta_{m_1}^1, \ldots, \beta_1^K, \ldots, \beta_{m_K}^K, \rho, \chi) =$$

$$= (\pi, \beta^1, \ldots, \beta^K, \rho, \chi) .$$

To denote the optimal levels of activities entering the optimal vector u^0 we shall use symbols $x^0 = [x_t^0]_{t=1,\ldots,T}$, $e^0 = (e_j^0)_{j=1,\ldots,n}$, $f^{10} = (f_j^{10})_{j=1,\ldots,n}$, $f_j^{20} = (f_j^{20})_{j=n+1,\ldots,N}$, $f^0 = [f^{10}, f^{20}]$.

If $x_t^0 > 0$, $e_j^0 > 0$, $f_j^{10} > 0$ or $f_j^{20} > 0$ we shall say that the corresponding production or foreign trade activities are *desirable*. The remaining activities will be called *undesirable*.

It is easy to see that the structure of the linear programming problem under consideration implies the following properties of the vector of dual values p^0.

(25) $\pi_j = c_j^0$ for all such $j \in Q$ that $y_j^0 > 0$.

This means that for commodities entering the optimal consumption basket, *their optimal prices coincide with their dual values associated with the optimal solution to the COP.* For *desirable* production activity $t \in$ $\in Z_k \cap S_j$ $(j = 1, \ldots, n)$

$$(26) \qquad \pi_j = \sum_{i=1}^{n} a_{it} \pi_i + \sum_{i=n+1}^{N} g_{it} \pi_i + \sum_{l=1}^{m_k} b_{lt}^k \beta_l^k + a_t^0 \rho \ . \ *$$

For commodity $j = 1, \ldots, n$, the export of which is *desirable*

$$(27) \qquad \pi_j = \eta_j \chi - a_j^e \rho \ .$$

For commodity $j = 1, \ldots, N$ the import of which is *desirable*

$$(28) \qquad \pi_j = \varphi_j \chi + a_j^f \rho \ .$$

For *non-desirable* production and import activities the relation "<" holds instead of equality relation. For non-desirable export activities instead of equality relation, the relation ">" holds.

These properties of the dual values are obvious, and need not to be explained here in detail. Let us only notice that ρ is the "shadow value" of the unit of labour.

The dual values will help us to introduce the concept of optimal prices of non-consumption commodities. We will identify the *optimal price vector of non-consumption commodities* with the vector (π_j), for $j \in Q$. As it turned out that $\pi_j = c_j^0$ for $j \in Q$, we may identify the *optimal price vector* (OP-vector) of all commodities with the vector π, including first N components of the dual vector p^0, and use the uniform notation π for all prices.

We have given some justification for the proposed definition of the OPC-vector. What is the justification of our definition of the OP-vector (including the former one)?

Roughly speaking the justification is as follows: if all commodities are bought and sold at optimal prices, and all producers, exporters and importers make decisions as to the level of their activities independently, then a suitable objective function may be defined so that decisions made by producers, exporters and importers maximizing this function would result in supplying the market with the optimal consumption basket or a basket *"not far"* from the optimal one.

---

* Let us remember (see Section 2.2, point) that if $t \in S_j$, then $a_{jt} = 0$.

At the same time profits accumulated in the whole economic system would suffice to cover all the *social expenditures**.

This point must be made clear, especially because we used (and we had to) the rather vague phrase "not far from the optimal". For any $t \in Z_k \cap S_j$ let us define the coefficient

$$(29) \qquad w_t = \pi_j - \sum_{i=1}^{n} a_{it} \pi_i - \sum_{i=n+1}^{N} g_{it} \pi_i - a_t^0 \rho .$$

w_t will be called the *"value added"* per unit level of the t-th production activity, which may be operated in the k-th enterprise and yields the j-th commodity. From the price of that commodity the value of all material inputs are subtracted as well as the "shadow value" of labour input.

Let us assume that the k-th enterprise decides independently which activities to operate, its decision being guided by the solution to the following linear programming problem

$$\sum_{t \in Z_k} w_t x_t^k = \text{maximum}, \quad B^k x^k \leqslant b^k, \quad x^k \geqslant 0 .$$

This problem will be referred to as the *local optimization problem of the k-th enterprise* (k-LOP).

Let us denote the set of indices of all *desirable* activities which may be operated in the k-th enterprise by P_k and the set of *undesirable* ones by $\bar{P}_k$.

Let us call two solutions ξ^* and ξ to the k-LOP *equivalent* (from the point of view of the use of the k-th enterprise's capacity), if $B^k \xi^* = B^k \xi$. The following theorem can be proved.

Theorem 3. *If $\xi^* = (\xi_t^*)$ and $\xi = (\xi_s)$ are equivalent solutions to k-LOP, and if $\xi_t^* > 0$ for $t \in P_k$ only, whereas at least one $\xi_s > 0$ for $s \in \bar{P}_k$, then the solution ξ^* is better than the solution ξ in the sense of the objective function of k-LOP (i.e. it brings more "value added").*

The proof is given in Appendix 2.

*The last term will be explained later.

The economic meaning of Theorem 3 is as follows: if enterprises aim at maximizing the "value added" calculated by means of optimal prices, then they would substitute the desirable activities for undesirable ones as far as their capacities and technology admit substitution. An undesirable activity may enter the optimal solution to the k-LOP only in case that there is no combination of desirable activities *equivalent* to a combination including some undesirable activity (as is the case e.g., if no desirable activity belongs to the set Z_k). As this must not be ruled out *a priori,* we cannot prove that no enterprise will operate any undesirable activity, but only that it will *try to avoid* it as much as possible. It also follows from the theorem that if a solution to the k-LOP exists which makes use of the *full capacity* of the k-th enterprise by operating desirable activities only, then no undesirable activity may appear in any optimal solution to the k-LOP. Analogous remarks are applicable to the decisions of exporters and importers.

In this sense the OP-vector favours the attainment of the short-term goal of the whole economic system which is to produce the optimal consumption basket, leaving aside a part of commodities produced for social accumulation. The OP-vector would stimulate producers (importers, exporters) to act so as to attain this goal, provided they are interested in maximizing the "value added".*

This does not mean that completely independent decisions of producers, importers and exporters maximizing the "value added" at optimal prices would automatically result in the optimal consumption basket y^0.

Firstly, we cannot prove that no undesirable activity will be operated by productive enterprises.

Secondly, even if productive enterprises operate only desirable activities,** and maximize the "value added", it does not mean that the sum

---

*How to make enterprises interested in maximizing the "value added" (or in any other objective function the maximization of which might turn out to be desirable from the point of view of working of the whole economic system) is a separate, and practically important, question which will not be dealt with here.

**I.e., $\xi_t^* > 0$ for $t \in Z_k$, only if $t \in P_k$.

of the optimal levels of all activities ξ_t^* for t belonging to S_j, reduced by the quantity v_j of the j-th commodity to be accumulated, would accurately equal y_j^0. The point is that the OP-vector may be (and under fairly general conditions will be) such that the k-LOP's will have several basic and infinitely many non-basic optimal solutions.* The combination chosen (out of many optimal combinations) by the k-th enterprise together with those chosen by the remaining ones may therefore not result in the (unique) optimal consumption basket y^0. We may only hope that it will be "not far" from it, due to the fact that the sets of optimal solutions of the k-LOP's will be "narrow". Otherwise some intervention of the centre would be needed to direct enterprises to choose some specific solutions out of the set of their optimal solutions. This is why we have said at the beginning that we may only expect that independent decisions of producers (exporters, importers) may result in supplying the market with the consumption basket "not far from the optimal one". The OP-vector does not, therefore, guarantee that the optimal consumption basket will appear on the market; it removes, however, the *inconsistency* between this goal and the interest of productive enterprises.

With respect to the foreign trade activities the optimal prices together with the foreign exchange rate χ and shadow value of the unit of labour ρ would distinguish the desirable export and import activities as activities for which equalities (27) and (28) are satisfied from undesirable export activities for which the relation ">" in (27) and from undesirable import activities for which the relation "<" in (28) would hold. The economic meaning is clear: no home-producible commodity should be exported if its optimal domestic price exceeds its foreign price converted into the domestic currency reduced by the labour cost of export. And no commodity should be imported if its optimal domestic price falls below its foreign price converted into the domestic currency increased by the labour cost of import.**

*This follows from the fact that the sum of the numbers of constraints in all LOP's will be, in general, less than the number of all constraints in the COP.

**Notice that labour costs of export and import are calculated at the "shadow value of the unit of labour" (other export or import costs are neglected).

This is, of course, a virtue of optimal prices (together with the foreign exchange rate and the shadow value of the unit of labour). They, however, only distinguish desirable foreign trade activities from undesirable ones, but do not indicate at what levels those activities should be operated. The only balance of foreign exchange constraint in the model does not guarantee that any choice of desirable import and export activities would be the optimal choice (i.e., that resulting in the optimal consumption basket y^0). This again shows that complete decentralization of decisions, even with the optimal price system, may not result in achieving the short-term goal of the whole economic system.

3.4. *Financial equilibrium of the economy with the optimal price system*

Using as before the symbol π to denote the OP-vector we shall also use the following notation

$$(30) \qquad \pi^0 = (\pi_j)_{j \in Q}, \quad \pi^1 = (\pi_j)_{j=1,\ldots,n}, \quad \pi^2 = (\pi_j)_{j=n+1,\ldots,N}.$$

It will also be convenient to use the symbol π_t to denote the price of the commodity being the (unique) output of the t-th activity. In other words we assume the following identity

$$(31) \qquad \pi_t = \pi_j \qquad \text{for} \qquad t \in S_j.$$

By well-known duality theorems of linear programming we have

$$(32) \qquad \pi^0 y^0 + \pi^1 v^1 + \pi^2 v^2 = \sum_{k=1}^{K} \beta^k b^k + \rho(R - R_0) + \chi H.$$

We shall make use of this equality proving that if the economy is savingless and all the transactions occur at optimal prices, then the sum of profits of all productive and foreign trade enterprises operating only desirable activities, plus the domestic value of the foreign credit will just cover all *social expenditures,* by which we mean expenses for social accumulation as well as the costs of maintaining labour force not employed in productive and foreign trade enterprises. By the *profit* of an enterprise we mean the surplus of all its returns over the material and labour outlays. Hence the profit of the k-th productive enterprise amounts to

$$\xi_k = \sum_{t \in P_k} \left(\pi_t - \sum_{i=1}^{n} a_{it}\,\pi_i - \sum_{i=n+1}^{N} g_{it}\,\pi_i - r a_t^0 \right) x_t^0 =$$

$$= \sum_{t \in P_k} \left(\pi_t - \sum_{i=1}^{n} a_{it}\,\pi_i - \sum_{i=n+1}^{N} g_{it}\,\pi_i - \sum_{l=1}^{m_k} b_{lt}^k \beta_l^k - \right.$$

(33)
$$\left. - \rho a_t^0 + \sum_{l=1}^{m_k} b_{lt}^k \beta_l^k + (\rho - r)a_t^0 \right) x_t^0 =$$

$$= \sum_{t \in P_k} \left(\sum_{l=1}^{m_k} b_{lt}^k \beta_l^k + (\rho - r)a_t^0 \right) x_t^0 =$$

$$= \beta^k b^k + (\rho - r) \sum_{t \in P_k} a_t^0 x_t^0 \,.$$

We made use here of the assumption that only desirable activities are operated (equality (26)). We also took into account that

(34)
$$\sum_{t \in P_k} b_{lt}^k x_t^0 < b_l^k \qquad \text{implies} \qquad \beta_l^k = 0\,.$$

Hence the sum of profits of all productive enterprises amounts to

(35)
$$\xi = \sum_{k=1}^{K} \xi_k = \sum_{k=1}^{K} \beta^k b^k + (\rho - r)a^0 x^0\,.$$

The sum of profits of the foreign trade enterprises amounts to:

for the export enterprise

(36)
$$\xi_E = (\chi \eta - \pi^1 - r a^e)e^0 = (\chi \eta - \pi^1 - \rho a^e + (\rho - r)a^e)e^0 =$$
$$= (\rho - r)a^e e^0\,;$$

for the import enterprise

(37)
$$\xi_F = [(\pi^1, \pi^2) - \chi(\varphi^1, \varphi^2) - r(a^1, a^2)]\begin{bmatrix} f^{10} \\ f^{20} \end{bmatrix} =$$

$$= [(\boldsymbol{\pi}^1 \cdot \boldsymbol{\pi}^2) - \chi(\boldsymbol{\varphi}^1, \boldsymbol{\varphi}^2) - \rho(a^1, a^2) + (\rho - r)(a^1, a^2)] \begin{bmatrix} f^{10} \\ f^{20} \end{bmatrix} =$$

$$= (\rho - r)[a^1 f^{10} + a^2 f^{20}] = (\rho - r)a^f f^0 \ .$$

Here again we used the assumption that only desirable processes are operated, and hence equalities (27) and (28) are applicable.

The domestic value of foreign credit is obviously equal to χH. Thus the sum of profits of productive and foreign trade enterprises plus the domestic value of foreign credit amounts to

$$\sum_{k=1}^{K} \beta^k b^k + \chi H + (\rho - r)[a^0 x^0 + a^e e^0 + a^f f^0] =$$

(38)

$$= \sum_{k=1}^{K} \beta^k b^k + \chi H + (\rho - r) R_1 \ ,$$

where, as before, we used R_1 to denote the labour force employed in productive and foreign trade enterprises.

As far as social expenditures are concerned two cases should be considered:

Case (a). The solution to the COP is such that the total labour force is employed. Then social expenditures amount to

(39) $\qquad \boldsymbol{\pi}^1 v^1 + \boldsymbol{\pi}^2 v^2 + r R_0 \ ,$

and at the same time

(40) $\qquad R_1 = R - R_0 \ .$

In this case the total wage fund amounts to rR, and this in the savingless economy is equal to $\boldsymbol{\pi}^0 y^0$. Hence by equality (32) both expressions (38) and (39) are equal to

(41) $\qquad \sum_{k=1}^{K} \beta^k b^k + \chi H + (\rho - r)(R - R_0) \ .$

Let us add that in the case (a) $\rho > 0$, but nothing can be said about the relation of ρ to r.

Case (b). The solution to the COP is such that labour force is not fully employed. Then $\rho = 0^*$, and

(42) $\qquad R_1 < R - R_0 $.

Let

(43) $\qquad L = R - R_0 - R_1$

be the unemployed labour force. Assuming that the unemployed labour force must be maintained by the economic system, and that the unemployment benefit is equal to the wage rate**, we would get for social expenditures the expression

(44) $\qquad \pi^1 v^1 + \pi^2 v^2 + r(R_0 + L)$.

The equality $rR = \pi^0 y^0$ again holds, although rR denotes now the wage fund increased by unemployment benefits. By equality (32) both expressions (38) and (44) are now equal to

(45) $\qquad \displaystyle\sum_{k=1}^{K} \beta^k b^k + \chi H - r R_1$.

So the financial equlibrium of the whole system will be attained in any case. Notice that we speak of the equilibrium of the system as a whole. We do not decide how to organize financial flows within the system, e.g., should the centre take over all the profits and cover social expenditures out of the central budget, or should it order enterprises to cover all or some expenses for investment or collective consumption, etc. Anyway, financial means accumulated in the whole system will suffice to cover all social expenditures, provided prices are optimal and economy is savingless.

---

*In general ρ and r need not coincide, and it cannot be postulated that the wage rate should be equal to the "shadow value" of the unit of labour. The basic reason is that ρ may turn out to be zero, and the wage rate must be positive.

**(See p. 155). If we consider the model with several types of labour force then the weaker assumption would suffice, viz., the assumption that the unemployment benefit equals the least wage rate (corresponding to the unskilled labour), which would be much more realistic.

Not much can be said if households save a part of their incomes. We do not even know whether the OP-vector exists. If it does, some redistribution of the funds would be necessary to assure financial equilibrium of the system. This point will not be dealt with here in detail.

4. CONCLUDING REMARKS

If the model presented above describes approximately how CP-economy works and if conditions under which OPC-vector exists are satisfied, the question may be asked how to find this vector.

Consider the following non-linear programming problem: to find a ν-dimensional vector c such that

(46)

    (a) $c \in \Lambda$

    (b) $d(c) \in Y$

    (c) $\min\limits_{z \in Y(c)} \delta(d(c), z) = \text{minimum}$.

Here δ stands for the distance between points in R^ν, and the set Λ has been defined in Appendix 1. If the economy is savingless, then by Theorem 1 and 2a the problem (46) has a solution c^* with $\delta(d(c^*), z^*) = = 0$ for some $z^* \in Y(c^*)$, and thus c^* is an OPC-vector. This vector would determine the dual vector π associated with the optimal solution to the COP at prices of consumption commodities c^* (including as its part the vector c^* itself), which would be the OP-vector. In this sense, the solution to the problem (46) would yield the OP-vector. These are, of course, purely theoretical speculations. Neither information available nor computing technique would allow nowadays to solve the problem (46)*.

We think, however, that the price vector called here optimal deserves its name, because, theoretically, it is the system of prices searched for by the economists of socialist countries who are used to say that prices should

---

*If economy is not savingless the problem (46) would also have a solution, but $\delta(d(c^*), z^*)$ may not attain the zero value. The solution c^* needs not be in such a case an OPC-vector, and the corresponding vector π — an OP-vector.

make possible "right economic calculations", enable the centre "the parametric control of the economy", induce enterprises to make "right decisions" etc. (see above, p. 146). We may therefore conclude, that — assuming we were right in what has been written above — "the price problem" in the centrally planned economy is theoretically solvable although not solvable practically at present (and in the foreseeable future)*. The only practical conclusion is that if we observe such symptoms as: disequlibrium on the market of consumption commodities — queues, stocks of unsold commodities in shops — or unnaturally high savings of households, or budget disequlibrium, then the system of prices is not optimal. This is, of course, what economists have been aware of since the origin of the discussion on the price problem in the CP-economy. One point, however, is worth being noticed. If the "price problem" in the CP-economy is to be considered at all, then it must be considered more or less in the way followed above, i.e. as the problem of choice of a *system* of prices on the ground of the comprehensive model of functioning of the whole economic system. I think that fruitless are discussions of the type: should prices be "value-prices", "production-prices", "average cost" or "marginal cost" prices. No simple formula may solve the "price problem". It seems to be no reason why prices of all commodities producible in a given economy should conform to a unique formula of this or that type. Only clear indication of technology, of export and import possibilities of predetermined decisions of the state (centre), of consumers' behaviour, of available resources and finally of the role the prices are expected to play in the economy, may raise hopes of solving the problem (in the theoretical meaning of the term). This is the way we tried to follow in our considerations. It is hardly believable that following this sort of way we may arrive at one simple, general formula of optimal price.

Finally, it must be stressed that our considerations show that even in very restrictive conditions (savingless economy, unique, non-degenerate solution to the COP) we must not hope that price system may be found which

---

*It must be stressed again that the system of prices called here optimal is a "short term" system. We did not investigate the problem, also widely discussed in the literature, what type of prices should be used in "long-term" planning, when "long-term" decisions are to be made on the basis of calcualtions involving future prices. We considered only the problem of "working" of the economy, and not that of its "growth".

would allow the centre to admit complete decentralization of decisions of productive (and foreign trade) enterprises, if some central goal is to be attained. It is not possible to prove that enterprises would operate only desirable activities precisely at the levels implied by the solution to the COP. Some degree of central intervention may by necessary, even if the optimal price system has been found and imposed on the economy.

APPENDIX 1

The proof of the existence of the APC-vector.

By assumptions (14) and (15) we may present Y (defined on p. 153) as a set of non-negative vectors y satisfying conditions

(I) $\quad \sum_{j \in Q} h_{kj} y_j \leqslant h_k \quad$ with some $\quad h_{kj} \geqslant 0$,

$\quad\quad h_k > 0$, for $\quad k = 1, \dots, L \quad$ at some $\quad L \geqslant 1$.

or conditions

(II) $\quad \sum_{j \in Q} \gamma_{kj} y_j \leqslant 1 \quad$ where $\quad \gamma_{kj} = h_{kj}/h_k$.

Let us consider the set Λ of price vectors $c = (c_j)$ defined as follows (for some given $D > 0$)

(III) $\quad c_j = D \sum_{k=1}^{N} \lambda_k \gamma_{kj} \quad$ with $\quad \lambda_k \geqslant 0, \quad \sum_{k=1}^{N} \lambda_k = 1$.

By (I)-(II) all vectors belonging to Λ are non-negative. Let $y \in Y$. Then for all $c \in \Lambda$

(IV) $\quad \sum_{j \in Q} c_j y_j = D \sum_{j \in Q} \sum_{k=1}^{L} \lambda_k \gamma_{kj} y_j = D \sum_{k=1}^{L} \lambda_k \sum_{j \in Q} \gamma_{kj} y_j \leqslant$

$\quad\quad \leqslant D \sum_{k=1}^{L} \lambda_k \leqslant D$,

which proves that price vectors c out of Λ satisfy the maximum choice postulate (β).

Let us consider the demand induced by an arbitrary price vector $c \in \Lambda$, $d(c)$. If it belongs to the interior of Y, then it satisfies the possible equilibrium condition (α). In the opposite case there exists a number ϑ_c, $0 < \vartheta_c \leqslant 1$, such that

(VI)
$$\vartheta d(c) \in Y \quad \text{for} \quad 0 \leqslant \vartheta \leqslant \vartheta_c \,,$$
$$\vartheta d(c) \bar{\in} Y \quad \text{for} \quad \vartheta > \vartheta_c \,.$$

Let us write for short

(VII) $q^c = \vartheta_c d(c)$.

The point q^c is the point in which the ray $Od(c)$ cuts the boundary of polyhedron Y. Its components q_j^c satisfy conditions

(VIII)
$$\sum_{j \in Q} \gamma_{kj} q_j^c \leqslant 1 \qquad \text{for} \quad k = 1, \ldots, L$$
$$\sum_{j \in Q} \gamma_{kj} q_j^c = 1 \qquad \text{for} \quad k \in L_c, \; L_c \text{ being a non-empty subset} \\ \text{of } \{1, \ldots, L\},$$

and so q^c belongs to Y. Were ϑ_c equal 1, then we would have $q^c = d(c)$ and, therefore, price vector c would satisfy the possible equilibrium postulate (α).

Consider the set of price vectors $\Lambda(c)$ defined as follows

(IX)
$$\bar{c} = (\bar{c}_j) \in \Lambda(c) \quad \text{if and only if}$$
$$\bar{c}_j = D \sum_{k \in L_c} \mu_k \gamma_{kj}, \quad \text{with} \quad \mu_k \geqslant 0, \quad \sum_{k \in L_c} \mu_k = 1 \,.$$

By (VIII) for any $\bar{c} \in \Lambda(c)$ the following equalities hold.

(X)
$$\sum_{j \in Q}' \bar{c}_j q_j^c = \sum_{j \in Q} D \sum_{k \in L_c} \mu_k \gamma_{kj} q_j^c =$$
$$= D \sum_{k \in L_c} \mu_k \sum_{j \in Q} \gamma_{kj} q_j^c = D \sum_{k \in L_c} \mu_k = D \,.$$

Obviously, $\Lambda(c) \subset \Lambda$. Both Λ and $\Lambda(c)$ are closed, bounded and convex sets. As the demand function is assumed to be continuous, the mapping $c \to \Lambda(c)$ is a semicontinuous mapping of Λ which assigns to any $c \in \Lambda$ a closed, convex and bounded subset of Λ. We may therefore make use of the Kakutani fixed point theorem, by virtue of which there exists a vector c^* out of Λ for which

(XI) $c^* \in \Lambda(c^*)$.

Taking the vector c^* for c, we may therefore also substitute c^* for $\bar{c}$ in (X), as this equality holds for any $\bar{c} \in \Lambda(c^*)$. we obtain

(XII) $$\sum_{j \in Q} c_j^* q_j^{c^*} = \vartheta_{c^*} \sum_{j=1}^{N} c_j^* d_j(c^*) = D \, .$$

As $0 < \vartheta_{c^*} \leqslant 1$, so by the property (10) of demand function, the last equality may be satisfied only in the case

(XIII) $\vartheta_{c^*} = 1$.

This implies that $q^{c^*} = d(c^*)$ and hence, by (VIII), $d(c^*) \in Y$. So the proof is completed, because the price vector c^* out of the set of vectors Λ satisfying the maximum choice postulates (β) satisfies at the same time the possible equilibrium postulate (α).

Let us stress that we have proved not only that the APC-vector exists, but also that at least one APC-vector belongs to the set Λ. The APC-vector needs not be unique.

APPENDIX 2

Proof of Theorem 3.

By assumption

(I) $$\sum_{t \in Z_k} b_{\cdot t} \xi_t^* = b^* = \sum_{s \in Z_k} b_{\cdot s} \xi_s \, ,$$

where $b_{\cdot t}$ stands for the column-vector $\begin{bmatrix} b_{1t}^k \\ \cdot \\ \cdot \\ b_{m_k t}^k \end{bmatrix}$.

(II) $\quad w_t = \beta^k b_{\bullet t}$ for *all* t *such that* $\xi_t^* > 0$ (as for all positive ξ_t^*, $t \in P_k$).

(III) $\quad w_s < \beta^k b_{\bullet s}$ for *some* s such that $\xi_s > 0$ (as for some positive ξ_s, $s \in \bar{P}_k$).

Suppose that the last inequalities hold for $s \in V_k$, whereas corresponding equalities hold for $s \in U_k$, where $U_k \cup V_k = Z_k$, and V_k is not empty. Then

(IV) $\quad w_s = \beta^k b_{\bullet s} - q_s$ for $s \in V_k$, and some $q_s > 0$.

We have

(V)
$$w^* = \sum_{t \in Z_k}' w_t \xi_t^* = \sum_{t \in Z_k}' \beta^k b_{\bullet t} \xi_t^* = \beta^k \sum_{t \in Z_k}' b_{\bullet t} \xi_t^* = \beta^k b^*.$$

$$w = \sum_{s \in Z_k}' w_s \xi_s = \sum_{s \in U_k}' w_s \xi_s + \sum_{s \in V_k}' w_s \xi_s =$$

$$= \sum_{s \in U_k}' \beta^k b_{\bullet s} \xi_s + \sum_{s \in V_k}' (\beta^k b_{\bullet s} - q_s) \xi =$$

(VI)

$$= \beta^k \sum_{s \in Z_k}' b_{\bullet s} \xi_s - \sum_{s \in V_k}' q_s \xi_s = \beta^k b^* - \sum_{s \in V_k}' q_s \xi_s =$$

$$= w^* - \sum_{s \in V_k}' q_s \xi_s < w^*.$$

This ends the proof. Notice that by the definition of w_t for any solution $x = [x_t]_{t \in Z_k}$ to the k-LOP

(VII)
$$\sum_{t \in Z_k}' w_t x_t \leqslant \sum_{t \in Z_k}' \beta^k b_{\bullet t} x_t = \beta^k \sum_{t \in Z_k}' b_{\bullet t} x_t \leqslant \beta^k b^k.$$

Hence if the solution ξ^* is such that $\sum_{t \in Z_k}' b_{\bullet t}^k \xi_t^* = b^* = b^k$, then by (V) $w^* = \beta^k b^k$, ξ^* is an optimal solution to the k-LOP (in which $\xi_t^* > 0$ only for $t \in P_k$), and no solution ξ for which at least one $\xi_s > 0$ appears for $s \in \bar{P}_k$ may be optimal.

So we have the following corollary: If a combination of desirable activities exists which exhausts all capacity of the k-th enterprise, then it is the optimal solution to the k-LOP.

Zbigniew Czerwiński

H Bonin 16/19, 60-658 Poznan, Poland.

MODELS FOR WATER DISTRIBUTION CONTROL IN THE TISZALÖK IRRIGATION SYSTEM

L. DÁVID — JUDIT MÓCSI — ERZSÉBET NAGY — J. STAHL

Our following models describe the operation of the Tiszalök Irrigation System (TÖR). The system belongs to the office of Tisza District Regional Waterworks and Watersupplies Enterprise in the city of Debrecen. The models were developed to improve the earlier, mainly empirical operation.

1. DESCRIPTION OF THE SYSTEM TO BE MODELLED

The irrigation system covers with its network an area of about 3000 km² at the east side of the river Tisza. Its components are the canals and the sluices connecting the individual canal sections and the meeting points of canals. In the sluices the operator can determine the transmitted water quantity, while in the meeting points of the canals the water flows continuously.

The clusters are certain connected canals. The system consists of three main branches (two main supply canals and a canal connecting them) and the clusters are located in the areas limited by these main canals. The irrigation system gets the water from the Tisza through two main sluices.

TÖR has numerous tasks. It has to provide with water an agricultural area of about 65.000 ha. This water serves for irrigation of agricultural cultures, water demands of fish-ponds etc. Moreover, in many points of the system there are demands for industrial and drinking-water, even water consumption for recreational purposes are arisen. The transfer of a rather large water quantity from the Tisza into the valley of the river Körös belongs also to the tasks of the system. The water quantity required to replace the water in the valley of the Körös burdens the system at two remove points. As a common effect of the Tisza water output, of the weather changes and of the emergency demands three operation states can be distinguished in the system.

The operation is *normal* when the water supply of the Tisza is sufficiently large for satisfying all demands and the system itself allows the transmission of necessary quantities everywhere. Experience shows that this is the case in 80% of the operations about.

The operation is *limited* when either from the Tisza the demanded water quantity can not be removed or, the water can be transmitted through the system is not enough to satisfy all the demands. About 5% of the whole operation period belongs to this state.

About 15% of all operations belongs to the *drainage* operation state taking place generally during extraordinary rainy periods.

Mathematical models are built for normal and limited operation states only. The drainage operation state has not been dealt with, because during it, the tasks of operation differ considerably from those of the two other operating states.

In normal and limited states, the entire or substantial satisfaction of the relatively large demands is the aim. In case of these operations only the demands can be reduced by the excess water. In case of excess water (drainage operation) the goal is to lead off this water which can cause great demage. In this period the demand is very small.

2. MODEL OF THE PHYSICAL BASES OF THE SYSTEM

To start with we give the physical characteristics of the system in the first two cases. Our models describe the operation of the system in successive periods of length T.

As previously stated, during a period there must be available water for the users and it is required to retrieve the leakage. Obviously, a certain time is needed to transfer the water through the system.

T has been chosen in order to make available the adequate water amount by the setting of the sluice at a moment of the previous period. Each calculation always refers to water quantities to be made available in a determined period, but on the basis of the results obtained, operative tasks must be done in two periods — the period in question and the previous one. Regarding, however, a certain object in the system, and the series of calculation this task is always either in the actual period or in the previous one. The system will be described by a directed graph $G = [N, A]$ containing no circle. The vertices are corresponding to certain sluices of the system, and to the crossing points of the canals, the arcs the corresponding to the clusters or sections of canals being between sluices.

The sluices taken into account in modelling were chosen according to operation standpoint instead of a modelling one. With our elaborated models also networks having more vertices and arcs can be handled.

The direction of the arcs is given by the water flow. The sluice corresponding to x of arc (x, y) will be called upper sluice, the one corresponding to y, lower sluice. Let S be a set of those points, which correspond to sluices where water may enter the system.

For every arc (x, y) the numbers $c_1(x, y)$ and $c_2(x, y)$ are given, which are well defined values characterising jointly the technical state of sluices corresponding to x and y, and of clusters or canals corresponding to (x, y). The $c_1(x, y)$ is the maximum amount of water can flow through the upper sluice corresponding to x during a time period of length T into the part represented by (x, y) of the system; $c_2(x, y)$ is

the maximum amount of water that can leave the part of system corresponding to (x, y) through the lower sluice corresponding to y during the
same period, G represents the system so, that demands are always assigned
to arcs, even in the case when of demand arises in a vertex of the original system (e.g. the water demand in the valley of the Körös). The sum of
water demands arising in the part of the system corresponding to (x, y)
will be denoted by $F(x, y)$. We should like to emphasize that $F(x, y) > 0$,
for every programmed time period and for every (x, y) because the leakage losses during operation of the system must be retrieved.

The seepage loss is considered previously fixed for every arc (x, y).
This hypothesis is realistic after a short, so called, time of saturation reck-
oned from the beginning of the growth season.

3. SOME IMPORTANT ASPECTS OF THE OPERATION OF THE SYSTEM

As explained, there is a given system of irrigation in certain places of
which water demands must be satisfied. Water is — partly or wholly —
available in the Tisza, but the water stocks must always be used economically. In the irrigation system the waterflow itself can be controlled with
the sluices.

We have the *task*, in the first place, to develop models for operating
the system. For these models the water quantities can be determined that
must be transmitted through the individual sluices. Thus we shall be able
not to violate the water transporting capacity of the system in some place
or other. All this must be solved to meet all the demands or a maximal
part of them, and to take off the Tisza only a water quantity satisfying
the user's demand. The system of such water quantities belonging to arcs
(x, y) will be named *feasible flow*.

In the present system of operation based on practical experiences the
solution of the above formulated task is not always possible.

From the two main points of the irrigation system the water must be
transmitted to about 40 user' points which are mostly located in the system

such a way that the adequate water quantity can not be transmitted to them through a single way. Provided that the ways through which we want to transmit the water to the users, have previously been determined, the capacity (during a period of time) in the common sections of the ways (of which we would have many) can make some trouble. As a consequence of this capacity problem the present operation system could not satisfy the demands in several cases, even if they should be satisfied by a better operation system.

This way of operation had another fault, of the same origin, i.e. it was operating with a large loss of water. The amount of water, lifted out of the river Tisza, exceeded essentially the sum of all water demands thus this excess amount of water flowed unnecessarily into the valley of the Körös. The constraints of our elaborated models assure to the use of all water, so this shortcoming of the operation can be eliminated.

4.1. *The model for the normal operation state*

In the above paragraph the aspects playing a very important part in elaborating the model were described. These aspects aim at meeting the users' demands and the economy with water stocks. Moreover, from operational aspects, only those were considered which according to the above conditions and physical characteristics, render possible the transmission of water in the irrigation system from the river Tisza to the users. The model of the normal operation state, however, takes into consideration other operational aspects, too.

For certain arcs (x, y) of the network a function $t_{(x,y)}(V)$ is given. Its value gives the moment at which the sluice corresponding to x must be opened, prior to the beginning of the examined period of length T if a quantity of water $- V$ must be passed through this sluice.

V corresponds to the sum of the users' demands arising on the edge, of losses due to seepage and of the quantities to be transmitted. The time interval T has been so chosen that $t_{(x,y)}(V) \leqslant T$. $t_{(x,y)}(V)$ is a monotone non-increasing function of V and $t_{xy}(V) > 0$.

Now we want to determine such a feasible flow, for which the earliest moment for setting any sluice before the beginning of the period takes place at the latest.

The mathematical model of the problem is going as follows: For every arc $(x, y) \in A$ a number $f(x, y) \geqslant 0$ (representing the sum of the proper water demands of the arc (x, y) and of the water quantities to be transmitted on the edge) must be determined which satisfy the following conditions:

(4.1) $f(x, y) \geqslant F(x, y) , \quad (x, y) \in A$

(4.2) $f(x, y) \leqslant c_1(x, y) , \quad (x, y) \in A$

(4.3) $f(x, y) - F(x, y) \leqslant c_2(x, y), \quad (x, y) \in A$

(4.4) $\displaystyle\sum_{y \in N^-(x)} (f(y, x) - F(y, x)) = \sum_{y \in N^+(x)} f(x, y) , \quad x \notin S$

$N^-(x) = \{y \mid (y, x) \in A\} , \quad N^+(x) = \{y \mid (x, y) \in A\}$

(4.5) $\displaystyle\sum_{s \in S} f(s, y) = \sum_{(x, y) \in A} F(x, y)$

(4.6) $\displaystyle\max_{(x, y)} t_{(x, y)}(f(x, y)) \to \min .$

The $f(x, y)$ values obtained solving the system (4.1)-(4.6) represent the water quantity to be let in at the upper sluice of arc (x, y), the values $t_{(x, y)}(f(x, y))$ give the times of interventions prior to the beginning of interval T.

4.2. Solution of the "normal model"

In the description until now the terminology of the book "Flows in Networks" by L.R. Ford and D.R. Fulkerson was followed, since for the solution we employ the out-of-kilter method contained therein.

For the solution procedure $G = [N, A]$ network is transformed as follows:

Every arc (x, y) is replaced with a pair of arcs $(x_1 y_1), (y_1, y)$. Let us denote by R^* the set of points of type y_2, by S^* the original set S. Let us complete our network with points r^* and s^*. Let $N^* = N \cup S^* \cup R^* \cup r^* \cup s^*$. Let an edge be led from each point $s \in S^*$ to s^*, from $r \in R^*$ to r^* and from r^* to s^*, and let A^* be the set of the edges.

On the edges of the $G^* = [N^*, A^*]$ a capacity function is defined as follows:

$$c^*(x^*, y^*) = \begin{cases} c_1(x, y) & \text{if } (x^*, y^*) \text{ edge is of } (x, y_1) \text{ type} \\ c_2(x, y) & \text{if } (x^*, y^*) \text{ edge is of } (y_1, y) \text{ type} \\ F(x, y) & \text{if } (x^*, y^*) \text{ edge is of } (y_1, r^*) \text{ type.} \end{cases}$$

We introduce also some lower bounds on the edges. (A lower bound on an edge means that at least as much water must be passed through it as the value of the lower bound.)

$$L^*(x^*, y^*) = \begin{cases} 0 & \text{if } (x^*, y^*) \neq (r^*, s^*) \\ \sum_{(x,y)} F(x, y) & \text{if } (x^*, y^*) = (r^*, s^*). \end{cases}$$

In this network a feasible flow corresponds, in an obvious manner, to a solution of the system (4.1)-(4.5).

The minimization of the objective function takes place by modifying the lower bounds, since in consequence of the monotonicity of the functions $t_{(x,y)}(V)$ a condition $t_{(x,y)} \leqslant \tau$ is equivalent to a constraint $f(x, y) \geqslant L(x, y)$. L is a monotone non-increasing function of τ here. This means that if we want to decrease the time point necessary to set upper sluice of an edge we must "compel" this arc to receive a larger and larger amount of water (of course $c_1(x, y)$ bounds in any case the value of $f(x, y)$ from above).

The solution can be obtained with the following algorithm:

4.a. There are given the network $G^* = [N^*, A^*]$, and the capacities

$c^*(x^*, y^*)$; $l^*(x^*, y^*) = 0$, if $(x^*, y^*) \neq (r^*, s^*)$;

$$l^*(r^*, s^*) = \sum_{(x,y) \in A} F(x, y) .$$

For certain edges there are given the functions $t_{(x,y)}$, Δt is a given value. $I = 1$.

4.b. With the help of the out-of-kilter algorithm we look for a feasible flow.

If such a flow does not exist, go to 4.d. Otherwise go to 4.c.

4.c. We choose the arc $(x, y) \in A$ for which

$$\tau = \max_{x \in X} \max_{y \in N^+(x)} t_{(x,y)}(f(x, y)) . \qquad \tau^* = \tau - \Delta t .$$

Let $l(x, y)$ be that V, for which $t_{(x,y)}(V) = \tau^*$, $(x, y) \in A$.

Let us continue from 4.b.

4.d. If $I = 1$, then the given demands cannot be met (limited operation state).

If $I > 1$, then from the system obtained at I-th step, we can obtain the water quantities to be passed through the sluices, and the moments of opening the sluices.

5. COMPUTATIONAL EXPERIENCES GAINED WITH THE "NORMAL MODEL"

In the summer of 1973 a trial operation lasting a week was carried out. The systematic programm runnings are expected in the summer of 1974. The experience gained by the trial operation can be considered favourable.

The algorithm has been programmed for an IBM 360/40 computer in FORTRAN-4 language. The extended G^* network has about 60 points and about 120 arcs. The function $t_{(x,y)}$ is given for about 20 arcs. (In 4.6 maximalization goes on these (x, y).) The process of seeking a feasible flow according to 4.b. requires at most 50 sec., for $I > 1$, generally, less than 10 sec. We had a maximum value of 5-6 for I thus the time necessary for the realization of the entire algorithm never surpassed 120 sec. The solution obtained by algorithm is only an approximate one, since the values were decreased by $\Delta t \cdot T = 6$ hours was programmed, between $I = 1$ and I, giving optimum, the value of the objective function decreased, generally, by 2 hours (from 5 to 3 hours).

Regarding operation we remark that, after all, users in connection with sluice settings considered only values $f(x, y)$. They used only the quantities to be let through the sluices, but the sluices were not set at the moments $t_{(x,y)}(f(x, y))$ determined by us. Thus, finally, every activity and process took place during the given time interval T. In spite of this, the application of our objective function was useful, because, as experience shows, it made more uniform the set of the sluices.

6. MODEL ELABORATED FOR THE LIMITED OPERATING STATE

As stated above, we call limited operating state a state if, either the water reserve of the Tisza is not sufficient to meet the sum of the demands, or the capacity, of the system sets limits to the demanded water quantity reaching every part of the system. It is not difficult to notice that both possibilities are the same from our standpoint, since the fact of the river Tisza water reservoir being small can be interpreted as the sluices having small capacity at S.

In elaborating this model, too, we considered our task to determine a feasible flow economizing on water. In this case, however, in interpretating the feasible flow, we had to disregard the demand that all users obtain all necessary water. We started from the general practice that in periods when water is scarce the water users' demands are categorized according to the character of consumption and among these categories a sequence of importance is determined. Water consumption is limited by prohibiting more and more sorts of water consumption according to the sequence of importance. This means that demands were arranged into 8 categories: in our system compensation of the seepage losses, demands for drinking and industrial water supply, water demands for gardening, irrigation of arable land, demands for rice growing, fish-ponds and recreational purposes. Within each category (with the exception of the seepage loss) demands were divided into two subcategories. Between the categories the sequence of importance coincides with the sequence of enumeration. The category of seepage loss in the most important one. Also the repartition among the categories is such that the satisfaction of the demands belonging to one category is more important than the satisfaction of the demands belonging to the other one. By means of the sequence of importance determined among the categories and subcategories a priority number (0 to 14) was assigned to each demand. The highest priority number was assigned to the water demands belonging to the category whose satisfaction we could at first disregard.

We should like to emphasize that on each arc there are, generally, several sorts of water demands too, but of course, it is not necessary that on each edge demands belonging to all categories should arise.

Subject to the following two conditions we have to determine those quantities of water which flow through the sluices. At first, taking into account the priority sequence demands must be met up to the highest extent in all parts of the system. Secondly, any water got into the system must be used up.

In addition to the former, the following new notations were introduced:

M the water stocks that can be taken off the Tisza, i.e. maximal water quantity that the capacity of the system allows of

$0, 1, \ldots, n$ let be all priority numbers

$k_{(x,y)}$ let mean the sorts of demands on arc (x, y). (That with the lowest priority number is the most important demand, $k_{(x,y)}$-th is the least important of all, regarding satisfaction.)

$F_j^i(x, y)$ let mean the extent of i-th demand arising on arc (x, y); j index means that this demand belongs to j-th priority level

$$i = 0, 1, \ldots, k_{(x,y)}$$

$$j \in \{0, \ldots, n\}$$

(to each $i_{(x,y)}$ uniquely corresponds a j).

The values

$$l_{(x,y)} \leqslant k_{(x,y)}, \qquad (x, y) \in A ,$$

$$f_j^i(x, y) \geqslant 0 , \qquad i = 0, \ldots, l_{(x,y)}, \ j \in \{0, \ldots, n\}, \ (x, y) \in A$$

$$f(x, y) \geqslant 0, \quad (x, y) \in A$$

must be determined, for which:

(6.1) $\quad f_j^i(x, y) \leqslant F_j^i(x, y) \qquad i = 0, \ldots, l_{(x,y)}, \ j \in \{0, \ldots, n\}$

(6.2) $\quad f(x, y) \leqslant c_1(x, y)$

(6.3) $\quad f(x, y) - \displaystyle\sum_{i=0}^{l_{(x,y)}} f_j^i(x, y) \leqslant c_2(x, y)$

(6.4) $\quad \displaystyle\sum_{y \in N^-(x)} \left[f(y, x) - \sum_{i=0}^{l_{(x,y)}} f_j^i(y, x) \right] = \sum_{y \in N^+(x)} f(x, y), \qquad x \notin S$

(6.5) $\quad \displaystyle\sum_{(x,y) \in A} \sum_{i=0}^{l_{(x,y)}} f_j^i(x, y) = M$

(6.6) $\quad \displaystyle\sum_{(x,y) \in A} \sum_{i=0}^{l_{(x,y)}} j f_j^i(x, y) \to$ minimal.

$f_j^{l_{(x,y)}}(x, y)$ gives that on arc (x, y) what quantity will be met from demands of j priority number.

$f(x, y)$ is the water quantity that has to be let into the part of the system represented by (x, y) at the sluice corresponding to x node.

Conditions (6.2)-(6.4) assure that values $f_j^i(x, y)$ and $f(x, y)$ represent a feasible flow. (6.5) assures the use of all available water.

(6.1)-(6.5) and the objective function together assure that by using up all available water, demands will be met from 0 priority level to the maximum highest level (in each part of the system).

Considering the priority number as "satisfying costs" of a demnad for a unit and requesting the use of all available water, we minimize this objective function. The solution will become such a one that on each edge, on each level that can be met (at the worst with the exception of the highest one), it meets entirely the demand and strictly takes into account the priority of demands in the system. The determined $l_{(x,y)}$, $(x,y) \in A$ shows on arc (x,y) (starting from 0 priority level) the number of priority levels that are entirely satisfied (at the very most, excepted the highest level).

7. SOLUTION OF THE LIMITED MODEL

The $G = [N, A]$ network is transformed now, too, for the solution. The difference between this and the previous ones is: the points $r \in R$ and the point r^* are connected by instead of one arc, so many arcs as many demands arise on the original arc (x, y). For these arcs the value of the capacity is $F_j^i(x, y)$. If on all other arcs the costs of transfer are considered 0, then we seek a feasible circulation at minimum expenses with out-of-kilter algorithm, thus reaching a solution of our problem.

L. Dávid

National Water Authority of Hungary, Budapest,

Judit Mócsi – Erzsébet Nagy – János Stahl

INFELOR, System Engineering Institute, H-1281 Budapest, P.o. Box 10.'.

DYNAMIC MODEL FOR LONG-TERM WATER RESOURCES DEVELOPMENT

L. DÁVID — F. SZIDAROVSZKY

1. INTRODUCTION

The purpose of this paper is to develop a dynamic model to compare alternative water resources development strategies under limited resources.

This model is based on the relationship of water management and socio-economic evolution, considering it as a coherent system. The main elements of the model and their interrelations are illustrated in Fig. 1, where the basic principles of development in water management are considered and the structure of the model is represented.

Socio-economic evolution in the region under consideration during the development period is represented in the model by the growth of regional income and population. Starting from the values applying to the beginning of the development period and with the annual growth rate envisaged it is possible to estimate both for any year of the development period. Socio-economic evalution represented by the growth of these two factors involves requirements to be satisfied by water management.

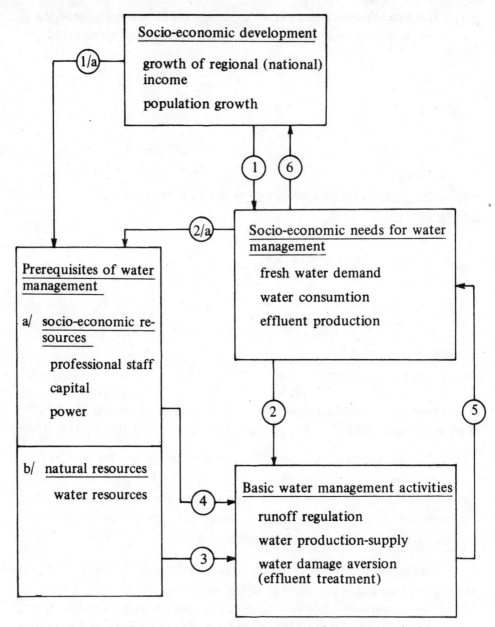

Note: figures indicate the preferable sequence of process analysis

Figure 1. Interrelations between the elements of the water
management development model

These requirements are expressed in the model by the freshwater demand, by water consumption and by effluent discharges. The desirable growth rate of the freshwater demand is estimated in terms of the growth rates of regional income and population. On this basis it is possible to estimate, starting from the initial value, the envisaged freshwater demand for any year of the development period. Consumption is expressed as a definite percentage of the freshwater demand, while the effluent discharge is the difference of the two.

For satisfying the social needs represented by these water volumes, the three fundamental activities of water management are runoff control, water production and supply and the aversion of water damages. All major activities of water management are substantially included in these three basic activities. Detailed informations on the basic activities can be found in the paper [2].

The resources required for realizing the fundamental activities are taken into account in the model as follows. Of the great number of resources involved the financial funds (capital), the number of professionals and the amount of power as social resources and the water supplies as natural resources are introduced into the computations. These may be regarded as the most important resources in performing the fundamental activities in water management. The necessary number of professionals and the power demand can be expressed as a percentage of the freshwater demand, while the capital demand as a percentage of the regional income, for any year in the development period. The funds include substantially all operating costs of water management, i.e., the sum of investment and operating costs. Water resources are characterized by the potential resources as the upper, and the minimum resources as the lower limit. The annual capital demand is expressed in thousand million Ft, the power demand in thousand million kWh and the necessary professionals in head/year as units.

For the desired development of the fundamental water management activities considered, all the above resources are necessary in the proper combination. For attaining a certain level of activity (e.g. a specific level of runoff control, meeting a specific freshwater demand, etc.) a certain amount of resources must be expended. To any particular amount of resources the corresponding level of activities can be determined.

If the resources made available to water management are adequate for performing the fundamental water management activities in the entire development period, then water management will be in accordance with the desired development, i.e., the desired socio-economic evolution of the region is ensured as for water management. On the other hand, where the resources are insufficient, water management is obviously incapable of satisfying the social requirements (e.g. it fails to meet the freshwater demand, or water consumption). This has adverse effects on socio-economic evolution retarding, or even halting it.

This attenuation, or delay is taken into consideration in the model by the fact that from the relative situation of freshwater demand, water consumption and available supplies different damage situations may arise year by year. If the available supplies are larger than the freshwater demand, no demage will obviously occur. On the other hand, in cases where the available supplies are less than either the freshwater demand, or water consumption, the consumers will suffer losses, the magnitude of which depends on their ability to compensate for shortages (shortage tolerance) and on the extent of recycling and repeated uses of water.

Depending on the characteristics of the particular damage situation, the impact of these losses will be reflected with a certain delay in a reduction of the growth rate of national income and of the population. As a result of the attenuated rate the actual income and population figures will ensue year by year. These latter will be clearly lower than the ideal ones.

In developing socio-economic systems with limited resources, these are in general insufficient for the ideal development envisaged. In long-term water management development planning, consideration must therefore be given to the possibility of developing water management under constraints imposed by insufficient resources. In such cases the development strategy adopted must be such that in the development period considered the loss in regional income and drop in population growth due to any failure of meeting the desired water demands should be minimized. In fact, at any given volume of resources the three fundamental activities in water management can be performed according to different strategies. The aim of the dynamic model of water management development is to select the optimum strategy of the potential alternatives, using the approach through systems engineering.

The fundamental purpose of the *development strategy* is to allocate the available resources among the fundamental water management activities during the development period.

In view of the system with limited resources, a loss in regional income and a drop in the rate of population growth relative to the ideal evolution envisaged may occur. Adding the annual figures the total loss is obtained for a particular strategy. Since there are two objective functions, it is necessary to specify a trade-off criteria for selecting an optimal strategy. The alternative strategies considered may be arranged separately according to both objective functions in sequences of growing magnitude. In this way two "order numbers" are obtained for each strategy. The optimal strategy will be choosen such that the sum of the two "order numbers" is minimized.

2. MATHEMATICAL MODEL

The parameters and variables of the model are functions of the time period t, choosen as one year in this model, and they are computed from year by year based on the data of the previous year during the entire development period extending to N years. The elements of the model to be described in detail below include: input variables, state variables and state transition functions including constraints, output variables and two objective functions.

(A) *Input variables* are the elements of the 3×3 matrix

$$(1) \qquad A(t) = \begin{pmatrix} a_t & b_t & c_t \\ A_t & B_t & C_t \\ \alpha_t & \beta_t & \gamma_t \end{pmatrix}$$

whose rows sum up to unity, thus we have six independent variables. The nine elements of matrix $A(t)$ correspond to a decision to allocate the three resources to three fundamental activities. For example C_t is the proportion of total manpower allocated to aversion of water damages.

(B) *State variables* can be divided into four groups.

(a) *Independent variables*

the regional income $T(t)$,

the population $L(t)$,

the fresh water demand $I(t)$,

the annual percentage growth coefficient of regional income $p(t)$,

the annual percentage growth coefficient of population $q(t)$,

the annual percentage growth coefficient of fresh water demand $r(t)$ which is assumed to be a given function of $p(t)$ and $q(t)$.

The value of $T(t)$ can be computed by the formula

$$(2) \qquad T(t) = T(t-1)\left(1 + \frac{p(t)}{100}\right),$$

and similar formulae can be used to compute $L(t)$ and $I(t)$.

(b) *Constraint variables* are $U(t), V(t), W(t)$. We assumed that the financial fund, the professional manpower available and the amount of power are $U(t), V(t)$ and $W(t)$ percentages of $T(t), I(t)$ and $I(t)$ respectively.

(c) *Dependent variables*

the consumptive water demand $H(t)$,

the volume of effluent discharge $SZ(t)$,

the volume of treated effluent discharge $K_t(t)$,

the percentage of runoff control X_t,

the potential amount of water available $K_{p,\,red}(t)$,

the capacity of water production and supply $K_k(t)$,

the water supply availabe $K_h(t)$,

the index of water consumption U_t,

the total capital available for socio-economic development $p(t)$,

the professional manpower available $Sa(t)$,

the power availabe $E(t)$;

the 3×3 matrix $B(t)$, the k-th element of the row i of $B(t)$ gives the value of i-th type of resources spent on k-th type of activity in the year t,

the 3×3 matrix $C(t)$ is the sum of the matrices $B(1), \ldots, B(t)$.

The values of the dependent variables can be computed by simple formulae. The consumptive water demand is defined by the equation

(3) $H(t) = U_t I(t) $,

and the volume of effluent discharge can be calculated using the formula

(4) $SZ(t) = I(t) - H(t) $.

The values of $P(t)$, $Sa(t)$, $E(t)$ are given by the constraint variables

(5) $p(t) = U(t) \dfrac{T(t)}{100}$

(6) $Sa(t) = V(t) \dfrac{I(t)}{100}$

(7) $E(t) = W(t) \dfrac{I(t)}{100} $.

The matrices $B(t)$ and $C(t)$ are defined by the following equations

(8) $B(t) = A(t) \begin{pmatrix} p(t) & 0 & 0 \\ 0 & Sa(t) & 0 \\ 0 & 0 & E(t) \end{pmatrix}$,

and

(9) $C(t) = B(1) + B(2) + \ldots + B(t) $.

We also assumed that x_t, $K_k(t)$ and $K_t(t)$ depend only on the elements of $C(t)$, and they can be computed by given formulae, which can be found in the paper [2].

We calculated $K_{p,\text{red}}(t)$ using the formula (Fig. 2)

$$(10) \qquad K_{p,\text{red}}(t) = K_p - SX_tK_p - \frac{[SZ(t) - K_t(t)]}{Z_t} \,,$$

where S is the coefficient of regulation losses, K_p is the potential water resources, Z_t is a number to indicate the unusable part to the total untreated effluent discharge.

We remark that all of these three coefficients are constant numbers.

The water supply available is defined by the equation

$$(11) \qquad K_h(t) = K_{\min} + X_t[K_{p,\text{red}}(t) - K_{\min}] \,,$$

where $K_{\min}$ is the minimal water resource.

(d) *Variable j of demage situation* is determined by considering the magnitude of the shortage relatively to "ideal" development variables which are denoted by a star. Five situations $j = 1, \ldots, 5$ can be distinguished (Fig. 3).

Situation $j = 1$

$$(12) \qquad K_h(t) > I^*(t) = K_k(t) > H^*(t) = H(t) \,.$$

The demand for fresh water being equal to the water producing-supplying capacity and the available water supplies being greater than these, involves no damage. Consequently the damage situation is a fictitious one.

Situation $j = 2$

$$(13) \qquad K_h(t) > I^*(t) > K_k(t) > H^*(t) > H(t) \,.$$

In this case, although the available water supplies are not utilized to their full extent, some slight damage may still be expected to occur, since the ideal freshwater demand is greater than that which can be met by the actual water producing capacity, even if shortage tolerance is allowed.

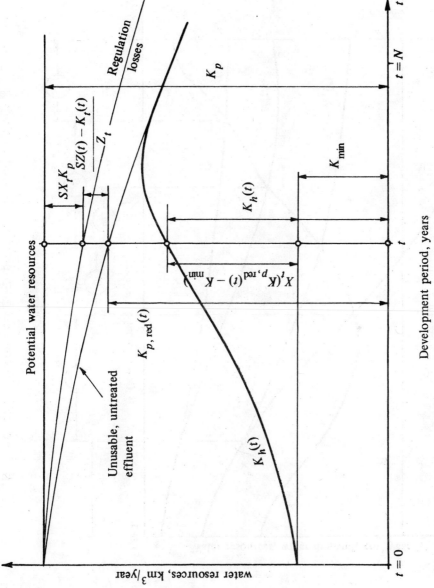

Figure 2. Estimation of usable water resources

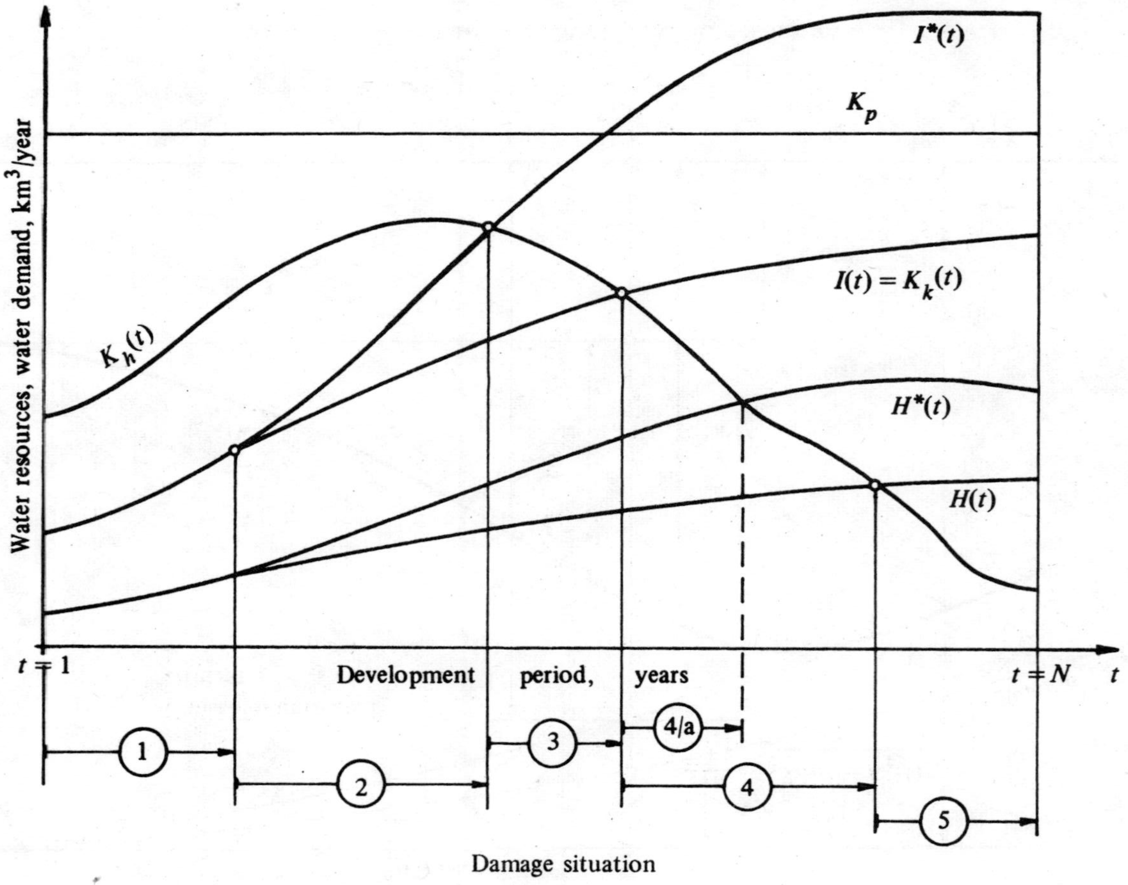

Figure 3. Theoretical description of damage situations

The effect on socio-economic evolution is perceptible with a great delay only, thus the growth rates p_t and q_t are reduced slightly with a long delay.

Situation $j = 3$

(14) $\qquad I^*(t) \geqslant K_h(t) > K_k(t) > H^*(t) > H(t)$

a damage of medium size and perceptible with a medium dealy is anticipated, since neither the water producing-supplying capacity, nor the available water supplies are sufficient for meeting the ideal fresh water demand. The reduction in p_t and q_t is a medium one.

Situation $j = 4$

(15) $\qquad I^*(t) > K_k(t) \geqslant K_h(t) > H^*(t) > H(t)$

or

(16) $\qquad I^*(t) > K_k(t) > H^*(t) \geqslant K_h(t) > H(t)$.

In this damage situation the available supplies are smaller than the actual freshwater demand characterized by the actual water producing-supplying capacity, or smaller than the ideal water consumption. For this reason little delay and heavy damages are likely to occur, i.e., both p_t and q_t are greatly reduced.

Situation $j = 5$

(17) $\qquad I^*(t) > K_k(t) > H^*(t) > H(t) \geqslant K_h(t)$

the damage is a very heavy one and occurs practically without delay, since the available supplies are insufficient to cover even the actual water consumption. The very great reduction is p_t and q_t occurs virtually without delay.

In estimating the damage situations the delay and the reduction in the rate of socio-economic evolution play roles of paramount importance. The delay in the reduction of the quantities p_t and q_t should be denoted by τ_j^p and τ_j^q, respectively and the extent of reduction thereof by d_j^p and d_j^q, respectively, in the damage situations $j = 1, 2, 3, 4$ and 5. The value of τ_j^p indicates the number of years following the occurrence of the damage situation j where the reduction in the growth rate of regional income becomes perceptible. The value of d_j^p on the other hand, indicates the percentage reduction in the growth rate of regional income in the damage situation j.

The magnitudes of d_j^p and d_j^q depend, however, also on the magnitude of the damage even within each damage situation. Thus

(18) $d_j^p = Y(\eta)D_j^p$ and $d_j^q = Y(\eta)D_j^q$

where D_j^p and D_j^q are the factors expressing the basic reduction depending on the damage situation, $Y(\eta)$ is a factor whose magnitude depends on the magnitude of water shortage within a particular damage situation, η is a factor expressing the magnitude of water shortage.

The magnitude of η is determined in the first three damage situations by the ratio $\dfrac{K_k(t)}{K_h(t)}$ in the fourth by $\dfrac{K_h(t)}{K_k(t)}$, while in the fifth by $\dfrac{K_h(t)}{H(t)}$. The criterion

$0 \leqslant \eta \leqslant 1$

is obviously satisfied. It is assumed further that in a damage situation of lower order the magnitude of the ensuing damage must not exceed the magnitude of damage ensuing in the damage situation of the next higher order.

(C) *The output variables are* $\tau_j^p, \tau_j^q, d_j^p, d_j^q$ $(1 \leqslant j \leqslant 5)$, and using the values of these variables the corrected growth coefficients $p_{t+\tau_j^p}$ and $q_{t+\tau_j^q}$ can be computed.

(D) *The two objective functions* $\delta(T)$ and $\delta(L)$ are defined by the equations

(19) $\delta(T) = \displaystyle\sum_{t=1}^{N} [T^*(t) - T(t)]$

(20) $$\delta(L) = \frac{1}{m} \sum_{t=1}^{N} [L^*(t) - L(t)] \, ,$$

where m is the average age in years,

The variables of the model and their relations are shown in Fig. 4.

The block diagram of computation for a potential development strategy is shown in Fig. 5.

3. PRACTICAL APPLICATION OF THE MODEL

As a practical test on the operation of the model and in the interest of improving long-term development planning in water management, further for exploring the new trends, development considerations and potential policies arising from the possibility of analysing a great number of competing alternatives, the development of water management has been examined in an assumed catchment, as in a socio-economic region, determining the optimal development strategy for the development period 1971 to 2020. The application of the model has been made necessary by the − assumed − fact that the resources necessary for the envisaged (ideal) development of water management in the region, determined in an earlier long-term development program, are not available. Thus the assumption of a developing socio-economic system with limited resources is justified in the present case.

The data and functions assumed in the model and the results can be found in the paper [2]. We considered 44 development strategies.

The comparison of optimum and poorest development alternatives are illustrated in Fig. 6. In development strategy 1 the bulk of resources is concentrated on runoff control over the full development period, devoting at the same time a considerable share to effluent treatment. As a consequence thereof, in the optimal alternative the available supplies exceed almost in the full development period the freshwater demand which can actually be met, although the latter is appreciably smaller than the ideal freshwater demand. In this way less severe demage situations occur. In 85% of

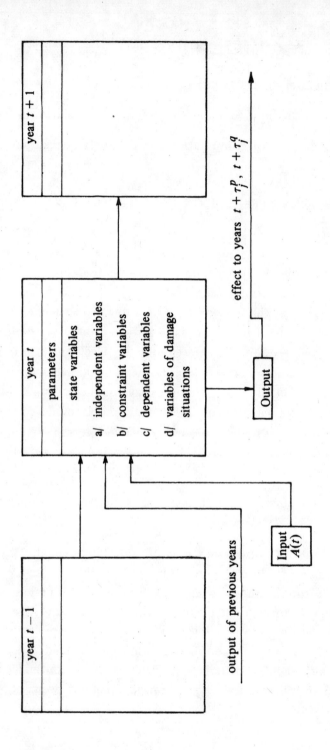

Figure 4. Systems model representation

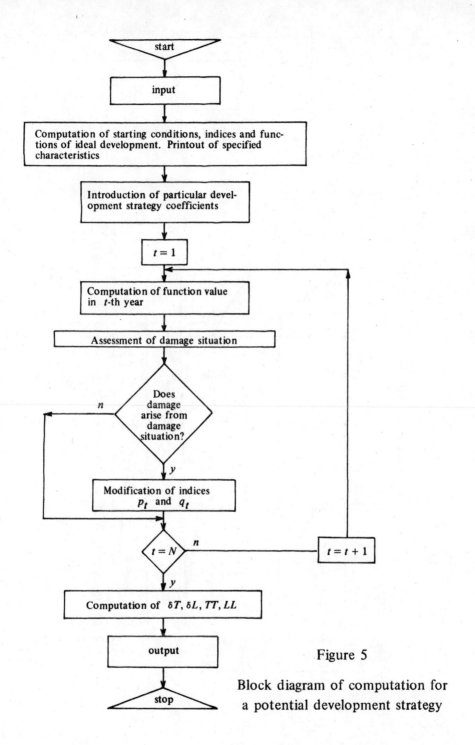

Figure 5

Block diagram of computation for a potential development strategy

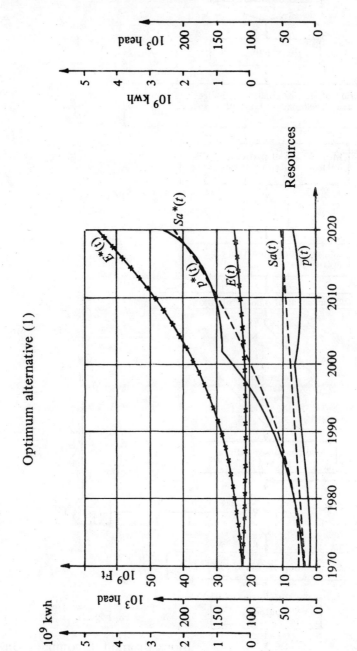

Optimum alternative (1)

10^9 head

10^9 kwh

Resources

$E^*(t)$

$Sa^*(t)$

$p^*(t)$

$E(t)$

$Sa(t)$

$p(t)$

10^9 Ft

10^3 head

10^9 kwh

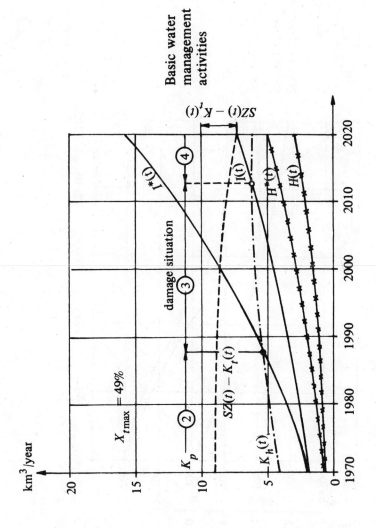

Basic water management activities

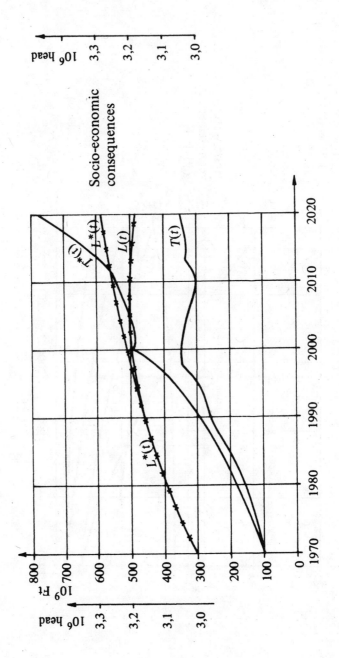

Socio-economic
consequences

Poorest alternative (2)

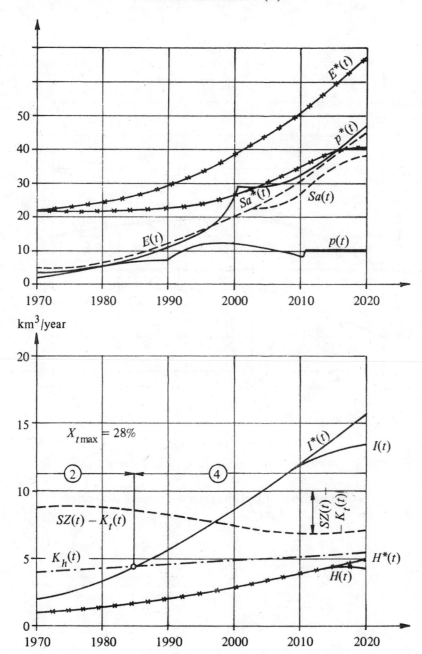

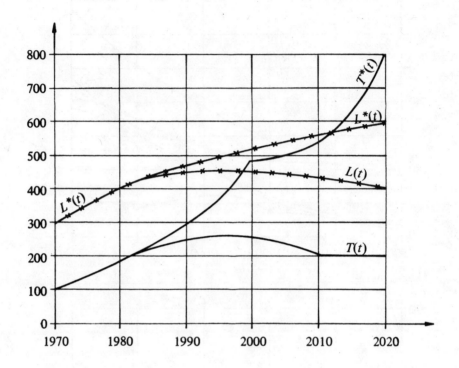

Figure 6

Comparison of optimum and poorest strategies

the period the damage situations 2 and 3 prevail, while the damage situation involving severe losses covers no more than 15% of the development period.

In contrast thereto the resources in development strategy 2 are concentrated highly on water-production-supply and effluent treatment, allocating small shares only to runoff control. Consequently in the poorest alternative the supplies which could be made available for utilization hardly increase and although the capacity for meeting the freshwater demand is virtually identical throughout with the ideal freshwater demand, the latter cannot be met over 70% of the period (damage situation 4).

4. DEVELOPMENT OF THE MODEL

The parameters and functions assumed in the model are uncertain, and can be considered as random variables and random functions. In this case both objective functions depend on these random variables and functions, thus they also are random variables. Considering this fact in the choice of optimal strategy the method of Bayesian Decision Theory can be applied [5].

5. SUMMARY

The natural-social coordination of water conditions calls for increasing resources, but these are available in limited quantities. The purpose of this paper is to develop a dynamic model to compare alternative water resources development strategies under limited resources.

The alternative development strategies are compared with respect to an objective function expressing the cost of not satisfying planned development socio-economic levels (opportunity loss); namely, because of water shortage, the population and regional economic income growth may be hindered. The best plan is the one for which this opportunity loss is minimum of monetary and population measures.

The model is discrete in time and continuous in state variables and has an advantage of combining social goals and regional economics with water resources in a dynamic mode with feedback.

A realistic example is presented. Seven alternative strategies are examined with a 50-year horizon under several different hypotheses for resources availability which yields 44 alternative cases of development. The computational algorithm is coded in ICL FORTRAN language.

It represents the first step toward a dual objective dynamic optimization model (income and population), in which uncertainty may be introduced.

REFERENCES

[1] Bureau of Reclamation: *Guidelines for implementing principles and standards for multiobjective planning of water resources*, Washington, 1972.

[2] L. Dávid — F. Szidarovszky, Long-range planning of water management development with dynamic model (in Hungarian, with English summary), *Hidrológiai Közlöny*, Budapest, 10-12 (1974).

[3] L. Dávid, The role of water management systems in water resources management, (in Hungarian), *Hidrológiai Közlöny*, 3 (1974).

[4] L. Dávid, Potential water resources and their role in water management development, (in Hungarian), *Vízügyi Közlemények*, 3 (1974).

[5] D.R. Davis — C.C. Kisiel — L. Duckstein, Bayesian decision theory applied to design in hydrology, *Water Resources Research*, 8, 1 (1972), 33-41.

[6] I. Dégen, *Water management*, Vol. I, *The economic foundations of water managemant*, (in Hungarian), Tankönyvkiadó, Budapest, 1972.

[7] I. Dégen, *Water management*, Vol. II, *Water resources management*, (in Hungarian), Tankönyvkiadó, Budapest, 1972.

[8] J. Dougles — R. Lee, *Economics of water resources planning*, McGraw-Hill, New York, 1971.

[9] M. Hufschmidt − M. Fiering, *Simulation techniques for design of water resources systems,* Harvard University Press, Cambridge, Mass. 1966.

[10] A. Kaufmann, *Methods and models of operation research,* (in Hungarian), Műszaki Kiadó, Budapest, 1968.

[11] E. Kuiper, *Water resources project economics,* Butterworths, London, 1971.

[12] A. Mass, et al, *Design of water resources systems,* Harvard University Press, Cambridge, Mass. USA. Fourth printing, 1970.

[13] H. Donella Meadows et al, *The limits to growth,* Potomac Associates Book, New York, 1972.

[14] D. Monarchi − C.C. Kisiel − L. Duckstein, Interactive multiobjective programming in water resources. A case study. *Water Resources Research,* 9 (1973).

[15] R. de Neufville − J. Stafford, *Systems analysis for engineers and managers,* McGraw-Hill Book Company, New York, 1971.

[16] F. Szidarovszky, *Introduction to numerical methods,* (in Hungarian), Közgazdasági és Jogi Kiadó, Budapest, 1974.

[17] F. Gilbert White, *Strategies of American water management,* Ann Arbor, The University of Michigan Press, 1970.

[18] T.L. Zolotarev − I.V. Obrezhkov, Planning of complex water resources schemes. Economic and technologic concepts (R. Dorfman). (In Russian). *Energoisdat,* Moscow − Leningrad, 1966.

László Dávid

National Water Authority of Hungary, Budapest,

Ferenc Szidarovszky

Eötvös Lóránd University, Budapest.

A BRANCH-AND-BOUND METHOD FOR SOLVING FIXED CHARGE NETWORK FLOW PROBLEMS

G. DEHNERT

1. THE PROBLEM

Let

$$N = (V, A, c, \lambda, \kappa)$$

be a finite, antisymmetrical, and capacitated flow network with

set of vertices V,

set of arcs A,

linear cost function c,

and upper and lower bounds κ and λ, respectively.

Let Q and T be nonempty disjoint subsets of V, the set of sources and sinks, respectively. Some of the arcs are potential arcs with fixed charges attached.

The problem is to find the configuration of the graph which yields a cost minimal flow from sources to sinks.

Practical examples. Transshipment problems with fixed charges, optimization of regional waste water treatment systems, optimization of regional water supply systems.

Figures 1 and 2 show an example of a regional waste water treatment system.

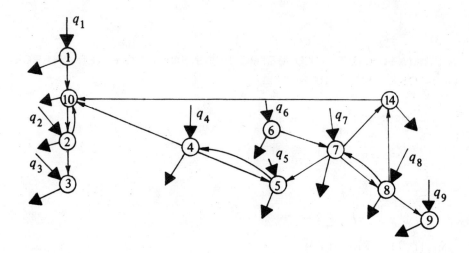

Fig. 1

Waste water treatment system with waste water
q_i at vertex i

Assumptions. (by transformations always to achieve)

(1) There are no negative cycles in the graph.

(2) The graph is antisymmetrical.

We formulate the problem as a mixed-binary optimization problem with the objective function

$$ZF = c\Phi + fy$$

and with the constraints:

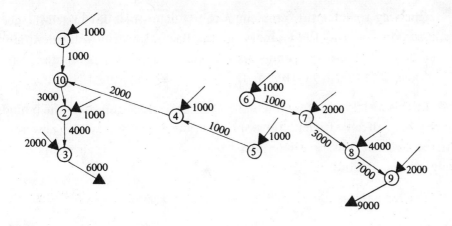

Fig. 2

Optimal solution of the example in Fig. 1

$$\lambda(u, v)y(u, v) \leqslant \varphi(u, v) \leqslant \kappa(u, v)y(u, v) \quad \forall (u, v) \in A$$

$$\sum_{v \in P(u)} \varphi(v, u) - \sum_{v \in S(u)} \varphi(u, v) = 0 \quad \forall u \in V - (Q \cup T)$$

$$\sum_{q \in Q} \left(\sum_{v \in S(q)} \varphi(q, v) - \sum_{v \in P(q)} \varphi(v, q) \right) =$$

$$= \sum_{t \in T} \left(\sum_{v \in P(t)} \varphi(v, t) - \sum_{v \in S(t)} \varphi(t, v) \right),$$

$$\varphi(u, v) \geqslant 0, \quad \forall (u, v) \in A, \quad y(u, v) \in \{0, 1\}.$$

Here

Q	is the set of sources,
T	is the set of sinks,
$P(u)$	is the set of all immediate predecessors of u,
$S(u)$	is the set of all immediate successors of u,
Φ	is the flow vector with the components
$\varphi(u, v)$	for $(u, v) \in A$.

One way to solve this problem is to use algorithms for mixed-integer optimization (such as the Gomory- or the Balas-algorithm with modifications). Some of these algorithms are implemented on large computers, like MPSX and UMPIRE from IBM or ILONA and FMPS from UNIVAC.

In this article we present a b-&-b-algorithm which generates the bounds by the help of an efficient flow-optimization algorithm, where new restricted optimal flows are determined using the already obtained open nodes of the solution tree.

The advantages of the method and the program are the following.

(1) Easy to manage if opposed to the software packages with standardized input-output.

(2) No danger of numerical inaccuracy, because of the only arithmetical operations of multiplying, comparing and adding of integers.

(3) An essential reduction of computing time demonstrated on examples.

2. THE B-&-B PRINCIPLE

The b-&-b principle is based upon Balinski's idea [2] for solving the transportation problem with fixed charges.

The following sets of indices are defined:

$$S^* = \{j \mid f_j > 0\}$$

set of all indices of arcs with 0-1-variables y_j;

$$S = \{j \mid y_j = 0 \vee y_j = 1\}$$

set of indices of fixed arcs;

$$S' = S^* - S.$$

At the beginning we have

$$S = \phi \quad \text{and} \quad S' = S^*.$$

For all $j \in S'$ the fixed-cost-function is linearized (see Fig. 3).

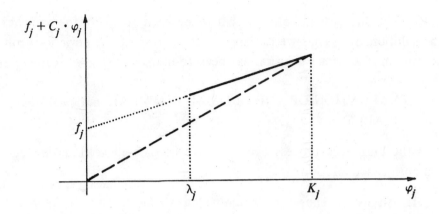

Fig. 3

Fixed-cost function and linearization

The linearized cost-coefficients are

$$cl_j = c_j + \frac{f_j}{\kappa_j} \quad j \in S'.$$

The linearized cost function coincides with the real one in two points: for $\varphi_j = 0$ and for $\varphi_j = \kappa_j$.

If this condition is satisfied for all φ_j $(j \in S')$, the solution φ is called an *exact* one. After solving the continuous problem with $S' = S^*$ a lower bound ZF_0 is known for the objective function and certain arcs are fixed:

$$\text{if} \quad y_j = 0 \quad \text{then} \quad cl_j = \infty$$

and

$$\text{if} \quad y_j = 1 \quad \text{then} \quad cl_j = c_j .$$

Then the optimal flow of the respective subproblem is determined and its exactness is checked.

An exact solution is optimal if its cost is less or equal than the costs of each previously generated inexact and other exact solutions.

The costs increase monotonically if we proceed on one of the branches of the solution tree. Thus we can give an estimation of the deviation from the optimum if an exact solution has been found.

3. EVALUATION OF THE OPTIMAL FLOWS AFTER FIXING OF ARCS

In the branching process two cases are considered after having obtained an inexact solution:

3.1. An arc j, chosen by a rule which will be formulated later, is fixed to 0, that is: it is closed for a flow. Hence we must bypass the flow which enters the vertex u of the arc $j = (u, v)$ in an optimal way.

We do this by using the incremental graph of the previously generated solution (see D o m s c h k e [10], [11]).

Figure 4 shows this principle.

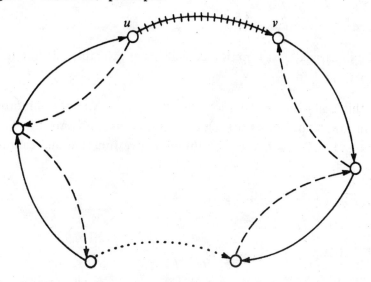

Fig. 4

Shortest path from u to v in this incremental graph

We determine the shortest path from u to v and correct the incremental graph along this path. If the flow $\varphi(u, v)$ is not yet reduced to zero after this correction, we have to repeat this procedure.

After reducing the flow $\varphi(u, v)$ we determine the optimal flow φ of this subproblem by the help of the increment graph, check the exactness of this solution and store the incremental graph for a backtrack to this node of the b-&-b-tree.

3.2. A chosen arc j is fixed to 1, that is: the linearized costs cl_j are replaced by the smaller costs c_j, and the fixed charge f_j has to be added completely to the objective function.

Decreasing the cost of the arc j a negative cycle can arise, which includes the arc j.

Thus we determine the shortest path from v to u. The length of this path is l.

There are two cases:

3.2.1.

$$c_j + l \geqslant 0 \,.$$

A flow correction along this path must be introduced only if previously we had $\varphi_j < \lambda_j$.

3.2.2.

$$c_j + l < 0 \,.$$

The flow in the negative cycle will be increased, by as much as possible.

Again we determine the shortest path in the corrected incremental graph and consider the two cases above.

We terminate

$$\text{if} \quad \varphi_j \geqslant \lambda_j \quad \text{in Case 1}$$

or

if $\varphi_j = \kappa_j$ in Case 2.

It is possible that we cannot find a feasible solution by this way. This means that we arrived at a node of the b-&-b-tree from which a further branching is not feasible.

After fixing, the index j is removed from the set S' and taken into S.

The solution is checked for its exactness. In the case of continuation we backtrack to an open node of the tree, where a new arc $j \in S'$ will be fixed.

4. CHOICE OF ARCS TO BE FIXED

Only the arcs j with

$$j \in S' \quad \text{and} \quad 0 < \varphi_j < \kappa_j$$

are candidate for fixing.

The choice of arcs does not influence the finiteness of the method but is important for the generation of the tree and hence influences the computer time.

Till now we have tested two rules:

4.1. Choice of j^* with

$$\varphi_{j*} = \min_{j \in S'} \left| \varphi_j - \frac{\kappa_j}{2} \right|.$$

In this case we fix at first those arcs where the greatest uncertainty exists, whether they will be fixed to 0 or 1.

4.2. Let

$$\psi_j = \begin{cases} \varphi_j & \text{if} \quad \varphi_j \leqslant \frac{\kappa_j}{2} \\ \kappa_j - \varphi_j & \text{otherwise.} \end{cases}$$

We choose the arc j^* with

$$\psi_{j^*} = \min_{j \in S'} \psi_j \, .$$

That is the arc with the flow closest to 0 or to the upper boundary of the capacity.

The relation between these choices and the b-&-b strategy applied is illustrated in the next section.

5. THE B-&-B STRATEGY

Several strategies are known for choosing the actual open node and for generating the b-&-b tree (see for example G e o f f r i o n & M a r s t e n [14]).

L a n d & D o i g [15] selected the node with the best objective function value, regardless of the values of the integer variables for that node.

Figure 5 shows such a tree.

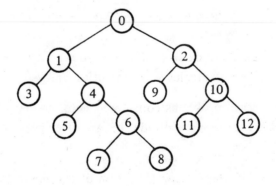

Fig. 5

B-&-b tree according to Land & Doig

The last in-first out rule by B e a l e & S m a l l [3] uses the branch postponement. When an integer solution has been found or no further progress can be made on the current branch the most recently created (and postponed) subproblem will be selected (Figure 6).

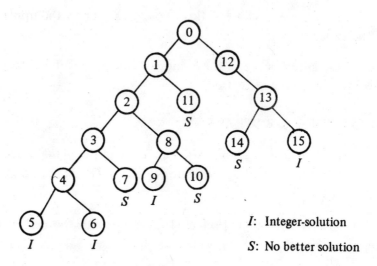

Fig. 6

B-&-b tree from Baale & Small

Furthermore there exist strategies with regard to the current values of the 0-1-variables (strategies with penalties or best projections).

In the practical problems considered here, however, we have no 0-1-variables because the upper bounds κ_j are often greater than the possible flow φ_j.

Therefore a strategy using the "sum of integer infeasibilities" see Forrest et al. [13], or the pseudocosts, see Benichou et al. [4], is not useful or even impossible.

In problems with few 0-1 variables (about up to 20) but with many nodes we used the strategy by Land & Doig. The first integer solution was often the optimal solution as well.

In problems with many 0-1-variables we were already satisfied with a good approximate solution (about a deviation of 3% from the optimum). Here we proceeded as follows:

(a) Solution of the continuous problem.

(b) Branching of j^* chosen like in 4.2 in *one* direction only, i.e

$$y_{j*} = \begin{cases} 0 & \text{if } \varphi_{j*} < \dfrac{\kappa_{j*}}{2} \\ 1 & \text{otherwise} \end{cases}$$

until an exact (= integer) solution has been obtained which has then the deviation d_k from the continuous optimum.

(c) Determination of

d_i = deviation from the continuous optimum

n_i = number of integer infeasibilities (= number of inexact arcs)

for all non-integer solutions i.

(d) Backtrack to that solution i^* where the deviation of the point (d_{i*}, n_{i*}) from the straight line $P_0 P_k$ is maximal.

Here we have

$$F_0 = (0, n_0) ,$$
$$P_k = (d_k, 0) .$$

Continue with (b) until an optimum is obtained or a cutoff criterion is satisfied.

Figures 7 and 8 show the situation after one or seven integer solutions has been found.

The ordinate axis shows the deviation $ZF_i - ZF_0$, while the abscissa axis shows the number of inexact arcs, i.e. the number of arcs where the exact objective function differs from the linearized one.

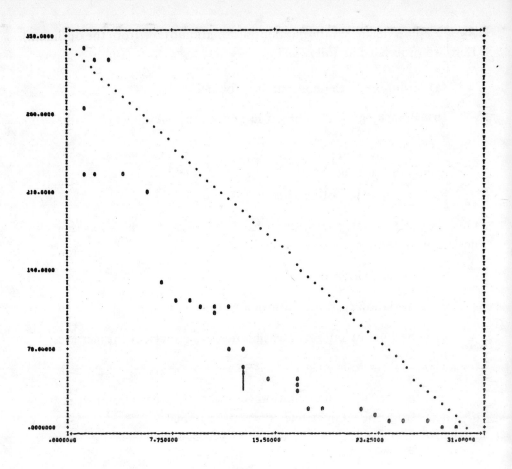

Fig. 7

Straight line of a continuous solution to the first
first integer solution and open nodes

The node with maximal deviation from the latest straight line is chosen for backtracking and it is marked by (↑).

Advantages

(1) We continue with the last generated solution until an exact solution has been obtained. Thus we do not need to restore the increment graph from external storage to core storage.

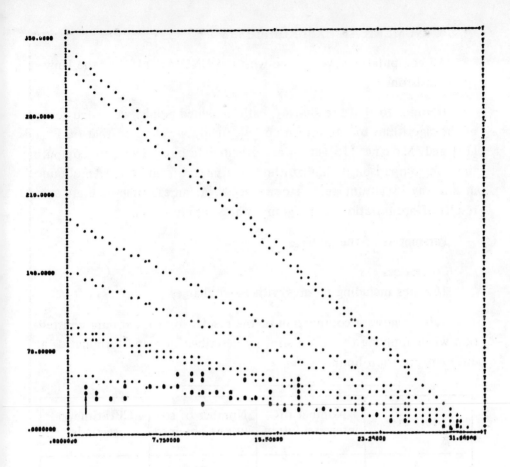

Fig. 8

Straight lines of continuous solutions to seven integer solutions
and open nodes

(2) We obtain quickly good approximations to the optimum. (In
practical examples the data has inaccuracies, so we are satisfied with good
approximations.)

Disadvantage

In order to obtain the global optimum we need much more time in
general than with the procedure by Land & Doig.

6. NUMERICAL EXPERIENCES

All computations were done with the UNIVAC 1108 of the University of Karlsruhe.

In order to find the shortest path in valued graphs we tested some of the algorithms of D o m s c h k e [9], finally we choosed that of F o r d [12] and M o o r e [16] in an arc oriented fashion. The best computing times in comparison with algorithms in a matrix form have been obtained in this way by advantageous storage needs. As an example here are some results of optimization of a regional water supply system.

Parameters of the graph:

70 vertices
169 arcs including 69 arcs with fixed charges.

Tab. 1 shows a compilation of the results for a fixed data constellation when applying the b-&-b strategy described in 5 and terminating at different precision limits.

Cutoff in %	Number of integer solution	Number of solutions obtained	CPU-time in seconds
15	1	55	45
10	4	137	91
5	6	156	97
3	9	290	199
1	11	439	297

Tab. 1

Results with different cutoffs

We also computed this example using the method of Land & Doig. The first integer solution was found after 3360 solutions, and then further execution was deleted. The CPU-time was 2340 seconds, the maximal possible deviation from the optimum was 0.01%.

Table 2 shows computing time for other practical problems (see Ahrens [1], Böttcher et al. [6], Dehnert [7], [8]).

Classification	arcs	nodes	pot. arcs	second CPU
Solid waste management	2039	126	20	560
Scrap car disposal	1730	123	10	320
Waste water disposal	29	15	19	11

Tab. 2

Results of different examples

Owing to the little number of fixed-cost-arcs, all these examples have been calculated by the strategy of Land & Doig.

For some examples we compared this CPU-time with the time required by the out-of-kilter-algorithm of Ford & Fulkerson [12] in the form given by Bray & Witzgall [5]. The running time with AOK was always greater, some of the problems have not been terminated within a reasonable time.

7. SUMMARY AND OUTLOOK

We have shown the solution of network flow problems with fixed charges with the aid of effective flow-optimization-algorithm. For the b-&-b-method a backtrack choice strategy was demonstrated, which yields in general in a short time good approximations for the optimum. As another problem we will consider inhomogeneous flows. Another point of application is the assumption of piecewise linear costs and the regard of logical restrictions.

REFERENCES

[1] W. A h r e n s, Optimierungsverfahren zur Lösung nichtlinearer Investitionsprobleme — angewandt auf das Problem der technischen und wirtschaftlichen Optimierung bei der Bildung von Zweckverbänden zur Abwasserbeseitigung, *Dissertation*, Universität (TH) Karlsruhe, 1974.

[2] M.L. B a l i n s k i, Fixed cost transportation problems, *Naval Res. Logist. Ouart.*, 8 (1961), 41-54.

[3] E.M.L. B e a l e — R.E. S m a l l, Mixed integer programming by a branch and bound technique, *Proc. IFIP Congress* 65, 2 (1966), 450-451.

[4] M. B e n i c h o u — J.M. G a u t h i e r — P. G i r o d e t — G. H e n t g e s — G. R i b i e r e — O. V i n c e n t, Experiments in mixed-integer linear programming, *Mathematical Programming*, 1 (1971), 76-94.

[5] T.A. B r a y — C. W i t z g a l l, Algorithm 336, *Collected Algorithms from CACM*, New York, 1968.

[6] H. B ö t t c h e r — G. D e h n e r t — W. D o m s c h k e, Verfahren zur Bestimmung optimaler Standorte für regionale Systeme, *Discussion Paper, Inst. f. Wirtschaftstheorie und OR*, Universität (TH) Karlsruhe, 1974.

[7] G. D e h n e r t, Anwendung von OR-Methoden bei der regionalen Planung von Anlagen zur Behandlung fester Abfallstoffe, *Technischer Bericht, Inst. f. Siedlungswasserwirtschaft*, Universität (TH) Karlsruhe, 1973.

[8] G. D e h n e r t, Eine Entscheidungshilfe für die Standort- und Kapazitätsplanung von Müllbehandlungsanlagen, *Technischer Bericht*, s. 7.

[9]   W. Domschke, Kürzeste Wege in Graphen: Algorithmen, Verfahrensvergleiche, *Mathematical Systems in Economics,* Heft 2, A. Hain Verlag, Meisenheim/Glan, 1972.

[10] W. Domschke, Two new algorithms for minimal cost flow problems, *Computing,* 11 (1973), 275-285.

[11] W. Domschke, *Graphentheoretische Verfahren und ihre Anwendungen zur Lösung von Zuordnungs- und Standortproblemen,* Habilitationsschrift, Univ. Karlsruhe, 1974.

[12] L.R. Ford — D.R. Fulkerson, *Flows in Networks,* Princeton, 1962.

[13] J.J.H. Forrest — J.P.H. Hirst — J.A. Tomlin, Practical solution of large mixed integer programming problems with UMPIRE, *Management Science,* 20, 5, Jan. 1974.

[14] A.M. Geoffrion — R.E. Marsten, Integer programming algorithms: A framework and state-of-the-art survey, *Management Science,* 18, 7, March 1972.

[15] A.H. Land — A.G. Doig, An automatic method of solving discrete programming problems, *Econometrica,* 28 (1960), 497-520.

[16] E.F. Moore, The shortest path through a maze, *The annals of the Computation Laboratory of Harvard University,* Vol. 30, Cambridge, 1959.

Gerd Dehnert

Institut für Siedlungswasserwirtschaft der Universität Karlsruhe, Kaiserstr. 12, D 75 Karlsruhe, B.R.D.

COLLOQUIA MATHEMATICA SOCIETATIS JÁNOS BOLYAI
12. PROGRESS IN OPERATIONS RESEARCH, EGER (HUNGARY), 1974.

NUMERICAL SOLUTION OF A STOCHASTIC CONTROL PROBLEM DERIVED FROM BENSOUSSAN — LIONS. INVENTORY MODEL

I. DÉKÁNY

INTRODUCTION

This paper is a contribution to the numerical aspects to one of J.L. Lions' and A. Bensoussan's stochastic control problems. This inventory holding problem is formulated as follows: find two series of optimal stopping times relative to a diffusion process.

In the first chapter we formulate in general the inventory holding problem, in the second we give the exact mathematical description of the model. The third chapter contains the basic theorems and tools for the resolution. In the fourth chapter we give a detailed numerical algorithm of the iteration procedure.

I am very thankfull for the help I have got from Professor Lions, Professor Bensoussan and from their colleagues at IRIA (Rocquencourt) as well as from Professor J. Mogyoródi at Eötvös L. University, Budapest.

I. GENERAL DESCRIPTION

We have an inventory of n goods. As a result of — during the time considered, altering — demand of the consumers, the stock level decreases. When it becomes too small, i.e. when there is a danger that we shall be unable further to satisfy our "clientèle", we may start a new re-production process in order to re-supply our stock. This way the stock level depends on two parameters

the demand

the production process.

The demand as we indicated is a random process with known parameters, which can be eventually functions of time too. We observe only a finite time period T. (This in practice is a week, a month, a year etc.) The production is a deterministic process which is characterised by the stopping or starting moments of the machines.

The emerging costs are of two types

the cost of maintaining a stock or the cost of rupture

the cost of the production.

A policy defined on $[0, T]$ is a sequence of starting and stopping moments of the producing unit. A policy is optimal if the associated cost is minimal.

II. MATHEMATICAL FORMULATION

The demand process satisfies the following stochastic differential equation

(1) $d\xi(t) = \mu(t)dt + \sigma(t)db(t)$.

$\mu(t) \in R^n$ is the deterministic part, the mean of the demand, $db(t)$ is a Gaussian random variable, with zero mean and of an $n \times m$ covariance matrix $\sigma(t)$.

The total demand on an interval $[t, s]$ is

$$(2) \qquad D(s, t) = \int_t^s \mu(\tau)d\tau + \int_t^s \sigma(\tau)db(\tau)$$

here $\int_t^s \sigma(\tau)db(\tau)$ is a Gaussian r.v. of zero mean and of $\int_t^s \sigma(\tau)\sigma^*(\tau)d\tau$ covariance matrix.

The production process is denoted by $v(t)$, $v(t) \in R^n$ and it is a deterministic function. The inventory holding costs at the moment t are

$$(3) \qquad f(y_{x_0}(t), t) = \text{stocking cost if } y_{x_0}(t) \geqslant 0$$
$$= \text{cost of rupture if } y_{x_0}(t) < 0$$

where $y_{x_0}(t)$ is the stock level at the moment t, if the initial state at time t_0 was x_0.

The productional cost is

$$(4) \qquad k(t, \Delta) > 0$$

which means the cost of starting the productional process at the moment t, for a length of time Δ.

We give two series of stopping times relative to the σ algebra generated by the demand process $\xi(t)$.

$$(5) \qquad \begin{aligned} &\vartheta_{xt}^1, \vartheta_{xt}^2, \vartheta_{xt}^3, \vartheta_{xt}^4, \vartheta_{xt}^5, \ldots \\ &\Delta_{xt}^1, \Delta_{xt}^2, \Delta_{xt}^3, \Delta_{xt}^4, \Delta_{xt}^5, \ldots \end{aligned}$$

with the following conditions

$$(6) \qquad \begin{aligned} &0 \leqslant \vartheta_{xt}^1 \leqslant \vartheta_{xt}^2 \leqslant \ldots \leqslant T \\ &\vartheta_{xt}^i < \vartheta_{xt}^i + \Delta_{xt}^i \leqslant \vartheta_{xt}^{i+1}. \end{aligned}$$

According to that the evolution of the stock level can be described by the following two equations:

$$(7) \qquad dy_{xt}(s) = [\mu(s) - v(s)]dt + \sigma(s)db(s) \qquad s \in [\vartheta_{xt}^i, \vartheta_{xt}^i + \Delta_{xt}^i]$$

$$(8) \qquad dy_{xt}(s) = \mu(s)dt + \sigma(s)db(s) \qquad s \in [\vartheta_{xt}^i + \Delta_{xt}^i, \vartheta_{xt}^{i+1}] .$$

Let's denote the policy assigned to a given initial stock x, at time t by

$$(9) \qquad V_{xt} = \{\vartheta_{xt}^1, \Delta_{xt}^1, \vartheta_{xt}^2, \Delta_{xt}^2, \ldots\} .$$

We introduce a discounting factor $\alpha > 0$ and so the objective function associated to a certain policy V_{xt} becomes

$$(10) \qquad J(V_{xt}) = E\left\{\sum_i e^{-\alpha(\vartheta^i - \Delta^i)} k(\vartheta_{xt}^i, \Delta_{xt}^i) \chi_{[0,T]}(\vartheta_{xt}^i) + \right.$$
$$\left. + \int_0^T e^{-\alpha s} f(y_{xt}(s), s)ds \right\} .$$

Here the first term represents the cost of production while the second corresponds to the inventory holding costs.

The optimal policy which gives the minimal cost is characterised by

$$(11) \qquad u(y_{xt}(s), s) = \inf_{V_{xt}} J(V_{xt}) .$$

V_{xt}^* is optimal if

$$(12) \qquad u(y_{xt}(s), s) = J(V_{xt}^*) .$$

III. SOLUTION

As our decisions consider always only the actual state of the stock, therefore this controlling policy does not change the Markovien character of the process. This way we can apply the usual dynamic programming scheme with Bellman's optimality principle.

Supposing that we are in a non-productive period then at the moment t we have to decide between two choices

C1. Start to produce for a time Δ and then the corresponding costs are the cost of stocking plus the cost of the production.

C2. Not to do anything for a small time δ

NB. After the validity of either decision expires we are supposed to follow an optimal policy!

The exact form of the cost functions corresponding to the two decisions are

(13)
$$\inf_{\substack{\Delta > 0 \\ \Delta \leqslant T - t}} E\Big\{k(t, \Delta) + \int_t^{t+\Delta} e^{-\alpha(s-t)} f(y_{xt}(s), s)\, ds +$$

$$+ e^{-\alpha\Delta} u(y_{xt}(t + \Delta), t + \Delta)\Big\} = K_1 .$$

For the first decision and

(14)
$$E\Big\{\int_t^{t+\delta} e^{-\alpha(s-t)} f(y_{xt}(s), s)\, ds + e^{-\alpha\delta} u(y_{xt}(t + \delta), t + \delta)\Big\} = K_2$$

for the second. They obviously have to satisfy the equation

(15)
$$[u(y_{x0}(t), t) - K_1][u(y_{x0}(t), t) - K_2] = 0$$

because

(16)
$$u(y_{x0}(t), t) \leqslant \min \begin{cases} K_1 \\ K_2 \end{cases}$$

for every $t \in [0, T]$.

Expanding the second equation in to Taylor series and applying Ito's theorem we get

(17)
$$- \frac{\partial u}{\partial t} + \frac{1}{2} \operatorname{spur} \langle \sigma(t)\sigma^*(t)\rangle \frac{\partial^2 u}{\partial x^2} + \Big\langle \mu(t) \frac{\partial u}{\partial x}\Big\rangle + \alpha u \leqslant f .$$

For later computational reasons we transform also the second equation into a differential equation by the same method as before. Then it will be

(18)
$$- \frac{\partial v}{\partial t} + (\mu(t) - v(t)) \frac{\partial v}{\partial x} + \frac{1}{2} \operatorname{spur} \sigma(t)\sigma^*(t) \frac{\partial^2 v}{\partial x^2} + \alpha v \leqslant$$

$$\leqslant f + \frac{\partial k}{\partial \Delta}\Big|_{\Delta = 0}$$

(19) $\qquad \lim_{\Delta \to 0} v(t + \Delta, x) = u(t, x).$

For the sake of simplicity let's denote the joined cost of inventory holding and producing for a time period Δ by

(20) $\qquad \tilde{k}(t, \Delta) = k(t, \Delta) + \int_t^{t+\Delta} e^{-\alpha(s-t)} f(y_{x0}(s), s) ds.$

To solve this system of differential inequalities we introduce two operators

(21) $\qquad a(u, v) = \sum_{i,j=1}^{n} \int_\theta a_{ij} \frac{\partial u}{\partial x_i} \frac{\partial v}{\partial x_j} dx + \sum_{j=1}^{n} \int_\theta a_j \frac{\partial u}{\partial x_j} v dx + \int_\theta a_0 uv dx$

(22) $\qquad M(v) = \inf_{\substack{\Delta \geqslant 0 \\ \Delta \leqslant T-t}} E\{\tilde{k}(t, \Delta) + \int_{R^n} v(\eta, t + \Delta) \pi(t, y, t + \Delta, d\eta)\}$

here the coefficients with the previous notations are

(23) $\qquad \{a_{ij}\} = \{\sigma_{ij}\}; \ \{a_j\} = \{\mu_j\} \qquad \eta = y_{x0}(t + \Delta)$

and π is the transition probability for the Gaussian process, from the state y, at time t, to η at the time $t + \Delta$. The classical variational formulation of the (15) and (16) problem is to find a u which satisfies

(24)
   (i) $\quad u \in \mathcal{H}^1(\theta) \cap \mathcal{L}^\infty(\theta) \qquad \theta \subset R^n$

   (ii) $\quad a(u, v - u) \leqslant (f, v - u)$

   (iii) $\quad u \leqslant M(u)$ for all $v \leqslant M(u)$

   (iv) $\quad f \in \mathcal{L}^\infty(\theta)$ and $(f, v) = \int_\theta fv dx.$

In order to solve this system of quasi-variational inequalities, (it is only quasi-variational because the second constraining set (iii), for the solutions, depends itself on the element we are searching for) we refer to J.L. Lions' and A. Bensoussan's works [2], [3]. We present here only the basic theorem in this domain, L i o n s – B e n s o u s s a n [1], which allows us to solve problems of this type.

Theorem. *We start from an approximate solution* $u_0 = \dfrac{1}{\alpha} \sup f$ *and then substituting it into (24) we get the next solution and so on. In general*

(25)
$$a(u^n, v - u^n) \leqslant (f, v - u^n)$$
$$u^n \leqslant M(u^{n-1}) \quad \text{for all} \quad v \leqslant M(u^{n-1}).$$

If the following conditions are satisfied

(i) $u: \mathscr{L}^\infty(\theta) \to \mathscr{L}^\infty(\theta)$

(ii) $M(\varphi) \geqslant 0$ *if* $\varphi \geqslant 0$ *a.e.*

(26)

(iii) $\varphi \geqslant \psi \Rightarrow M(\varphi) \geqslant M(\psi)$ *a.e.*

(iv) *if* $\varphi^n \searrow \varphi$ *a.e. and in* $\mathscr{L}^P(\theta)$ *and if* $M(\varphi^n) \searrow \chi$ *a.e. and in* $\mathscr{L}^P(\theta)$ *then* $\varphi \leqslant M(\varphi)$

then the sequence of the solutions $u_0, u_1, u_2, u_3, \ldots$ *satisfies*

(I) $u_0 \geqslant u_1 \geqslant u_2 \geqslant u_3 \geqslant \ldots \geqslant 0$

(27)   (II) $\exists c$ const. $\| u^n \| \leqslant c \; \forall n$

(III) $u^n \searrow u$ *in* $\mathscr{H}^1(\theta)$ *weakly.*

However it is necessary to notice that it can not be directly applied to our problem, since e.g. the operator (21) is not coercive, i.e. $a(u, u) \geqslant \lambda u^2$ is not true, therefore further investigations are necessary. For a more detailed discussion see [3], [4], [5].

The numerical algorithm, based on this "theorem" is convergent for all examples we have studied.

IV. COMPUTATION

For numerical computation we use the method of finite differences, in order to find a solution of the problem (13)-(16). In one dimension the method is the same as in higher dimensions, yet the organisation of the program is more complicated, therefore we executed the numerical calculations in one dimension.

$$\theta = [a, b] \quad a, b \in R$$

(28) $\qquad h =$ one step in space

$\qquad \Delta t =$ one step in time.

We discretise the equation (17) with the following final and boundary conditions:

(29)
$$-\frac{u_i^k - u_i^{k-1}}{\Delta t} + \frac{\sigma^2(t^k)}{2h^2} [u_{i+1}^k - 2u_i^k + u_{i-1}^k] -$$

$$-\frac{\mu(t^k)}{2h} [u_{i+1}^k - u_{i-1}^k] + \alpha u_i = f_i$$

(30) $\qquad$ (a) $u(T, x) = 0$ $\qquad$ (b) $\left. \dfrac{\partial u}{\partial v} \right|_{\Gamma} = 0$ $\qquad$ (normal derivative on the

boundary).

Then we start "backwards" in time by a variant of the Gauss – Seidel method with relaxation and with a certain kind of projection.

The solution of (24) has to satisfy the condition (16). To accelerate the algorithm's convergency we choose at each iterational step the minimal one from the present solution and from the solution of the discretised form of (18). This is

(31)
$$-\frac{v_i^k - v_i^{k-1}}{\Delta t} + \frac{\sigma^2(t^k)}{2h^2} [v_{i+1}^k - 2v_i^k + v_{i-1}^k] -$$

(31)

$$- [\mu(t^k) - v(t^k)](v_{i+1}^k - v_{i-1}^k) + \alpha v_i = f_i + l^k$$

with the final and border conditions (19) and (30 (a), (b)). Here

(32) $\qquad l^k = \left. \dfrac{\partial k(t^k, \Delta)}{\partial \Delta} \right|_{\Delta = 0} .$

So the successive steps of the algorithm are

1. At the final time T, $u_i^1 = 0$ for all i. $(u(T, x) = 0)$.

2. At the k-th step for the equation (29) the initial values are u_i^{k-1} for all i.

3. At the k-th step for the equation (31) we choose the initial values according to (13) and (19) in the following way:

we discretise in time according to Δ by the same way as for t. Therefore we solve (31) k times and the l-th time, $1 \leqslant l \leqslant k$ the initial values are u_i^l for all i.

4. We solve (31) k times with relaxation, i.e.

$$(33) \qquad v_{i,j}^k = v_{i,j-1}^k \omega + v_{i,j}^k (1 - \omega) \qquad 0 < \omega < 1$$

where j marks the j-th iterational step in the Gauss-- Seidel process. For the optimal value of ω see Varga [13].

5. From the sequence $v_i^1, v_i^2, \ldots, v_i^k$ we got in 4, we choose the minimal v_i^* for all i. (i.e. in practice the optimal Δ according to (13)).

6. We solve now the equation (29) by Gauss $-$ Seidel relaxated but at each iterational step we "project" on the previous solution, i.e. we choose always the $\min(u_i, v_i^*)$ for all i, in order to satisfy (16).

7. Start again from 2 while T does not become 0.

V. NUMERICAL EXAMPLE

We present here the result of a computer program executed on an ODRA-1304.

The data are the following:

The cost function

$$f = (l - \text{sign}(x))99 + (1 + \text{sign}(x))(x^2 + x + 2)$$

demand

$$\mu(t) = 12{,}5 + 2 \, \text{sign}(6\pi t)$$

production

$$v(t) = 25(1 + 0{,}1t) .$$

The production cost derivative $l(t, \Delta) = 280 \log (1 + \Delta)$

$$\theta = [a, b] = [- 0.5, 2.5] \qquad \omega_1 = 0.6$$

$$\Delta t = 0.02 \qquad\qquad \omega_2 = 0.35$$

$$h = 0.075 \qquad\qquad \epsilon_1 = \epsilon_2 = 0.05.$$

Computation time cca 12 min.

Then the optimal continuation set is the following:

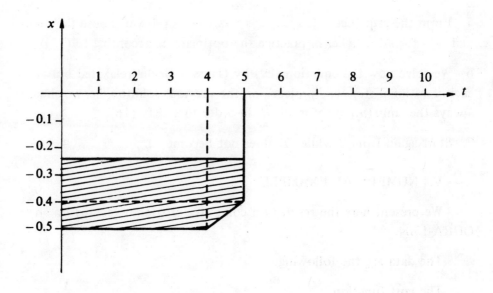

REFERENCES

[1] A. Bensoussan – J.L. Lions, Nouvelle formulation de problèmes de contrôle inpulsionnel et applications. *Compt. Rendus,* 276 (1973), 1189.

[2] A. Bensoussan – M. Goursat – J.L. Lions, Contrôle impulsionnel et inequations quasi-variationnelles stationnaires. *C.R.A.S.,* 276 (1973), 1279.

[3] J.L. Lions, Lectures held at the College de France in 1973/74.

[4] A. Bensoussan – J.L. Lions, Some questions about the optimal control (in Russian), *UMN,* 1974. March-April.

[5] J.L. Lions – G. Stampacchia, Variational inequalities, *Comm. Pure Appl. Math.,* (1967), 493-519.

[6] H. Scarf, *Math. Meth. in the Social Sciencies,* Stan. Univ. Press, 1960.

[7] R. Bellman, *Dynamic Programming,* Princeton, 1957.

[8] H. Chernoff, Optimal stochastical control, *Sankhya,* Serie A, 30 (1968).

[9] W.H. Fleming, The Cauchy problem for degenerate parabolic equations, *J. Math. Mech.,* 13, 6 (1964).

[10] A. Friedman, *Partial differential equations of parabolic type,* Prent. Hall, 1964.

[11] K. Ito – H.P. McKean, *Diffusion processes and their sample paths,* Springer, 1965.

[12] I.T. Gichman – A.V. Skorochod, *Stoch. differential equations,* Moscow, 1963.

[13] R.S. Varga, *Matrix iterative analysis,* New Yersey, 1962.

[14]   A. Friedman, On quasi-linear parabolic equations of the second order, *J. Math. Mech.,* 9 (1960), 539-556.

István Dékány

Eötvös Lóránd University of Sciences, 1088 Budapest, VIII. Múzeum krt. 6-8, Hungary.

COLLOQUIA MATHEMATICA SOCIETATIS JÁNOS BOLYAI

12. PROGRESS IN OPERATIONS RESEARCH, EGER (HUNGARY), 1974.

OPTIMUM DESIGN OF A MULTI-PURPOSE RESERVOIR APPLYING CONTROL THEORY

B. DJORDJEVIĆ — S. OPRICOVIĆ

1. INTRODUCTION

The extremely rapid rise of water consumption and the alarming rate at which existing reserves are being exhausted and/or polluted has brought practically all countries up against a serious water supply problem. Water demands can now only be met by construction of more and more complex water engineering systems and efficient utilization of the available resources. This situation has made it essential to introduce into water management planning a number of new mathematical and cybernetic methods: systems analysis, control theory, operations research, etc.

Many papers have appeared recently dealing with the application of new methods in water management planning, and also some monographs which offer a systematic presentation of the state of the art in water engineering systems modelling and optimization (Hall and Dracup, [1]; Buras, [2], etc.). At the symposium on water resources systems planning in Washington (1974) the participants exchanged experience in this domain and reviewed the lines to be followed in future research (general reports by Emsellem, Rydz, Djordjevic, Vasilchenko, Caldwell, and Uzunov). It was agreed that there are great opportunities for the application of modern methods and computer techniques in water resources planning, and the discussion particularly turned on various numerical and methodological problems: too many dimensions involved in the problems, the question of the choice of optimization criteria, difficulties in defining ecological and sociological constraints, the problem of the sensitivity of optimum solutions, various types of indeterminacy in problem formulation, problems of gathering and transmitting information relevant to system control, etc.

Of the factors influential in the application of modern methods of designing and operating water engineering systems the following are fundamental:

water resources systems (WRS's) are becoming more and more complex, with even more complex interactions between component parts within the system and between systems as a whole;

less and less water of good quality is becoming available for more and more consumers. Therefore compound systems must be designed to optimally compromise the conflicting interests of different users and to make the most economical distribution of water among users, as a function of time and space. Multi-purpose systems are therefore generally preferable;

the key elements of compound WRS's are reservoirs, which according to modern design philosophy usually fulfil a number of functions. Only they allow the most economical distribution referred to above;

reliability is becoming a more and more critical factor for WRS's. With increasing urbanization and economic growth reliability demands are becoming increasingly stringent — be they for various kinds of water supply, or for effective flood control. Since even a slight increase in the reliability criterion greatly increases the cost of a WRS, it is clear too that mathematical methods must be brought into the problem so that the reliability could be estimated as reliably as possible.

Optimal control problems of WRS's have two types:

(a) Optimal synthesis problems (design problems): for a given input (deterministic or stochastic) and defined users (required output defined), find the WRS and the control which will optimally satisfy the specified water resources engineering demands with the required operation reliability for each user.

(b) Optimal analysis problems (operational optimization): given the input and the system (WRS), find the optimal control which makes the objective function an extremum.

The control of a WRS is an integral process, the system is always being controlled, only in the design stage the number of control coordinates is greater because they also include the system parameters (the parameters of the system and their ratios have to be optimized, e.g. dimensioning reservoirs, channels, etc.).

2. FORMULATION OF THE PROBLEM

Specific design (synthesis) assignments for some compound reservoir systems brought the authors up against an optimization problem which had not previously been solved. This is the problem of the optimal control of a multi-purpose reservoir with a hydroelectric plant and a number of direct and indirect users. The system configuration is shown in Fig. 1.

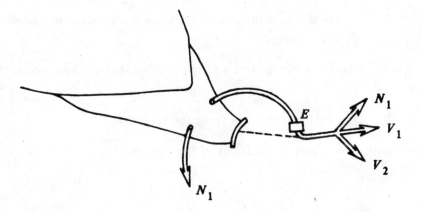

Fig. 1

From the aspect of control theory it is fundamental that the reservoir has both direct and indirect users: indirect users are those who take water downstream of the hydro.

Let us formulate the optimal synthesis problem of a multi-purpose reservoir which has K direct and I indirect (downstream) users. Optimal synthesis requires the simultaneous solution of the following problems

determination of the optimum reservoir volume,

determination of the optimal control: time-dependent distribution of available water to the $K + I$ users,

check the reliability with which the demands of the various users are met.

The control model derived from the water accounting equation of the reservoir can be written in the discrete form

$$(1.1) \qquad V_{m+1} = V_m + Q_m - Cq'_m - Dq''_m - g_m$$

where

m \qquad denotes the m-th time interval $(m \in \overline{1, M})^*$

$V \triangleq$ \quad state vector – volume of water in the reservoir

$Q \triangleq$ \quad random input vector – reservoir recharge

$q' \triangleq$ \quad K-dimensional control vector defining the water allocated to each of the K direct users

$q'' \triangleq$ \quad I-dimensional control vector of deliveries to the I indirect users

$g \triangleq$ \quad vector of water losses from the reservoir

C and $D \triangleq$ \quad control matrices of the system.

*$\overline{1, M}$ denotes the set $\{1, 2, \ldots, M\}$.

The model also includes relations expressing power production, in the general form

$$(1.2) \qquad E_m = E(V_{m+1}; V_m; q'_{e,m})$$

where $q'_{e,m} \triangleq$ the discharge through the hydro in the m-th time interval.

The optimal synthesis criterion involves two conditions:

(1) make the objective function, which expresses the economic goals of optimization, an extremum

(2) ensure the required reliability for all WRS users.

The objective function can be written in the general form

$$(2.1) \qquad J(W; q) = \sum_{m=1}^{M} \sum_{j=1}^{K+I} D_{j,m}(\bar{V}_m; q_{j,m}; m) - T(W)$$

where

$D_{j,m} \triangleq$ profit from the j-th user of the reservoir in the m-th interval

$T(W) \triangleq$ costs of the reservoir as function of its volume W.

The reliability criterion can be expressed in the form

$$(2.3) \qquad \begin{aligned} P_k\{q'_k = p_k\} &\geqslant P_k^{\min}; &\quad k &= 1, \ldots, K \\ P_i\{q''_i = p_i\} &\geqslant P_i^{\min}; &\quad i &= 1, \ldots, I \end{aligned}$$

where

P_k and $P_i \triangleq$ probability of occurrence of $\{\ldots\}$;

p_k and $p_i \triangleq$ quantities of water required by the k-th direct and the i-th indirect user

$P_k^{\min}$ and $P_i^{\min} \triangleq$ required reliability for the k-th direct and i-th indirect user.

To solve this optimization problem, it include constraints on the state and control coordinates. The constraints on the state coordinates have the general form

(3.1)
$$V_m^{\min} \leqslant V_m \leqslant W$$
$$0 \leqslant W \leqslant W^{\max}$$

where

$W^{\max} \triangleq$ greatest storage volume which could be achieved with the given dam site.

The constraints on the control coordinates have the general form

(3.2)
$$p_{k,m}^{\min} \leqslant q_{k,m}' \leqslant p_{k,m}$$
$$p_{i,m}^{\min} \leqslant q_{i,m}'' \leqslant p_{i,m}$$

where

$p_{k,m}$ and $p_{i,m} \triangleq$ the quantities of water required for the k-th and i-th user in the m-th time interval

$p_{i,m}^{\min}$ and $p_{k,m}^{\min} \triangleq$ the absolute minimum quantities which must be delivered to these users.

Now the optimal synthesis problem for the multi-purpose reservoir can be formulated: find the reservoir volume W and the operational control $q_j(t)$, $j = 1, \ldots, K + I$ which make the objective function (2.1) a maximum while satisfying the criteria of control quality (reliability) (2.3) and the constraints on the state and control coordinates (3.1 and 3.2). Hence the optimization criterion can be written in the form

(4.1)
$$\max_{\{W, q_{j,m}\}} \left\{ \sum_{m=1}^{M} \sum_{j=1}^{K+I} D_{j,m} (V_m; q_{j,m}; m) - T(W) \right\}.$$

Thanks to the fact that $T(W)$ is independent of the control, the problem formulated by (4.1) can be broken down into two simpler problems, formulated by the expression

$$(4.2) \qquad \max_{W} \left\{ -T(W) + \max_{\{q_{j,m}\}} \sum_{m=1}^{M} \sum_{j=1}^{K+I} D_{j,m} (V_m; q_{j,m}; m) \right\}.$$

Let us introduce the function $F(W)$, the profit yielded by optimal control for a given W

$$(4.3) \qquad F(W) = \max_{\{q_{j,m}\}} \sum_{m=1}^{M} \cdot \sum_{j=1}^{K+I} D_{j,m} (V_m; q_{j,m}; m).$$

Then by substituting from (4.3) into (4.2) gives the criterion functional

$$(4.4) \qquad J^* = \max_{W} \{ F(W) - T(W) \}.$$

Thereby the closed-loop optimal synthesis (dimensioning) problem is reduced to a two-step optimization. In the first step the optimal control is determined according to (4.3) for some fixed W. By doing this for various values of W we get the function $F(W)$. The second step involves optimization at a higher level of the hierarchy, as formulated by (4.4), to determine the optimal W.

In the case of more than one indirect user the optimization problem cannot be solved by means of the classical recurrence relations of dynamic programming, since the amount of water allocated to the indirect users depends on the control of the direct user (in this case the hydro). We have worked out a procedure for solving such problems using dynamic programming according to a three-level strategy: at the first level optimize the distribution of available water among time intervals (months); at the second level allocate water to direct users in one time interval; at the third level allocate water used by a direct user (the hydro) to indirect users taking water further downstream. The operational control of the system is thus determined by a three-run algorithm, which also overcomes the problem of the excessive number of dimensions involved. At the first level, in the first run, the optimum system trajectory is found (volume of water in the reservoir for each month), while the second and third levels determine the optimal control for direct and indirect users, respectively.

The corresponding recurrence relations derived according to Bellman's optimality principal are presented below.

Equation 1.1 for practical cases can be written in the modified form

$$(5.1) \qquad V_{m+1} = V_m^+ - \sum_{k=1}^{K} q'_{k,m}$$

where $V_m^+ = V_m + Q_m - g_m \overset{\Delta}{=}$ the net quantity of water available in the m-th time interval.

Let $Y_m = \sum_{k=1}^{K} q'_{k,m}$ denote the total quantity of water delivered in the m-th time interval and whose distribution among the direct users has to be optimalized. The profit derived from this total Y_m is given by

$$(5.2) \qquad D_m(Y_m) = \max_{\{q'_{k,m}; q''_{i,m}\}} \sum_{k=1}^{K} \{D_{k,m}(q'_{k,m}; V_m; V_{m+1}; m) + \\ + \sum_{i=1}^{I} D_{i,m}(q''_{i,m}; m)\}; \qquad m = 1, M.$$

With regard to (5.1) and (5.2), the maximum of the profit function achieved by optimal operational control for a fixed W and a given initial state of the reservoir V_0 is

$$(6.3) \qquad F^*(W, V_0) = \max_{V_1,\ldots,V_M} \sum_{m=1}^{M} D_m(V_m^+ - V_{m+1}).$$

Hence the decision-making problem at the first level reduces to determining the trajectory of optimal states $\{V_1^*, \ldots, V_M^*\}$.

From the principle of optimality a recurrence relation for the first strategic level can be derived in the form

$$(6.4) \qquad F_m(v_m) = \max_{v_{m-1}} \{D_m(v_{m-1}^+ - v_m) + F_{m-1}(v_{m-1})\}$$

where v_m denotes a variable which can take values in the range V_m.

The maximum has to be achieved while at the same time satisfying conditions (5.1) and constraints (3.1) and (3.2).

It may be seen from the recurrence relation that a forward dynamic programming algorithm is used here. For $m = 1$, since $v_1 = V_0 = \text{const.}$, and it is reasonable to assume that there is no initial profit, $F_0 = 0$, (6.4) becomes

(6.5) $\qquad F_1(v_1) = D_1(v_0^+ - v_1)$.

Let $v_{m-1}^*(v_m)$ denote the value of v_{m-1} yielding a maximum in (6.4). All the $v_{m-1}^*(v_m)$, $m = 1, \ldots, M$ are stored in the computer memory. The optimum value V_M^* at the end of the ordered time set m is that value of v_M which satisfies the relation

(6.6) $\qquad F^* = \max_{\{v_M\}} F_M(v_M)$.

The other optimal states are determined from the stored data: $V_m^* = v_m^*(V_{m+1}^*)$ for $m = M-1, M-2, \ldots, 1$.

$D_m(v_{m-1}^+ - v_m)$ in (6.4) is determined in the computation of the second strategic level. At this level the distribution of the available water within a given time interval is optimized, so for convenience the time index m can be omitted. Then the criterion function of the second level can be written

(7.1) $\qquad D(Y) = \max_{\{q_k', q_i''\}} \left\{ \sum_{k=1}^{K} D_k(q_k') + \sum_{i=1}^{I_k} D_i(q_i'') \right\}$.

V_m and V_{m-1} do not figure in (7.1) because at the second level their values are known. I_k denotes the number of indirect users which get their water from the k-th direct user.

(7.1) can be written

(7.2) $\qquad D(Y) = \max_{\{q_k'\}} \left\{ \sum_{k=1}^{K} \left[D_k(q_k') + \max_{\{q_i''\}} \sum_{i=1}^{I_k} D_i(q_i'') \right] \right\}$.

We have to introduce a new function $R_k(q_k')$ which expresses the indirect profit from the direct allocation q_k' if it is optimally distributed among the I_k indirect users

(7.3) $\qquad R_k(q_k') = \max_{\{q_i''\}} \sum_{i=1}^{I_k} D_i(q_i'')$.

The determination of this profit is left for the third level. Substituting in (7.2) then yields

$$(7.4) \qquad D(Y) = \max_{q'_1,\dots,q'_K} \sum_{k=1}^{K} [D_k(q'_k) + R_k(q'_k)]\]$$

with the condition (5.1).

The lumped allocation Y is given by the first level calculation.

Now the second-level optimization problem can be concisely formulated: find the control $\{q'_1,\dots,q'_K\}$ which makes the profit defined by (7.4) a maximum.

In order to derive recurrence relations for the second-level optimization let us introduce the function $D_j(y)$ which expresses the maximum profit obtainable when a part y of the total available Y is allocated to the first j of K users, i.e.

$$(7.5) \qquad D_j(y) = \max_{\{q'_1,\dots,q'_j\}} \sum_{k=1}^{j} [D_k(q'_k) + R_k(q'_k)]$$

under the condition

$$\sum_{k=1}^{j} q'_k = y .$$

Applying the principle of optimality and the usual procedure for constructing recurrence relations, we have for optimization at the second level

$$(7.6) \qquad D_j(y) = \max_{\{q'_j\}} \{D_j(q'_j) + R_j(q'_j) + D_{j-1}(y - q'_j)\}$$

and hence the total profit at the second level is

$$(7.7) \qquad D_K(Y) = \max_{\{q'_K\}} \{D_K(q'_K) + R_K(q'_K) + D_{K-1}(Y - q'_K)\} .$$

The profit function for indirect users in eq. (7.6) is evaluated at the third level of optimization. This part of the task can be turned into the static problem of distributing of water q'_j among I_j users. The procedure for deriving the recurrence relation is the same (for convenience we can now omit the index j which was dealt with in the second-level optimization). We introduce a new symbol for the allocation to the i-th user $z_i \equiv q''_{i,m}$. Then (7.3) can be written

$$(8.1) \qquad R(q) = \max_{\{z_1,...,z_I\}} \sum_{i=1}^{I} D_i(z_i) \, .$$

Denote the total water available for distribution among the I_j indirect users by $Z = q'_j$. Then the recurrence relation for the third level which optimizes this distribution is

$$(8.2) \qquad R_i(Z) = \max_{\{z_i\}} \{D_i(z_i) - R_{i-1}(Z - z_i)\} \, .$$

Application of (8.2) yields the desired value of $R_j(q'_j)$

$$(8.3) \qquad R_I(\bar{q}) = \max_{\{z_I\}} \{D_I(z_I) + R_{I-1}(\bar{q} - z_I)\}$$

where $\bar{q}$ is the total quantity of water available for distribution to downstream users, i.e. the condition

$$\sum_{i=1}^{I_j} z_i = \bar{q} \leqslant q'_j$$

must also be satisfied.

The flow chart of the control optimization computation is shown in Fig. 2.

3. APPLICATION

It has already been mentioned that this optimization model was developed in order to solve certain practical design problems of multi-purpose reservoirs in the Vardar basin (Yugoslavia). This basin is an area of water deficit, while on the other hand a very big rise in water consumption is envisaged for the future. Therefore a very complex WRS is being designed with reservoirs which supply many users simultaneously.

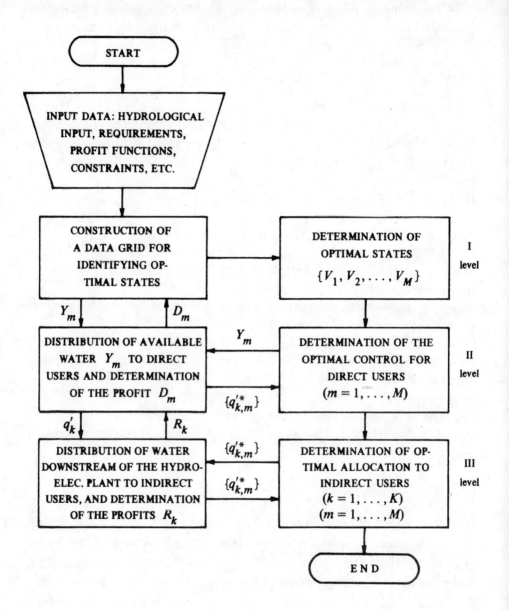

Fig. 2

The complex planning problem of this WRS was solved in two stages:

optimization of each reservoir individually, where they were isolated, or of cascades of reservoirs where not, examination of maximum water engineering capacities and local optima of these component systems considered in isolation;

optimal synthesis of the entire system of reservoirs.

The first stage of the planning problem consisted in processing 12 reservoirs by the procedure described above, which proved highly successful. Here we shall discuss only some of the practical problems of optimal synthesis solved in this way.

Figure 1 shows the configuration of one particular reservoir which supplies two irrigation systems (N_1 and N_2), a municipal and an industrial water supply, and produces electric power (E). It also fulfils a flood control function, attenuating flood waves.

Given: hydrological input sequence (monthly streanflow for 20 years); monthly consumption requirements (corresponding to input); the area F_1 of irrigation system N_1; profit functions for all users in terms of the amount of water delivered to them; costs of the reservoir as a function of its volume; price of electrical energy (variable over the year); constraints on the state and control coordinates.

Tasks.

(a) what downstream area F_2 can be irrigated, with a reliability of 75%

(b) optimal synthesis (i.e. dimensions) of the reservoir and optimal allocation of the available water

(c) to check functional reliability for all users and determine flood routing effects

(d) investigate sensitivity of the optimal solution (optimum volume) to changes in the economic functions and key constraints.

These tasks were successfully executed by employing the optimization procedure described above. First task (a) was solved by trial-and-error (nine runs), i.e. the relation $F_2 = f(W)$ was derived for a reliability of irrigation N_2 of 75%. Then the optimal synthesis problem yielding the optimum reservoir volume and optimal control was solved with this $F_2 = f(W)$.

The optimal state and control having been found for the given 20-year series, the results were subjected to a probabilistic analysis. Figure 3 shows the probability graph for optimal states of the reservoir, which can be very useful for constructing a rule curve. Analysis of the control solutions yielded the reliabilities of allocations to all users, satisfying condition (2.3). Also the routing effect was calculated for some synthetic flood waves and various storage states (Fig. 4).

In view of the difficulty of reliably estimating economic functions, the sensitivity of the optimal storage volume to changes in these functions was investigated. This was done by repeating the optimization computations for various economic functions within a certain domain, and yielded the limits of the economic parameters within which the optimal solution would be stable.

The algorithm presented here has been successfully employed in solving optimal synthesis problems of multiple-purpose reservoirs, it can also be applied to some other problems of optimal control of resources.

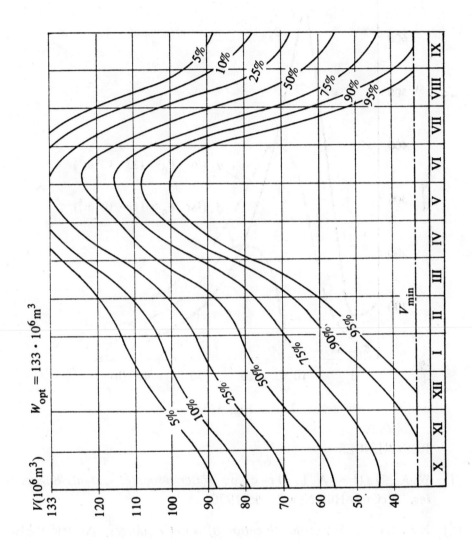

Fig. 3.

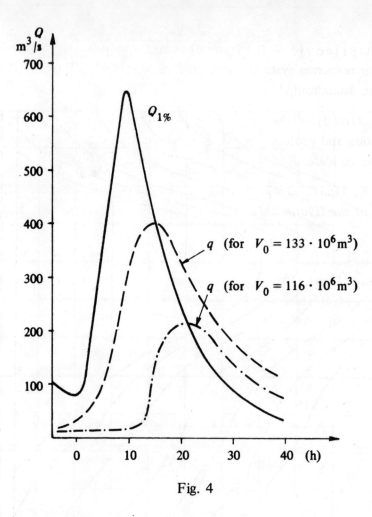

Fig. 4

REFERENCES

[1] W.A. Hall — A.J. Dracup, *Water resources systems Engineering,* McGraw-Hill, New York, 1970.

[2] N. Buras, *Scientific allocation of water resources,* American Elsevier, New York, 1972.

[3] B. Djordjević, Socio-economic models for planning WRS's, General report, *Symposium on the use of computer techniques for WRS's,* Washington, D. C. 1974.

[4] S. Opricović — B. Djordjević, Analysis and synthesis of water resources systems by systems engineering, *XV-th IAHR Congress*, Istamboul, 1973.

[5] B. Djordjević, The development of methods for planning of utilisation and protection of Yugoslav water resources, *Internat. Congress on Water Resources Planning*, Mexico, 1972.

[6] W.A. Hall, Optimum design of a multiple-purpose reservoir, *Journal of the Hydraulics division, ASCE*, 90, 1964.

Serafim Opricović
Dr. Ivana Ribara 159/43, 11070 Beograd, Yugoslavia
Branislav Djordjević
Toneta Tomxice 2/41, 11 000 Beograd, Yugoslavia.

COLLOQUIA MATHEMATICA SOCIETATIS JÁNOS BOLYAI

12. PROGRESS IN OPERATIONS RESEARCH, EGER (HUNGARY), 1974.

CHEMICAL INDUSTRIAL PRODUCTION PLANNING BY DYNAMIC PROGRAMMING

L. DOMOKOS — G.E. VERESS

SUMMARY

The problem is the production planning for the Chemical Industrial Enterprise at Borsod, that is to determine the amounts of the products for marketing and those of intermediates for producing. This paper gives a solution for this problem.

Using the linear input-output model of the plant, the plant production is characterized by the intensity of the production, and the decision variables of the plant model are the distribution of the products at a given level of the production intensity. On the basis of the plant models, the enterprise model can be considered as a multi-stage optimization problem. This multi-stage optimization problem was solved by a nonserial discrete dynamic programming algorithm.

1. INTRODUCTION

The problem to be examined is the production planning for the Chemical Industrial Enterprise at Borsod, that is to determine the amounts of the products for marketing and those of intermediate materials for producing. The planning period is a quarter (of a year) or a year. This production planning problem is a part of the task to carry out a computer-aided management decision system.

There are some possible ways to solve this problem (e.g. linear programming), but because of the multistage character of the problem, it is solved by nonserial discrete dynamic programming.

In spite of the fact that the application of the discrete dynamic programming is very spread we are ignorant of its application in solving such problems.

2. BASIC ASSUMPTIONS FOR MODELLING

In order to creat a mathematical model of the production planning problem, the following basic assumptions are taken into consideration:

the object of the production planning is to maximize the profit,

only the effect of production activity is to be examined and the change of the production activity has no influence on the other activities,

at the given period the state transition and the change of stock do not depend on the change of production,

varying the production only the actual material, the energy costs and the product revenue are changing,

the material and energy demands are changing linearly with the production in the neighbourhood of the setpoint, that is they can be calculated with the "specifics".

3. THE PLANT MODEL

The plants of the Chemical Industrial Enterprise at Borsod produce only one product (or at least one product and a "twice"-product).

The plant "i" can be considered as the following transport theoretical system:

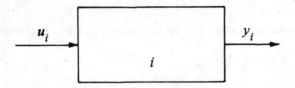

where the input resource amount is denoted by u_i and the amount of the product by y_i. For the product amount the following constraint must be valid:

$$y_i^a \leqslant y_i \leqslant y_i^f .$$

The return function is given as follows

$$v_{y_i} \cdot y_i - v_{u_i} \cdot u_i .$$

From the point of view of control theory, the plant can be regarded as the following control theoretical system:

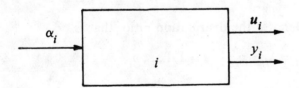

where the production intensity is denoted by α_i, that is the amount of the used resources and of the product are functions of the production intensity:

$$u_i = u_i(\alpha_i)$$

$$y_i = y_i(\alpha_i) .$$

The production intensity can be defined as

$$\alpha_i \equiv \frac{y_i}{y_i^f}$$

so the following inequalities must be satisfied:

$$\frac{y_i^a}{y_i^f} \leqslant \alpha_i \leqslant 1 \ .$$

Using the above relations, the resource and the production are

$$u_i = a_i \cdot \alpha_i \cdot y_i^f$$
$$y_i = \alpha_i \cdot y_i^f$$

where a_i denotes the specific resource demand vector.

The decision for the product distribution can be considered as the following control theoretical system:

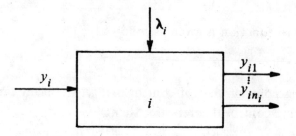

where λ_i denotes the distribution ratio, that is

$$y_{ij} = \lambda_{ij} \cdot y_i \qquad j = 1, \ldots, n_i$$

where

$$\sum_{j=1}^{n_i} \lambda_{ij} = 1$$

$$0 \leqslant \lambda_{ij} \leqslant 1 \qquad j = 1, \ldots, n_i \ .$$

Using the usual notations of the multi-stage problems, the plant i can be considered as the i-th stage,

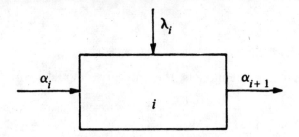

where α_i is the state variable, and λ_i is the decision variable. The i-th stage problem is:

$$\max_{\alpha_i, \lambda_i} \left\{ v_{y_i} \left(\sum_{j=1}^{n_i} \lambda_{ij} \cdot \alpha_i \cdot y_i^f \right) - v_{u_i} \cdot a_i \cdot \alpha_i \cdot y_i^f \right[$$

$$\left| \sum_{j=1}^{n_i} \lambda_{ij} = 1, \quad 0 \leqslant \lambda_{ij} \leqslant 1, \quad \frac{y_i^a}{y_i^f} \leqslant \alpha_i \leqslant 1 \right\}.$$

It can be seen that a plant itself is uninterested in the optimization of the components of λ_i, but it will be important for the whole enterprise.

4. THE ENTERPRISES MODEL

In order to create the enterprise model on the basis of the plant models, we must take into consideration the connection between the plants.

We suppose that one of the distributed outputs $(y_{i,i+1})$ of the plant i is equal to one of the inputs $(u_{i+1,i})$ of the plant $i+1$, that is

$$y_{i,i+1} = u_{i+1,i}.$$

Using this relation, the connection between the plants can be expressed by the formula

$$\alpha_{i+1} = \frac{\lambda_{i,i+1}}{a_{i+1,i}} \cdot \frac{y_i^f}{y_{i+1}^f} \cdot \alpha_i$$

because

$$y_{i,i+1} = \alpha_i \cdot \lambda_{i,i+1} \cdot y_i^f$$

and

$$u_{i+1,i} = a_{i+1,i} \cdot \alpha_{i+1} \cdot y^f_{i+1} \ .$$

Applying the plant models, the enterprise model is the following:

$$\max_{\substack{\alpha_1,\ldots,\alpha_N \\ \lambda_1,\ldots,\lambda_N}} \left\{ \sum_{i=1}^{N} \left[v_{y_i} \left(\sum_{j=1}^{n_i} \lambda_{ij} \cdot \alpha_i \cdot y^f_i \right) - v_{u_i} \cdot a_i \alpha_i \cdot y^f_i \right] \right|$$

$$\left| \sum_{j=1}^{n_i} \lambda_{ij} = 1, \quad 0 \le \lambda_{ij} \le 1, \quad \frac{y^a_i}{y^f_i} \le \alpha_i \le 1, \right.$$

$$\alpha_{i+1} = \frac{\lambda_{i,i+1}}{a_{i+1,i}} \cdot \frac{y^f_i}{y^f_{i+1}} \cdot \alpha_i \bigg\} \ .$$

5. THE DYNAMIC PROGRAMMING RECURSIVE EQUATION

Since the enterprise model can be considered as a multi-stage optimization problem, where the stage model is the plant model, the production planning problem can be formulated as the following discrete dynamic programming recursive equation:

$$F_i(\alpha_i) = \max_{\lambda_i} \left\{ v_{y_i} \left(\sum_{j=1}^{n_i} \lambda_{ij} \cdot \alpha_i \cdot y^f_i \right) - \right.$$

$$- v_{u_i} \cdot a_i \cdot \alpha_i \cdot y^f_i + F_{i+1}(\alpha_{i+1}) \bigg| \sum_{j=1}^{n_i} \lambda_{ij} = 1 \ ,$$

$$0 \le \alpha_{ij} \le 1 \ , \quad \frac{y^a_i}{y^f_i} \le \alpha_i \le 1 \ , \quad \alpha_{i+1} = \frac{\lambda_{i,i+1}}{a_{i+1,i}} \cdot \frac{y^f_i}{y^f_{i+1}} \cdot \alpha_i \bigg\}$$

$$i = N, \ldots, 1$$

where

$$F_{N+1} \equiv 0 \ ,$$

and F_1 is the optimal enterprise return using the optimal production planning policy.

This recursive equation forms a serial problem, but this can be generalized without difficulties to a nonserial one.

6. APPLICATION OF THE ALGORITHM

Using the nonserial version of the above dynamic programming recursive equation computer programs were written in FORTRAN language running on CDC 3300 and on ICL 1903/A for solving the production planning problem of the Chemical Industrial Enterprise at Borsod.

To solve our problem by nonserial discrete dynamic programming algorithm seemed to be very useful, because the dimension of the state variable was only one (in the case of serial connection), the number of the stages was 8, while the number of the plants was 15, and the number of the products was 12.

One of the problems of the algorithm application is to pick up the actual enterprise data. Using the actual data, the running time was about two minutes. The results were checked by an enterprise input-output model.

The results of the algorithm were applied for preparing the management decisions and analysing the sensitivity of plan capacities.

Acknowledgements. The authors are very thankful for the help of Mr. József Gazda and Mrs. Klára Mosonyi of Chemical Industrial Enterprise at Borsod in solving the problems of application.

Gábor E. Veress, and

László Domokos

Institute for General and Analytical Chemistry, Technical University Budapest, H-1111 Budapest, Műegyetem rkp. 3.

COLLOQUIA MATHEMATICA SOCIETATIS JÁNOS BOLYAI

12. PROGRESS IN OPERATIONS RESEARCH, EGER (HUNGARY), 1974.

NEW ALGORITHMS FOR MINIMAL COST FLOW PROBLEMS AND THEIR APPLICATIONS

W. DOMSCHKE

1. THE FLOW PROBLEM AND SOME DEFINITIONS

The flow problem that we will consider is the following: Given a finite antisymmetrical lower and upper bound capacitated flow network N with a source s and a sink t, find a minimal cost flow f from s to t in N.

Detailed description of the problem:

We consider a *finite antisymmetrical flow network* $N = (V, A, c, a, b)$ with

the *finite set of nodes or vertices* V (in general we set

$$V = \{1, 2, \ldots, n\} \subset N),^*$$

---

* N = Set of all natural numbers,

R = Set of all real numbers,

Z = Set of all integer numbers.

the *set of arcs* $A \subset V \times V$ with the properties

$$(u, u) \notin A \quad \text{for all} \quad u \in V \quad \text{and}$$

$$(u, v) \in A \Rightarrow (v, u) \notin A \quad \text{for all} \quad u, v \in V \quad \text{(antisymmetry)},$$

the *cost function* $c: A \to R,$

the *lower capacity bound* $a: A \to Z_+$ and

the *upper capacity bound* $b: A \to Z_+$

with $\quad 0 \leqslant a(e) \leqslant b(e) \quad$ for all $\quad e \in A$.

The network N may contain a source s and a sink t, that is $\mathscr{P}(s) = \mathscr{S}(t) = \phi$, where we denote the set of all immediate predecessors of a node v by $\mathscr{P}(v)$ and the set of all immediate successors of a node v by $\mathscr{S}(v)$.

The problem is to find a *minimal cost flow* f from s to t in N, that is, we want to find a function $f: A \to Z_+$ with the properties

(1) $$\sum_{v \in \mathscr{S}(s)} f(s, v) = \sum_{u \in \mathscr{P}(t)} f(u, t) \quad (\geqslant 0);$$

(2) $$\sum_{u \in \mathscr{P}(v)} f(u, v) = \sum_{u \in \mathscr{S}(v)} f(v, u) \quad \text{for all} \quad v \in V - \{s, t\};$$

(3) $$a(e) \leqslant f(e) \leqslant b(e) \quad \text{for all} \quad e \in A;$$

(4) There is no function $f': A \to Z_+$ with properties (1)-(3) and

$$\sum_{e \in A} f'(e) \cdot c(e) < \sum_{e \in A} f(e) \cdot c(e).$$

A function $f: A \to Z_+$ with properties (1)-(3) but not (4) is said to be a *feasible flow* from s to t in N.

Further definitions.

We define a path in a network by its nodes $(v_1, v_2, \ldots, v_i)$, where $(v_j, v_{j+1}) \in A$ for all $j = 1(1)i - 1$.

The *length* of a path $p = (v_1, v_2, \ldots, v_i)$ is $c(p) = \sum_{j=1}^{i-1} c(v_j, v_{j+1})$.

p^* is a *shortest path* from node u to node v in a network, if there is no path p going from u to v with $c(p) < c(p^*)$. A path $p = (v_1, v_2, \ldots, v_i)$ with $v_1 = v_i$ is said to be a cycle; p is a *negative cycle* if $c(p) < 0$.

For every flow network $N = (V, A, c, a, b)$ and every $f: A \to Z_+$ we introduce an *incremental network* $I(N, f) = (V, \bar{A}, \bar{c}, cp)$ with the nodes V, the arcs $\bar{A}$, the costs $\bar{c}$, and the *residual capacities cp*, defined as follows:

$$(u, v) \in \bar{A} \Leftrightarrow \begin{cases} \text{(a)} \ (u, v) \in A & \text{and} \quad f(u, v) < b(u, v) \\ & \text{or} \\ \text{(b)} \ (v, u) \in A & \text{and} \quad f(v, u) > a(v, u) \end{cases}$$

$\bar{c}: \bar{A} \to R$ with

$$\bar{c}(u, v) = \begin{cases} c(u, v) & \text{if} \quad (u, v) \in A \\ -c(v, u) & \text{if} \quad (v, u) \in A \end{cases}$$

$cp: \bar{A} \to Z_+$ with

$$cp(u, v) = \begin{cases} b(u, v) - f(u, v) & \text{if} \quad (u, v) \in A \\ f(v, u) - a(v, u) & \text{if} \quad (v, u) \in A. \end{cases}$$

One can recognize that the incremental network $I(N, f)$ consists of the same nodes as N. For every arc (u, v) of N it contains

(a) an arc (u, v) if and only if $f(u, v)$ less $b(u, v)$. It carries the costs $\bar{c}(u, v) = c(u, v)$ and the residual capacity $cp(u, v) = b(u, v) - f(u, v)$. The flow $f(u, v)$ can be increased by $cp(u, v)$ without hurting the upper capacity bound $b(u, v)$.

(b) an arc (v, u) if and only if $f(u, v)$ greater $a(u, v)$. It carries the costs $\bar{c}(v, u) = -c(u, v)$ and the residual capacity $cp(v, u) = f(u, v) - a(u, v)$. The flow $f(u, v)$ can be decreased by $cp(v, u)$ without hurting the lower capacity bound $a(u, v)$. By decreasing $f(u, v)$ by one unit $c(u, v)$ units of money can be *saved*.

Concluding we illustrate the definition of the incremental network by means of an example: Figure 1 shows a flow network $N = (V, A, c, a, b)$ with flow $f: A \to Z_+$, in Figure 2 the corresponding incremental network $I(N, f)$ is given.

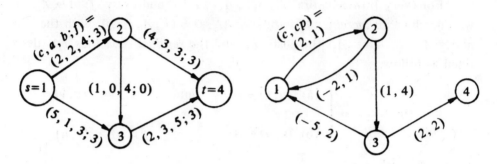

Figure 1   Figure 2

2. THE ALGORITHM

Given a finite antisymmetrical flow network $N = (V, A, c, a, b)$ with a source s and a sink t, one finds a minimal cost flow f from s to t with the help of the following algorithm. The algorithm consists of two parts:

Part I. Search for a feasible flow f';

Part II. Search for a minimal cost flow f by starting with and improving a feasible flow f' found in Part I.

Part I. It consists of three steps.

Step 1. Set $f(u, v) = a(u, v)$ for all $(u, v) \in A$.

Compute the *"flow difference"*

$$fd(v) = \sum_{u \in \mathscr{P}(v)} f(u, v) - \sum_{u \in \mathscr{S}(v)} f(v, u) \quad \text{for all} \quad v \in V - \{s, t\}.$$

Set up $I(N, f)$ and go to Step 2.

Step 2. Find a node i with $fd(i) > 0$ (if none exists, go to Step 3). Find a path* p from i to a node j with $fd(j) < 0$ in $I(N, f)$.

If such a path cannot be found or if $fd(j) \geqslant 0$ for all $j \in V - \{s, t\}$ then find a path from i to the sink t in $I(N, f)$.

If such a path also cannot be found, then there does not exist a feasible flow from s to t in N.**

Otherwise evaluate

$$m = \begin{cases} \min (fd(i), \min_{(u,v) \in p} cp(u, v)), & \text{if } t \text{ is end node} \\ \min (fd(i), -fd(j), \min_{(u,v) \in p} cp(u, v)), & \text{if } j \text{ is end node.}*** \end{cases}$$

Set $fd(i) = fd(i) - m$ and, if j is end node of p, $fd(j) = fd(j) + m$.

Alter f as follows:

  Increase $f(u, v)$ by m, if $(u, v) \in p$,

  decrease $f(u, v)$ by m, if $(v, u) \in p$;

for all other arcs of N the flow f rests unchanged.

Correct $I(N, f)$ — see its definition — and go to Step 2.

Step 3. Find a node j with $fd(j) < 0$ (if none exists a feasible flow has already been found; go to Part II).

Find a path p from source s to j in $I(N, f)$.

If such a path cannot be found, then there does not exist a feasible flow from s to t in N.**

---

*This path may or may not be a shortest one. See also Chapter 3.

**See the proof in Domschke [9], Chapter 4.4.

***$(u, v) \in p$ means (u, v) is an arc of p.

Otherwise evaluate $m = \min(-fd(j), \min_{(u,v)\in p} cp(u,v))$.

Set $fd(j) = fd(j) + m$. Alter f as described in Step 2, correct $I(N, f)$, and go to Step 3.

Part II. Suppose there is given a feasible flow f determined by the help of Part I. In Part II this flow will be improved successively until a minimal cost flow has been reached.

Part II consists of two steps:

Step 1. Find a negative cycle z in $I(N, f)$.*

Choose the source s as starting node for this procedure.**

Three cases are possible:

Case 1. One finds a negative cycle $z = (v_i, v_{i+1}, \ldots, v_j)$.

If $m = \min_{(u,v)\in z} cp(u,v)$, then alter f as described in Step 2 of **Part** I, correct $I(N, f)$, and go to Step 1.

Case 2. One does not find a negative cycle but paths of negative length from source s to sink t. Let p be the shortest of them, then:

Evaluate $m = \min_{(u,v)\in p} cp(u,v)$, alter f as described in Step 2 of Part I, correct $I(N, f)$, and go to Step 1.

Case 3. One finds no negative cycle and no path of negative length from source s to sink t. Go to Step 2.

Step 2. First determine the set M of those nodes which could not be reached from s in the last run of Step 1.

---

*Choose, for example, one of the two methods in D o m s c h k e [6]. One of these methods uses the shortest path algorithm of F o r d (or M o o r e, see D o m s c h k e [5]); the other is an advancement of the method given by D a n t z i g, B l a t t n e r and R a o [2] and uses the algorithm of D i j k s t r a [4].

**In practice one saves computing time by changing the starting node from run to run of Step 1. Only the last runs must be started with s for the detection of paths of negative length from s to t.

$\oplus$ Find negative cycles in $I(N, f)$ by choosing any element i of M as starting node.

If a negative cycle z can be found, alter f by $m = \min_{(u,v) \in z} cp(u, v)$ as described in Step 2 of Part I, correct $I(N, f)$, and go to $\oplus$.

If no negative cycle can be found, reduce M by all nodes which could be reached from i; start again with $\oplus$ if $M \neq \phi$, otherwise the present flow f is a minimal cost flow.

3. THREE VARIATIONS OF THE ALGORITHM

Essentially we can distinguish three variants of the algorithm. Their greatest difference lies in Step 2 and Step 3 of Part I because one can use paths of different kind for the compensation of the flow differences $fd(v)$ of all nodes $v \in V - \{s, t\}$. The type of the paths chosen in Part I has also consequences for Part II.

Variant 1. The compensation of the flow differences takes place via paths determined by the Moore-algorithm without consideration of the costs, i.e. the paths are determined within incremental networks $I(N, f)' = = (V, \bar{A}, \bar{c}', cp)$ with $\bar{c}'(u, v) = 1$ for all arcs $(u, v) \in \bar{A}$ (see for instance Domschke [5], pp. 11-14). In comparison with Variants 2 and 3 computational time for Part I is short but the feasible solution f at the end of Part I is bad with many negative cycles in $I(N, f)$.

Variant 2. It is just the opposite of Variant 1. We compensate the flow differences via *shortest paths*. If there are no negative cycles* in the given flow network N, then there are also no negative cycles in $I(N, f)$ at the end of Part I. Part II then shrinks to one step:

$\oplus$ Find the shortest path p from source s to sink t in $I(N, f)$. If p has negative length, then alter f by $m = \min_{(u,v) \in p} cp(u, v)$ as described in Step 2 of Part I, correct $I(N, f)$, and go to $\oplus$; otherwise a minimal cost flow has been found.

*This is no restriction if you want to solve economic problems.

In comparison with Variants 1 and 3 the computational time for Part I is high but the feasible solution f at the end of Part I is almost optimal or optimal.

Variant 3. It is a compromise between Variant 1 and 2. We compensate the flow differences via *conditionally shortest paths.* * Such paths we get, for instance, if we always choose that path between two nodes of an incremental network $I(N, f)$ which we find first of all (e.g. with the algorithm of F o r d (resp. M o o r e) or with the method of D i j k s t r a)*.

4. COMPUTATIONAL EXPERIENCES

For Variant 1 and Variant 2 of the flow algorithm an ALGOL-procedure has been developed.** They have been compared with the ALGOL-procedure "NETFLOW" for the Out-of-Kilter-algorithm developed by B r a y and W i t z g a l l [1]. For these comparisons we built up more than 200 antisymmetrical flow networks with $10 \leqslant n = |V| \leqslant 100$ by the aid of random numbers. The "relative number of arcs" $= |A|/n(n-1)$ was between 0.12 and 0.45, on the average 0.32.

For every example both variants of the flow algorithm needed less computing time than NETFLOW. Variant 1 was better than Variant 2.

On the average Variant 1 required $1/2 - 1/3$ of the computing time of NETFLOW.

Nevertheless further tests are necessary, e.g. for flow networks with small relative numbers of arcs. In the procedures for the flow algorithm we store matrices for $\bar{c}$ and cp, possibly it is better to store the vector (initial node, end node, $\bar{c}, cp$) for each arc. Furthermore it should be tested whether a program for Variant 3 does not attain better results than programs for Variant 1 and 2. This is possible by virtue of the experiences with transportation and assignment problems.

*See also the solution method for the assignment problem, Chapter 5.

**The procedure for Variant 2 has been published in D o m s c h k e [7].

5. APPLICATIONS OF THE ALGORITHM

The algorithm can be used, for instance, to solve assignment, transportation, traveling salesman, and location problems. In the following specialized solution methods for assignment and location problems will be given.

5.1. *A solution method for the assignment problem**

The problem: n jobs can be done by n workers. If worker i does job j this causes costs of $c(i, j)(= c_{ij})$ units. Which worker has to do which job so that the sum of the costs for carrying out all jobs is minimal?

We can construct the very simple flow network $N = (V, A, c, a, b)$ of Figure 3.

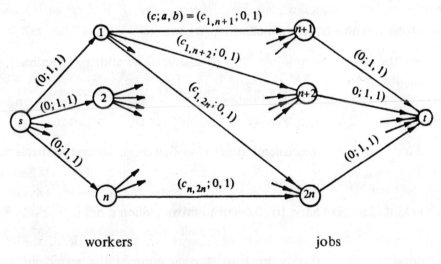

workers   jobs

Figure 3

By determining a minimal cost flow from s to t in N we get an optimal solution for the assignment problem.

*See also D o m s c h k e and W e u t h e n [10].

The solution method* consists of three steps:

Step 1. The same as the first step of Part I of the flow algorithm:

We set $f(u, v) = a(u, v)$ for all $(u, v) \in A$ and get

$$fd(i) = 1 \qquad \text{for all} \qquad i = 1(1)n \qquad \text{and}$$

$$fd(j) = -1 \qquad \text{for all} \qquad j = n + 1(1)2n .$$

We get a very special incremental network $I(N, f)$. In this network as well as in the other we get in the course of the algorithm one can neglect the source s and the sink t.

Step 2. Compensation of the flow differences like in Step 2 of Part I according to the rule: The flow difference $+ 1$ of node i $(= 1(1)n)$ has to saturate the difference $- 1$ of node $i + n$ $(= n + 1(1)2n)$; the compensation has to take place via *shortest paths of* $I(N, f)$ *with three arcs at most* (conditionally shortest paths).

At the end of Step 2 we have a feasible flow and a corresponding incremental network $I(N, f)$. Now it is possible to reduce $I(N, f)$ to a network with only n nodes and at most $n(n - 1)$ arcs (see D o m s c h k e [9], Chapter 5.1.3).

Step 3. Find and eliminate successively all negative cycles of the reduced incremental network $I(N, f)$ with n nodes and $n(n - 1)$ arcs at most (see part II of the flow algorithm). We use the Method 2 (Zyklus Dijkstra) in D o m s c h k e [6] to find negative cycles.

If each worker is able to do each work, then any node of the incremental network can be chosen as starting node of the search process.

Computational experiences with an ALGOL-procedure:

For the solution method described above there have been developed two distrinct ALGOL-procedures. In the first we use incremental networks with $2n$ nodes (see D o m s c h k e and W e u t h e n [10]), in the second

---

*A similar solution method for this special network flow problem has been given by K l e i n [11].

we work with reduced incremental networks with n nodes (see Domschke [9], Chapter 7.3). Both procedures have been compared with — probably the best — procedure for the Hungarian Method, developed by Pape and Schön [14], on a Univac 1108. Each program has been tested by means of 20 problems of the dimension $n = 20, 40, 60$ and 80 with cost-values c_{ij} equally distributed in the intervals $[0, 99]$, $[0, 1000]$, $[0, n^2 - 1]$ and $[0, n^3]$ respectively.

On the average our first procedure needed more computing time than the second (with incremental networks with n nodes). The quotients "time for Hungarian Method/time for our second procedure" that we got are given in Table 1.

Inter-val n	$[0, 99]$	$[0, 1000]$	$[0, n^2 - 1]$	$[0, n^3]$
20	0.933	1.188	1.133	1.250
40	0.750	1.524	1.559	1.646
60	0.617	1.652	1.981	2.285
80	0.570	1.791	2.481	2.651

Table 1

5.2. *A Solution Method for Location (Fixed-Charge) Problems*

The flow algorithm can be turned to account for the solution of location problems of the following type:

For the production of some good a company possesses p *factories* $P = \{P_1, P_2, \ldots, P_p\}$. Factory P_h $(h = 1(1)p)$ is able to produce at least ap_h and at most bp_h units of the good per period with costs of cp_h dollars per unit of the good.

There are k *customers* $K = \{K_1, K_2, \ldots, K_k\}$. Customer K_j $(j = 1(1)k)$ can be supplied with at least ak_j and at most bk_j units of the good per period and pays ck_j dollars per unit.

The company wants to establish *warehouses*. There are l potential locations $L = \{L_1, L_2, \ldots, L_l\}$. If in L_i $(i = 1(1)n)$ a warehouse will be established then the flow of goods per period has to be al_i units at least and bl_i units at most; the variable costs are cl_i dollars per unit; furthermore there appears a *fixed charge* of f_i dollars per period.

The *charges for transshipment* from the factories to the warehouses and from those to the customers are proportional to the transshipped quantities. They are c_{hi} dollars for the transport of one unit from factory P_h to location L_i and $\tilde{c}_{ij}$ dollars for the transport of one unit from L_i to customer K_j. There are no capacity constraints for the transshipment.

The problem is: Where has the company to establish warehouses, how much shall be produced in the various factories, delivered by the various warehouses, delivered to the various customers, and transported via the various routes so that the profit (proceeds minus costs) of the company is a maximum or – what's the same – so that costs minus proceeds are minimal?

It is obvious that if all fixed charges would be zero the minimum problem could be solved by determining a (or the) minimal cost flow from source s to sink t in the flow network $N = (V, A, c, a, b)$ of **Figure 4**. For every potential location L_i the network contains two nodes L_i and L_i' and an arc (L_i, L_i').

But also within the solution method for the fixed charge problem (with charges $\geqslant 0$) one takes advantage of the flow algorithm.

For a short description of the solution method* it is useful to look at the mathematical formulation of the problem. We have to minimize

*A detailed description of the algorithm you find in Domschke [8] and Domschke [9], Chapter 6.

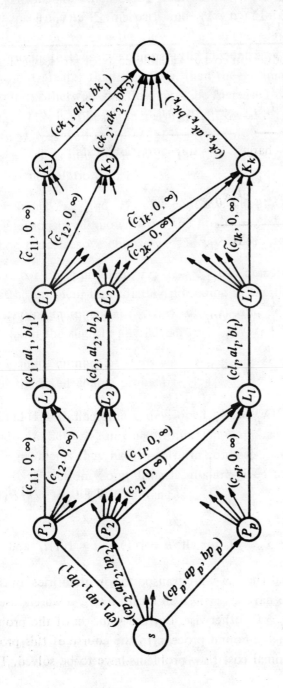

Figure 4

$$(1) \qquad Z = \underbrace{\sum_{h=1}^{p} \sum_{i=1}^{l} cp_h x_{hi} +}_{\text{production cost}} \underbrace{\sum_{h=1}^{p} \sum_{i=1}^{l} cl_i x_{hi} +}_{\text{variable cost for stock-keeping}}$$

$$+ \underbrace{\sum_{i=1}^{l} f_i y_i +}_{\text{fixed charge}} \underbrace{\sum_{h=1, i=1}^{p} \sum_{i=1}^{l} c_{hi} x_{hi} + \sum_{i=1}^{l} \sum_{j=1}^{k} \tilde{c}_{ij} \tilde{x}_{ij} -}_{\text{transportation costs}}$$

$$\underbrace{- \sum_{i=1}^{l} \sum_{j=1}^{k} ck_j \tilde{x}_{ij}}_{\text{proceeds}}$$

subject to

$$(2) \qquad ap_h \leqslant \sum_{i=1}^{l} x_{hi} \leqslant bp_h \qquad\qquad \text{for all} \ \ h = 1(1)p$$

$$(3) \qquad al_i y_i \leqslant \sum_{h=1}^{p} x_{hi} \leqslant bl_i y_i \qquad\qquad \text{for all} \ \ i = 1(1)l$$

$$(4) \qquad ak_j \leqslant \sum_{i=1}^{l} \tilde{x}_{ij} \leqslant bk_j \qquad\qquad \text{for all} \ \ j = 1(1)k$$

$$(5) \qquad \sum_{h=1}^{p} x_{hi} = \sum_{j=1}^{k} \tilde{x}_{ij} \left.\begin{array}{c} \\ \\ \\ \\ \\ \end{array}\right\}$$

$$\qquad\qquad\qquad\qquad\qquad\qquad\qquad \text{for all} \ \ i = 1(1)l$$

$$(6) \qquad y_i \in \{0, 1\}$$

$$(7) \qquad x_{hi} \geqslant 0, \ \tilde{x}_{ij} \geqslant 0 \ \ \text{for all} \ \ h = 1(1)p, \ \ i = 1(1)l, \ \ \text{and} \ \ j = 1(1)k,$$

where the x_{hi} and the $\tilde{x}_{ij}$ are transportation quantities. In the solution of the problem we have $y_i = 1$ if in location L_i a warehouse has to be established and $y_i = 0$ otherwise. For the solution of the problem we carry out a branch-and-bound process. In the course of this process a lot of (linearized) minimal cost flow problems have to be solved. These flow problems (or *subproblems*) differ from each other and from the fixed charge problem by distinct assumptions in restriction (6). In each subproblem there are

(1) some y_i we set equal 0, i.e. we assume that L_i gets no warehouse. The network N for the solution of the subproblem does not contain the arc (L_i, L_i').

(2) some y_i we set equal 1; i.e. we assume that L_i gets a warehouse. The network N contains the arc (L_i, L_i') with the variable costs cl_i, the lower bound al_i, and the upper bound bl_i.

(3) some y_i we let vary in $[0, 1]$ (we set $0 \leqslant y_i \leqslant 1$), i.e. we did not decide already whether L_i gets a warehouse or not. The network N contains the arc (L_i, L_i') with *the cost* $(cl_i + f_i/bl_i)$, *the lower bound* 0, *and the upper bound* bl_i.

By carrying out the branch-and-bound process we get a solution tree as represented in Figure 5. To each node of the tree there corresponds a special sub (= flow)-problem.

For each problem Pr_i of the tree the following statement holds:

If Pr_i is a problem of plane j then there are exactly j of the y_i fixed to 0 or 1.

Therefore we start with problem Pr_1 with the condition

$$(6') \qquad 0 \leqslant y_i \leqslant 1 \quad \text{for all} \quad i = 1(1)l.$$

We solve Pr_1 with one of the variants of the flow algorithm. If Pr_1 has a solution and if in the optimal solution there are y_i's not equal to 0 or 1 we define the subproblems Pr_2 and Pr_3 by setting $y_r = 0$ in Pr_2 and $y_r = 1$ in Pr_3 for one $r \in \{1, 2, \ldots, l\}$ with $0 \neq y_r \neq 1$ in the optimal solution for Pr_1.

Both problems can be solved by the flow algorithm without regarding the solution of Pr_1 and the corresponding incremental network $I(N, f)$.

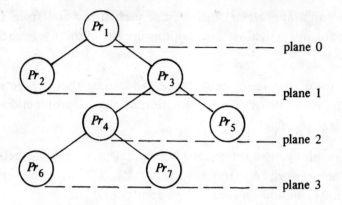

Pr_1

Pr_2 Pr_3

Pr_4 Pr_5

Pr_6 Pr_7

plane 0

plane 1

plane 2

plane 3

Figure 5

But it is worthwhile to start with these results of Pr_1. We alter the values of the arcs between L_r and L'_r in $I(N, f)$, necessary by reason of fixing y_r to 0 or 1. Furthermore we expand $I(N, f)$ by adding the two arcs (s, t) and (t, s) with $\bar{c}(s, t) = \bar{c}(t, s) = 0$ and $cp(s, t) = = cp(t, s) = \infty$ between the source s and the sink t. Then we get the optimal solutions for Pr_2 and Pr_3 within a few steps of determining shortest paths in the altered $I(N, f)$.

Reasons for this statement relating Pr_2

By setting $y_r = 0$, i.e. elimination of the arc (L_r, L'_r) in $I(N, f)$, we get the flow differences $fd(L_r) = - fd(L'_r) > 0$. We compensate these differences via *shortest paths* form L_r to L'_r in $I(N, f)$ (see Variant 2 of the flow algorithm). If the full compensation — possibly in more than one step — is not possible, then Pr_2 has no solution; otherwise we get an (or the) optimal solution for Pr_2.

Reasons for the fore-going statement relating Pr_3

We set $y_r = 1$, i.e. we decrease the costs from $(cl_r + f_r/bl_r)$ to cl_r and introduce the lower bound al_r. On account of the reduction of the costs it is possible that $I(N, f)$ now contains negative cycles including the arc (L_r, L'_r). This we examine by determining the *shortest path* from L'_r to L_r in $I(N, f)$. If this path and (L_r, L'_r) form a negative cycle we eliminate it by increasing the flow along the cycle and begin again with our examination; otherwise we compare the current flow in (L_r, L'_r) with al_r: Is al_r not greater than this flow, then the optimal solution for Pr_3 has been found; otherwise the flow must be increased until it turns to be equal to al_r. This is done by increasing the flow along the *shortest path* from L'_r to L_r as well as in (L_r, L'_r). If in this way — possibly in more than one step — it is impossible to set the flow of (L_r, L'_r) equal to al_r, then Pr_3 has no solution.

After solving Pr_2 and Pr_3 we continue the branching process by one of the methods well-known from the literature.* Without regarding the branching processes we choose we can say:

The sub-(or flow)-problem Pr_i $(i \geqslant 2)$ can be solved by using the solution of the problem immediately preceding in the branching tree and the corresponding incremental network $I(N, f)$ and determining a few shortest paths in the slightly altered network $I(N, f)$.

After a finite number of steps we get — if one exists — the optimal solution for the fixed charge problem.

Böttcher and Dehnert have developed an ALGOL-procedure for a specialization of the fore-going algorithm. They applied this program to fixed-charge problems they had to solve in connection with the analysis of solid waste collection. Computing results are given in D e h n e r t [3] (see also D o m s c h k e [9], Chapter 6).

---

*See for instance L a n d and D o i g [13].

Several branching methods are discussed by D e h n e r t [3].

REFERENCES

[1]   J.A. Bray – C. Witzgall, Algorithm 336, netflow, *Communications of the ACM,* 11 (1968), 631-632.

[2]   G.B. Dantzig – W.O. Blattner – M.R. Rao, All shortest routes from a fixed origin in a graph. In: V. Rosenstiehl (Ed.):
Théorie des graphes, journées internationales d'étude, Rome, Juillet
1966, Paris – New York, 1967, 85-90.

[3]   G. Dehnert, A branch and bound (b-&-b) method for solving
network flow problems with fixed costs, This volume.

[4]   E.W. Dijkstra, A note on two problems in connection with
graphs, *Numerische Mathematik,* 1 (1959), 269-271.

[5]   W. Domschke, *Kürzeste Wege in Graphen: Algorithmen, Verfahrensvergleiche. Mathematical Systems in Economics,* Anton
Hain Verlag, Meisenheim/Glan, 1972.

[6]   W. Domschke, Zwei Verfahren zur Suche negativer Zyklen in
bewerteten Digraphen, *Computing,* 11 (1973), 125-136.

[7]   W. Domschke, Two new algorithms for minimal cost flow
problems, *Computing,* 11 (1973), 275-285.

[8]   W. Domschke, Verfahren zur Bestimmung optimaler Betriebs-
und Lagerstandorte. In: E. Bahke (Ed.): *Materialflussysteme,* Bd.
II: Materialflussmodelle. Krausskopf Verlag, Mainz, 1975, Chapter 5.

[9]   W. Domschke, Graphentheoretische Verfahren und ihre Anwendungen zur Lösung von Zuordnungs- und Standortproblemen.
Mathematical Systems in Economics, Anton Hain Verlag, Meisen-
heim/Glan, 1976.

[10]   W. Domschke – H.-K. Weuthen, Ein effizientes Verfahren zur Lösung des Zuordnungsproblems, *Operations Research-Ver-
fahren,* (Ed. by R. Henn), 18 (1974), 42-56.

[11]   M. Klein, A primal method for minimal cost flows with applications to the assignment and transprotation problems, *Management Science*, 14 (1967), 205-220.

[12]   H. Kuhn, The Hungarian method for the assignment problem, *Nav. Res. Log. Quart.*, 2 (1955), 83-97.

[13]   A.H. Land – A.G. Doig, An automatic method of solving discrete programming problems, *Econometrica*, 28 (1960), 497-520.

[14]   U. Pape – B. Schön, Verfahren zur Lösung von Summen- und Engpass-Zuordnungsproblemen, *Elektronische Datenverarbeitung*. 4 (1970), 149-163.

Wolfgang Domschke

Hochschule der Bundeswehr Hamburg, Holstenhofweg 85, D-2 Hamburg 70.

GENERALIZED UNIMODAL FUNCTIONS

G. DONATH — K.H. ELSTER

1. INTRODUCTION

When considering optimization problems of the form

(1) $\min \{f(x) \mid x \in G\}$ with $G \subseteq R^n$

we have to answer the following fundamental questions

(a) What are the necessary conditions for a point $x^* \in G$ to be a global minimum of problem (1), i.e.

(2) $f(x^*) \leqslant f(x)$ $\forall x \in G$?

(b) Is it possible to avoid the use of derivatives (which can be obtained from the given function only approximately by computers) in the procedures which solve the problem?

If

$$G = \{x \in D, \ g_j(x) \leqslant 0, \ j \in J\} \,,$$

$$D \subseteq R^n, \quad D \text{ is open}; \quad J = \{1, \dots, m\}$$

f, g_j have continuous derivatives in D, f is pseudoconvex in D, the g_j are quasiconvex in D, $j \in J$ (cf. e.g. M a n g a s a r i a n [11]) the question (a) is answered by the Kuhn — Tucker theory.

The problem mentioned in question (b) has been approached by applying "direct methods". First they were developed for the one dimensional case, where efficient procedures have been given by K i e f e r [8] and others (like Fibonacci search). Later different procedures have been found for the n-dimensional case, but they converge* more slowly than the methods using derivatives.

In general, the references on direct methods do not contain conditions for the convergence of the methods or the conditions they propose are not satisfactory, mainly because they are too strong.

2. UNIMODAL FUNCTIONS

In the one dimensional case many of the direct methods start with a compact interval $G = [a, b] \subset R$ and construct a sequence of intervals, which captures exactly one $x^* \in G^*$ (see D o n a t h — E l s t e r [3]).

Here it is important that f has in each closed subinterval $I \subseteq [a, b]$ only such minimum points which have this property for I as well. This is the case for unimodal functions.

Definition 1. We say that $f: x \to R$ with $[a, b] \subseteq x \subseteq R$ is *unimodal in $[a, b]$* if there exists an $x^* \in [a, b]$ such that f is strictly decreasing in $[a, x^*]$ and strictly increasing in $[x^*, b]$.

Then we have

---

*Suppose $G^* = \{x^* \in G \mid x^*$ satisfies (2)$\}$. Then we say that a procedure is convergent in the sense of Z a n g w i l l [16] if in order to reach an $x^* \in G^*$ the procedure constructs a sequence $(x^k) \subset R^n$ satisfying the conditions

    (a) $x^k \in G^* \Rightarrow x^{k+1} \in G^*$ $\forall k \geqslant 1$,

    (b) if $x^k \notin G^*$ $\forall k \geqslant 1$, then for every convergent subsequence $(x^{k_r}) \subset (x^k)$ we have $\lim_{r \to \infty} x^{k_r} \in G^*$.

+**Theorem 1.*** *If f is unimodal in [a, b] then f is unimodal in all closed subintervals $I \subseteq [a, b]$.*

Unimodal functions are closely connected with certain generalized convex functions:

Definition 2. We say that $f: x \to R$ with $[a, b] \subseteq x \subseteq R$ is strictly explicitly quasiconvex in $[a, b]$ (or also x-convex) if

$$x_1, x_2 \in [a, b], \quad x_1 \neq x_2, \quad f(x_2) \leqslant f(x_1), \quad \alpha \in (0, 1)$$

imply

$$f(\alpha x_1 + (1 - \alpha)x_2) < f(x_1)$$

(see B e c t o r [1]).

Then we have

+**Theorem 2.** *If f is unimodal in [a, b] then f is strictly explicitly quasiconvex in [a, b].*

Obviously, continuity properties of f have no part here. On the other hand, the following proposition is valid:

Theorem 3. *Suppose that f is lower semicontinuous in [a, b]. Then f is unimodal in [a, b] iff f is strictly explicitly quasiconvex in [a. b].*

The converse of Theorem 2 does not hold if the strictly explicitly quasiconvex function f is not bounded below in $[a, b]$ or if it does not reach its infimum in a closed subinterval $I \subseteq [a, b]$. But both cases are impossible if f is a lower semicontinuous function in $[a, b]$.

One possibility of generalizing direct methods to the *n-dimensional case* is to apply an elimination principle (like the nest of intervals in the one dimensional cases). A generalization of the Fibonacci search using this principle has been found by K r o l a k and C o o p e r [9] and S u g i e [13] for $G = \{x \in R^n \mid a \leqslant x \leqslant b\}$. It can be applied to linear unimodal functions.

*The proofs of the theorems marked with + can be found in D o n a t h − E l s t e r [2].

Definition 3. A function $f: x \to R$ with $G \subseteq x \subseteq R^n$, G is closed, bounded, and convex, is said to be *linear unimodal* on G, if f is unimodel in $\text{conv}\,(x^1, x^2)$ for any $x^1, x^2 \in G^*$.

The crucial property which ensures the application of the elimination principle is here, too, the following

Theorem 4. *If f is linear unimodal in G then it is linear unimodal in every closed, convex subset $G' \subseteq G$.*

Definition 2 can be generalized to the case $n \geqslant 2$ by replacing $[a, b]$ by a closed, bounded, and convex set G with $G \subseteq x \subseteq R^n$ and by putting x^i for x_i, $i = 1, 2$. Then the following theorems can be proved similarly to Theorems 2 and 3.

+**Theorem 5.** *If f is linear unimodal in G then f is strictly explicitly quasiconvex in G*

Theorem 6. *Suppose that f is lower semicontinuous in G. Then f is linear unimodal in G iff f is strictly explicitly quasiconvex in G.*

Direct methods based on the elimination principle — even for small values of n — require to calculate the function-value so many times that the compute-time becomes irreal (see K u z o v k i n [10]).

Direct methods based on the climbing principle are more efficient. Using comparisons of function values they produce a sequence $(x^k) \subset G$ such that

$$f(x^{k+1}) < f(x^k) \qquad \forall k \geqslant 1 .$$

For this purpose the notion of unimodality in the one dimensional case can be extended to a form which is weaker than linear unimodality.

---

*This statement means that the function
$$F(t) = f(x(t)) \quad \text{with} \quad x(t) = tx^1 + (1 - t)x^2 \quad t \in [0, 1]$$
is unimodal in $t \in [0, 1]$ in the sense of Definition 1.

Definition 4. A function $f: x \to R$ with $G \subseteq x \subseteq R^n$, G is closed, bounded, and connected, is said to be unimodal in G if there exists an $x^* \in G$ such that for any $x \in G$ $(x \neq x^*)$ there exists a piece of a Jordan curve $J(x, x^*) \subset G$ such that f is strictly decreasing in $J(x, x^*)$.

The following proposition is of interest:

+Theorem 7. *If f is unimodal on G then f has a unique local minimum x^*, where f takes on its global minimum, too.*

The connection between Definition 4 and Definition 1 is given by

+Theorem 8. *f is unimodal in G iff there exists an $x^{**} \in G$ such that an arbitrary pair of points (x^1, x^2) can be connected by a piece of a Jordan curve $J \subset G$ with $x^{**} \in J$ so that f is unimodal in J.** *

Finally one can prove the connection with linear unimodal functions which has been told about before Definition 4:

+Theorem 9. *If f is linear unimodal in G, then it is unimodal in G.*

3. GENERALIZATIONS OF UNIMODAL FUNCTIONS

A very important property of the modifications of unimodal functions described in Section 2 is the uniqueness of their global minimum points in $x^* \in G$. Giving up this property, many of those solution methods remain still available which converge in case of unimodal functions. These investigations are interesting from the practical point of view: frequently it is sufficient to find for the objective function F and $x^* \in G$ such that

$$F(x^*) \leqslant C$$

where C is a constant given in advance.

---

*This proposition means that the function $F(t) = f(x(t))$, $t \in [0, 1]$ with
$$J = \{x(t) \mid t \in [0, 1], \; x(0) = x^1, \; x(1) = x^2\}$$
is unimodal in $t \in [0, 1]$ in the sense of the Definition 1.

Whenever such points exist, the problem mentioned above can be transformed into an equivalent one of the form (1)

$$f(x) = F(x) - C + |F(x) - C|.$$

In [3] the authors have shown that for example in the one dimensional case the direct methods using a nest of intervals are convergent for quasiunimodal functions, too.

Definition 5. A function $f: x \to R$ with $[a, b] \leqslant x \subseteq R$ is said to be quasiunimodal in $[a, b]$ if there exists an (open, semiopen or closed) interval $I^* \subseteq [a, b]$ such that

(3) $\qquad f(x)$ is $\begin{cases} \text{strictly decreasing in } [a, c] \\ \text{constant, but } \leqslant \min \{f(c), f(d)\} \text{ in } I^* \\ \text{strictly increasing in } [d, b] \end{cases}$

where $c = \inf I^*$, $d = \sup I^*$.

Putting $I^* = \{x^*\}$ it is easy to see that every unimodal function in $[a, b]$ is quasiunimodal as well.

It is again important that there are no closed subintervals of $[a, b]$ admitting local but not global minima, as is shown by the following two theorems.

‡**Theorem 10.*** *Suppose that f is quasiunimodal in $[a, b]$. Then f attains its global minimum in the subinterval $I^* \subseteq [a, b]$. There are no other local minima in $[a, b]$.*

‡**Theorem 11.** *If f is quasiunimodal in $[a, b]$ then it is quasiunimodal in every closed subinterval $I \subseteq [a, b]$.*

Now we have again a close connection with certain generalized convex function.

Definition 6. We say that a function $f: x \to R$ with $[a, b] \subseteq x \subseteq R$ is quasiconvex in $[a, b]$ if

*The proof of theorems marked with ‡ can be found in Donath – Elster [3].

$$x_1, x_2 \in [a, b]$$
$$f(x_2) \leqslant f(x_1) \left.\right\} \Rightarrow f(\alpha x_1 + (1 - \alpha)x_2) \leqslant f(x_1)$$
$$\alpha \in [0, 1]$$

(see M a r t o s [12]).

Definition 7. $f: x \to R$ with $[a, b] \subseteq x \subseteq R$ which is quasiconvex in $[a, b]$ is said to be explicitly quasiconvex in $[a, b]$ if

(4)
$$x_1, x_2 \in [a, b]$$
$$f(x_2) < f(x_1) \left.\right\} \Rightarrow f(\alpha x_1 + (1 - \alpha)x_2) < f(x_1)$$
$$\alpha \in (0, 1)$$

(see G r e e n b e r g — P i e r s k a l l a [5]).

One can show

‡**Theorem 12.** *If f is quasiunimodal in $[a, b]$ then it is explicitly quasiconvex in $[a, b]$.*

Definition 8. We say that $f: x \to R$ with $[a, b] \subseteq x \subseteq R$ is strictly quasiconvex in $[a, b]$ if it satisfies (4).

Finally the following proposition can be shown like in Theorem 3 by noting that the properties "explicitly quasiconvex" and "strictly quasiconvex" coincide if f is semicontinuous.

Theorem 13. *Suppose that f is lower semicontinuous in $[a, b]$. Then f is quasiunimodal in $[a, b]$ iff it is strictly quasiconvex in $[a, b]$.*

The properties of f introduced in Section 2 can also be generalized to this case for $n \geqslant 2$, and they remain sufficient to ensure the convergence of certain methods. For example, the generalized Fibonacci search converges for linear quasiunimodal functions, too.

Definition 9. A function $f: x \to R$ with $G \subseteq x \subseteq R^n$, G is closed, bounded and convex is said to be linear quasiunimodal in G if for any $x^1, x^2 \in G$ it is quasiunimodal in $\text{conv}(x^1, x^2)$.

Taking into consideration the connection between quasiunimodal and unimodal functions in the one dimensional case, we can easily prove that every linear unimodal function is linear quasiunimodal, and we can also prove an assertion analogous to Theorem 4 for linear quasiunimodal functions.

Definitions 6-8 can be generalized to the case $n \geqslant 2$ by replacing $[a, b]$ by a closed, bounded, and convex set G with $G \subseteq x \subseteq R^n$ and by putting x^i for x_i, $i = 1, 2$. Then the following theorems can be proved similarly to Theorems 12 and 13.

Theorem 14. *If f is linear quasiunimodal in G then it is explicitly quasiconvex in G.*

Theorem 15. *Suppose that f is lower semicontinuous in G. Then f is linear quasiunimodal in G iff it is strictly quasiconvex in G.*

Another extension of the notion of quasiunimodality from the one dimensional case has also proved to be useful:

Definition 10. A function $f: x \to R$ with $G \subseteq x \subseteq R^n$, G closed, bounded, and connected, is said to be quasiunimodal in G if there exists a subset $G^* \subseteq G$, $G^* \neq \phi$ such that for every $x \in G \setminus \mathrm{cl}\, G^*$ there exist an $\tilde{x} \in \mathrm{bd}\, G^*$ and a piece of a Jordan curve $J(x, \tilde{x}) \subset G$ such that f is strictly decreasing in J.

If $x^* \in G^*$ then

$$f(x^*) = \text{const} \leqslant \inf \{ f(\tilde{x}) \mid \tilde{x} \in G^* \} .$$

With $G^* = \{x^*\}$ every unimodal function is quasiunimodal.

It is obvious that f attains its global minimum on the set G^*, which must be connected. Together with the following theorem, this corresponds to Theorem 7.

Theorem 16. *If f is quasiunimodal then it has no local minima in $G \setminus G^*$.*

In the case of quasiunimodal functions Theorem 8 has the following form:

Theorem 17. *f is quasiunimodal in G iff there exists a set* $G^{**} \subseteq G$, $G^{**} \neq \phi$ *such that any* $x^1, x^2 \in G$ $(x^1 \neq x^2)$ *can be connected by a piece of a Jordan curve* $J \subset G$, $J \cap G^{**} = \phi$ *in such a way that f is quasiunimodal in J.*

The proof is similar to that of Theorem 8. Finally we obtain, similarly to Theorem 9,

Theorem 18. *If f is linear quasiunimodal in G then it is unimodal in G.*

Another possibility of generalizing unimodality of functions is to omit the condition on the connectedness of G, which ensures the applicability of direct methods to discrete optimization problems. In a stricter sense this is also necessary when realizing the methods on digital computers because of their discrete domain of operation. However, in the n-dimensional case only such properties are of sense which relay on the corresponding ones in the one dimensional case, that is they concern $\text{conv}(x^1, x^2) \cap G$ for any $x^1, x^2 \in G$.

4. APPLICATION OF GENERALIZED UNIMODAL FUNCTIONS. AN EXAMPLE

In order to solve problems of the form*

$$\min \{f(x) \mid x \in R^n\}$$

one generally uses the pattern search method. (See H o o k e — J e e v e s, [7]).

By using a sequence of $(n + 1)$-tuples $((t^{m0}, t^{m1}, \ldots, t^{mn}))$ of temporary optimal points it constructs a sequence b^m of basispoints. These temporary optimal points are defined for any $\delta > 0$ as follows:

$$b^1 \in R^n$$

---

*Having a solution $x^* \in \text{int } G$, the problem can be solved in case of $G \in R^n$, too, by a simple extension of the algorithm.

is arbitrary,

$$t^{1,0} = b^1 ,$$

and by

$$t_+^{mi} = (t_1^{mi}, \ldots, t_{i+1}^{mi} + \delta, \ldots, t_n^{mi})' \in R^n ,$$

$$t_-^{mi} = (t_1^{mi}, \ldots, t_{i+1}^{mi} - \delta, \ldots, t_n^{mi})' \in R^n$$

$$i = 0, \ldots, n-1; \quad m = 1, 2, \ldots$$

we define

(a) for determining the direction

$$t^{m,i+1} = \begin{cases} t_+^{mi} & \text{if } f(t_+^{mi}) < f(t^{mi}) \text{ and } f(t_+^{mi}) \leqslant f(t_-^{mi}) \\ t_-^{mi} & \text{if } f(t_-^{mi}) < \min \{f(t^{mi}), f(t_+^{mi})\} \\ t^{mi} & \text{otherwise,} \end{cases}$$

$$i = 0, \ldots, n-1; \quad m = 1, 2, \ldots .$$

(b) for steplength:

$$b^{m+1} = \begin{cases} t^{mn} & \text{if } f(t^{mn}) < f(b^m) \\ b^m & \text{otherwise,} \end{cases}$$

$$t^{m+1,0} = 2b^{m+1} - b^m , \quad m = 1, 2, \ldots .$$

If for some $m \geqslant 1$ we have

$$t^{m0} = b^{m+1} = b^{m+2} ,$$

then for the given $\delta > 0$ there is no basispoint with a smaller value of the function.

Then we go on by applying a smaller value of δ until we reach the prescribed bound.

In [7] it was announced that no practically satisfactory conditions for the success of the method had been found so far, and that the method could yield only a unique global minimum. W i l d e [14] and W i l d e —

Beightler [15] also described the method without mentioning any condition on its convergence. Himmelblau [6] gives some possible criteria for stopping, it remains open, however, whether a global minimum has been reached.

Now we can show that if the described method converges, then the function f must satisfy certain properties which lead to quasiunimodal functions. In fact, we can give the following necessary condition on the convergence:

Theorem 19 (see [4]). *If the pattern search method converges in the sense of Zangwill, independently of the choice of the point b^1 and of the value of $\delta > 0$, then every local minimum of the objective function is a global minimum as well.*

This assertion can be proved in an indirect way. For this end choose b^1 so that for every x in a δ_0-neighbourhood of b^1 we have

$$f(x) \geq f(b^1)$$

but there exists an $x^* \in R^n$ such that $f(x^*) < f(b^1)$. Choose now a $\delta \leq \delta_0$ then it can be seen from the given procedure that the generated sequence (b^m) does not have the δ_0-neighbourhood of b^1, thus neither the convergence criterium (a) nor (b) is satisfied.

$$\text{Q.e.d.}$$

If the level hyperplanes

$$A(y) = \{x \in R^n \mid f(x) = f(y)\}$$

contain singular points for some y then these sequence may become stationary before reaching a global minimum. Consequently, the quasiunimodality of f is not sufficient for the convergence of the method. In this context we can show that the following generalization of unimodality yields a sufficient condition for avoiding the case described above, hence for the convergence of the method.

Definition 11. A function $f: R^n \to R$ which has a continuous derivative is said to be *differentiably quasiunimodal* if there exists a set

$G^* \subseteq R^n$, $G^* \neq \phi$ such that for every $\bar{x} \in R^n \setminus G^*$ there exist an $\tilde{x} \in$ $\in bdG^*$ and a smooth piece of a Jordan curve $J(\bar{x}, \tilde{x})$ from $\bar{x}$ to $\tilde{x}$ such that

$$\frac{\partial f(x)}{\partial u} < 0 \quad \forall x \in J(\bar{x}, \tilde{x}), \quad x \neq \tilde{x}$$

where u is the direction of the semitangent J in x for increasing values of the parameter.

For $x^* \in G^*$ we have:

$$f(x^*) = \text{const} < f(x) \quad \forall x \in R^n \setminus G^*.$$

It is obvious that every differentiably quasiunimodal function is quasiunimodal, since we can set $G = R^n$ in Definition 10. Now we have

Theorem 20 (see [4]). *Suppose that* $f: R^n \to R$ *is differentiably quasiunimodal. Then the pattern search method converges in the sense of Zangwill, independently of the choice of the point* b^1 *and of the value of* $\delta > 0$.

Proof. Condition (a) is satisfied obviously. In order to check condition (b), consider a convergent subsequence $(b^{m_k}) \subset (b^m)$, $b^m \notin G^*$ $\forall m$, with

$$\lim_{k \to \infty} b^{m_k} = b'.$$

For differentiably quasiunimodal objective functions this subsequence can always be chosen in such a way that for a suitable $\epsilon(m_k) > 0$ we have

(5) $\qquad f(b^{m_k + 1}) + \epsilon(m_k) = f(b^{m_k}).$

Now let $b' \notin G^*$. Then it can be shown that

$$f(b^{m_k}) < f(b') + \epsilon(m_k)$$

for sufficiently large m_k. Then, using (5), we obtain

(6) $\qquad f(b^{m_k + 1}) < f(b').$

On the other hand, one can see from the described procedure that $(f(b^m))$ is decreasing sequence. By Lemma 4.1 in [16] (page 89) it follows for continuous functions f that

$$\lim_{m \to \infty} f(b^m) = f(b') \,,$$

a contradiction to (6), hence we have $b' \in G^*$.

REFERENCES

[1] C.R. Bector, On convexity, pseudo-convexity and quasiconvexity of composite functions, *Res. Rep.,* 10 (1971), Fac. of Com., University of Manitoba, Winnipeg.

[2] G. Donath – K.-H. Elster, Über Eigenschaften unimodaler Funktionen, *Wiss. Z.,* TH Ilmenau 18, 3 (1972), 103-120.

[3] G. Donath – K.-H. Elster, Über eine verallgemeinerung unimodaler Funktionen, *Godišnik na visšite techničeski učebni zavedenija* (Matematika), IX, 3 (1973), 7-21.

[4] G. Donath – K.-H. Elster, Zur Konvergenz eines Verfahrens der nichtlinearen optimierung, (in preparation).

[5] H.J. Greenberg – W.P. Pierskalla, A review of quasiconvex functions, *Op. Res.,* 19 (1971), 1553-1570.

[6] D.M. Himmelblau, *Applied nonlinear programming,* McGraw-Hill, Inc., New York 1972.

[7] R. Hooke – T.A. Jeeves, "Direct Search" solution of numerical and statistical problems, *Journ. ACM,* 8 (1962), 212-229.

[8] J. Kiefer, Sequential minimax search for a maximum, *Proc. Am. Math. Soc.,* 4 (1953), 502-506.

[9] P. Krolak – L. Cooper, An extension of Fibonaccian search to several variables, *Comm. ACM,* 6 (1963), 639-641.

[10] A.I. Kuzovkin, Obobščenie poiska fibonačči na mnogomernyj slučaj, *Ékon, i mat. metody,* 4 (1968), 931-940.

[11] O.L. Mangasarian, Pseudo-convex functions, *SIAM Journ. Contr.,* 3 (1965), 281-290.

[12] B. Martos, Quasi-convexity and quasi-monotonicity in non-linear programming, *Studia Sci. Math. Hungar.,* 2 (1967), 265-273.

[13] N. Sugie, An extension of Fibonaccian searching to multidimensional cases, *IEEE Transact. Autom. Contr.,* 9 (1964), 105.

[14] D.J. Wilde, *Optimum seeking methods,* Prentice-Hall, Inc., Englewood Cliffs, N.J. 1964.

[15] D.J. Wilde — C.S. Beightler, *Foundations of optimization,* Prentice-Hall, Inc., Englewood Cliffs, N. J. 1967.

[16] W.I. Zangwill, *Nonlinear programming — A unified approach,* Prentice-Hall, Inc., Englewood Cliffs, N.J. 1969.

K.H. Elster

Sektion Mathematik, Rechnentechnik und ökonomische Kybernetik. Technische Hochschule, 63 Ilmenau, DDR P.o. Box 327.

MINIMAX STOCHASTIC PROGRAMS WITH NONCONVEX NONSEPARABLE PENALTY FUNCTIONS

JITKA DUPAČOVÁ

1. We shall consider the situation where in the linear program

(1) $Ax = b$, $x \in \mathfrak{M}$, $c^T x = \text{maximum}$,

$\mathfrak{M}$ is a given bounded convex polyhedron whereas $A(m, n)$, $b(m, 1)$,
$c(n, 1)$ are random matrices, and the decision $x \in \mathfrak{M}$ is to be chosen independently on realization of these random matrices. One possible way
how to deal with such a situation is to penalize the violation of the constraints by a penalty function $\varphi(x, A, b)$ which is to be subtracted from
the corresponding value of the gain $c^T x$.

As to the functional form of the penalty, a quadratic function of the
discrepancy may be considered, or the proportionality to absolute value of
the discrepancy, i.e., the function $\varphi(x, A, b) = \sum_{i=1}^{m} q_i \left| \sum_{j=1}^{n} a_{ij} x_j - b_i \right|$,
$q_i \geqslant 0$, $1 \leqslant i \leqslant m$ (see D e m p s t e r [1]). The symmetry of the latter
function is often undesirable and the sign of the discrepancy is distin-
guished by different proportionality factors:

$$\varphi(x, A, b) = \sum_{i=1}^{m} q_i \left(\sum_{j=1}^{n} a_{ij}x_j - b_i \right)^- +$$

$$+ \sum_{i=1}^{m} q_{m+i} \left(\sum_{j=1}^{n} a_{ij}x_j - b_i \right)^+ ,$$

with $q_i + q_{m+i} \geqslant 0$, $1 \leqslant i \leqslant m$. (Here, u^+ stands for max $(0, u)$ and u^- for max $(0, -u)$.) The aim to get a sufficiently general form of the penalty and at the same time not to move far from the primary linear programming model has led to the choice of the penalty function $\varphi(x, A, b)$ as an optimal solution of the program

$$\min \{q^T y: \; My = b - Ax, \; y \geqslant 0\}$$

where M and q are given nonstochastic matrix and vector, respectively, i.e. to the two-stage problem with fixed recourse (Walkup and Wets [6]). Note that in all mentioned cases, the penalty function $\varphi(x, A, b)$ is for fixed A, b a convex function in x.

As to the simultaneous distribution F of the random matrices A, b, c suppose that our knowledge is not complete but limited only to the fact that the distribution F belongs to a given set $\mathscr{F}$. In such situations, it is possible to use Wald's minimax criterion, i.e., to choose the optimal decision $x \in \mathfrak{M}$ maximizing

$$\min_{F \in \mathscr{F}} E_F \{c^T x - \varphi(x, A, b)\} .$$

For the case of convex function φ, the problem was studied and formulated as a two-person zero-sum game in its normal form

$$G = \{\mathfrak{M}, \; \mathscr{F}, H\} ,$$

where for $x \in \mathfrak{M}$, $F \in \mathscr{F}$, the payoff function H equals

$$H(x, F) = E_F \{c^T x - \varphi(x, A, b)\}$$

(see Iosifescu and Theodorescu [2], Žáčková [7]). In some cases, the solution (= the optimal pure strategy of the first player) can be found by solving an ordinary (deterministic) linear program (see Žáčková

[7]). Theodorescu [5] generalized the results for the case of concave criterion function and concave constraints.

We shall treat the problem for a special class of penalty functions which are neither convex nor separable.

2. For the set of distributions $\mathcal{F}$ with a convex compact range $\mathcal{R} \subset E_N$ and a fixed mean value and for the class of functions ψ bounded on $\mathcal{R}$, it is possible to evaluate the maximal mean value $\max\limits_{F \in \mathcal{F}} E_F \psi(r)$ when generalizing Richter's approach formulated originally for the one-dimensional case (see R i c h t e r [4], I s i i [3]).

Theorem 1. *Suppose that*

(i) *$\mathcal{F}$ is a set of distribution functions of the random vector $r \in E_N$ with a convex compact range $\mathcal{R}$ and fixed mean value $E_F r = \bar{r}$ for all $F \in \mathcal{F}$; let $\bar{r} \in \text{int } \mathcal{R}$.*

(ii) *ψ is a bounded nonnegative function on $\mathcal{R}$.*

Let

$$\mathcal{L} = \left\{ l = (l_0, l_1, \ldots, l_N)^T : \sum_{i=1}^{N} l_i r_i + l_0 \geq \psi(r) \quad \text{for all } r \in \mathcal{R} \right\}.$$

Then

$$\max_{F \in \mathcal{F}} E_F \psi(r) = \inf_{l \in \mathcal{L}} \left[\sum_{i=1}^{N} l_i \bar{r}_i + l_0 \right].$$

Heuristically. The set $\mathcal{L}$ contains all hyperplanes in E_{N+1} that are above the graph of ψ. Then, evidently, the inequality

$$\max_{F \in \mathcal{F}} E_F \psi(r) \leq \inf_{l \in \mathcal{L}} \left[\sum_{i=1}^{N} l_i \bar{r}_i + l_0 \right]$$

is true. (Notice that the set $\mathcal{F}$ is convex and compact and $E_F \psi(r)$ is continuous on $\mathcal{F}$.)

Under additional assumption, we shall construct a discrete distribution $F^* \in \mathcal{F}$ and a vector $l^* \in \mathcal{L}$ such that

$$\max_{F \in \mathcal{F}} E_F \psi(r) = E_{F*} \psi(r) = \sum_{i=1}^{N} l_i^* \bar{r}_i + l_0^*$$

and, moreover, we shall see that the $\max\limits_{F \in \mathcal{F}} E_F \psi(r)$ can be evaluated as an optimal value of a linear program.

Theorem 2. *Let assumptions* (i), (ii) *of Theorem 1 hold. Suppose further that there is a nonoverlapping decomposition of* $\mathcal{R}$ *into convex compact polyhedrons* $\mathcal{R}_k$, $1 \le k \le K$, *and that there are convex continuous functions* ψ_k *with domains* $\mathcal{R}_k$, $1 \le k \le K$, *respectively, such that*

$$\psi(r) = \psi_k(r) \qquad \text{for} \qquad r \in \text{int } \mathcal{R}_k, \ 1 \le k \le K,$$

and on the boundary points

(2) $\qquad \psi(r) = \max \{\psi_k(r): k \in \{1, \dots, K\} \text{ such that } r \in \mathcal{R}_k \}.$

Let $r^{(h)}$, $1 \le h \le H$ *be all different extremal points of the polyhedrons* $\mathcal{R}_k$, $1 \le k \le K$.

Then $\max\limits_{F \in \mathcal{F}} E_F \psi(r)$ *equals to the maximal value of*

(3) $\qquad \sum_{h=1}^{H} y_h \psi(r^{(h)})$

subject to

(4) $\qquad \sum_{h=1}^{H} y_h r_i^{(h)} = \bar{r}_i, \qquad 1 \le i \le N$

(5) $\qquad \sum_{h=1}^{H} y_h = 1$

(6) $\qquad y_h \ge 0, \qquad 1 \le h \le H.$

Proof. Using Theorem 1 for the evaluation of $\max\limits_{F \in \mathcal{F}} E_F \psi(r)$ we have to find the minimum of

(7) $\qquad \sum_{i=1}^{N} l_i \bar{r}_i + l_0$

subject to $l \in \mathcal{L}$; i.e., subject to

(8) $\qquad \displaystyle\sum_{i=1}^{N} l_i r_i + l_0 \geqslant \psi(r) \qquad$ for all $\qquad r \in \mathcal{R}$.

Let $r^{(h)}$, $h \in \mathcal{H}_k \subset \{1, \ldots, H\}$ be all extremal points of the polyhedron $\mathcal{R}_k$, $1 \leqslant k \leqslant K$. Under our assumptions on the function ψ, condition (8) is equivalent to

(9) $\qquad \displaystyle\sum_{i=1}^{N} l_i r_i^{(h)} + l_0 \geqslant \psi_k(r^{(h)}), \qquad h \in \mathcal{H}_k, \quad 1 \leqslant k \leqslant K$.

Using (2), system (9) can be written as

$$\sum_{i=1}^{N} l_i r_i^{(h)} + l_0 \geqslant \psi(r^{(h)}), \qquad 1 \leqslant h \leqslant H,$$

and the problem reduces to a linear program; its dual program is the program (3), (4), (5), (6), which has evidently a nonempty bounded solution set, so that there exists the finite minimum of $\displaystyle\sum_{i=1}^{N} l_i \bar{r}_i + l_0$ on $\mathcal{L}$.

The optimal solution y^* of the program (3)-(6) produces the discrete distribution concentrated in the points $r^{(h)}$ with probabilities y_h^*, $1 \leqslant h \leqslant H$ which belongs to the subset of discrete distributions $\mathcal{F}^* \subset \mathcal{F}$ and realizes the maximal mean value $\max_{F \in \mathcal{F}} E_F \psi(r)$. There exists a basic optimal solution of (3)-(6) which does not contain more than $N + 1$ nonzero elements y_h what together with the Duality theorem of linear programming gives

Corollary. *Under assumptions of Theorem* 1

$$\max_{F \in \mathcal{F}} E_F \psi(r) = \max_{F \in \mathcal{F}^{(N+1)}} E_F \psi(r) = \min_{l \in \mathcal{L}} \left[\sum_{i=1}^{N} l_i \bar{r}_i + l_0 \right]$$

where $\mathcal{F}^{(N+1)} \subset \mathcal{F}$ is a set of all discrete distributions concentrated in at most $N + 1$ points.

Theorem 3. *Under assumptions of Theorem* 2, *let $\mathcal{R}$ be an N-dimensional interval and ψ be a nondecreasing function on $\mathcal{R}$, i.e., the implication*

(10) $z \leqslant y \Rightarrow \psi(z) \leqslant \psi(y)$

holds.

   Then there exists an optimal solution of (7), (8) *with* $l_i \geqslant 0$
$1 \leqslant i \leqslant N.$

   Proof. Let $\displaystyle\sum_{i=1}^{N} l_i \bar{r}_i + l_0$ attends its minimum on $\mathscr{L}$ for l^* such
that $l_k^* < 0, \ k \neq 0.$ Define

$$l_0^1 = l_0^* + l_k^* \bar{r}_k$$
$$l_i^1 = l_i^* \qquad 1 \leqslant i \leqslant N, \ i \neq k$$
$$l_k^1 = 0.$$

For all $r \in \mathscr{R}$ with $r_k \geqslant \bar{r}_k$

(11) $\displaystyle \psi(r) \leqslant \sum_{i=1}^{N} l_i^* r_i + l_0^* = \sum_{i \neq k} l_i^* r_i + l_0^* + l_k^* r_k \leqslant \sum_{i=1}^{N} l_i^1 r_i + l_0^1 .$

Let us consider now an arbitrary $r \in \mathscr{R}$ with $r_k \leqslant \bar{r}_k.$ Let
$\rho = (r_1, \ldots, r_{k-1}, \bar{r}_k, r_{k+1}, \ldots, r_N)^T.$ According to our assumptions
(namely, $\bar{r} \in \text{int } \mathscr{R}, \ \mathscr{R}$ interval), $\rho \in \mathscr{R}$ holds. Now, using (10), (11)

$$\sum_{i=1}^{N} l_i^1 r_i + l_0^1 \geqslant \psi(\rho) \geqslant \psi(r).$$

We have proved that $l^1 \in \mathscr{L};$ moreover,

$$\sum_{i=1}^{N} l_i^1 \bar{r}_i + l_0^1 = \sum_{i=1}^{N} l_i \bar{r}_i + l_0 = \min_{l \in \mathscr{L}} \left[\sum_{i=1}^{N} l_i \bar{r}_i + l_0 \right].$$

In the case when there is a $l_j^1 < 0, \ j \neq 0,$ we shall repeat the same procedure.

   3. Before discussing the possibility of using the results in stochastic
programming models we shall introduce an example which shows that the
nonconvex nonseparable penalty functions of considered type may be of
economic interest.

Example. Let the original linear program describe the problem of maximizing the gain $\sum_{j=1}^{n} c_j x_j$ subject to

(12) $Ax \leqslant \tilde{b}$

(13) $0 \leqslant x \leqslant b$

where constraints (12) are the (deterministic) conditions on the production process whereas the demand vector b in (13) varies randomly. Suppose that $c_j \geqslant 0$, $1 \leqslant j \leqslant n$, are given coefficients and that the producer knows only the mean value and the range of the random demand b, namely,

$$\beta_i' \leqslant b_i \leqslant \beta_i'' , \qquad a.s., \qquad Eb_i = \beta_i , \qquad 1 \leqslant i \leqslant n .$$

The excessive production is stored. The producer is in possession of one store-room and he rents additional ones according to his instantaneous need. In the latter case, the whole capacity of rented store-rooms is charged. The order of the available store-rooms is given in advance, e.g., in contracts or according to their quality.

This situation is described by the penalty function

$$\varphi(x, b) = 0 \qquad \text{for } \sum_{i=1}^{n} h_i^{(1)}(x_i - b_i)^+ < \alpha_1$$

$$= a_1 \qquad \text{for } \sum_{i=1}^{n} h_i^{(1)}(x_i - b_i)^+ \geqslant \alpha_1$$

$$\text{and } \sum_{i=1}^{n} h_i^{(2)}(x_i - b_i)^+ < \alpha_2$$

$$\cdots\cdots\cdots$$

$$= a_1 + \ldots + a_k \quad \text{for } \sum_{i=1}^{n} h_i^{(k)}(x_i - b_i)^+ \geqslant \alpha_k$$

$$\text{and } \sum_{i=1}^{n} h_i^{(k+1)}(x_i - b_i)^+ < \alpha_{k+1}$$

$$\cdots\cdots\cdots$$

$$= \sum_{k=1}^{K} a_k \qquad \text{for } \sum_{i=1}^{n} h_i^{(K)}(x_i - b_i)^+ \geqslant \alpha_K ,$$

where

$a_k > 0$ is the storage-charge for the k-th storage room,
$1 \leqslant k \leqslant K$

$h_i^{(k)} > 0, \ 1 \leqslant i \leqslant N, \ 1 \leqslant k \leqslant K$

and

$$0 < \frac{\alpha_1}{h_i^{(1)}} < \frac{\alpha_2}{h_i^{(2)}} < \ldots < \frac{\alpha_K}{h_i^{(K)}} \ , \qquad 1 \leqslant i \leqslant n \ .$$

The considered penalty function $\varphi(x, b) = \psi(r)$ is a piecewise linear, quasiconvex funttion in $r_i = (x_i - b_i)^+, \ 1 \leqslant i \leqslant n,$ and satisfies the assumptions of Theorem 2 and 3.

The transformed objective function

$$\min_{F \in \mathscr{F}} E_F \left\{ \sum_{j=1}^{n} c_j x_j - \varphi(x, b) \right\} = \sum_{j=1}^{n} c_j x_j - \max_{F \in \mathscr{F}} E_F \varphi(x, b) \ ,$$

where $\mathscr{F}$ is the set of distribution functions defined by (14), is to be maximized on the set $\mathfrak{M} = \{x \in E_n : x \geqslant 0, \ Ax \leqslant \tilde{b}\}$.

4. In the problem (1), let $a_{ij}, \ 1 \leqslant i \leqslant m, \ 1 \leqslant j \leqslant n,$ as well as $c_j,$ $1 \leqslant j \leqslant n,$ be given constants whereas $b_i, \ 1 \leqslant i \leqslant m,$ be random variables such that

(14) $Eb_i = \beta_i, \ \beta_i' \leqslant b_i \leqslant \beta_i'' \qquad a.s., \qquad \beta_i' < \beta_i'', \qquad 1 \leqslant i \leqslant m$

(herewith the set $\mathscr{F}$ is defined). Let the violation of constraints $Ax \leqslant b$ be penalized by the amount

(15) $\varphi(x, b) = \psi(r)$

where $r_i = \left(\sum_{j=1}^{n} a_{ij} x_j - b_i \right)^+, \ 1 \leqslant i \leqslant m,$ and the function ψ is a nonnegative nondecreasing piecewise convex function on $E_m^+, \ \psi(0) = 0,$ which satisfies the conditions of Theorem 2.

The original objective function $\sum_{j=1}^{n} c_j x_j$ is now transformed into a substantially new one

$$(16) \qquad \min_{F \in \mathcal{F}} E_F \left\{ \sum_{j=1}^{n} c_j x_j - \varphi(x, b) \right\} = \sum_{j=1}^{n} c_j x_j - \max_{F \in \mathcal{F}} E_F \varphi(x, b)$$

and the problem is to maximize function (16) subject to $x \in \mathfrak{M}$.

For fixed $x \in \mathfrak{M}$, the penalty function $\varphi(x, b)$ is a nonnegative, piecewise convex function of b. When applying Theorem 2 to the problem of maximizing the mean value $E_F \varphi(x, b)$ over set $\mathcal{F}$ with b in the place of r, the choice of $x \in \mathfrak{M}$ will affect the matrix of coefficients in the program (3)-(6). Any direct discussion of the solution and the optimal value of the program (3)-(6) with respect to parameter will be difficult (with exception of case $m = 2$). However, the procedure may evaluate the worst expected penalty for the given decision yielded by solving an ordinary linear program with suitable chosen right sides, e.g., with β_i', or β_i'', $1 \leq i \leq m$.

Another possibility is to apply Theorem 2 directly to the random discrepancies r and to the function $\psi(r)$ defined by (15). For fixed $x \in \mathfrak{M}$, assumption (14) evidently implies

$$(17) \qquad \left(\sum_{j=1}^{n} a_{ij} x_j - \beta_i'' \right)^+ \leq r_i \leq \left(\sum_{j=1}^{n} a_{ij} x_j - \beta_i' \right)^+ \qquad a.s., \qquad 1 \leq i \leq m$$

$$(18) \qquad \begin{aligned} \left(\sum_{j=1}^{n} a_{ij} x_j - \beta_i \right)^+ &\leq E r_i \leq \lambda_i \left(\sum_{j=1}^{n} a_{ij} x_j - \beta_i'' \right)^+ + \\ &+ (1 - \lambda_i) \left(\sum_{j=1}^{n} a_{ij} x_j - \beta_i' \right)^+, \qquad 1 \leq i \leq m, \end{aligned}$$

where

$$(19) \qquad \lambda_i = \frac{\beta_i - \beta_i'}{\beta_i'' - \beta_i'}, \qquad 1 \leq i \leq m.$$

According to Theorem 3, the maximal value of $E_G \psi(r)$ on the set of distributions $\mathscr{G}^x$ defined by (17), (18), (19) is attained for the distribution with mean values

$$
\begin{aligned}
Er_i = \bar{r}_i(x) &= \lambda_i \Big(\sum_{j=1}^n a_{ij} x_j - \beta_i'' \Big)^+ + \\
&+ (1 - \lambda_i) \Big(\sum_{j=1}^n a_{ij} x_j - \beta_i' \Big)^+ , \qquad 1 \leqslant i \leqslant m .
\end{aligned}
$$

(20)

The decision vector x appears on the right side of constraints (4) and because of (17), it may affect some of coefficients $r_i^{(h)}$, too. In the case considered now it is much easier to draw conslusions concerning the $\max\limits_{G \in \mathscr{G}^x} E_G \psi(r)$ than in the case mentioned before. Unfortunately, even for fixed $x \in \mathfrak{M}$, there is not one-to-one correspondence between the sets of distributions $\mathscr{G}^x$ and $\mathscr{F}$, so that the

$$
\max_{x \in \mathfrak{M}} \Big\{ \sum_{j=1}^n c_j x_j - \max_{G \in \mathscr{G}^x} E_G \psi(r) \Big\}
$$

underestimates the optimal value of the objective function (16) on $\mathfrak{M}$ and the procedure yields a suboptimal solution only.

For fixed $x \in \mathfrak{M}$, it is possible to give an assumption under which the equality

$$
\max_{G \in \mathscr{G}^x} E_G \psi(r) = \max_{F \in \mathscr{F}} E_F \varphi(x, b)
$$

holds.

Theorem 4. Let $x \in \mathfrak{M}$ be fixed, $\sum_{j=1}^n a_{ij} x_j \leqslant \beta_i''$, $1 \leqslant i \leqslant m$. Let in the problem (3)-(6)

$$
r_i^{(h)} = 0 \qquad \text{for} \qquad h \in N_i
$$

$$
r_i^{(h)} > 0 \qquad \text{for} \qquad h \notin N_i ,
$$

where $N_i \subset \{1, \ldots, H\}$, $N_i \neq \phi$, $1 \leqslant i \leqslant m$, and y_h^x, $1 \leqslant h \leqslant H$, be the optimal solution, i.e.

$$\max_{G \in \mathscr{G}^x} E_G \psi(r) = \sum_{h=1}^{H} y_h^x(r^{(h)}) \, .$$

Then the condition

(21)
$$\sum_{h \in N_i} y_h^x \geqslant \lambda_i, \qquad 1 \leqslant i \leqslant m \, ,$$

is necessary and sufficient for the equality

$$\max_{G \in \mathscr{G}^x} E_G \psi(r) = \max_{F \in \mathscr{F}} E_F \varphi(x, b)$$

to hold.

Proof. Define

(22)
$$b_i^{(h)} = \sum_{i=1}^{n} a_{ij} x_j - r_i^{(h)} \, , \qquad h \notin N_i, \ 1 \leqslant i \leqslant m \, .$$

In case $h \in N_i$, there is no one-to-one correspondence between $r_i^{(h)}$ and $b_i^{(h)}$, but evidently

(23)
$$\sum_{j=1}^{n} a_{ij} x_j \leqslant b_i^{(h)} \leqslant \beta_i'' \, , \qquad 1 \leqslant i \leqslant m \, .$$

We search for a discrete distribution belonging to the set $\mathscr{F}$ which is concentrated with probabilities y_h^x in the points $b^{(h)}$ that satisfy (22), (23). If there is such a distribution, it realizes the maximal mean value $E_G \psi(r)$ evaluated through solving the program (3)-(6).

The points $b^{(h)}$ satisfying (22), (23) belong to the range prescribed by (14). It remains to check the condition

$$\sum_{h=1}^{H} y_h^x b^{(h)} = \beta \, .$$

Evidently, using (22) and (4)

$$\sum_{h=1}^{H} y_h^x b_i^{(h)} = \sum_{h \in N_i} y_h^x b_i^{(h)} + \sum_{h \notin N_i} y_h^x \sum_{j=1}^{n} a_{ij} x_j - \sum_{h \notin N_i} y_h^x r_i^{(h)} =$$

$$= \sum_{h \in N_i} y_h^x b_i^{(h)} + (1 - \mu_i) \sum_{j=1}^{n} a_{ij} x_j - \sum_{h=1}^{H} y_h^x r_i^{(h)} =$$

$$= \sum_{h \in N_i} y_h^x b_i^{(h)} + (1 - \mu_i) \sum_{j=1}^{n} a_{ij} x_j - \bar{r}_i \, ,$$

where $\mu_i = \sum_{h \in N_i} y_h^x, \quad 1 \leqslant i \leqslant m.$

According to (23),

$$\sum_{j=1}^{n} a_{ij} x_j - \bar{r}_i \leqslant \sum_{h=1}^{H} y_h^x b_i^{(h)} \leqslant \mu_i \beta_i'' + (1 - \mu_i) \sum_{j=1}^{n} a_{ij} x_j - \bar{r}_i \, .$$

The necessary condition for the assertion of Theorem 4 to hold is

(24) $$\sum_{j=1}^{n} a_{ij} x_j - \bar{r}_i \leqslant \beta_i \leqslant \mu_i \beta_i'' + (1 - \mu_i) \sum_{j=1}^{n} a_{ij} x_j - \bar{r}_i \, , \quad 1 \leqslant i \leqslant m \, .$$

For $\sum_{j=1}^{n} a_{ij} x_j \leqslant \beta_i'$, $\bar{r}_i = 0$ and $\mu_i = 1$, so that both inequalities in (24) are satisfied.

Let $\sum_{j=1}^{n} a_{ij} x_j > \beta_i';$ then

$$\sum_{j=1}^{n} a_{ij} x_j - \bar{r}_i = \sum_{j=1}^{n} a_{ij} x_j - (1 - \lambda_i) \Big(\sum_{j=1}^{n} a_{ij} x_j - \beta_i' \Big) =$$

$$= \lambda_i \sum_{j=1}^{n} a_{ij} x_j + (1 - \lambda_i) \beta_i' \leqslant \beta_i \, .$$

The equality sign holds for $\sum_{j=1}^{n} a_{ij} x_j = \beta_i''$. As to the second inequality in (24), we have

$$\mu_i \beta_i'' + (1 - \mu_i) \sum_{j=1}^{n} a_{ij} x_j - \bar{r}_i = \mu_i \Big(\beta_i'' - \sum_{j=1}^{n} a_{ij} x_j \Big) +$$

$$+ \sum_{j=1}^{n} a_{ij} x_j - (1 - \lambda_i) \Big(\sum_{j=1}^{n} a_{ij} x_j - \beta_i' \Big) =$$

$$= (\mu_i - \lambda_i) \Big(\beta_i'' - \sum_{j=1}^{n} a_{ij} x_j \Big) + \beta_i \geqslant \beta_i$$

iff the condition (21) holds. The equality sign occures for $\mu_i = \lambda_i$ or

$$\sum_{j=1}^{n} a_{ij} x_j = \beta_i''.$$

The condition (21) is sufficient: keep (22) and define for $h \in N_i$

$$b_i^{(h)} = \nu_i \max \left(\sum_{j=1}^{n} a_{ij} x_j, \beta_i' \right) + (1 - \nu_i) \beta_i'', \qquad 1 \leqslant i \leqslant m,$$

where $\nu_i = 1 - \dfrac{\lambda_i}{\mu_i}$.

Then $\displaystyle\sum_{h=1}^{H} y_h^x b^{(h)} = \beta$.

Irrespective of Theorem 4, the possibility of making decisions by means of the described procedure remains still open from the numerical point of view.

REFERENCES

[1] M.A.H. Dempster, On stochastic programming I. Static linear programming under risk, *J. Math. Analysis Appl.*, 21 (1968), 304-343.

[2] M. Iosifescu – R. Theodorescu, Sur la programmation linéaire, *C.R. Acad. Sci. Paris,* 256 (1963), 4831-4833.

[3] K. Isii, Inequalities of the types of Chebyshev and Cramér – Rao and Mathematical Programming, *Ann. Inst. Stat. Math.,* XVI (1964), 277-293.

[4] H. Richter, Parameterfreie Abschätzung und Realisierung von Erwartungswerten, *Bl. Dtsch. Ges. Versicherungsmath.,* 3 (1957), 147-162.

[5] R. Theodorescu, Minimax solutions of random convex programs, *Atti Acad. Naz. Lincei,* Ser. 8, 46 (1969), 689-692.

[6] D. Walkup – R. Wets, Stochastic programs with recourse, *J. SIAM Appl. Math.,* 15 (1967), 1299-1314.

[7] J. Žáčková, On minimax solutions of stochastic linear programming problems, *Časopis pro pěstování matematiky*, 91 (1966), 423-430.

Jitka Dupačová

Charles University 18600 Praha 8, Sokolovská 83, Czechoslovakia.

COLLOQUIA MATHEMATICA SOCIETATIS JÁNOS BOLYAI

12. PROGRESS IN OPERATIONS RESEARCH, EGER (HUNGARY), 1974.

GPSTEM: AN INTERACTIVE MULTI-OBJECTIVE OPTIMIZATION METHOD

J. FICHEFET

ABSTRACT

The purpose of this paper is to develop, for the linear multiobjective programming (MOP) problem, an interactive method of solution which makes allowance for the decision-makers' psychological characteristics. At first we present some suggestions made by several authors to improve the classical theory of firms. In the light of those suggestions, we next discuss some methods of solution of the MOP problem, particularly the goal programming and STEM methods. We then propose our method named GPSTEM as it is based on goal programming and STEM. GPSTEM explores the efficient solutions that give to the objective functions values close to satisfying levels imposed by the decision-makers, it also provides an equilibrium solution resulting from a bimatrix game which can be useful in the case of complete desagreement among the decision-makers.

1. INTRODUCTION

In the classical theory of firms, the hypotheses about the entrepreneur's rationality can be reduced to two assertions [6]: (i) the entrepreneur tries to maximize profit; (ii) he has a perfect knowledge of the market. This means that the entrepreneur knows all alternatives and their consequences and that, confronted with a pair of alternatives, he will choose the one which yields the larger profit.

As Simon points out [19], the theory assumes nothing about the psychological characteristics of the entrepreneur. The factors that determine his behaviour (apart from those already mentioned) are entirely external to him. He is faced with determinate supply schedules for factors of production, demand schedules for his products, and a technologically determined production function. But neither his intelligence nor his personality are taken into account by the theory in order to predict his behaviour. This is the reason why several authors have proposed to improve the classical theory by substituting the principle of rationality by a principle of bounded rationality [19]: "The capacity of the human mind for formulating and solving complex problems is very small compared with the size of the problems whose solution is required for objectively rational behaviour in the real world — or even for a reasonable approximation to such objective rationality". Two consequences follow immediately: (i) the entrepreneur behaves rationally with respect to a simplified model of the real situation, the construction of which is certainly related to his psychological properties as a perceiving, thinking and learning animal; (ii) human rationality is subject to practical limits which are not static but depend upon the organizational environment in which decision-making takes place. We make two main assumptions [6]:

(i) Profit is important but the entrepreneur may not care to maximize it. Instead he wants to attain a satisfactory level of profit (Gordon, Simon and Marpolis). As Simon writes [20], models of satisfactory behaviour are richer than models of maximizing behaviour, because they treat not only the equilibrium but also the method of reaching it. He also notes that psychological studies of the formation and change of aspiration levels provide the propositions:

(a) When performance falls short of the level of aspiration, search behaviour (particularly search for new alternatives of action) is induced;

(b) At the same time, the level of aspiration begins to adjust itself downward until goals reach levels that are practically attainable. Here, it has to be noticed that the classical theory leaves ambiguous whether it is a short-term profit or a long-term profit that is to be maximized [20]. But in the case of a satisfactory profit, the level from which the profit becomes satisfactory is variable [6] and, in the short-term, an utility function can be defined: this function can take two values depending on whether the profit is sufficient or not.

(ii) The firm is a cooperative system (Papandréou). But a firm being an organization, the groups forming the coalition may enter into conflict as they have a real need for common decisions, different goals and different faculties of perceiving reality [19]. For example, if we are interested in models of prices and production, we may suppose that the firm is formed with three groups: the first one has a profit objective, the second one a sales objective and the third one a production objective. It is not vain to suppose that each group is able to find a satisfactory level for his objective: production may not vary too much from one period to the following one, it has to take at least a minimum value, etc... It can thus be supposed that the firm is a learning being [6] and that, for a given period, the objectives are functions: (a) of the objectives during the last period, (b) of the experience of the firm (groups forming it) concerning the pursuit of the objectives during the last period, and (c) of the experience of similar firms.

The assimilation of a firm to a cooperative system leads naturally to problems which are termed multi-objective programming (MOP) problems in mathematical programming. In a MOP problem, each decision-maker i among a body of N decision-makers wants to maximize an objective function $f_i(x)$ when x is restricted to vary in a subset X of R^n.

The are several methods of solution of the MOP problem (for a survey, see [18]). By the light of the above considerations, we shall discuss some of these methods — particularly the goal programming approach and the

STEM approach – in Section 2. The discussion will help us to derive in Section 3 a new method which we have called GPSTEM (Goal Programming Step Method). We shall suppose that the decision-makers' objective functions are linear:

$$f_i(x) = \sum_{j=1}^{n} c_j^i x_j, \quad x = (x_1, x_2, \ldots, x_n)' \in X \subset R^n ,$$

$$i = 1, 2, \ldots, N ,$$

and that X is a convex subset of R^n determined by linear constraints and constraint $x \geqslant 0$ for each $x \in X$.

2. DISCUSSION OF SOME METHODS OF SOLUTION OF THE MOP PROBLEM

2.1. *Goal programming* [5], [13]

In this approach, evey decision-maker i settles a satisfactory level (called a goal) M_i for his objective. The body of decision-makers tries then to determine a point $x^* \in X$ so that, in the space R^N of values of the objectives, the point $f(x^*) = (f_1(x^*), \ldots, f_N(x^*))'$ be as close to the point $M = (M_1, \ldots, M_N)'$ as possible. This means that the decision-makers choose a metric in R^N:

$$\forall u, v \in R^N : d_p(u, v) = \left(\sum_{i=1}^{N} |u_i - v_i|^p \right)^{\frac{1}{p}} , \quad 1 \leqslant p < \infty ,$$

or

$$\forall u, v \in R^N : d_\infty(u, v) = \max_{i \in \{1, \ldots, N\}} |u_i - v_i| ,$$

and then seek a point $x^* \in X$ such that

$$d_p[f(x^*), M] = \min_{x \in X} d_p[f(x), M] ,$$

or

$$d_\infty[f(x^*), M] = \min_{x \in X} d_\infty[f(x), M] .$$

For example, if $p = 1$, the optimization problem is equivalent to the linear program

$$(1) \qquad \min \sum_{i=1}^{N} (y_i^+ + y_i^-)$$

subject to the linear constraints

$$(2) \qquad f_i(x) - y_i^+ + y_i^- = M_i \, ,$$

$$(3) \qquad x \in X, \ y_i^+ \geqslant 0, \ y_i^- \geqslant 0, \quad i = 1, 2, \ldots, N \, .$$

The variables y_i^+ and y_i^- may eventually be weighted.

In this method, the M_i must be considered as the best satisfactory levels for the objectives. The use of satisfactory levels is an advantage of the method since a linear program such as (1)-(3) will generally provide a solution that is reasonable in practice. The main disadvantage is that the decision-makers are forced to choose a metric in R^N. For example, although they are regularly equivalent, the metric d_1, d_2 and d_∞ will not give in general the same solutions and a priori it can not be said that one metric will furnish a more reasonable solution than another metric. Of course, each decision-maker i could fix an interval of variation for M_i and then the body of decision-makers could investigate the solutions corresponding to different values of the M_i but the goal programming approach does not supply any systematic way for doing this.

We think that another disadvantage of the method is that decision-makers ignore the maximum values $\bar{f}_i$ of their objectives $f_i(x)$ when $x \in X$. Indeed we believe that the knowledge of these $\bar{f}_i$ could be a good stimulus for the decision-makers to search for new alternatives of action.

2.2. STEM *Method* [4]

STEM is an iterative method. Each iteration step consists of two phases: a calculation phase and a decision phase. Before the first iteration step, the linear programs

$$\max_{x \in X} f_i(x), \qquad i = 1, \ldots, N \, ,$$

should be solved ($\tilde{x}^i$ will denote hereafter their optimal solutions) and a payoff table T should be constructed. The element in the i-th row and i-th column of T is the value of $f_j(x)$ for $x = \tilde{x}^j$. The point $\tilde{x} = = (\tilde{x}^1, \ldots, \tilde{x}^N)$ is called the "ideal solution" or the "shadow maximum".

Calculation phase

In the k-th iteration step the decision-makers seek the feasible solution x^k which is the "nearest", in the minimax sense, to the shadow maximum $\tilde{x}$, i.e. the solution of the linear program

$$\min z$$

subject to

$$z \geqslant w_j[\bar{f}_j - f_j(x)], \qquad j = 1, \ldots, N,$$

$$z \geqslant 0, \ z \in X^k.$$

$X^0 = X$ and the w_j are local weights defined from the payoff table and give the relative importance of the distances to the optima:

$$w_j = \frac{p_j}{\sum\limits_{i=1}^{N} p_i}, \quad p_j = \frac{\bar{f}_j - m_j}{\bar{f}_j} \frac{1}{\left(\sum\limits_{i=1}^{N} (c_i^j)^2\right)^{\frac{1}{2}}},$$

where m_j is the minimum value in row j of table T.

Decision phase

The compromise solution x^k is proposed to the body of decision-makers. If some values $f_j(x^k)$ are satisfactory and others are not, one decision-maker, let him be m, must accept a certain amount of relaxation Δf_m of his satisfactory level $f_m(x^k)$. The weight w_m is then set to 0 and the feasible region

$$X^{k+1} = \{x \in X^k \mid f_m(x) \geqslant f_m(x^k) - \Delta f_m \qquad \text{and}$$

$$f_j(x) \geqslant f_j(x^k) \qquad \text{for} \qquad j \neq m\}$$

is prepared for the next iteration step.

Let us note that

(i) STEM makes implicit allowance for the psychological characteristics of the decision-makers (see decision phase);

(ii) the metric chosen in the calculation phase has but a local importance since the method provides in fact the possibility of exploring a set of compromise solutions called efficient solutions. Let us recall that a point $x^* \in X$ is *efficient* if and only if there exists no other point $x \in X$ such that

$$f_i(x) \geqslant f_i(x^*) \quad \text{for all} \quad i \in \{1, \dots, N\},$$

$$f_i(x) > f_i(x^*) \quad \text{for at least one} \quad i \in \{1, \dots, N\};$$

(iii) a possible disadvantage of STEM is that, in the 0-th iteration step, the decision-makers obtain a compromise solution x^0 such that many of the $f_i(x^0)$ are very far from satisfactory levels; this may lead in particular to a complete disagreement among the decision-makers after some iteration steps.

2.3. *Other methods*

We shall indicate some other methods of solution of the MOP problem:

(i) Exterior branching method [1], [15]: it is a STEM-like method for the nonlinear MOP problem.

(ii) Interactive multi-objective optimization method of Geoffrion, Dyer and Feinberg [7], [8], [11]: the method supposes the existence of a preference function defined on the set of values of the objective functions; although that preference function remains implicit, the body of decision-makers must be able to provide some information about it in each iteration step.

(iii) Methods derived from the simplex method that calculate efficient solutions [9], [17]: although they furnish compromise solutions, they do not include a process to explore the set of efficient solutions.

(iv) A method derived from game theory [2]: the method constructs N efficient solutions in considering the payoff table of the STEP method as the matrix of game but the decision-makers do not control the exploration of the set of efficient solutions.

3. THE GPSTEM METHOD

We shall suppose here that:

(i) $f_i(x) < +\infty$ for each $i \in \{1, \ldots, N\}$ and each $x \in X$;

(ii) the set of efficient solutions corresponding to the linear objective functions $f_i(x)$, $x \in X$, is not empty; this is the case for example when X is not empty and is bounded;

(iii) the polar set

$$C^* = \{u \in R^n \,|\, u'c \geqslant 0 \quad \text{for all} \quad c \in C\}$$

of the set $C = \{c^1, c^2, \ldots, c^N\}$ is a polyhedral cone, this assumption allows us to assert [17] that an optimal solution of the linear program

$$\max_{x \in X} \sum_{j=1}^{N} \lambda_j f_j(x), \quad \text{with all} \quad \lambda_j > 0,$$

is efficient;

(iv) for a reason which will be evident later, there are more than two decision-makers (when $N = 2$, it is possible to generate all efficient solutions through simple parametric linear programming [10]).

At the start of GPSTEM, each decision-maker i is asked to fix a best satisfactory level M_i $(i = 1, \ldots, N)$ for his objective. Then GPSTEM explores a set of compromise solutions which will be referred as M-efficient solutions, where $M = (M_1, \ldots, M_N)'$.

By definition, a point $x^* \in X$ is an *M-efficient point* if there exists no $x \in X$ such that

$$|M_i - f_i(x)| \leqslant |M_i - f_i(x^*)| \quad \text{for all} \quad i \in \{1, \ldots, N\},$$

$$|M_i - f_i(x)| \leqslant |M_i - f_i(x^*)| \quad \text{for at least one} \quad i \in \{1, \ldots, N\}.$$

We shall first prove some interesting properties of M-efficient solutions.

Theorem 1. *Let* $U = \{f(x) = (f_1(x), \ldots, f_N(x))' | x \in X\}$. *If* $M \in U$, *then a point* $x^* \in X$ *such that*

$$f_i(x^*) = M_i, \quad i = 1, \ldots, N,$$

is an M-*efficient point.*

Proof. Let us suppose that x^* is not M-efficient. Then there exists at least one $x \in X$ such that

$$|M_i - f_i(x)| \leqslant |M_i - f_i(x^*)| = 0 \quad \text{for all} \quad i \in \{1, \ldots, N\},$$

$$|M_i - f_i(x)| < |M_i - f_i(x^*)| = 0 \quad \text{for at least one}$$

$$i \in \{1, \ldots, N\}.$$

The last inequality is impossible so that x^* is necessarily M-efficient.

Theorem 2. *Let* V *be the set of points* $v \in R^N$ *such that*

$$v_i \leqslant \max_{x \in X} f_i(x) = \bar{f}_i, \quad i = 1, \ldots, N$$

and such that the system

$$f_i(x) \geqslant v_i, \quad \text{for all} \quad i \in \{1, \ldots, N\},$$

$$f_i(x) > v_i, \quad \text{for at least one} \quad i \in \{1, \ldots, N\},$$

has no solution in x. *If* $M \in V$, *then every* M-*efficient point is efficient.*

Proof. Let us suppose that $x^* \in X$ is M-efficient but not efficient. Then, by definition of an efficient point, there exists an $x \in X$ such that

(4) $\qquad f_i(x) \geqslant f_i(x^*) \quad \text{for all} \quad i \in \{1, \ldots, N\},$

(5) $\qquad f_i(x) > f_i(x^*) \quad \text{for at least one} \quad i \in \{1, \ldots, N\}.$

But $M \in V$ so that, for each $x \in X$

(6) $\quad\bullet\qquad f_i(x) \leqslant M_i \quad \text{and} \quad f_i(x^*) \leqslant M_i \quad \text{for all} \quad i \in \{1, \ldots, N\},$

It follows from (4)-(6) that

(7) $\quad |M_i - f_i(x)| \leqslant |M_i - f_i(x^*)| \quad$ for all $\quad i \in \{1, \ldots, N\}$,

$\quad\quad\quad |M_i - f_i(x)| < |M_i - f_i(x^*)| \quad$ for at least one $\quad i \in \{1, \ldots, N\}$,

which contradicts the fact that x^* is M-efficient and thus proves the theorem.

Theorem 3. *An optimal solution of the program*

(8) $\quad \min\limits_{x \in X} d_p[f(x), M], \quad 1 \leqslant p < \infty,$

is M-efficient.

Proof. Let us suppose that $x^* \in X$ is an optimal solution of program (8) but is not M-efficient. Then, there exists $x \in X$ such that

$\quad\quad |M_i - f_i(x)|^p \leqslant |M_i - f_i(x^*)|^p \quad$ for each $\quad i \in \{1, \ldots, N\}$,

$\quad\quad |M_i - f_i(x)|^p < |M_i - f_i(x^*)|^p \quad$ for at least one $\quad i$.

Adding these inequalities, we get

$$\sum_{i=1}^{N} |M_i - f_i(x)|^p < \sum_{i=1}^{N} |M_i - f_i(x^*)|^p$$

which contradicts the fact that x^* is an optimal solution of program (8).

The following theorem will also be basic in GPSTEM

Theorem 4. *If x^* is an optimal solution of the program*

(9) $\quad \min\limits_{x \in X} d_1(M, f) = \min\limits_{x \in X} \sum_{i=1}^{N} |M_i - f_i(x)|,$

then x^* is also optimal for the program

(10) $\quad \min \sum_{i \neq j} |M_i - f_i(x)| + |M_j - \Delta M_j - f_j(x)|,$

where

$$\Delta M_j = M_j - f_j(x^*).$$

– 326 –

Proof. Let us first note that

$$\sum_{i \neq j} |M_i - f_i(x^*)| + |M_j - \Delta M_j - f_j(x^*)| = \sum_{i \neq j} |M_i - f_i(x^*)| .$$

It follows that if x^* is not optimal for (10), then there exists $\bar{x} \in X$ such that

$$\sum_{i \neq j} |M_i - f_i(\bar{x})| + |M_j - \Delta M_j - f_j(\bar{x})| < \sum_{i \neq j} |M_i - f_i(x^*)| .$$

But

$$|M_j - \Delta M_j - f_j(\bar{x})| \geqslant |M_j - f_j(\bar{x})| - |\Delta M_j|$$

so that

$$\sum_{i=1}^{N} |M_i - f_i(\bar{x})| - |\Delta M_j| < \sum_{i \neq j} |M_i - f_i(x^*)|$$

and

$$\sum_{i=1}^{N} |M_i - f_i(\bar{x})| < \sum_{i=1}^{N} |M_i - f_i(x^*)|$$

which contradicts the fact that x^* is optimal for (9).

We can now describe the GPSTEM method

Step 0. Find the optimal solutions $\bar{x}^i$ of the linear programs

$$\max_{x \in X} f_i(x) , \qquad i = 1, \ldots , N$$

and form the payoff matrix A in which the element in row i and column j has value $f_i(\bar{x}^j)$ $(i, j = 1, 2, \ldots , N)$.

Step 1. Ask the decision-makers to provide their best satisfactory levels M_i for their respective objectives and choose metric d_1 to find a first compromise solution x^0, i.e. solve*

---

*The y_i^+ and y_i^- variables may eventually be weighted.

$$(11) \qquad \min z = \sum_{i=1}^{N} (y_i^+ + y_i^-)$$

$$(12) \qquad f_i(x) - y_i^+ + y_i^- = M_i$$

$$(13) \qquad x \in X, \ y_i^+ \geqslant 0, \ y_i^- \geqslant 0, \qquad i = 1, \ldots, N.$$

Since the decision-makers are thinking people, we can suppose that $M \in U \cup V$, i.e. the y_i^+ variables in the optimal solution of (11)-(13) have zero value.*

If $y_i^- > 0$ for at least one i, set $E = \phi$ and go to Step 2. If $y_i^- = 0$ for each i, go to Step 5 with $x^e = x^0$.

Step 2. For each $j \in \{1, \ldots, N\} \setminus E$, solve the parametric linear program $(\Theta_j \geqslant 0)$

$$\min z_j = \sum_{i=1}^{N} y_i^-$$

$$f_i(x) - y_i^- = M_i - \Theta_i \delta_{ij}$$

$$x \in X, \ y_i^- \geqslant 0, \qquad i = 1, \ldots, N,$$

to find the value Θ_{j_m} for which $z_j = 0$. Save the intervals of variation of Θ_j

$$[0, \Theta_{j_1}], [\Theta_{j_2}, \Theta_{j_3}], \ldots, [\Theta_{j_{n-1}} - \Theta_{j_m}]$$

the end-points of which imply changes of basis and save also the corresponding simplex tables. The optimal solutions of the above linear programs for $\Theta_j = 0$ are x^k. The value

$$\bar{M}_j(k) = M_j - \Theta_{j_m}$$

would be the worst result obtained by decision-maker j if the other decision-makers force him to relax his claim to the maximum, i.e. as far as his $y_j^- = 0$. Hereafter, $\tilde{x}^j$ will denote the solution corresponding to $\Theta_j = \Theta_{j_m}$.

---

* *If always $y_i^+ > 0$ for at least one i, give x^0 to the decision-makers and then stop.

Step 3. Form the matrix B in which the element in the i-th row and j-th column is $f_i(\tilde{x}^j)$. Then determine an equilibrium of the bimatrix game (A, B), i.e. a pair of mixed strategies (u^*, v^*) such that, for any other mixed strategies, u and v,

$$u'Av^* \leqslant (u^*)'Av^* \, ,$$

$$(u^*)'Bv \leqslant (u^*)'Bv^* \, .$$

This can be done by means of L e m k e 's and H o w s o n 's algorithm [16].

Step 4. Solve the linear program

$$\max_{x \in X} \sum_{i=1}^{N} u_i^* f_i(x) \, .$$

Its optimal solution x^e will be called an equilibrium efficient solution.

Step 5. Propose x^k and x^e to the decision-makers. If they find x^k satisfactory, stop. If not, there are three possibilities:

(i) All y_i^- corresponding to x^k are 0. Then prepare an exploration of the efficient points "close to" x^k through determining, for each i and with the help of parametric linear programming, the maximum possible value of M_i for which y_i^- still remains 0. If all these maximum values are equal to their respective M_i, then the decision-makers have to adopt x^e as a compromise solution. If not, set $E = \phi$ and $k = 0$, replace each M_i by its possible maximum value and go to Step 2.

(ii) If $y_i^- > 0$ for at least one i and if a decision-maker, let him be q, agrees to relax his satisfactory level M_q, go to Step 6.

(iii) If $y_i^- > 0$ for at least one i and if no decision-maker agrees to relax his satisfactory level, then the decision-makers have to adopt x^e as a compromise solution.

Step 6. Let

$$\Delta M_q > M_q - f_q(x^k)$$

be the amount of relaxation of the level M_q. Find the interval

$I = [\Theta_{q_r}, \Theta_{q_{r+1}}]$ such that $\Delta M_q \in I$. The basic compromise solution x^{k+1} of the next iteration step follows immediately. Replace M_q by $M_q - \Delta M_q$, k by $k+1$ and set $E = \{q\}$ and $\bar{M}_q(k) = \bar{M}_q(k-1)$. Then go to Step 2.

The GPSTEM method has not yet been tested with large real multi-objective problems. However, as the decision-makers provide their best satisfactory levels, we think that GPSTEM will guide them to adopt a compromise solution within fewer iteration steps than STEM. On the other hand, the bimatrix games (A, B), although being not of prime importance in GPSTEM, seem interesting to us. In fact, some decision-makers might fear to arrive at a complete disagreement and to be forced to adopt a prejudicial equilibrium efficient solution. Thus they might prefer to relax their claims.

The bimatrix games (A, B) are to be considered as games opposing the body of decision-makers to nature. A is the payoff matrix of the decision makers and B is the payoff matrix of nature. Nature tries to guide the body of decision-makers to the least satisfactory objective levels. The results of the parametric programming Step 2 may considerably help the decision-makers in their exploration.

REFERENCES

[1] J.P. Aubin, Closest efficient decisions to the shadow minimum for a multiobjective problem, *WP* 72-6, *European Institute for Advanced Studies in Management*, Brussels, February 1972.

[2] S.M. Belenson − K.C. Kapur, An algorithm for solving multicriterion linear programming problems with examples, *Operational Research Quartely*, 24 (1973), 65-77.

[3] R. Benayoun − J. Tergny, Mathematical programming with multi-objective functions: a solution by P.O.P. (Progressive Orientation Procedure), *Revue Metra*, 9 (1970), 279-299.

[4] R. Benayoun – J. de Montgolfier – J. Tergny – O. Laritchev, Linear programming with multiple objective functions: step method (STEM), *Mathematical Programming,* 1 (1971), 366-375.

[5] A. Charnes – W.W. Cooper, *Management models and industrial applications of linear programming,* Vol. 1, John Wiley, New York, 1961.

[6] R.M. Cyert – J.G. March, *A behavioral theory of the firm,* Prentice-Hall, Englewood Cliffs, New Jersey, 1963.

[7] J. S. Dyer, Interactive goal programming, *Management Science,* 19 (1972), 62-70.

[8] J.S. Dyer, A time-sharing computer program for the solution to the multiple criteria problem, *Management Science,* 19 (1973), 1379-1383.

[9] J.P. Evans – R.E. Steuer, A revised simplex method for linear multiple objective programs, *Mathematical Programming,* 5 (1973), 54-72.

[10] A.M. Geoffrion, Solving bicriterion mathematical programs, *Operations Research,* 15 (1967), 39-54.

[11] A.M. Geoffrion – J.S. Dyer – A. Feinberg, An interactive approach for multi-criterion optimization, with an application to the operation of an academic department, *Management Science,* 19 (1972), 357-368.

[12] S.C. Huang, Note on the mean-square strategy for vector-valued objective functions, *Journal of Optimization Theory and Applications,* 9 (1972), 364-366.

[13] Y. Ijiri, *Management goals and accounting for control,* North-Holland, Amsterdam, 1965.

[14] J.G. March – H.A. Simon, *Organizations,* John Wiley, New York, 1958.

[15] B. Naslund, A method for solving multicriteria problems, *WP* 72-8, *European Institute for Advanced Studies in Management,* Brussels, February 1972.

[16] T. Parthasarathy — T.E.S. Raghavan, *Some topics in two-person games,* American Elsevier, New York, 1971.

[17] J. Philip, Algorithms for the vector maximization problem, *Mathematical Programming,* 2 (1972), 207-229.

[18] B. Roy, Problems and methods with multiple objective functions, *Mathematical Programming,* 1 (1971), 239-266.

[19] H.A. Simon, *Models of man,* John Wiley, New York, 1957.

[20] H.A. Simon, Theories of decision-making in economics and behavioral science, in *G.P.E. Clarkson (ed.), Managerial economics.* Selected readings, Penguin Books, Harmondsworth, Middlesex, England, 1968, 13-49.

[21] H.A. Simon, Theories of bounded rationality, in *C.B. McGuire and R. Radner* (eds.), *Decision and organization,* North-Holland, Amsterdam, 1972, 161-176.

J. Fichefet

Facultés Universitaires Notre-Dame de la Paix, Institut d'Informatique, 21, rue Grandgagnage, B 5000 Namur (Belgium).

SOME TRANSFORMATIONS OF INTEGER PROGRAMMING PROBLEMS

F. FORGÓ

1. INTRODUCTION

Garfinkel and Nemhauser [1] discusses the interrelationship between certain integer programming problems. Transformations of equality constrained binary integer linear programming problems (ILP) to set covering (SC), set partitioning (SPO), set packing (SPA), vertex packing (VP) and vertex covering (VC) problems are also included. The particular transformation reduces an ILP to an SPO, SPA, SC, VC and VP so that the number of variables (vertices) of the new problems is a function of the ILP data. Granot and Hammer [3] transform special ILP's to SC's without increasing the number of variables. Their coefficient matrix also depends on the problem data.

In the first part of this paper we give a simple transformation of an integer quadratic programming (IQP) problem to an SPO, SPA, SC, VC and VP such that the number of variables and the structure of the coefficient matrix of the new problems depends only on n, the number of variables in the original IQP. More specifically, the number of constraints and variables of the SPO, SPA, SC, VC and VP is of order n^2.

In the second part a method is given capable of reducing an IQP to a fixed cost transportation problem with a cost matrix of order $n \times n$.

2. TRANSFORMATION OF AN IQP TO ILP'S WITH A $0-1$ COEFFICIENT MATRIX

Let us consider the following

IQP: $0 \leqslant x_j \leqslant 1$ $\quad x_j = $ integer $\quad (j = 1, \ldots, n)$

$$(1) \qquad \sum_{j=1}^{n} a_{ij} x_j = b_i \qquad (i = 1, \ldots, m)$$

$$z(x) = \sum_{k=1}^{n} \sum_{j=1}^{n} c_{kj} x_k x_j \rightarrow \max$$

where all constants a_{ij}, c_{kj}, b_i are integers.

In the special case, when $c_{kj} = 0$ for all $k \neq j$ (1) is an ILP.

The following problems are of special interest since all of them have features not shared by general ILP's. These might be of use for constructing efficient algorithms for their solution.

SC: $0 \leqslant x_j \leqslant 1$ $\quad x_j = $ integer $\quad (j = 1, \ldots, n)$

$$\sum_{j=1}^{n} a_{ij} x_j \geqslant 1 \qquad (i = 1, \ldots, m)$$

$$\sum_{j=1}^{n} c_j x_j \rightarrow \min.$$

a_{ij} is either 0 or 1 for all i and j, $c_j > 0$ for all j.

SPO: $0 \leqslant x_j \leqslant 1$ $\quad x_j = $ integer $\quad (j = 1, \ldots, n)$

$$\sum_{j=1}^{n} a_{ij} x_j = 1 \qquad (i = 1, \ldots, m)$$

$$\sum_{j=1}^{n} c_j x_j \to \min .$$

The constants a_{ij} are either 0 or 1, c_j's are arbitrary.

SPA: $0 \leqslant x_j \leqslant 1$ $\quad x_j = $ integer $\quad (j = 1, \ldots , n)$

$$\sum_{j=1}^{n} a_{ij} x_j \leqslant 1 \quad (i = 1, \ldots , m)$$

$$\sum_{j=1}^{n} c_j x_j \to \max .$$

The constants a_{ij} and c_j have the same properties as in SPO.

VP: The same as SPA except $[a_{ij}]$ is an edge-vertex incidence matrix of a graph.

VC: The same as SC, $[a_{ij}]$ being an edge-vertex incidence matrix of a graph.

The following theorem is our main result.

Theorem 1. *Problem* (1) *can be transformed to an* SC, SPO, SPA, VP *and* VC *in such a way that the number of variables and that of the constraints for these problems is of order* n^2.

(Transformation here means assuring equivalence among these problems in a sense that by solving any of them an optimal solution to the others can be obtained.)

Proof. First we get rid of the constraints in (1) by choosing a large enough integer constant R and creating the problem

$$0 \leqslant x_j \leqslant 1 \quad x_j = \text{integer} \quad (j = 1, \ldots , n)$$

(2) $\quad v_R(x) = \sum_{k=1}^{n} \sum_{j=1}^{n} c_{kj} x_k x_j - R \sum_{i=1}^{m} \left(b_i - \sum_{j=1}^{m} a_{ij} x_j \right)^2 \to \max .$

Hammer and Rudeanu [17] have shown, that for an R

$$R \geqslant \lambda^+ - \lambda^- + 1$$

where λ^+ and λ^- satisfy for any binary x the inequalities

$$\lambda^- \leqslant z(x) \leqslant \lambda^+$$

the set of optimal points of (1) and (2) is the same provided the feasible set of (1) is nonempty. (We will assume this without loss of generality. The case when (1) has no feasible solution can be handled in a similar way).

We may rewrite (2) in a more convenient form

(3)
$$0 \leqslant x_j \leqslant 1 \qquad x_j = \text{integer} \qquad (j = 1, \ldots, n)$$

$$v(x) = d_0 + \sum_{k=1}^{n} \sum_{j=1}^{n} d_{kj} x_k x_j \rightarrow \max$$

where the integer constants d_0, d_{kj} are determined by c_{kj}, b_i, a_{ij} and R. Let us introduce $\dfrac{n(n-1)}{2}$ new binary variables u_{kj} $(k \neq j)$ and $n(n-1)$ constraints of the form

(4)
$$0 \leqslant x_k + x_j - 2u_{kj} \leqslant 1 \qquad (k, j = 1, \ldots, n; \; k < j) .$$

It can very easily be seen that $u_{kj} = 1$ if and only if both x_k and x_j are 1. (Transformation of polinomials of binary variables to linear functions was first shown by W a t t e r s [4].) Since $d_{kk} x_k^2 = d_{kk} x_k$ and $d_{kj} x_k x_j = d_{kj} u_{kj}$ for x_k, x_j, u_{kj} satisfying (4) thus (3), (2) and (1) are equivalent to the ILP

(5)
$$0 \leqslant x_j \leqslant 1 \qquad x_j = \text{integer} \qquad (j = 1, \ldots, n)$$

$$0 \leqslant u_{kj} \leqslant 1 \qquad u_{kj} = \text{integer} \qquad (k, j = 1, \ldots, n; \; k < j)$$

$$0 \leqslant x_k + x_j - 2u_{kj} \leqslant 1 \qquad (k, j = 1, \ldots, n; \; k < j)$$

$$d_0 + \sum_{k=1}^{n} d_{kk} x_k + \sum_{k=1}^{n} \sum_{j=1}^{n} d_{kj} u_{kj} \rightarrow \max \qquad (k < j) .$$

Consider the following system of inequalities

$$x_k + x_j - u_{kj} \leqslant 1$$

(6) $\qquad x_k \geqslant u_{kj} \qquad\qquad (k, j = 1, \ldots, n; \ k < j) .$

$$x_j \geqslant u_{kj}$$

We will show that (4) and (6) are equivalent. Clearly, if $\bar{x}_k, \bar{x}_j, \bar{u}_{kj}$ satisfy (6), then adding $\bar{x}_k \geqslant \bar{u}_{kj}; \ \bar{x}_j \geqslant \bar{u}_{kj}$ we get $\bar{x}_k + \bar{x}_j - 2\bar{u}_{kj} \geqslant 0$ and $\bar{x}_k + \bar{x}_j - \bar{u}_{kj} \leqslant 1$ implies $\bar{x}_k + \bar{x}_j - 2\bar{u}_{kj} \leqslant 1$. On the other hand if x_k', x_j', u_{kj}' satisfy (4), then $x_k' < u_{kj}'$ would imply $x_k' = 0, \ u_{kj}' = 1$ violating $0 \leqslant x_k' + x_j' - 2u_{kj}'$. If $x_k' + x_j' - u_{kj}' > 1$, then $x_k' = x_j' = 1$ and $u_k' = x_j' = 1$ and $u_{kj}' = 0$ which violates $x_k' + x_j' - 2u_{kj}' \leqslant 1$.

Introducing the variables $y_j = 1 - x_j \ (j = 1, \ldots, n)$ the inequalities $x_k \geqslant u_{kj}$ and $x_j \geqslant u_{kj}$ of (6) can be written as

(7) $\qquad \begin{aligned} y_j + u_{kj} &\leqslant 1 \\ y_k + u_{kj} &\leqslant 1 \end{aligned} \qquad (k, j = 1, \ldots, n; \ k < j)$

and adding slack variables s_{kj} and t_{kj} we get

(8) $\qquad \begin{aligned} y_j + u_{kj} + s_{kj} &= 1 \\ y_k + u_{kj} + t_{kj} &= 1 \end{aligned} \qquad (k, j = 1, \ldots, n; \ k < j)$

inequalities

$$x_k + x_j - u_{kj} \leqslant 1$$

become

$$y_k + y_j + u_{kj} \geqslant 1 .$$

Expressing y_j from the first equation of (8) and $u_{kj} + y_k$ from the second one we have

(9) $\qquad s_{kj} + u_{kj} + t_{kj} \leqslant 1 \qquad (k, j = 1, \ldots, n; \ k < j)$

and adding the slack variable r_{kj} we get the equation

(10) $\qquad s_{kj} + u_{kj} + t_{kj} + r_{kj} = 1 \qquad (j, k = 1, \ldots, n; \ k < j) .$

Of course, all the slack variables have 0 coefficients in the objective function.

Since (8) and (10) define a feasible region of an SPO, and the number of variables is $2n^2 - n$ and that of the constraints is $\frac{3}{2}(n^2 - n)$, we have shown the equivalence of (1) to an SPO.

Garfinkel and Nemhauser show in [1] and [2] that an SPO can be converted to an SC and SPA by adding suitable positive numbers to each coefficient of the objective function (thereby preserving the structure — variables and coefficient matrix — of the problem and making each coefficient of the objective function positive). They also show that an SPA can be transformed to a VP by splitting each inequality into as many inequalities as the number of pairs of 1's in a row of the SPA. This means that if

(11) $\qquad \sum_j a_{kj} x_j \leqslant 1$

is a constraint of the SPA, and $a_{kj_i} = 1$ $(i = 1, \ldots, t)$, then (11) can be replaced by the system

(12) $\qquad a_{kj_i} x_{j_i} + a_{kj_s} x_{j_s} \leqslant 1 \qquad (i, s = 1, \ldots, t; \ i < s)$.

This transformation leaves the variables unaltered while the number of constraints increases. Since in our SPA problem there are precisely three 1's in a row (slack variables r_{kj} need not be considered when transforming from SPO to SPA) each row should be taken three times when going from (11) to (12) thereby obtaining a VP with $\frac{9}{2}(n^2 - n)$ constraints. Thus we have transformed (1) into a VP having variables and constraints of order n^2. Since any VP can be converted to a VC by simply taking the complement of each variable, the equivalence of (1) and a VC is obvious.

Having proved the equivalence of (1) to the problems SC, SPO, SPA, VP and VC we are done.

Although no immediate computational advantages can be taken of Theorem 1, it might be of some value as a tool for gaining additional in-

Theorem 1, it might be of some value as a tool for gaining additional insight into the structure of integer programming problems. In this direction we would like to make a few comments.

1. It is remarkable that the SC, SPO, SPA, VP and VC problems have the same structure for fixed n. Two arbitrary IOP's of n variables, when transformed to any of these problems differ only in the objective function. Thus it is sufficient to determine the convex hull of the feasible points of these problems for a fixed n only once, the power of linear programming can then be applied for their solution.

Since for any of these problems there is an underlying graph (for SC, SPO, SPA, see [5], for VP and VC a graph can be associated in an obvious way) and for each n there is only one to be considered, further research can be focused to investigate the structure of that particular problem. For $n = 2, 3, 4$ we give the coefficient matrices of the SC, SPO, SPA, and for $n = 2, 3$, the matrix and the associated graph of the VP and VC (see the Appendix).

2. L e b e d e v and S t y r i k o v i c [7] report good computational results for problems slightly different from an SPA with the Gomory cutting plane algorithm. For the 14 test problems of sizes ranging from 11×22 to 33×91 no more than 7 cuts were needed to scive them. It would deserve some research to find out why the Gomory algorithm performs quite well for these kinds of problems while being ineffective for general ILP's.

M a r s t e n [8] reports very encouraging computational results with an enumeration algorithm for SPO's and SC's with sparse coefficient matrices. By the construction of our transformations none of our transformed problems has more than four 1's in a row thereby the coefficient matrix is very sparse.

3. The transformation to a VC may provide some information to decide whether a solution is not optimal. B a l i n s k i [9] gives a necessary condition for a solutionsof a VC to be optimal which is unfortunately not

sufficient. If the dual of the VC which is apparently a generalized matching problem — solvable by a polynomial-time algorithm (see E d m o n d s and J o h n s o n [6]) — has a unique optimum, then the application of Balinski's criterion is very simple.

4. B a l a s and P a d b e r g [10], [11] have established some useful and interesting results for SPO's and have given an algorithm which is capable of finding a better basic integer solution of an SPO starting from a given basic integer solution. Our transformation to an SPO makes it possible to combine Balas's method with any method for an IQP. E.g. any time an enumeration algorithm gets stuck (that means: finds no improvement and fails to verify optimality through a number of steps) we may recourse to the transformed SPO and apply Balas's method to find a better solution. Of course computational experience is needed to evaluate the possible gains and losses that can be obtained by this policy.

5. It should be mentioned that the VC has a property common with the well solvable vertex matching problem (VM) which can be stated as

(13)
$$x \geqslant 0$$
$$Ax \leqslant 1$$
$$x = \text{integer}$$
$$1^*x \to \max$$

where A is a vertex-edge incidence matrix of a graph. Consider the polyhedron of the corresponding VC

(14)
$$A^*y \geqslant 1$$
$$y \geqslant 0$$

(* stands for transposition). The following theorem is an analogue of Theorem 10 in [2]; page 85.

Theorem 2. *Let* y *be a basic feasible solution to* (14) *and* B *be a nonsingular matrix of rows in* $A' = \begin{bmatrix} A^* \\ E \end{bmatrix}$ *which are binding at* y. *Each*

component of B^{-1} *is* 0 *or* $\frac{1}{2}$ (mod 1) *and each component of* y

is $0, \frac{1}{2}$ *or* 1.

Proof. It is clear that $y \leqslant 1$. Let the matrix of rows binding at y be B

$$ B = \begin{bmatrix} A_{11}^* & A_{21}^* \\ 0 & E \end{bmatrix} $$

and b be the corresponding vector of 1's and 0's from the right-hand side of (14). Thus $y = B^{-1}b$. But B^* is a basis matrix for (13) known to have the property that each of its components is 0 or $\frac{1}{2}$ (mod 1). Since $y \leqslant 1$ and $y = B^{-1}b$ we have that $y_j = 0$ or $\frac{1}{2}$ (mod 1) ($j = 1, \ldots, n$) which completes the proof the theorem.

This property does not carry over to the corresponding SC, SPO, SPA, but it does to the VP.

6. When transforming an ILP to the SC, SPO, SPA, VP or VC problems the continuous optimum may be quite different from that of the original problem and therefore the optimal basis is not the same for the original and the transformed problem. This fact can be useful if the determinant of the new basis is of much lower magnitude. There are algorithms for the ILP (for reference see e.g. [2] [1] [6]) where the magnitude of this determinant plays a crucial role.

3. TRANSFORMATION OF AN IQP TO FIXED COST TRANSPORTATION PROBLEMS

It is known that the so-called "fixed cost transportation" problem [12] being a special fixed charge problem can be represented as a mixed integer programming problem. It is however true the opposite, that is, a broad class of integer programming problems can be reduced to one or more fixed cost transportation problems.

For easy reference we recall the definition of the fixed cost transportation problem.

Find $x_{ij} \geq 0$ $(i = 1, \ldots, m, \ j = 1, \ldots, n)$ satisfying

$$\sum_{i=1}^{m} x_{ij} = r_j \qquad (i = 1, \ldots, m)$$

$$\sum_{j=1}^{n} x_{ij} = f_i \qquad (j = 1, \ldots, n)$$

and minimizing

$$\sum_{i=1}^{m} \sum_{j=1}^{n} c_{ij} x_{ij} + \sum_{i=1}^{m} \sum_{j=1}^{n} b_{ij} y_{ij}$$

where c_{ij} and b_{ij} are constants $(b_{ij} \geq 0)$ and

$$y_{ij} = \begin{cases} 0 & \text{if} \quad x_{ij} = 0 \\ 1 & \text{if} \quad x_{ij} > 0. \end{cases}$$

Theorem 3. *The solution of an IQP can be reduced to the solution of at most $n - 1$ fixed cost transportation problems.*

Proof. Our proof will be constructive. We will show how this reduction can be done. Let us adjoin the constraint

(15) $$\sum_{j=1}^{n} x_j = t$$

to the constraint set of (1), (2) and (3). t is an integer parameter $0 \leq t \leq n$. If we denote the optimal objective function value of (1) for a given t by z_t $(z_t = -\infty$ by definition if the feasible set of (1) is empty for a given t), then

$$z_0 = \max_{0 \leq t \leq n} z_t$$

gives the optimum of (1) if $z_0 > -\infty$ otherwise (1) has no solution. The case when $t = 0$ and $t = n$ is trivial therefore it is enough to consider (1) for $1 \leq t \leq n - 1$. Let us now consider a fixed cost transportation problem given by the cost matrix and the amounts of supply and demand at each location displayed at the right-hand and lower boundary of the cost matrix.

A typical entry of the cost matrix looks like this

$$\begin{array}{l} \qquad \textcircled{c} \\ a \\ \qquad \boxed{b} \end{array}$$

where a is the variable (linear cost per unit, b is the fixed cost and c is an upper bound for the corresponding variable. The notation $\textcircled{\times}$ means a large number which drives the corresponding variable to zero in every optimal solution. M denotes a positive number satisfying

$$M > Dn^2 \qquad D = \max_{k,j} |d_{kj}|$$

where d_{kj} is the same as in (3).

$$K > (D + M)n^2 .$$

We are going to show that for any given t $(1 \leqslant t \leqslant n - 1)$ the solution of problem (1) together with the constraint (15) can be reduced to the following fixed cost transportation problem given by the $(n + 1) \times (n + 1)$ cost matrix

$$
\begin{array}{ccccc|c}
-d_{11}^{\textcircled{1}} & (-d_{12}+M)^{\textcircled{1}} & \cdots & (-d_{1n}+M)^{\textcircled{1}} & 0_{\boxed{K}} & t \\
(-d_{21}+M)^{\textcircled{1}} & -d_{22}^{\textcircled{1}} & \cdots & (-d_{2n}+M)^{\textcircled{1}} & 0_{\boxed{K}} & t \\
& & \cdots\cdots\cdots & & & \vdots \\
(-d_{n1}+M)^{\textcircled{1}} & (-d_{n2}+M)^{\textcircled{1}} & \cdots & -d_{nn}^{\textcircled{1}} & 0_{\boxed{K}} & t \\
0_{\boxed{K}} & 0_{\boxed{K}} & \cdots & 0_{\boxed{K}} & \textcircled{\times} & (n-t)t \\
\hline
t & t & \cdots & t & (n-t)t & 2nt-t^2
\end{array}
$$

(16)

    Let x^0 be an optimal solution of (1). It is therefore optimal for (3) for some t. Define $x_{kj}^0 = x_k^0 x_j^0$ $(k = 1,\dots,n; \ j = 1,\dots,n)$ and $x_{k,n+1}^0 = 0$ if $x_k^0 = 1$, $x_{k,n+1}^0 = t$ if $x_k^0 = 0$, $x_{n+1,j}^0 = 0$ if $x_j^0 = 1$, $x_{n+1,j}^0 = t$ if $x_j^0 = 0$. It is clear that $\{x_{kj}^0\}$ defined above is a feasible solution to (16) with the objective function value

(17) $$-\sum_{k=1}^{n} \sum_{j=1}^{n} d_{kj} x_{kj}^{0} + Mt(t-1) + 2(n-t)K$$

where r denotes the number of positive y_{kj}^{0}'s for which $k \neq j$ $(k, j = 1, \ldots, n)$ and s is the total number of positive $y_{n+1,j}^{0}$'s. By the construction of (16) $s \geqslant 2(n-t)$. In fact $s = 2(n-t)$ because of the definition of K. This means that for a row or column of (16) either $y_{k,n+1}^{0} = 0$ or $y_{k,n+1}^{0} = t$ and $y_{n+1,j}^{0} \propto 0$ or $y_{n+1,j}^{0} = t$.

Thus (17) reduces to

(18) $$-\sum_{k=1}^{n} \sum_{j=1}^{n} d_{kj} y_{kj}^{0} + rM \leqslant -\sum_{k=1}^{n} \sum_{j=1}^{n} d_{kj} x_{kj}^{0} + Mt(t-1)$$

$r \geqslant t(t-1)$ since otherwise there were more than t positive y_{kk}^{0} implying that both $y_{k,n+1}^{0} = 0$ and $y_{n+1,k}^{0} = 0$ for more than t elements which is impossible. But by the definition of M $r > t(t-1)$ is incompatible with (18), thus $r = t(t-1)$ and

(19) $$-\sum_{k=1}^{n}{}' \sum_{j=1}^{n} d_{kj} y_{kj}^{0} \leqslant -\sum_{k=1}^{n} \sum_{j=1}^{n} d_{kj} x_{kj}^{0} .$$

We have seen that there are exactly t positive y_{kk}^{0}'s. Define $y_{k}^{0} = 1$ if $y_{kk}^{0} = 1$ and $y_{k}^{0} = 0$ if $y_{kk}^{0} = 0$. Then (19) can be rewritten as

(20) $$\sum_{k=1}^{n}{}' \sum_{j=1}^{n} d_{kj} x_{k}^{0} x_{j}^{0} \leqslant \sum_{k=1}^{n}{}' \sum_{j=1}^{n} d_{kj} y_{k}^{0} y_{j}^{0}$$

which means that $y^{0} = [y_{1}^{0}, y_{2}^{0}, \ldots, y_{n}^{0}]$ is optimal for (1), (2) and (3). By solving (16) for each $1 \leqslant t \leqslant n-1$ and by taking into account the trivial cases $t = 0$ and $t = n$ we can choose that (those) solution(s) which optimizes (3) and thereby (1) and (2). This completes the proof of Theorem 3.

As a consequence any method suitable for solving the fixed cost transportation problem can be used for the IQP. For such methods see references [12] [13] [14]. Since there are numerous well known types of ILP's where the constraint (15) is a part of the original formulation of the problem. (See e.g. [15]) it is sufficient to solve (16) only for one value of t. In these cases (1) is equivalent to a single fixed cost transportation problem.

APPENDIX

The structure of transformed problems

$n = 2$

The coefficient matrix of the SPO, SPA and SC (In case of the SPA the column associated with the r_{ij}'s can be omitted)

y_1	y_2	u_{12}	s_{12}	t_{12}	r_{12}
1		1	1		
	1	1		1	
		1	1	1	1

The coefficient matrix of the VP and VC

	y_1	y_2	u_{12}	s_{12}	t_{12}
	1		1		
	1			1	
			1	1	
		1	1		
		1			1
			1		1
*			1	1	
*			1		1
				1	1

(Redundant constraints are marked by an asterisk and left out of further consideration.)

The associated graph is the following (the nodes assigned to the variables are numbered from 1 to 5).

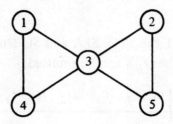

$n = 3$

Matrix of the SPO, SPA and SC

y_1	y_2	y_3	u_{12}	u_{13}	u_{23}	s_{12}	s_{13}	s_{23}	t_{12}	t_{13}	t_{23}	r_{12}	r_{13}	r_{23}
1			1			1								
	1		1						1					
1				1			1							
		1		1						1				
	1				1			1						
		1			1						1			
			1			1			1			1		
				1			1			1			1	
					1			1			1			1

The matrix of the VP and VC

	1	2	3	4	5	6	7	8	9	10	11	12
	y_1	y_2	y_3	u_{12}	u_{13}	u_{23}	s_{12}	s_{13}	s_{23}	t_{12}	t_{13}	t_{23}
	1			1								
	1						1					
				1			1					
		1		1								
		1								1		
				1						1		
	1				1							
	1							1				
					1			1				
			1		1							
			1								1	
					1						1	
		1				1						
		1							1			
						1			1			
			1			1						
			1									1
						1						1
*				1			1					
*				1						1		
							1			1		
*					1			1				
*					1						1	
								1			1	
*						1			1			
*						1						1
									1			1

The associated graph is the following

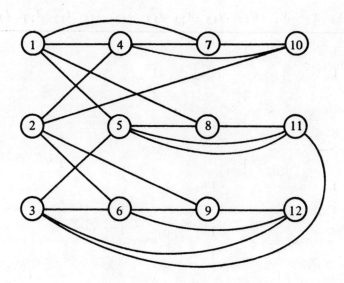

$n = 4$

Matrix of the SPO, SPA and SC

$y_1 \; y_2 \; y_3 \; y_4 \; u_{12} \; u_{13} \; u_{14} \; u_{23} \; u_{24} \; u_{34} \; s_{12} \; s_{13} \; s_{14} \; s_{23} \; s_{24} \; s_{34} \; t_{12} \; t_{13} \; t_{14} \; t_{23} \; t_{24} \; t_{34} \; r_{12} \; r_{13} \; r_{14} \; r_{23} \; r_{24} \; r_{34}$

REFERENCES

[1] R.S. Garfinkel – G.L. Nemhauser, A survey of integer programming emphasizing computation and relations among models, in *Mathematical Programming, ed.* by Hu and Robinson, 77-155.

[2] R.S. Garfinkel – G.L. Nemhauser, *Integer programming,* John Wiley and Sons, New York, 1972.

[3] F. Granot – P.L. Hammer, On the role of generalized covering problems, *Centre de Recherches Mathematiques,* Universite de Montreal, CRM-220 1972. Sept.

[4] L.J. Watters, Reduction of integer polynomial programming problems to zero-one linear programming problems, *Operations Research,* 15 (1967), 1171-1174.

[5] J. Edmonds, Covers and packings in a family of sets, *Bull. Am. Math. Soc.,* 68 (1962), 494-499.

[6] J. Edmonds – E.L. Johnson, Matching: A well solved class of integer linear programs, *Proc. of the Calgary Int. Conf. on Comb. Structures and Their Appl.,* Gordon and Breach, 89-92.

[7] B.D. Lebedev – R.S. Styrikovic, The effectiveness of the Gomory method for a certain class of integer programming problems, (in Russian) *Ekonom. i. Mat. Metody,* 7 (1971), 769-772.

[8] R.E. Marsten, An implicit enumeration algorithm for the set partitioning problem with side constraints, *Ph. D. Dissertation,* Univ. of Calif. Los Angeles, 1971.

[9] M.L. Balinski, On maximum matching, minimum covering and their connections, In *Proceedings of the Prineeton Symposium on Mathematical Programming,* (ed. Kuhn) 303-312. Princeton University Press, 1970.

[10] E. Balas – M. Padberg, On the set covering problem, *Operation Research,* 20 (1972).

[11]   E. Balas − M. Badberg, On the set covering problem II. An algorithm. *Carnegie-Mellon University, Management Sciences, Report* 295 (1972).

[12]   M.L. Balinski, Fixed cost transportation problems, *Naval Research Logistics Quarterly,* 11 (1961), 41-54.

[13]   L. Cooper − C. Drebes, An approximate solution method for the fixed charge problem, *Naval Research Logistics Quarterly,* 14 (1967), 101-115.

[14]   K.G. Murty, Solving the fixed charge problem by ranking the extreme points, *Operation Research,* 16 (1968), 268-280.

[15]   W.C. Jr. Healy, Multiple choice programming, *Operations Research,* 12 (1964), 122-138.

[16]   J.F. Shapiro, Group theoretic algorithms for the integer programming problem I-II, *Operations Research,* 16 (1968), 91-102 and 928-947.

[17]   P.L. Hammer − S. Rudeanu, *Boolean methods in Operations Research and Related Areas,* Springer Verlag, Berlin, 1969.

Ferenc Forgó

Department of Mathematics Karl Marx University of Economics Budapest, 1093 Budapest, IX. Dimitrov tér 8.

COLLOQUIA MATHEMATICA SOCIETATIS JÁNOS BOLYAI

12. PROGRESS IN OPERATIONS RESEARCH, EGER (HUNGARY), 1974.

COMPUTER AIDED MANAGEMENT OF INDUSTRIAL RESEARCH THE METHOD LOGEL

P. FUTÓ

SUMMARY

The paper presents new models, algorithms, and computer programs for solving topical problems of research management. These methods have been developed in the Hungarian Institute for Building Science. After a short demonstration of a few models and algorithms a detailed description of the program system follows and its use in research management is mentioned. The Appendix contains an effective algorithm for optimal bisection of a graph.

1. PREFACE

Both the advanced and developing countries use about 2 to 4 per cent of their national incomes for scientific research. For the allocation of this vast amount of money, that is, for research planning and control, the methods used for industrial and military purposes have been adopted; these, however, study research only from an external economic management point of view, do not take into consideration the special character of scientific research and do not even attempt to make use of the internal logic of research for the planning and control purposes.

Applying some methods and results of operations research, logic of science, and information science, the method LOGEL has been developed by a team of the Hungarian Institute for Building Science for supporting the solving the problems of research management, taking into consideration the internal logic of scientific research. [3], [9], [10]. The method LOGEL is a system of mathematical models, algorithms, and computer programs, based on logical models (wherefrom its name *logical model*) of topical structures in science.

The method LOGEL has already been employed successfully in the evaluation of the Hungarian building research activities, [8], for the elaboration of their long-term 15-year draft plan, [10], for their co-ordination, and for outlining the situation of the international building research activities [6].

Reeently, application of the method was started in environment protection, mechanical engineering, and medical research fields as well.

2. MODELS, ALGORITHMS

Mathematical models and algorithms are the fundamentals of the methods evolved for solving the problems of research management.

The operations research literature generally considers that the concept of the model consists of the system of requirements and of the objective function, too.

Further we separately discuss the objective functions and algorithms from the systems of requirements (further called models) because for solving the practical problems we can combine the models with different objective functions.

In the following a few of the elements and the relations of the graph models will be defined, 5 of the 16 models and 3 of the 8 algorithms used will be demonstrated shortly, by way of illustration. A detailed description of a model and an algorithm can be seen in the Appendix.

2.1. *Elements*

Cognitive unit: means any elementary unit of scientific cognition (individual scientific results, laws, hypotheses, problems, noncomplex research objectives, projects).

Cognitive system: means complex units of scientific cognition (disciplines, scientific trends, ranges of problems, programmes).

Terms (keywords, descriptors): by the aid of which the essence of the content of the cognitive unit can be described.

2.2. *Relations*

Relation of *affiliation* exists

(a) between a term and a cognitive unit if and only if we have used the term for describing the content of the cognitive unit.

(b) between two terms if and only if there exists at least one cognitive unit whose content has been described by using these terms together.

(c) between two cognitive units if and only if there exists at least one term which has been used for describing the content of both of these cognitive units.

Generic relation exists between the terms t_i and t_j if and only if t_i is a broader term of t_j, t_j is a narrower term of t_i.

Relation of *explanation* exists between the cognitive units C_i and C_j if and only if the relation of premise and conclusion holds between the two cognitive units in the cognitive system including them.

Relation of *effectuation* exists between the cognitive units C_i and C_j if and only if the realization of C_i is the condition of the realization of C_j.

2.3. *Models*

M6. Model of a cognitive system using cognitive units and the relation of affiliation. The model is a graph, its vertices are cognitive units connected pairwise by edges, the number of which equals to the number of common terms of the two cognitive units represented by the two vertices.

M7. Model of a cognitive system using terms and the relation of affiliation. The model is a graph, its vertices are terms connected pairwise by edges, the number of which equals to the number of cognitive units described by the common use of the terms represented by the two connected vertices.

M8. Model of a cognitive system using terms and the generic relation.

The model is a directed graph without circuits, its vertices are terms connected pairwise by a directed arc representing the generic relation.

M15. Model of a cognitive system using cognitive units and the relation of explanation.

The model is a directed graph. Its vertices are cognitive units (data, experimental laws, hypotheses or theorems and axioms, respectively).

The arcs represent the relation of explanation.

M16. Model of a cognitive system using cognitive units and the relation of effectuation.

The model is a tripartite directed graph. Its vertices are cognitive units (expenditures, objectives, benefits).

The arcs represent the relation of effectuation.

2.4. *Algorithms*

A1. Algorithm for determining the densest subgraphs of a graph.

The algorithm solves this seeking problem in the case when the maximum number of vertices of the examined subgraphs are 2, 3, 4, 5.

A2. Algorithm for determining the optimal bisection of a graph.

The algorithm determines the minimal cut of a graph separating two disjoint subsets of edges. The algorithm is based on the transformation of the optimal bisection problem into the maximal pairing problem of supply and demand. In this way the algorithm will be swift and small computer storage oriented. The detailed description of the algorithm can be seen in the Appendix.

A6. Algorithm for determining optimal subgraphs of a tripartite directed graph.

The aim of this algorithm is to find the optimal subset of a set of proposed projects, when optimizing from the point of view of expenditures and benefits.

3. COMPUTER PROGRAMS

The basic condition of using our methods is a proper topical information about the cognitive units of the examined cognitive system.

Since the number of logical model elements may amount to several thousands, data storage and handling are best performed by a computer, using the thesaurus of terms.

Our computer programs aid the composition of subject matter statistics and the optimization of the research control decisions. These programs are written in FORTRAN language for a CDC 3300 and a SIEMENS 4004 computer.

Furtherly we sketch the aims of the programs.

LOGEL 01 gives the list and frequency of terms describing the cognitive units of the cognitive system, in order of occurrence.

LOGEL 02 gives the list and frequency of terms in alphabetical and frequency order.

LOGEL 03 gives a number for each pair of terms to be examined. This number showes how many cognitive units have been described by the common use of these pairs of terms. That is to say, the program defines the graph model M7.

LOGEL 04 determines the number of the common terms for the pairs of cognitive units to be examined.

This program defines the graph model M6.

LOGEL 05 looks for the densest subgraphs of a graph, using the algorithm A1.

LOGEL 06 determines the minimal cut of a graph separating two disjoint subsets of edges, using the algorithm A2.

The following diagram showes the relations of our programs written in FORTRAN for a CDC 3300 computer.

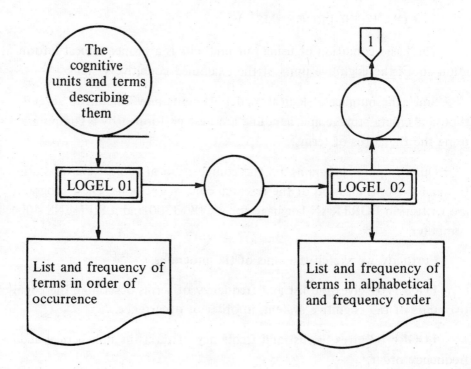

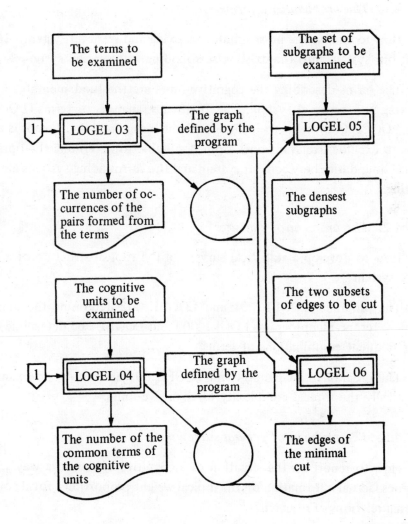

4. USE OF COMPUTER PROGRAMS IN SOLVING TOPICAL PROBLEMS OF RESEARCH MANAGEMENT

4.1. *The problem of information*

How to choose the most suitable indexing and retrievel system? How to fit our system into the existing surrounding information systems?

The terms describing the cognitive units are the fundamentals of the indexing and retrievel system. The frequency analysis of terms (LOGEL 001, LOGEL 002) helps to include relevant terms into the thesaurus and helps to exclude irrelevant ones from it suitable to determine the optimal topical boundaries between our system and the surrounding systems already existing.

4.2. *The problem of statistics*

How to develop a statistical survey on the topical structure of a cognitive system?

The programs LOGEL 001 and LOGEL 002 determine the most frequent terms. The programs LOGEL 003 and LOGEL 005 determine the most frequent combinations of terms.

The programs LOGEL 004 and LOGEL 005 are suitable to examine statistically the topical complexity of cognitive units.

4.3. *The problem of general survey*

How to report on the situation of a cognitive system in a way which provides factual information on the topical weight proportions, focal points, internal relations of research?

The outputs of programs LOGEL 003, LOGEL 004, and LOGEL 005 give important information for general survey.

4.4. *The problem of forecasting*

How to forecast the development of a cognitive system on the basis of existing topical information?

Good forecasting can be done by extrapolating the topical statistics and graph models (given by the programs LOGEL) of the cognitive system examined at different times.

4.5. *The problem of coordination*

How to discover the cognitive units to be coordinated by all means? How to divide cognitive units among research institutes?

The program LOGEL 005 is very considerable to discover the cognitive units to be coordinated.

The use of program LOGEL 006 is an effective mean of optimal topical division of cognitive units.

4.6. *The problem of concentration*

How to concentrate resources in the case of a cognitive system planned or formed spontaneously?

The programs LOGEL 003, LOGEL 004, and LOGEL 005 give important information to help the decision of concentration in the case of spontaneously formed systems.

In the case of planned systems, algorithm A3 can be used as a method of finding the optimal use of resources.

Management tasks 4.3, 4.4, 4.5, 4.6 have to be supported by analyses based on the use of models M15 and M16.

5. APPENDIX.
ALGORITHM FOR OPTIMAL BISECTION OF A GRAPH

5.1. *Basic concepts*

Let us denote by $[N, A]$ an undirected graph without loops.

$$N = \{n_1, \ldots, n_j, \ldots, n_n\}$$

is the set of the nodes of the graph;

$$A = \{a_1, \ldots, a_i, \ldots, a_m\}$$

is the set of the undirected arcs of the graph.

Let $c(a_i)$ $(i = 1, \ldots, m)$ be positive real numbers (capacities) associated with every arc.

Let us define the matrix $(A \times A) = \{d_{ij}\}$ $i = 1, \ldots, m;$ $j = 1, \ldots, m$

$$d_{ij} = \begin{cases} 1 & \text{if } a_i \in A \text{ and } a_j \in A \text{ arcs are adjacent or } i = j \\ 0 & \text{otherwise.} \end{cases}$$

Remark. If $S \subset A$, $T \subset A$ then $(S \times T) \subset (A \times A)$.

If all of the cells of the submatrix $(S \times T)$ contain 0, then the latter is called *zero homogeneous*.

Further denote by S and T the parts of A and by Z a zero homogeneous submatrix of A.

If $(S \times T)$ zero homogeneous and $(A \times A)$ does not contain any other zero homogeneous submatrices containing $(S \times T)$, then we call $(S \times T)$ *prime*.

Let us define the measure of $(S \times T)$

$$\| (S \times T) \| = \sum_{a_i \in S} c(a_i) + \sum_{a_i \in T} c(a_i)$$

Remark. $[N, A]$ can be either the model M6 or M7

5.2. *Discussion of the problem*

Let $0 \neq S_0 \subset A$ and $0 \neq T_0 \subset A$ be given sets of arcs which are not adjacent, that is $(S_0 \times T_0) = Z$.

The task is to look for the sets $\bar{S} \subset A$ and $\bar{T} \subset A$ which satisfy the following constraints:

1. $S_0 \subset \bar{S}$; $T_0 \subset \bar{T}$,

2. $\bar{S}$ and $\bar{T}$ are not adjacent, that is $(\bar{S} \times \bar{T}) = Z$.

The objective function to be maximized is the following:

$$\| (\bar{S} \times \bar{T}) \| = \sum_{a_i \in \bar{S}} c(a_i) + \sum_{a_i \in \bar{T}} c(a_i) \,.$$

It is easy to see that this task corresponds to the maximal flow minimal cut problem.

This paper examines the problem only from the point of view of the minimal cut and gives another effective algorithm for solving the problem.

Remark. $(\bar{S} \times \bar{T})$ is a prime submatrix, because $c(a_i) > 0$ and $(\bar{S} \times \bar{T})$ is zero homogeneous with maximal measure.

Denote by

$\hat{S}$ the maximal subset of arcs which are not adjacent to the arcs of T_0,

$\hat{T}$ the maximal subset of arcs which are not adjacent to the arcs of S_0.

Remark. $\bar{S} \subset \hat{S}$, $T \subset \hat{T}$, and so

$$(\bar{S} \times \bar{T}) \subset (\hat{S} \times \hat{T}) \,.$$

Theorem. *All prime submatrices of* $(\hat{S} \times \hat{T})$ *contain the submatrix* $(S_0 \times T_0) = Z$.

Proof. Let $(S \times T)$ be an arbitrary prima submatrix of $(\hat{S} \times \hat{T})$.

$$S \subset \hat{S} \Rightarrow (S \times T_0) = Z \,,$$

$$T \subset \hat{T} \Rightarrow (S_0 \times T) = Z \,.$$

If $S \subset S_0$ then $Z = (S_0 \times \hat{T}) \supset (S \times \hat{T}) \supseteq (S \times T)$, so $(S \times T)$ cannot be a prime submatrix.

If $T \subset T_0$ then $Z = (\hat{S} \times T_0) \supset (\hat{S} \times T) \supseteq (S \times T)$, so $(S \times T)$ cannot be a prime submatrix. Consequently, $S \supset S_0$; $T \supset T_0$; q.e.d. (Figure 1.)

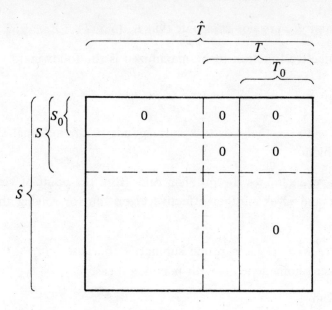

Figure 1

5.3. *Algorithm*

Consider the matrix $(\hat{S} \times \hat{T})$ as a qualification matrix of a supply-demand task.

If $a_i \in \hat{S}$ then $c(a_i)$ means the supply of the factory a_i;

If $a_j \in \hat{T}$ then $c(a_j)$ means the demand of the shop a_j.

$$d_{ij} = \begin{cases} 1 & \text{if the factory } a_i \text{ can transport to the shop } a_j \text{ ;} \\ 0 & \text{if the factory } a_i \text{ cannot transport to the shop } a_j \text{ .} \end{cases}$$

The theorem of König — Hall declares that the whole supply can be transported if and only if for an arbitrary $P \subset \hat{S}$ one has

$$\sum_{a_i \in P} c(a_i) \leqslant \sum_{a_j \in R} c(a_j) ,$$

where R is the set of shops to which we can transport from at least one of the factories $a_i \in P$.

Remark. $(\hat{S} \times \hat{T})$ does not satisfy the assumption of the theorem of König – Hall, because if

$$P = S_0 \quad \text{then} \quad (S_0 \times \hat{T}) = Z, \quad \text{so} \quad R = \phi,$$

consequently,

$$\sum_{a_i \in P} c(a_i) > \sum_{a_i \in R} c(a_j) = 0$$

Let us prepare the network to be seen of Figure 2 to the supply-demand problem.

Denote by $C(a, b)$ the capacity of the directed arc (a, b).

$$C(s, a_{i_k}) = c(a_{i_k}) \quad \text{if} \quad a_{i_k} \in \hat{S},$$

$$C(a_{j_l}, t) = c(a_{j_l}) \quad \text{if} \quad a_{j_l} \in \hat{T},$$

$$C(a_{i_k}, a_{j_l}) = \infty \quad \text{iff} \quad d_{i_k j_l} = 1.$$

Notations.

(1) (V, U) a cut separating s and t

(2) (V^*, U^*) a minimal cut separating s and t

(3) $P = V \cap \hat{S}$

(4) $P^* = V^* \cap \hat{S}$

(5) $R = V \cap \hat{T}$

(6) $R^* = V^* \cap \hat{T}.$

Remark. Since the assumption of the König – Hall theorem is not satisfied, the value of the maximal flow of the above prepared network is less than

$$\sum_{a_{i_k} \in \hat{S}} c(a_{i_k}),$$

so, according to the Ford – Fulkerson theorem, the value of the minimal cut (V^*, U^*) is less than

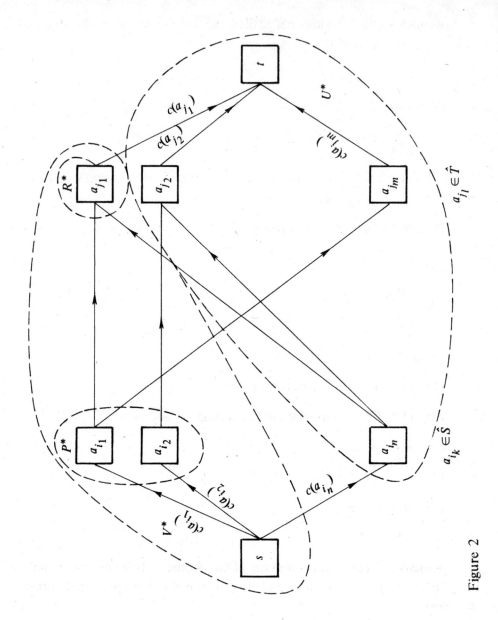

Figure 2

$$\sum_{a_{i_k} \in \hat{S}} c(a_{i_k}), \quad \text{consequently,} \quad P^* \neq \phi.$$

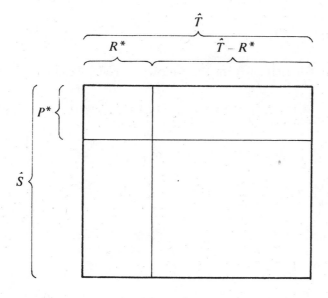

Figure 3

Theorem.

$$P^* = \bar{S}, \quad \hat{T} - R^* = \bar{T}$$

are the solutions of our problem, that is to say

$$(P^* \times \hat{T} - R^*)$$

is the prime submatrix of $(\hat{S} \times \bar{T})$ which maximizes the objective function.

Proof.

(1) We cannot transport from the factory $a_i \in P^*$ to the shop $a_j \in \hat{T} - R^*$ because otherwise $c(a_i, a_j)$ would be ∞ which contradicts that (V^*, U^*) is a minimal cut.

Consequently, $(P^* \times \hat{T} - R^*)$ is a zero homogeneous submatrix.

(2) Since (V, U) is an arbitrary an (V^*, U^*) is a minimal cut separating s and t, so

$$\sum_{a_i \in \hat{S} - P^*} c(a_i) + \sum_{a_j \in R^*} c(a_j) \leqslant \sum_{a_i \in \hat{S} - P} c(a_i) + \sum_{a_j \in R} c(a_j).$$

Subtracting this inequality from the following trivial equality

$$\sum_{a_i \in \hat{S}} c(a_i) + \sum_{a_j \in \hat{T}} c(a_j) = \sum_{a_i \in \hat{S}} c(a_i) + \sum_{a_j \in \hat{T}} c(a_j),$$

we obtain

$$\sum_{a_i \in P^*} c(a_i) + \sum_{a_j \in \hat{T} - R^*} c(a_j) \geqslant \sum_{a_i \in T} c(a_i) + \sum_{a_j \in \hat{T} - R} c(a_j).$$

This means that

$$\| (P^* \times (T - R^*)) \| \geqslant \| (P \times (T - R)) \| .$$

consequently, $(P^* \times (T - R^*))$ is a zero homogeneous submatrix of $(\hat{S} \times \hat{T})$ with maximal measure. q.e.d.

It is a trivial consequence that

$(P^* \times T - R^*)$ is prime.

The solution of the problem:

(1) Consider the matrix $(\hat{S} \times \hat{T})$ as a qualification matrix of a supply demand problem.

(2) Using the algorithm of the supply-demand problem [5] search the maximal matching (P^*, R^*).

(3) Then $(P^* \times \hat{T} - R^*)$ is the optimal solution of our problem, that is to say

$$P^* = \bar{S} \qquad \hat{T} - R^* = \bar{T}.$$

Remark. The algorithm can be smaller computer storage oriented if we examine the qualification matrix $(\hat{\hat{S}} \times \hat{T})$ (where $\hat{\hat{S}} = \hat{S} - S_0$ and

$\hat{\hat{T}} = \hat{T} - T_0$) instead of the matrix $(\hat{S} \times \hat{T})$. Let us denote the minimal cut of the network prepared for solving this supply-demand problem $(\hat{V}^*, \hat{U}^*)$,

$$\hat{P}^* = \hat{V}^* \cap \hat{S}, \quad \hat{R}^* = \hat{V}^* \cap \hat{\hat{T}}. \quad \text{(Figure 4.)}$$

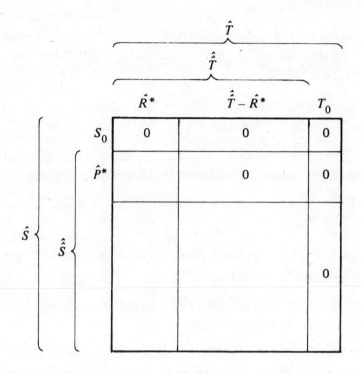

Figure 4

(1) If $\hat{P}^* = 0$ then the optimal solution of the original problem is $(S_0 \times \hat{T})$.

(2) If $\hat{P}^* = \hat{S}$ then $\hat{\hat{T}} - \hat{R}^* = \phi$, so the optimal solution of the original problem is $(\hat{S} \times T_0)$.

(3) If $0 \subset \hat{P}^* \subset \hat{\hat{S}}$ then the optimal solution of the original problem is

$$((\hat{P}^* \cup S_0) \times (\hat{\hat{T}} - \hat{R}^* \cup T_0)).$$

It is an essential advantage of the described method that the computer program of the algorithm of the supply-demand problem is contained by the program libraries of modern computers as a standard routine.

REFERENCES

[1] R.L. Ackoff — S.V. Gupta — I.S. Minas, *Scientific Method: Optimizing applied research decision,* John Wiley and Sons Inc., New York, 1962.

[2] M. Bunge, *Scientific Research, I. The search for system. II. The search for truth,* Springer Verlag, Berlin, New York, 1967.

[3] P. Futó, *Management information system relating to building research,* Hungarian Institute for Building Science, Budapest, 1973.

[4] T.C. Hu, *Integer programming and network flows,* Addison-Wesley, Reading, 1969.

[5] E. Klafszky, *Network flows* (in Hungarian) Bolyai János Mathematical Society Budapest, 1969.

[6] Gy. Kunszt, Main fields and problems of building research, *CIB Report* No. 10, CIB, Rotterdam, 1967.

[7] Gy. Kunszt — P. Futó, A simplified graph model of building tested with system engineering and information theory consideration for clearing up the role of data banks, *CIB Report,* Rotterdam, 1970.

[8] Gy. Kunszt — L. Szepeslublói — P. Futó — A. Kiss, Analysis of hungarian building research in the years 1968-69 by means of descriptor statistics, (in Hungarian), *Report of the Hungarian Institute for Building Science,* Budapest, 1970.

[9] Gy. Kunszt, The use of logical models in solving topical problems of research management, *Report of the Hungarian Institute for Building Science,* Budapest, 1971.

[10]   Gy. Kunszt, Logical models and topical management of scientific research, A general theory and applications to building science (in Hungarian), *Report of the Hungarian Institute for Building Science,* Budapest, 1973.

[11]   L. Szepeslublói – Gy. Kunszt – I. Révész – J. Dávid – P. Futó – A. Kiss, Drafting a long-range research plan for the hungarian building research by the application of descriptor statistical methods, (in Hungarian), *Report of the Hungarian Institute for Building Science,* Budapest, 1970.

[12]   B. Vickery, *On retrieval system theory,* Butterworths, London, 1961.

P. Futó

Hungarian Institute for Building Science, 1113 Budapest, Hungary, Dávid Ferenc u. 6.

COLLOQUIA MATHEMATICA SOCIETATIS JÁNOS BOLYAI
12. PROGRESS IN OPERATIONS RESEARCH, EGER (HUNGARY), 1974.

OPTIMIZATION OF URBAN PUBLIC UTILITY NETWORKS BY DISCRETE DYNAMIC PROGRAMMING

L. GARBAI — L. MOLNÁR

The urban gas, fresh water supply and district heating systems are very expensive, their investment lies in the order of some ten million dollars.

When designing such systems during the first step the traces of the consumer's pipelines are determined, the feed points are selected and the diameters are calculated.

The usual procedures concerning the design of the pipeline networks of different kinds result in solutions answering technical problems only. The criteria of optimality, the selection of the most economic solution is neglected, though nowadays the optimization of the extremely expensive networks is a real possibility. When optimizing the urban public utility networks, in the general case, the diameters of the single pipe sections and the arrangement of network are selected resulting in minimum investment and operating costs.

According to the practice the following basic problems occur:

optimization of the network with fixed layout,
optimization of the layout too e.g. in case of a new residential area.

The optimization of the public utility networks with fixed layout is a pure discrete programming problem, namely there are different design restrictions and the possible diameters are discrete, standard values.

The optimization of the network's layout, however, can be considered as a problem of the graph theory.

Notation.

d_{j_k}, d'_{j_k} standard diameters within the j-th pipe section of the k-th main (decision variables within the j-th stage of k-th branch)

Δp_{jk} pressure loss within the j-th pipe section of the k-th main

c constant

K_{1,j_k} pumping cost within the j-th section of the k-th main

K_{2,j_k} investment cost of the j-th section of the k-th main

$h^*_{j_k}$ pressure in the function points within the j-th section of the k-th main (state variables within the j-th stage of the k-th branch)

$\dot{m}_{j_k}$ mass flow in the j-th section of the k-th main

R_{j_k} limit

o_{j_k} optimum cost for the stages $j_{k+1}, \ldots, N_k$

$\vec{G}_{i_z}(A = \{A_1, \ldots, A_n\} | A_k \in A)$ directed tree fitted to the points $A_1, \ldots, A_n$, and having initial point A_k

K_{3,j_k} cost from heat loss or other special cost.

1. OPTIMIZATION OF UTILITY NETWORKS WITH FIXED LAYOUT

In this case standard diameters are selected for the single pipe sections resulting in minimum investment and operating costs. This problem can be solved by the different discrete programming methods, essentially by the enumerative algorithms. Among the methods tested (branch and bound procedure, Gomory-type algorithm, simplex method, complete enumeration, discrete dynamic programming, etc.) the discrete dynamic programming proved to be the most efficient one without limitations and completely satisfying the technical requirement.

When using the discrete programming the optimization problem — as a discrete programming problem — is transformed into a discrete deterministic decision process according to the connections of the network's elements.

Within the series of decisions the criterium of every decision is the satisfaction of the Bellman's principle of optimality of the dynamic programming.

According to the principle of optimality the decisions in the single stages should be made considering the possibilities of the whole series, and these must be optimum comparing by the given state of the system. The decision, mathematically, satisfy a recursive function equation.

The decision system of the optimization of radial type networks is shown in Fig. 1 using the so-called black boxes.

The decision variables (d_{j_k} and d'_{j_k}) of the single stages (the elements of the system) are the sets of the standard diameters ordered to the pipe section symbolized by the black box.

The results of our decisions (f_{j_k} and $f^*_{j_k}$) considering the standard diameters are the costs relating to the given stage (pipe section).

These costs of type f_{j_k} for the given section considering one of the standard diameters include the total costs from investment, pumping and

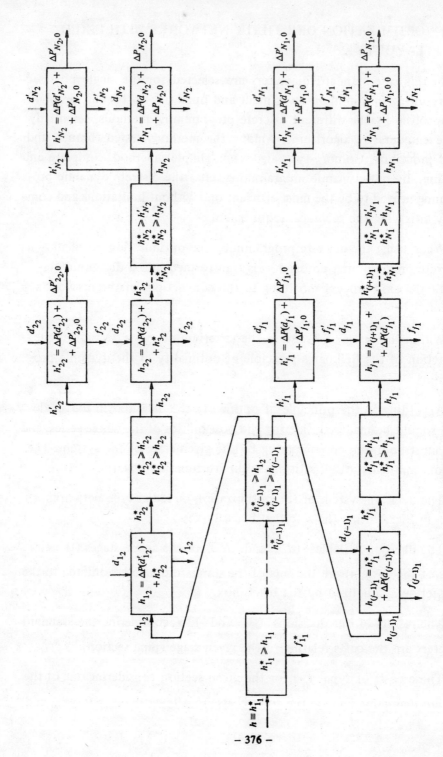

Decision model for optimization of radial-type piping systems with fixed flow arrangement

Fig. 1

heat loss during the life period in such a form, which enables comparison. This is calculated as follows

(1) $$f_{j_k} = \underbrace{K_{1,j_k}(\Delta p_{j_k}(d_{j_k})) + K_{2,j_k}(d_{j_k})}_{c \cdot \Delta p_{j_k}(d_{j_k})} + K_{3,j_k}(d_{j_k}).$$

The cost of type $f_{j_k}^*$ includes the necessary throttle and excess pumping power to establish the necessary flow. The black boxes symbolize the junction points of the pipe sections.

(2) $$f_{j_k}^* = c \cdot (h_{j_k}^* - \min\{h_{j_k}, h_{j_k}'\}) \cdot (\dot{m}_{j_k} \quad \text{or} \quad \dot{m}_{j_k}').$$

The values of the pressure at the ends of the single sections are prescribed by

(3) $$\Delta p_{j_k,0}' = \text{const.}$$

The pressure in the different junction points should not be higher than the given limit

(4) $$h_{j_k}^* \leqslant R_{j_k}.$$

The total cost of the network, naturally, can be computed by summarizing those of the sections. The criterium of the network's optimality is therefore

(5) $$f = f_{N_2} + f_{N_2}' + f_{N_2}^* + f_{N_2-1} + f_{N_2-1}' + f_{N_2-1}^* + \dots$$
$$\dots + f_{j_k} + f_{j_k}' + f_{j_k}^* + \dots + f_{1_1} + f_{1_1}' + f_{1_1}^* \to \min!$$

For the sake of the optimization a recursive function equation is formulated. As a state variables among the elements of the system the pressures $h_{j_k}^*$ in the junction points were selected, therefore

(6) $$o(h_{j_k}^*) = \min(f_{j_k}(d_{j_k}) + f_{j_k}^*(h_{j_k}^*, h_{j_k}, h_{j_k}') + o_{j_k}(h_{j_k}') + o(h_{j_k+1}^*)).$$

The relations between the variables, i.e. the state transformations are

(7) $\qquad h'_{j_k} \leqslant h^*_{j_k}$,

(8) $\qquad h_{j_k} = h^*_{j_k + 1} + \Delta p_{j_k}(d_{j_k}) \leqslant h^*_{j_k}$.

By the state transformations connections among the pressures in the junction points are created. The satisfaction of the consumer's consumption, i.e. the adjustment of the flows within the pipe sections is possible, generally, by throttle in one of the pipe sections. The pressure in the junction point is determined either by the friction losses in the consumer's pipe section or in the main which is bigger.

To adjust the desired flow throttle is necessary in the pipe section of smaller resistance.

The above mentioned are expressed by (7) and (8), postulating that the pressure in a junction point may not be less than the sum of the pressure in the preceding point and the friction loss of the pipe section between these points.

The decision system shown in Fig. 1 gives information both for the decision about the optimum diameters and adjustment of the network.

Fig. 2 was formulated to a model of the decisions about the network's optimization only, while those about the adjustment of the network are not shown. The excess pumping power cost from the adjusment is considered by the resultant feed pressure. Namely the pumping power in a network is an uniter, monotonously increasing function of the feed pressure. In the decision system, therefore, the pumping power cost may be ordered to the costs of the first box as a function of the feed pressure.

The cost of the first element (box) therefore

(9) $\qquad f^*_{1_1} = c \cdot h^*_{1_1}$,

while those of the other elements are

(10) $\qquad f_{j_k} = K_{2,j_k}(d_{j_k}) + K_{3,j_k}(d_{j_k})$.

The pumping power calculated by the feed pressure includes a priori the excess pumping power from the adjustment, too, therefore

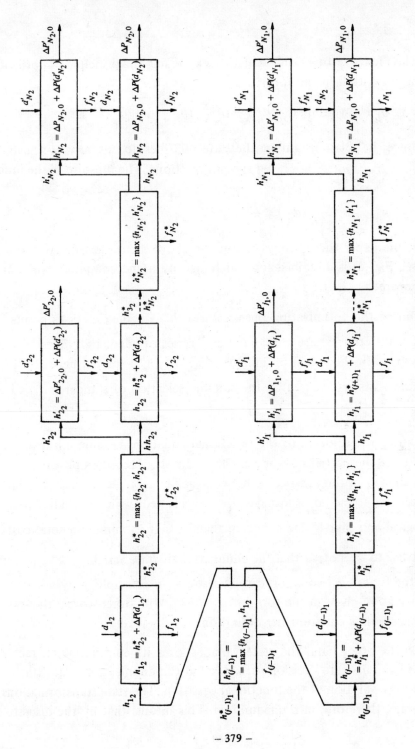

Decision model for optimization of radial-type piping systems with fixed flow arrangement

Fig. 2

(11) $f_{j_k}^* \equiv 0$.

The recursive functional equation expressing the principle of optimality can be written in the form

(12) $o_{j_k}(h_{j_k}^*) = \min(f_{j_k}(d_{j_k}) + o_{j_k+1}(h_{j_k+1}^*) + o'_{j_k}(h'_{j_k}))$.

Since the relations among the state variables do not vary, we have

(13) $h'_{j_k} \leqslant h_{j_k}^*$,

(14) $h_{j_k+1}^* + \Delta p_{j_k}(d_{j_k}) \leqslant h_{j_k}^*$.

In the paper the optimization of the above mentioned decision system (see Fig. 2) is described for which algorithm and computer program was prepared.

During the optimization the pressures $h_{j_k}^*$ in the junctions points (pressure differences) are considered as a series of adequately dense discrete values. In the actual optimizing stage $o_{j_k}(h_{j_k}^*)$ partial networks of minimum costs are created by the suitable selection of standard d_{j_k} diameters.

During the solution of the functional equation, i.e. minimization of the costs of the partial network as far as the stage those empirical costs of the already optimized partial network as far as $j_k + 1$ and of the pipe diameters d_{j_k} and d'_{j_k} in stage j_k are selected, which consider the topological and pipe-laying conditions, and result in minimum total costs.

It has to be noted, that the elimination of state variables $h_{j_k+1}^*$ and h'_j in the functional equation can be made — in principle — by a state transformation given in the form of equation. With other words: the state transformation is equation per definitionem.

On the other hand the state variable loses its continuous character owing to the discrete decision variables and the enumerating algorithm used for the solution of the functional equation. The state transformations degenerate, therefore, into unequilibria. This means, that by the discrete variables and their a prioiri values the error was introduced into the optimum, this error, however, can be reduced by densification of state variable's series and can be eliminated.

More accurately, the problem was transformed into the determination of the optimum route. The optimum route is determined on the graph fitted onto the points of the discrete variables (pressures in the junction points). In this problem the state transformation given by the hydraulic functions loses its original importance.

The a priori values of the state variables (pressures in the junction points) are the upper limits in the given range of the possible values of the state variables. By the "state transformations", strictly speaking, these ranges are ordered to each other. When looking for the optimum route a point of the graph represents such a range. By the a posteriori values of the state variables (i.e. by a value of the ranges) the state transformation is realized in form of equilibrium.

II. OPTIMIZATION OF THE NETWORK'S LAYOUT*

In the most general case, different network layouts are possible, therefore the arrangement of the network and the feed point can be optimized too. During the overall optimization, therefore, the constrant topology of the network's graph is realized.

During the overall optimization of radial-type piping networks the traces of the consumer's pipelines, the feed point and the diameters of the pipe sections have to be selected in such a manner, that the investigated cost items (i.e. pumping, investment and heat loss) result in minimum.

The determination of the optimum graph (layout) and the feed point is equivalent with the determination of a simple, continuous graph, which — ordering the optimum diameters to each link — can not improved further. The optimum graph is interpreted together with the optimum diameters only. This means, that the determination of the optimum graph of

*This problem was solved for radial-type networks only.

a network can not be separated from the determination of the optimum diameters. It has to be emphasized, that looking for the optimum graph the calculations has to be made on the graph of the network's flows and not on the topologic graph of the network.

In this paper a recursive optimizing theorem is described on basis of which an exact, partial enumerating algorithm is composed optimizing the network's layout.

The algorithm is constructive, namely, by the series of decision stages the optimum graph for the ever increasing number of consumers is determined, which in the last decision stage considers the whole consumer's system.

The recursive optimizing theorem (with the symbols of Fig. 3) can be defined as follows:

If $G_{(i+1)_j}$ is optimum (i.e. the costs of the network represented by it are optimal) for the set of graphs* $\{\vec{G}_{(i+1)_k}\}$ fitting to the points (consumers) $A_1, A_2, \ldots, A_n, A_{n+1}$, then $\vec{G}_{i_z}$ is optimum for the set of graphs $\{\vec{G}_{i_z}\}$ having A_1 rootes and fitting to the points $A_1, A_2, \ldots \ldots, A_n$.

Argumentation. If there is a $\vec{G}_{i_p} \in \{\vec{G}_{i_z}\}$ graph, which is better than $\vec{G}_{i_s}$ (i.e. the cost of the network represented by $\vec{G}_{1_p}$ is less than that of $\vec{G}_{i_s}$), then according to the principle of optimality of the dynamic programming a graph** $\vec{g} \cup \vec{G}_{1_p}$ can be composed having lower costs than those of $\vec{G}_{(i+1)_j}$. This is against our assumption, therefore only $\vec{g} \cup \vec{G}_{i_p} \equiv \vec{G}_{(i+1)_j}$ is possible, and therefore $\vec{G}_{i_s}$ is really optimum.

---

*Every graph represents an in itself optimum network (having optimum diameters).

**Strictly speaking by $(\vec{g} \cap \vec{G}_{2_j}) \cup \vec{G}_{i_p}$ relation, with the a posteriori values of the graphs.

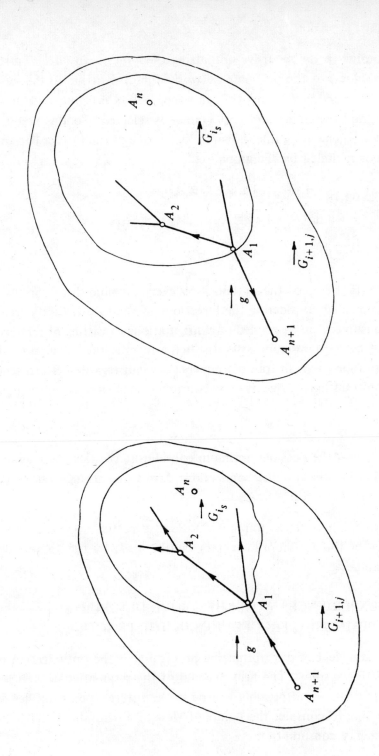

Recursive composition of the graph of radial-type network flows

Fig. 3

According to the recursive optimizing theorem, in any decision stage, the costs (values) of the optimum networks (graphs) fitting to the same points (consumers) and having the same feed points are compared, and the network (graph) of minimum cost (value) is selected. To this graph, according to the generating rule shown in Fig. 3, one of the further consumers is added not included by the graph yet,

$$\{\vec{G}_{(i+1)_s}\} = G_{(i+1)_s}(A \cup (A_s \notin A)) =$$

(15)
$$= (\min_z \{\vec{G}_{i_z}(A = \{A_1, \ldots, A_n\} | A_k \in A)\}) \cup$$

$$\cup \vec{g}(B = \{A_k, A_s \notin A\}); \quad \forall A_k \, .$$

As the first step of the optimization every possible three consumers are interconnected considering the directions of fluid flow. Configurations of four consumers are assembled of configurations consisting of three consumers and having minimum costs. In such a manner the calculation of all possible configurations of four consumers can be disregarded. The assembly of configurations having five or more consumers is obvious from the before-going.

The interconnection of two consumers (as a link of the given graph), naturally, means the possible optimum considering the fact, that within a given residential area the interconnections have to be arranged along the streets.

The calculation of the minimum costs of a partial graph, i.e. the determination of the optimum diameters, can be made by the discrete dynamic programming.

III. EXPERIENCES WITH THE ABOVE DESCRIBED OPTIMIZING PROCEDURES IN THE PRACTICE

The main field of our optimizing procedures is the optimization of district heating systems. The heat demand of the residential areas in Budapest is at present — and possible will be in the future, too — fulfilled by district heating to consider the points of view of environment and to reduce the energy consumption.

In Budapest the experts have to design the heating of about 15000 flats. This requires enormous preliminary and design work and − simultaneously − investment, too. The investment of the pipelines of the heating systems only is about 7 million US$.

The methods of operation research − especially those of discrete programming − as well as the big computers made possible the substitution of the earlier design methods by newer optimizing ones as a result of which the investment of the systems could be drastically reduced and the efficiency of the design work could be increased.

The work on the optimizing programs utilizing the discrete dynamic programming on basis of technical and economic decision models was started in 1974. The programs were used for the optimization of the district heating systems in the III and XIV district of Budapest. The same systems were designed by the conventional method too not considering the economic criteria.

Comparing the costs the advantage of the computer could be pointed out. The result − which was quite astonishing − proved the advantages of the operation research and design combined with optimization.

In the paper the optimization of the district heating system in the XIV district is outlined. The heating system consists of a boiler plant and pipelines interconnecting the former with the flats. The pipeline network is of fixed layout. The total length of the single pipe sections is about 13800 meters.

In the boiler plant hot water of 150°C is produced and pumped to the consumers. The sketch of the network is shown in Fig. 4. The number of flats connected to the system is about 15000. The total heat demand is $138 \cdot 10^6$ kcal/hr which requires the circulation of about 2000 m^3/hr hot water. The pressure maximum at the discharge side of the circulating pump is 6 bars.

The task was to select a standard diameter for every pipe section to assure minimum total costs. The input data were the total water flow, the

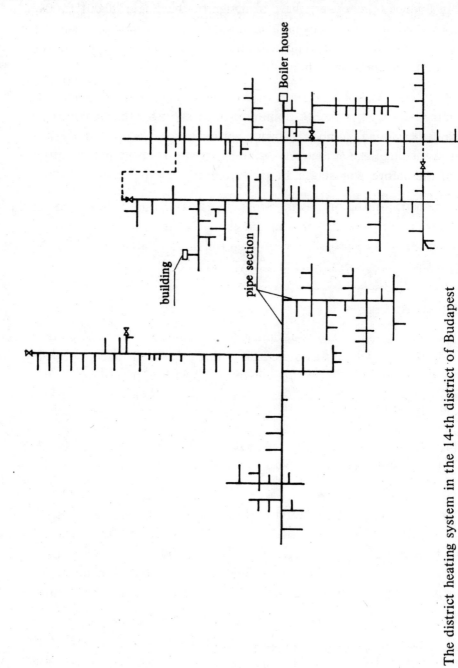

The district heating system in the 14-th district of Budapest

Fig. 4

heat demands of the different consumers and the pressure maximum of 6 bars.

The problem was solved by discrete dynamic programming. The program was written in FORTRAN IV for the computer CDC 3300.

On basis of heuristic principles it was achieved, that maximum 6 discrete potential values were enough for the calculation of state variables which were computed recursively by the program from the pressure potentials of the beforegoing stages. In such a manner the time requirement of the optimization of an extremely large system was reduced to 6 minutes and no background memory was used.

In the given case the reduction of the investment owing to the optimization was about one million US$. For the sake of comparison: the reduction of the investment in the III district, where the network was similar, was about 1.2 million US$. Both values are about 20% of the total costs.

Both systems were investigated for different parameters, e.g. which would be the costs in tase of higher inlet pressure, in case of 180 or 130°C hot water instead of 150°C temperature. The variation of these factors results in different water flows which, however, transform the dimensions of pipe sections.

The results as well as the variation of investment costs are summarized in Fig. 5 and 6.

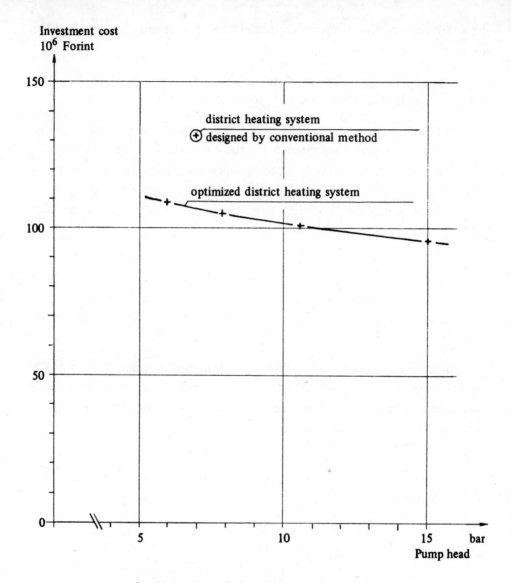

Optimization of the district heating system
in the 14-th district of Budapest

Fig. 5

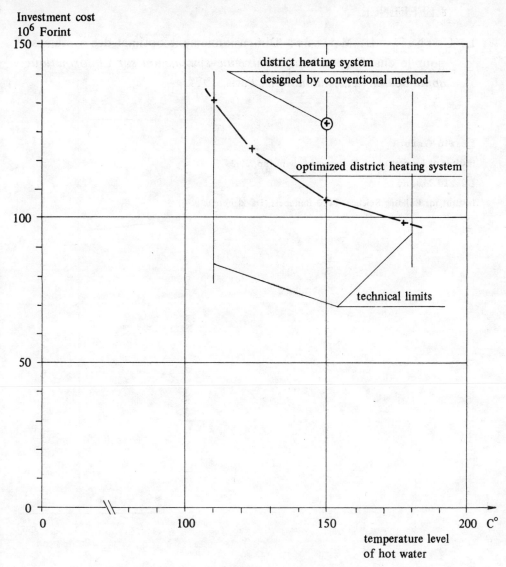

Optimization of the district heating system
in the 4-th district of Budapest

Fig. 6

REFERENCE

L. Garbai – L. Molnár, Dimensionnement optimal des systèmes pour le chauffage urbain, *Deuxième symposium sur l'informatique appliquée en genie climatique,* Paris, 1974.

László Garbai

Institut of Energetics, 1027 Budapest, Bem rkp. 33/34

László Molnár

Institut for Building Science, 1113 Budapest, Dávid Ferenc u. 6.

SOLVING AN OVERALL PRODUCTION PLANNING PROBLEM IN
A SIMPLE JOB-SHOP

L.F. GELDERS

ABSTRACT

Recently, a formal model of the one-machine job-shop scheduling problem with variable capacity was presented by Gelders and Kleindorfer (see *Operations Research,* Vol. 22, No. 1, 1974, pag. 46-60). Its primary interest focuses on the trade-off between overtime and detailed scheduling costs. The detailed scheduling problem considered is minimizing the sum of weighted tardiness and weighted flow-time costs for a given capacity plan.

This paper presents some results of further research in the above area, the aggregate cost function now being much more complex. On the basis of computational experience thus far available, we conjecture that the Gelders − Kleindorfer approximation to the detailed scheduling problem represents the cost and structural elements of the overall scheduling inter-actions sufficiently closely so as to ensure that the aggregate plan developed using this linear-programming (or transportation) representation of the de-tailed problem will be near optimal.

THE GELDERS – KLEINDORFER MODEL

The GK-model (4) is applied in a one-machine job-shop. To be specific, consider following smoothing problem

(1)
$$\min_{\pi \in \Pi} \left\{ \sum_{k=1}^{K} (c^+ \delta_k^+ + c^- \delta_k^- + b_k^1 \rho_k + b_k^1 x_k^1 + b_k^2 x_k^2) + \right.$$

$$\left. + \sum_{j \in N} (p_j T_j + h_j F_j) \right\} = \min_{\pi \in \Pi} \ G(x, \pi)$$

subject to

$$\sum_{j \in N} t_j \leqslant \sum_{k=1}^{K} (\rho_k + x_k^1 + x_k^2)$$

$$x_k^2 \leqslant \alpha(\rho_k + x_k^1) \qquad \text{for} \qquad k = 1, 2, \ldots, K$$

(2)
$$x_k^1 + x_k^2 \leqslant x_{mk} \qquad \text{for} \qquad k = 1, 2, \ldots, K$$

$$x_k^1 - x_{k-1}^1 = \delta_k^+ - \delta_k^- \qquad \text{for} \qquad k = 1, 2, \ldots, K$$

$$x_0^1 \qquad \text{given}$$

all variables $\geqslant 0$

all variables integer

where

ρ_k fixed regular time in period $k = 1, \ldots, K$

$x^1 = (x_1^1, x_2^1, \ldots, x_K^1)$ variable regular time capacity vector

x_{mk} maximum capacity available, period k

$x^2 = (x_1^2, x_2^2, \ldots, x_K^2)$ overtime capacity vector

δ_k^+ positive variation in regular capacity (e.g. manpower), period k

δ_k^- negative variation in regular capacity in period k

c^+ per unit regular capacity change cost for capacity increases

c^- per unit regular capacity change cost for capacity decreases

b_k^1 per unit cost of regular time capacity, period k

b_k^2 per unit cost of overtime capacity, period k

α allowable overtime per period as a fraction of regular time $(0 \leqslant \alpha \leqslant 1)$.

j job index

N job set $= \{1 \ldots n\}$

C_j completion time of job j

d_j due date of job j $(d_j \geqslant 0)$

T_j tardiness of job $j = \max (0, C_j - d_j)$

p_j tardiness penalty per unit time $(p_j \geqslant 0)$

F_j flow time of job $j = C_j$

h_j holding cost per unit time $(h_j \geqslant 0)$

Π set of feasible schedules π.

Models of the above form would be appropriate, for example, for scheduling a facility having a standard backlog of customer-specific orders in which the primary method of absorbing load fluctuations is to adjust manpower capacity (in terms of, say, manhours of regular time and overtime).

The lower bounding function for this problem is given by

$$
(3) \qquad
\begin{aligned}
G'(x, \Upsilon') = {} & \sum_{k=1}^{K} (c^+ \delta_k^+ + c^- \delta_k^- + b_k^1(\rho_k + x_k^1) + b_k^2 x_k^2) + \\
& + L(q(\tau, x^1 + x^2)\Upsilon')
\end{aligned}
$$

where $x = (x^1, x^2)$, where δ_k^+, δ_k^- are respectively $\max (x_k^1 - x_{k-1}^1, 0)$ and $\max (x_{k-1}^1 - x_k^1, 0)$.

$L(q(\tau, x), \Upsilon')$ is a transportation representation of the above combinatorial scheduling problem. Gelders and Kleindorfer proved the following property (see [2]).

Consider a scheduling problem (P) as defined above, namely

$$\min_{\pi \in \Pi} \sum_{j \in N}' (p_j T_j + h_j F_j)$$

(see Fig. 1 and 2).

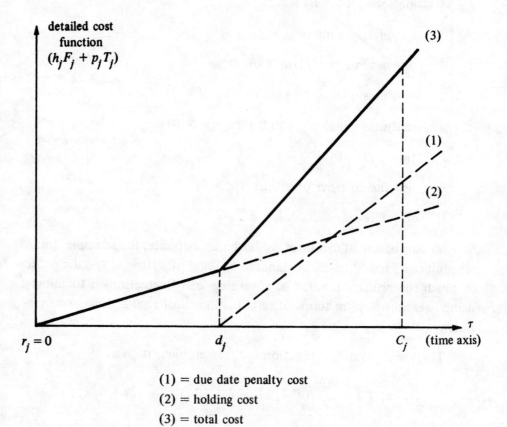

(1) = due date penalty cost
(2) = holding cost
(3) = total cost

Convex piecewise linear cost function

Fig. 1.

Then, consider a transportation problem (P1), defined as follows

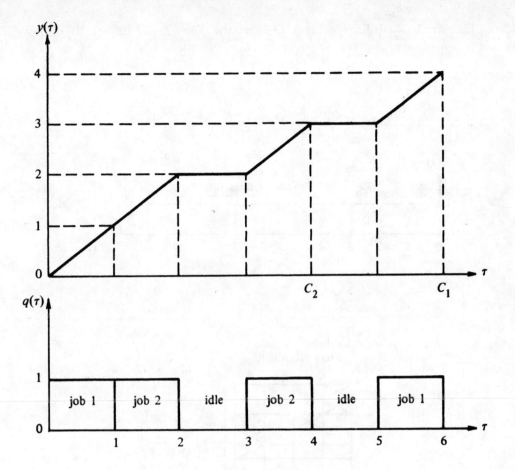

Illustrating completion time determination

Fig. 2

$$L(q, \Upsilon') = \min \sum_{i=1}^{\nu} \sum_{j=1}^{n} a_{ij} w_{ij}$$

(see Fig. 3)

subject to

$$\sum_{j=1}^{n} w_{ij} \leqslant s_i \qquad i = 1, 2, \ldots, \nu$$

$$\sum_{i=1}^{\nu} w_{ij} = t_j \qquad j = 1, \dots, n$$

$$w_{ij} \geqslant 0 \qquad \text{all} \quad i, j$$

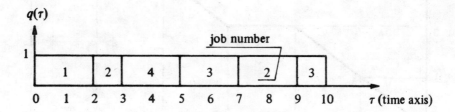

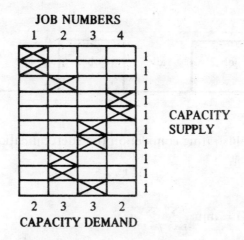

Preemptive schedule $\pi = 1 - 1 - 2 - 4 - 4 - 3 - 3 - 2 - 2 - 3$

The scheduling decision as a transportation decision

Fig. 3.

where

w_{ij} amount of capacity used by job j in timeslot i

s_i capacity supply in timeslot i

t_j capacity demand of job j = processing time of job j

$$\Upsilon' = (\tau_1, \tau_2, \ldots, \tau_\nu \mid 0 = \tau_1 \leqslant \tau_2 \leqslant \ldots \leqslant \tau_\nu \leqslant H)$$

is any arbitrary division of time horizon H into time slots i

$$a_{ij} \triangleq \begin{cases} \{1 + [(\tau_i - d_j)/t_j]\}p_j + \{1 + [\tau_i/t_j]\}h_j & \text{for} \quad \tau_i \geqslant d_j \\ \{1 + [\tau_i/t_j]\}h_j & \text{otherwise.} \end{cases}$$

Property. The optimal solution value of problem (P1) is always a lower bound on the optimal solution of problem (P).

Omitting integrity restrictions, the definition of $L(q, \Upsilon')$ and (1)-(3) imply that the minimum of the lower bounding curve G' is determined by the following *linear program*

(4)
$$\min \Big\{ \sum_{k=1}^{K} (c^+ \delta_k^+ + c^- \delta_k^- + b_k^1(\rho_k + x_k^1) + b_k^2 x_k^2) + \sum_{\substack{i=1 \\ j \in N}}^{2K} a_{ij} w_{ij} \Big\}$$

subject to

(5)
$$\sum_{j \in N} t_j \leqslant \sum_{k=1}^{K} (\rho_k + x_k^1 + x_k^2)$$

$$x_k^2 \leqslant \alpha(\rho_k + x_k^1) \qquad \text{for} \quad k = 1, 2, \ldots, K$$

$$x_k^1 + x_k^2 \leqslant x_{mk} \qquad \text{for} \quad k = 1, 2, \ldots, K$$

$$x_k^1 - x_{k-1}^1 = \delta_k^+ - \delta_k^- \qquad \text{for} \quad k = 1, 2, \ldots, K$$

$$\sum_{i=1}^{2K} w_{ij} = t_j \qquad \text{for all} \quad j \in N$$

$$\sum_{j\in N} w_{ij} \leqslant \rho_k \qquad\qquad \text{for } i = 2k - 1 \text{ and } k = 1, 2, \ldots, K$$

$$\sum_{j\in N} w_{ij} \leqslant x_k^1 + x_k^2 \qquad \text{for } i = 2k \text{ and } k = 1, 2, \ldots, K$$

x_0^1 given

all variables $\geqslant 0$.

Because of the separable nature of the constraints (5) (x^1 and x^2 enter only as supplies in the transportation constraints) and because of the ease of evaluating $L(q, \Upsilon')$ via the transportation algorithm, it seems a distinct possibility that decomposition techniques could be used to find the optimal solution to this LP. In fact, the above problem has a structure very similar to the combined production-distribution problem.

The following conjecture was verified (see [4])

$$G(x, \pi(x)) \cong G(x^*, \pi^*)$$

where

x is the optimal solution to (4)-(5), suitably rounded to achieve feasibility if necessary

$\pi(x)$ is determined by $G(x, \pi(x)) = \min_{\pi\in\Pi} G(x, \pi)$

(x^*, π^*) represents the overall optimum.

Example. Consider following data

j	1	2	3	4	5	6	7	8	9	10
d_j	10	12	18	20	20	24	30	36	44	48
p_j	5	2	5	3	4	1	2	2	1	4
t_j	3	7	4	6	5	5	6	4	7	3

$n = 10$ $\qquad\qquad\qquad\qquad$ $h_j = 0$ for all $j\in N$

$$H = 60, \quad K = 5$$

$$p_k = 8, \quad k = 1, 2, 3, 4, 5$$

$$x_{mk} = 4 \text{ for } k = 1, 2, 3, 4, \quad x_{m5} = 0$$

$$\alpha = 0.25$$

$$b^1 = 2, \quad b^2 = 3, \quad c^- = 16, \quad c^+ = 4.$$

The corresponding lower bounding problem (4)-(5) was solved as an integer linear program because of the low levels of admissible variable capacity. A gross time partition $\Upsilon' = (0, 8, 12, 20, 24, \ldots, 60)$ was used to determine the costs a_{ij}. Solving this ILP yielded

$$\min_X G(x, \Upsilon') = G(x, \Upsilon') = 174$$

where $x = (x^1, x^2) = ((1, 1, 1, 1, 0), (2, 2, 2, 0, 0))$.

The corresponding schedule was preemptive. From this preemptive schedule a non-preemptive schedule $\bar{\pi}$ was extracted, yielding a solution $G(x, \bar{\pi}) = 194$. Detailed search by our branch and bound algorithm, for the given capacity plan x, yielded

$$\pi(x) = 1 - 2 - 3 - 5 - 4 - 7 - 8 - 6 - 10 - 9$$

and

$$G(x, \pi(x)) = 192.$$

Then a one unit partition Υ'' was introduced in order to improve the lower bounding surface (and to eliminate some of the admissible x vectors). Intelligent enumeration of the remaining vectors (admissible and unbounded) yielded following overall optimum

$$x^* = (x^1, x^2) = ((1, 1, 1, 1, 0), (2, 2, 2, 1, 0))$$

$$\pi^* = 1 - 2 - 3 - 5 - 4 - 7 - 8 - 6 - 10 - 9 = \pi(x)$$

$$G(x^*, \pi^*) = 190.$$

The total cost $G(x^*, \pi^*)$ may be subdivided as follows

fixed regular capacity cost $= \sum \rho_k b^1 = 40.2 = 80$

hiring and firing cost $= c^- + c^+ = 16 + 4 = 20$

variable regular capacity cost $= \sum x_k^1 b^1 = 4.2 = 8$

overtime cost $= \sum x_k^2 b^2 = 7.3 = 21$

detailed scheduling cost $= \sum (p_j T_j + h_j F_j) = 61$.

The benefits of jointly solving both aggregate and detailed objectives may be demonstrated. Indeed, let us solve both aggregate and detailed problems separately. The aggregate problem to be solved may be represented by (1) and (2) after having deleted the detailed cost $\sum\limits_{j \in N} (p_j T_j + h_j F_j)$ in the objective function.

The optimal solution of this aggregate problem is

$$x^{\circ \circ} = ((0, 0, 0, 0, 0), (2, 2, 2, 2, 2))$$

and the corresponding cost is 110.

Solving the detailed scheduling problem with our branch and bound procedure yields an optimal sequence $\pi^{\circ \circ}$ with detailed solution cost 94.

As a result, the total cost of this solution is

$$G(x^{\circ \circ}, \pi^{\circ \circ}) = 110 + 94 = 204, \quad \text{while} \quad G(x^*, \pi^*) = 190.$$

It is interesting to notice that the capacity plan $x^{\circ \circ}$ is very different from the optimal plan x^*.

Comments. The essence of the GK-conjecture is the following

The transportation problem approximation to the detailed scheduling problem represents the cost and structural elements of the overall scheduling interactions sufficiently closely so as to ensure that the aggregate plan developed using this representation of the detailed problem will be near optimal.

Explorations of more complex aggregate costs and constraints and a variety of alternative assumptions concerning the underlying detailed scheduling problem corroborate this conjecture. The significance of this for problems of realistic size and complexity is evident, since it would imply that

A linear programming formulation (see (4)-(5)) could easily determine a near optimal aggregate plan to which detailed search could then be limited in determining the overall production and capacity schedule.

The implication is that, although our optimum seeking method may be unfeasible for large scale problems, real benefit may be gained from the possibility of delineating excellent capacity plans at low computational cost.

As a matter of fact, the complexity of the detailed scheduling problem led to the generalized use of dispatching rules (applied to the capacity plan derived from the medium term model). The most commonly used dispatching rules are the SPT (shortest processing) rule, the WSPT (weighted SPT) rule, the DD (due date) rule and the COVERT (c over t) rule. A considerable improvement may be expected when applying these dispatching rules at capacity plan x instead of the capacity plan resulting from the aggregate model alone.

REFERENCES

[1] E.H. Bowman, Production scheduling by the transportation method of linear programming, *Operations Research*, 4, 1 (1956).

[2] L.F. Gelders – P.R. Kleindorfer, Coordinating aggregate and detailed scheduling in a one-machine job-shop, Part I: Theory, *Operations Research*, 22, 1 (1974).

[3] L.F. Gelders – P.R. Kleindorfer, Coordinating aggregate and detailed scheduling in a one-machine job-shop, Part II: Computation and Structure, *Operations Research*, 23, 2 (1975).

[4] L.F. Gelders, *Coordinating aggregate and detailed scheduling in a one-machine job-shop*, unpublished Ph. D. thesis, Kath. Univ. Leuven, May 1973.

[5] F. Hanssmann — S.W. Hess, A linear programming approach to production and employment scheduling, *Management Technology*, January 1960.

Ludo F. Gelders

Commanderijstraat 19, B-3800, Sint-Truiden, Belgium.

(Katholieke Universiteit Leuven)

COLLOQUIA MATHEMATICA SOCIETATIS JÁNOS BOLYAI

12. PROGRESS IN OPERATIONS RESEARCH, EGER (HUNGARY), 1974.

A SECOND ORDER TECHNIQUE FOR THE SOLUTION OF NONLINEAR OPTIMIZATION PROBLEMS

L. GERENCSÉR

1. INTRODUCTION

In this paper we shall develop a second order technique based on a perturbation method, which is generally called SUMT method. The idea will be discussed in connection with the general problem of nonlinear programming. Further examples of applications such as discrete and continuous control problems, variational problems, two-stage decision problems will be discussed in a forthcoming paper.

The problem of nonlinear programming will be given in the form

(1.1) $\qquad \min f(x)$

subject to

(1.2) $\qquad g_i(x) = 0 \qquad i = 1, \ldots, m$.

We restrict ourselves to the case, when all constraints are given by equalities. Here x is an n-dimensional vector-variable. A local solution of the problem will be denoted by x^*. We make the following assumptions

(1.3) the functions f, g_i are twice continuously differentiable in some neighbourhood of x^*.

(1.4) second order sufficient condition of optimality is satisfied in x^*.

(1.5) the vectors $\nabla g_1(x^*), \ldots, \nabla g_m(x^*)$ are linearly independent.

To solve problem (1.1), (1.2) we take a penalty approach. We form an auxiliary function $P(x, r)$ containing quadratic penalty terms:

$$(1.6) \qquad P(x, r) = f(x) + r^{-1} \sum_{i=1}^{m} g_i^2(x) \qquad (r > 0).$$

Under assumptions (1.3), (1.4) and (1.5) the following theorem can be proved

Theorem 1. *The function $P(x, r)$ has a single local minimum, say $x(r)$ in some neighbourhood of x^*, if r is sufficiently small. The curve $x(r)$ is continuously differentiable for $r \geqslant 0$, where $x(0) = x^*$ by definition.*

(The theorem is essentially proved in the book of F i a c c o and M c C o r m i c k .)

Relying on this theorem an extrapolation technique can be developed. Namely the first order Taylor expansion of $x(r)$ around $x(0)$ gives

$$(1.7) \qquad x^* \approx x(r) - rh$$

where

$$(1.8) \qquad h(r) = \frac{dx(r)}{dr}.$$

The error of approximation (1.7) is of order r^2. In the next section we shall derive a system of linear equations whose solution is h.

2. DEFINING EQUATION FOR h

Let us go back to formula (1.6). The vector $x(r)$ was defined as the minimizer of $P(x, r)$, hence it is obtained from the equation

$$(2.1) \qquad \nabla P(x(r), r) = \nabla f(x(r)) + 2r^{-1} \sum_{i=1}^{m} g_i(x(r)) \nabla g_i(x(r)) = 0 .$$

Introduce the variables

$$(2.2) \qquad u_i(r) = 2r^{-1} g_i(x(r)) \qquad i = 1, \ldots, m .$$

It is easily shown that $u_i(r) \to u_i^*$ as $r \to 0$, where u_i^* denotes the Lagrange multipliers appearing in the first order necessary condition of optimality. They are uniquely defined because of condition (1.5).

Differentiating (2.1) with respect to r we get

$$(\nabla^2 f(x(r))) + \sum_{i=1}^{m} u_i(r) \nabla^2 g_i(x(r)) +$$

$$(2.3) \qquad + 2r^{-1} \sum_{i=1}^{m} \nabla g_i(x(r)) \nabla' g_i(x(r))) h(r) =$$

$$= 2r^{-1} \sum_{i=1}^{m} u_i(r) \nabla g_i(x(r)) .$$

We simplify this expression by introducing a few notations. The Lagrangian of the problem (1.1), (1.2) will be denoted by $L(x, u)$, i.e.

$$(2.4) \qquad L(x, u) = f(x) + \sum_{i=1}^{m} u_i g_i(x) .$$

Here u denotes an m-vector with components $u_1, \ldots, u_m$.

The $n \times m$ matrix, whose coloumns are $\nabla g_1(x(r)), \ldots, \nabla g_m(x(r))$ will be denoted by $N(x(r))$, i.e.

$$(2.5) \qquad N(x(r)) = (\nabla g_1(x(r)), \ldots, \nabla g_m(x(r))) .$$

Now if we multiply equation (2.3) by r and use the new notations we get

$$(2.6) \qquad (r \nabla_{xx}^2 L(x(r), u(r)) + 2N(x(r)) N'(x(r))) h(r) = 2N(x(r)) u(r) .$$

This is a system of linear equations for the unknown vector $h(r)$. Unfortunately this equation becomes highly ill-conditioned as $r \to 0$. In fact the limit for $r \to 0$ of the coefficient matrix equals $2N(x^*) N'(x^*)$, which is singular if $m < n$. We shall see, however, that the special structure of equation (2.6) allows to develop a stable method of solution.

3. SOLUTION OF THE LINEAR EQUATION (2.6)

The main idea is to collect and separate the small terms in the coefficient-matrix (2.6). The first step is to apply a Householder-triangularization to the matrix $N(x(r))$. This gives

$$(3.1) \qquad Q(x(r))N(x(r)) = \begin{pmatrix} R(x(r)) \\ 0 \end{pmatrix}.$$

Here $Q(x(r))$ is an orthogonal $n \times n$ matrix, and $R(x(r))$ is an upper-triangular, nonsingular $m \times m$ matrix. (We suppose that the order of columns in $N(x(r))$ is such that no permutation is needed to carry out the transformation (3.1)).

To simplify notations we shall omit the arguments $r, x(r)$ in the subsequent computations, whenever this does not lead to confusion. The parameter r may be thought fixed for a while. Now multiply equation (2.6) from the left by Q. Further introduce the new variable

$$(3.2) \qquad l = Qh,$$

which is the same as

$$h = Q'l.$$

We then obtain

$$(3.3) \qquad (rQ\nabla^2 LQ' + 2QNN'Q')l = 2QNu.$$

The point of this transformation is that matrix $QNN'Q'$ has the structure

$$(3.4) \qquad \begin{pmatrix} \overset{m}{\overbrace{RR'}} & 0 \\ 0 & 0 \end{pmatrix} {\scriptstyle \}m}.$$

We split the matrix $Q\nabla^2 LQ'$ in a similar manner and denote the partitioned form as

$$\overbrace{}^{m}$$

(3.5) $\begin{pmatrix} B_1 & B_2 \\ B_2' & B_3 \end{pmatrix} \}m$.

Finally we split l as

(3.6) $l = \begin{pmatrix} l_1 \\ l_2 \end{pmatrix} \}m$.

Thus equation (3.3) is replaced by the following two equations

(3.7) $\quad rB_1 l_1 + rB_2 l_2 + 2RR' l_1 = 2Ru$

(3.8) $\quad rB_2' l_1 + rB_3 l_2 = 0 .$

These two equations can be handled separately. In fact equation (3.7) differs slightly from the equation

(3.9) $\quad 2RR' l_1 = 2Ru .$

The error of this approximation is of order r, since RR' is nonsingular. The approximate value of l_1 is then obtained from

(3.10) $\quad R' l_1 = u .$

Since R' is a lower triangular matrix, this equation is easily solved.

All the small terms of the coefficient matrix of the system (3.7), (3.8) are condensed in equation (3.8). However this equation is equivalent to the equation

(3.11) $\quad B_2' l_1 + B_3 l_2 = 0 .$

The factor r does not appear in this equation and the only thing we have to show is that the coefficient matrix B_2 is nonsingular. Then we can substitute the value l_1 obtained from (3.10) and then calculate l_2 from (3.11).

In order to show that B_2 is nonsingular let us recall that we required the fulfilment of condition (1.4). In a more detailed form we suppose that for any v for which

(3.12) $\nabla' g_i(x^*)v = 0$ $i = 1, \ldots, m$

we have

(3.13) $v' \nabla^2 L(x^*, u^*)v \geqslant \mu \|v\|^2$

where μ is some positive number.

Equation (3.12) is equivalent to

(3.14) $N'(x^*)v = 0$

which is the same as

(3.15) $N'(x^*)Q'(x^*)Q(x^*)v = 0$.

Let us partition the transformed vector $w = Q(x^*)v$ in to two parts

(3.16) $w = \begin{pmatrix} w_1 \\ w_2 \end{pmatrix} \}k$.

According to (3.1) and (3.15) we have

(3.17) $R'(x^*)w_1 = 0$,

hence $w_1 = 0$.

In short the set of feasible vectors described by (3.14) are vectors of the form

(3.18) $w = \begin{pmatrix} 0 \\ w_2 \end{pmatrix} \}k$

in the transformed coordinate system. But then the inequality (3.13) is the same as

(3.19) $w_2' B_3(x^*)w_2 \geqslant \mu \|w_2\|^2$.

(The constant μ is unchanged as orthogonality of Q implies that $\|v\|$ and $\|w\|$ are equal.)

Since the functions f, g_i are twice continuously differentiable the inequality (3.19) remains true if we replace x^* by some $x(r)$ sufficiently close to x^*, and decrease somewhat the value μ. Thus we proved that $B_3(x(r))$ is positive definite hence nonsingular.

The analysis given above enables us to prove Theorem 1 as well, but we shall omit this proof.

So far we were concerned with the calculation of the tangent of a single curve $x(r)$. It is easily seen that the above method extends for the case, when a succesive extrapolation technique is used, as described in [2].

4. RELATION TO THE METHOD OF MULTIPLIERS

A recently popular method of solving problem (1.1), (1.2) is the method of multipliers discovered by several authors. See [4]. In this method we use the augmented Lagrangian function

$$(4.1) \qquad Q(x, w, k) = f(x) + \sum_{i=1}^{m} w_i g_i(x) + k \sum_{i=1}^{m} g_i^2(x)$$

instead of the penalty funttion $P(x, r)$ defined by (1.6). The remarkable properties of this function are expressed in

Theorem 2. *Suppose that conditions* (1.3), (1.4), (1.5) *are satisfied. Then*

$$(4.2) \qquad \nabla_x Q(x^*, u^*, k) = 0$$

and

$$(4.3) \qquad \nabla_{xx}^2 Q(x^*, u^*, k)$$

is positive definite if k is sufficiently large.

The proof of the theorem is based on the Finsler-lemma. The advantage of the new approach is that there is no need to increase infinitely the parameter k when building an iterative method.

According to Theorem 2 the function $Q(x, w, k)$ will have an unconstrained minimum in x only if w is close to u^* and k is sufficiently large. Denote this point by $x(w)$, then $x(w)$. satisfies.

(4.4) $Q_x(x(w), w, k) = 0$.

The problem of finding x^* can be reformulated as follows: solve the system of nonlinear equations

(4.5) $g_i(x(w)) = 0$ $i = 1, \ldots, m$.

If some initial guess for the solution $w = u^*$ is known, then a correction δw can be obtained by Newton-method. The mapping $w \to x(w)$ defines a correction vector δx.

On the other hand for any point $x(r)$ defined in previous sections a correction δx^0 is obtained using extrapolation. This vector is clearly defined as

(4.6) $\delta x^0 = - rh^0(r)$

where $h^0(r)$ denotes the approximate value of $h(r)$ computed above. We shall prove the following

Theorem 3. *The vectors δx and δx^0 are identical in $x = x(r) = x(w)$.*

Proof. Let us find a detailed expression for the correction vector δx. We have to compute the Jacobian of the system (4.5). But first let us find the Jacobian $\dfrac{\delta x(w)}{\delta w}$ from (4.4). Differentiating with respect to w we get

(4.7) $\dfrac{\delta x}{\delta w} = - (\nabla^2_{xx} Q)^{-1} \nabla^2_{xw} Q$.

Clearly

(4.8) $\nabla^2_{xw} Q(x(w), w, k) = N(x(w))$

where $N(x(w))$ was defined under (2.5). Let us introduce the notation

(4.9) $F(w) = \nabla^2_{xx} Q(x(w), w, k)$.

Then instead of (4.7) we can write

(4.10) $\dfrac{\delta x}{\delta w} = - F^{-1} N$.

The Jacobian (4.5) is then

$$(4.11) \qquad N' \frac{\delta x}{\delta w} = - N' F^{-1} N .$$

The correction vector obtained from the Newton-method is

$$(4.12) \qquad \delta w = (N' F^{-1} N)^{-1} g$$

where

$$g = \begin{pmatrix} g_1 \\ . \\ . \\ . \\ g_m \end{pmatrix} .$$

In fact we are interested in the correction vector δx generated by the mapping $x \rightarrow x(w)$. Obviously we have

$$(4.13) \qquad \delta x = - F^{-1} N \delta w = - F^{-1} N (N' F^{-1} N)^{-1} g .$$

A simpler way of speaking is the following: δx is a tangent vector of the "dual surface" formed by the points $x(\nu)$ and it satisfies the equality

$$(4.14) \qquad N' \delta x = - g .$$

This characterization uniquely defines δx, as for any nonzero tangent vector

$$(4.15) \qquad \delta y^* = - F^{-1} N \delta \nu$$

the "projection"

$$(4.16) \qquad N' \delta y^* = - N' F^{-1} N \delta \nu$$

is nonzero. The hyperplane spanned by the vectors $\nabla g_1 (x(w)), \ldots$ $\ldots, \nabla g_m (x(w))$ thus serves for a natural parameter region of the "dual surface".

On the other hand the correction δx^0 obtained in the extrapolation technique satisfies

(4.17) $N'\delta x^0 = - rN'h = - rN'Q'Qh = - rR'l_1 = ru = - g$

according to the analysis following equations (3.7), (3.8). Since N' is a full-rank matrix it follows that δx and δx^0 are identical.

5. NEW METHOD FOR FINDING NEWTON-DIRECTIONS

The result of the preceding section can be interpreted as an alternative way of finding Newton-correction vectors δx, at least along the curve $x(r)$. The attractive feature of this computation is that no initial guess for the constant k is needed. The question arises if it is possible to carry out this computation in points different from $x(r)$.

We shall show that this is possible, that is a new way of evaluation the vector δx defined by (4.13) will be given. Let us split the matrix Q into two parts

(5.1) $Q = \begin{pmatrix} Q_1 \\ Q_2 \end{pmatrix} \begin{matrix} \}m \\ \ \end{matrix}$

and introduce the vector

(5.2) $\delta y = \begin{pmatrix} \delta y_1 \\ \delta y_2 \end{pmatrix} \begin{matrix} \}m \\ \ \end{matrix} = Q\delta x$

we will show that δy_1 can be computed from the equation

(5.3) $R'\delta y_1 = - g$.

In fact

(5.4) $R'\delta y_1 = R'Q_1 \delta x$

and from equation (3.1) we get

(5.5) $R'Q_1 = (R', 0)Q = N'$.

Thus

(5.6) $R'\delta y_1 = N'\delta x = - N'F^{-1}N(NF^{-1}N)^{-1}g = - g$

as stated.

The next step is to determine δy_2.
Introduce the matrices

(5.7) $B_3 = Q_2 F Q_2'$

and

(5.8) $B_2' = Q_2 F Q_1'$.

We shall show that the relation

(5.9) $B_2' \delta y_1 + B_3 \delta y_2 = 0$

holds. At the end of this section we also verify, that in formulas (5.7), (5.8) F can be replaced by $\nabla^2 L$.

To prove equality (5.9) we first discuss a simple identity for orthogonal matrices. We state that

(5.10) $Q_1' Q_1 + Q_2' Q_2 = E$,

where E denotes the $n \times n$ unit matrix.

The proof is quite simple. Because of orthogonality the following equations are valid

(5.11) $Q_1'(Q_1 Q_1') = Q_1'$

$Q_1'(Q_1 Q_2') = 0$

$Q_2'(Q_2 Q_1') = 0$

$Q_2'(Q_2 Q_2') = Q_2'$.

The first two equations yield

(5.12) $Q_1' Q_1 (Q_1', Q_2') = (Q_1', 0)$

while the second two equations yield

(5.13) $Q_2' Q_2 (Q_1', Q_2') = (0, Q_2')$.

Adding the last two equalities we get

(5.14) $(Q'_1 Q_1 + Q_2 Q'_2)Q' = Q'$

which is equivalent to (5.10).

Going back to (5.9) we have

(5.15)
$$B'_2 \delta y_2 + B_3 \delta y_3 = Q_2 F Q'_1 Q_1 \delta x + Q_2 F Q'_2 Q_2 \delta x =$$
$$= Q_2 F (Q'_1 Q_1 + Q'_2 Q_2) \delta x = Q_2 F \delta x .$$

Substituting the expression (4.13) for δx yields

$$Q_2 F \delta x = - Q_2 N (N' F^{-1} N)^{-1} g$$

but

$$Q_2 N = 0$$

thus equality (5.9) is proved.

There is one problem left: we have to verify that B_3 and B'_2 are unchanged when replacing F by $\nabla^2 L$. We show this for B_3, the case of B'_2 is similar. Remembering the definition of F (see (4.9)) we have

(5.16) $B_3 = Q_2 (\nabla L + 2kNN') Q'_2$

and since

(5.17) $Q_2 N = 0$

we get

(5.18) $B_3 = Q_2 \nabla^2 L Q'_2 .$

The interesting feature of this approach is that the parameter k is completely eliminated. We need not be concerned about its appropriate choice.

REFERENCES

[1] A.V. Fiacco – G.P. McCormick, *Nonlinear programming: sequential unconstrained minimization techniques,* Wiley, New York – London, 1968.

[2] L. Gerencsér, Extension of the extrapolation technique in the SUMT method, *Problems of Control and Information Theory* (to appear).

[3] R. Fletcher – A.P. McCann, Acceleration techniques for nonlinear programming. In Fletcher, R. (ed.) *Optimization,* Academic Press, London – New York, 1969.

[4] M.J.D. Powell, A method for nonlinear constraints in minimization problems. In Fletcher, R. (ed.) *Optimization,* Academic Press, London – New York, 1969.

László Gerencsér

Computer and Automation Institute of the Hungarian Academy of Sciences, 1014 Budapest, I.
Uri u. 49. Hungary.

COLLOQUIA MATHEMATICA SOCIETATIS JÁNOS BOLYAI
12. PROGRESS IN OPERATIONS RESEARCH, EGER (HUNGARY), 1974.

A STOCHASTIC PROCESS TO DESCRIBE THE VIRTUAL WAITING TIME IN A DISCRETE-TIME QUEUEING SYSTEM

T. GERGELY — T.L. TÖRÖK

1. INTRODUCTION

A GI/G/1 system is investigated i.e. the moments of arrivals form a renewal process $(\tau_1, \tau_2, \ldots)$ and the service times are independent, identically distributed random variables (χ). Each variable emerging during the investigation is a discrete one, namely

(1)
$$P\{\tau_n - \tau_{n-1} = k\} = P\{\sigma = k\} = a_k;$$
$$P\{\chi = k\} = b_k; \qquad k = 0, 1, 2, \ldots .$$

One of the important characteristics of the systems is the virtual waiting time. This is a random variable indicating how long a customer — eventually arriving at the time point n — has to wait before being served (W_n). Significance of this variable is supported by its connection with the busy period and with the actual waiting time.

To investigate queueing systems it is a useful method to construct stochastic processes describing the characteristics of the system. The consistent application of this method can be seen in [1]. In this paper a Markov chain with discrete interference is given.

2. BASIC PROCESS

Let $\{\zeta_n, \eta_n\}$ be a two component Markov chain taking values in the state space $N \times N$ $(N = \{0, 1, 2, \ldots\})$ with the following transition probabilities

$$P\{\zeta_n = j, \; \eta_n = l \mid \zeta_{n-1} = i, \; \zeta_{n-1} = k\} =$$

(2)
$$= \begin{cases} p_{ij}\alpha_k & \text{if} \quad l = k+1; \; n \geqslant 1 \\[2mm] \sum_{r=0}^{\infty} q_{ir}p_{rj}\beta_k & \text{if} \quad l = 0; \; i,j \geqslant 0 \\[2mm] 0 & \text{otherwise} \end{cases}$$

where $\sum_{j=0}^{\infty} q_{ij} = \sum_{j=0}^{\infty} p_{ij} = 1$ and $\alpha_k + \beta_k = 1$ if $i, k = 0, 1, \ldots$.

A process like this can be given as follows

Consider a homogeneous Markov chain $\{\xi_n\}$ with the transition probability-matrix $P = \| p_{ij}; \; i,j \geqslant 0 \|$.

Let $\{t_n\}$ be a sequence of timepoints, where $v_n = t_{n+1} - t_n$ are independent identically distributed random variables (v) and $P\{v_n = k\} = = h_k$. At these time points the transition of the Markov chain $\{\xi_n\}$ evenmore is changed by a discrete Markovian interference having the transition probability matrix $Q = \| q_{ij}; \; i,j \geqslant 0 \|$ i.e. at the moment t_n the probability of the transition $i \to j$ is $\sum_{k=0}^{\infty} p_{ik}q_{kj}$ instead of p_{ij}. This means that the modified process (denoted by $\{\zeta_n\}$) is a superposition of a homogeneous Markov chain and a semi-Markov chain. The imbedded Markov chain of $\{\zeta_n\}$ is $\zeta_n^* = \zeta_{t_n}$ with the transition probability matrix $H(P)Q$ where $H(P) = \sum_{k=1}^{\infty} h_k P^k$ and the contributory process of $\{\zeta_n\}$ is $\{\zeta_n, \eta_n\}$ where $\eta_n = n - \max\{t_k; \; t_k \leqslant n\}$, $n \geqslant 0$. Thus we attain to the process given in (2) with

(3) $$\alpha_k = \left(1 - \sum_{l=1}^{k+1} h_l\right)\left(1 - \sum_{l=1}^{k} h_l\right)^{-1},$$

and

$$\beta_k = h_k\left(1 - \sum_{l=1}^{k} h_l\right)^{-1}, \qquad k \geqslant 0.$$

A simple function of $\{\zeta_n\}$ and its construction are illustrated in Fig. 1.

If $p_{ij} = \delta_{ij}$ or $q_{ij} = \delta_{ij}$ (where δ_{ij} is Kronecker's symbol) we get a special semi-Markov process or a homogeneous Markov chain respectively as special cases. Let

(4) $$\Phi(n) = \|\varphi_{ij}(n); \ i,j \geqslant 0\| = \|P\{\zeta_n = j \mid \zeta_0 = i\}; \ i,j \geqslant 0\|$$

Theorem. *If* $\pi = \{\pi_0, \pi_1, \ldots, \pi_n, \ldots\}$ *is the stationary distribution vector of the imbedded Markov chain* $\{\zeta_n^*\}$ *(i.e.* $\pi = \pi H(P)Q)$ *then* $\varphi_{ik} = \lim_{n \to \infty} \varphi_{ik}(n)$ *exists and*

(5) $$\varphi_{ik} = \varphi_k = \frac{1}{\mathsf{E}(\nu)} \sum_{j=0}^{\infty} \pi_j \rho_{jk}, \qquad k = 0, 1, 2, \ldots$$

where

(6) $$R = \|\rho_{ij}; \ i,j \geqslant 0\| = \sum_{r=0}^{\infty} \mathsf{P}\{\nu > r\}P^r.$$

Proof. Let denote $\{C\}_{i,j}$ the entry γ_{ij} of an arbitrary matrix $C = \|\gamma_{ij}; \ i,j \geqslant 0\|$. On the basis of the theorem of total probability

$$\varphi_{ik}(n) = \mathsf{P}\{\nu > n\}\{P^n\}_{ik} +$$

$$+ \sum_{t=1}^{n} \mathsf{P}\{\nu = t\} \sum_{j=0}^{\infty} \{P^t\}_{ij} \sum_{r=0}^{\infty} \{Q\}_{jr} \varphi_{rk}(n - t)$$

or in matrix form

$$\Phi(n) = \sum_{i=n+1}^{\infty} h_i P^n + \sum_{t=1}^{n} h_t P^t Q \Phi(n - t).$$

Multiplying both sides by s^n and summing for all $n = 0, 1, 2, \ldots$ we obtain

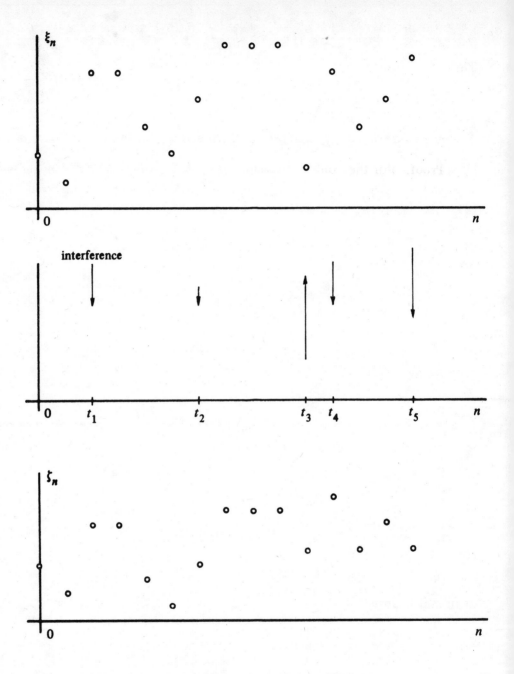

Figure 1. The construction of the process $\{\zeta_n\}$

$$\Phi(s) = \sum_{n=0}^{\infty} \Phi(n)s^n = \frac{I - H(sP)}{I - sP} + H(sP)Q\Phi(s) .$$

Thus

(7)
$$\lim_{n \to \infty} \Phi(n) = \lim_{s \to 1} (1-s)\Phi(s) =$$

$$= (1-s)(I - H(sP)Q)^{-1}(I - H(sP))(I - sP)^{-1} .$$

On one hand it is obvious that

(8)
$$\lim_{s \to 1} \frac{I - H(sP)}{I - sP} = \sum_{l=0}^{\infty} P\{v > l\}P^l .$$

On the other hand let

$$A(s) = (1-s)(I - H(sP)Q)^{-1} .$$

From this at the point $s = 1$ we get

(9)
$$A(1) = A(1)H(P)Q$$

(10)
$$\{A(1)\}_{ij} = a_{ij} = \sum_{k=0}^{\infty} a_{ik} \{H(P)Q\}_{kj} ,$$

which is a system of linear equations for all fixed i. Since the matrix of the system $(H(P)Q)$ is just the transition probability matrix of the imbedded Markov chain the stationary distribution vector of which is π it follows

(11)
$$a_{ij} = c_i \pi_j \qquad i, j \geqslant 0$$

where c_i are fixed positive constants for all $i \geqslant 0$.

According to (7), (8), (10), (11) we obtain

(12)
$$\lim_{n \to \infty} \varphi_{ij}(n) = \sum_{k=1}^{\infty} c_i \pi_k \sum_{l=0}^{\infty} P\{v > l\}p_{kj}^{(l)} = \sum_{k=1}^{\infty} c_i \pi_k \rho_{kj} .$$

Summing for all $j \geqslant 0$

$$1 = \sum_{k=1}^{\infty} c_i \pi_k \sum_{l=0}^{\infty} P\{v > l\} = c_i E(v) \qquad \text{for all} \qquad i \geqslant 0 .$$

From this and (12) the theorem follows.

Remark. In the Markovian case $(q_{ij} = \delta_{ij})$ the theorem gives the well known result for Markov chains. When $p_{ij} = \delta_{ij}$ then we obtain a semi-Markov process with identical holding times ν. The theorem accords to the ergodic theorem of such processes.

3. THE VIRTUAL WAITING TIME

Consider the above mentioned GI/G/1 queueing system. If W_n is the waiting time of the customer eventually arriving at the moment n the following equation is wellknown [1].

$$W_{n+1} = \begin{cases} [W_n - 1]^+ & \text{if there is no income at the} \\ & \text{moment } n \\ [W_n - 1]^+ + \chi & \text{if a customer arrives at the} \\ & \text{moment } n \end{cases}$$

where $[x]^+ = \max\{0, x\}$.

It is easy to see that the process $\{W_n\}$ is a Markov chain with discrete interference namely

$$P = \begin{bmatrix} 1 & 0 & 0 & 0 & \cdots \\ 1 & 0 & 0 & 0 & \cdots \\ 0 & 1 & 0 & 0 & \\ 0 & 0 & 1 & 0 & \\ \vdots & & & & \end{bmatrix}, \quad h_k = a_k, \ k = 0, 1, 2, \ldots$$

and

$$Q = \begin{bmatrix} b_0 & b_1 & b_2 & \cdots \\ 0 & b_0 & b_1 & \cdots \\ 0 & 0 & b_0 & \cdots \\ & \ddots & & \end{bmatrix}.$$

The imbedded Markov chain is just the actual sojourn time of the n-th customer (W_n). It is well known in the theory of queues ([2]) that the stationary distribution vector $(\widetilde{\pi})$ of $\widetilde{W}_n$ exists for both of the cases

(a) finite waiting time (loss system) with traffic intensity

$$\rho = \frac{E(\chi)}{E(\sigma)} < \infty \, ,$$

(b) arbitrary waiting time with $\rho < 1$.

If one of the two conditions (a), (b) is satisfied then applying the theorem we can obtain

$$\lim_{n \to \infty} P\{W_n = k\} = \frac{1}{E(\sigma)} \sum_{j=0}^{\infty} \pi_j \sum_{r=0}^{\infty} P\{\sigma > r\} \{P^r\}_{jk} =$$

$$= \begin{cases} \dfrac{1}{E(\sigma)} \displaystyle\sum_{r=0}^{\infty} \sum_{l=0}^{k+r} \pi_l \sum_{i=r+1}^{\infty} a_i & \text{if} \quad k = 0 \\[2em] \dfrac{1}{E(\sigma)} \displaystyle\sum_{r=0}^{\infty} \pi_{k+r} \sum_{i=r+1}^{\infty} a_i & \text{if} \quad k > 0 \, . \end{cases}$$

REFERENCES

[1] D.V. Lindley, The theory of queues with a single server, *Proc. Cambridge Phil. Soc.*, 48 (1952).

[2] J.W. Cohen, *The single server queue*, North-Holland, 1969.

Tamás Gergely
Central Research Institute for Physics 1121 Budapest, Konkoly Thege M. u.
Turul László Török
Central Research Institute for Physics 1121 Budapest, Konkoly Thege M. u.

FINDING MINIMUM SPANNING TREES WITH A FIXED NUMBER OF LINKS AT A NODE

F. GLOVER — D. KLINGMAN

ABSTRACT

This paper addresses a variant of the minimum spanning tree problem in which a given node is required to have a fixed number of incident edges. We show that this problem, which is combinatorially a level of complexity beyond the ordinary minimum spanning tree problem, can be solved by a highly efficient "quasi-greedy" algorithm. Applications include a tele-communication linking problem and a new relaxation strategy for the traveling salesman problem via appropriately defined order-constrained one-trees.

1. INTRODUCTION

The minimum weight spanning tree problem has enjoyed a good deal of notoreity ever since K r u s k a l first provided a greedy algorithm for solving it [12]. Interest in the problem at least in the beginning, appeared to center primarily around the novelty that something with a nontrivial statement could be solved by an "almost trivial" procedure. Philosophically, this was both intriguing and unsettling, and other manifestations and generalizations of greedy algorithms were sought [1, 13]. A broad characterization of such methods in the context of matroid theory was accomplished by E d m o n d s [3], who coined the term "greedy algorithm."

With rare exception (e.g., [4]), the precise form assumed by a greedy algorithm is usually one of the first possibilities that springs to mind, and the validity of such an approach can typically be established without notable effort. The early applications seemed for some time to have little practical significance and little relevance outside their immediate contexts. Recently, however, things have changed. Practical applications in such diverse areas at least cost electrical wiring, minimum cost connecting communication and transportation networks and minimum stress networks have found their way into the literature and textbooks (see e.g. [10a], [11], [15]). A variation of the minimum spanning tree problem, called the minimum "1-tree" problem was shown by H e l d and K a r p [8], [9] to be extremely useful as a relaxation of the traveling salesman problem. In addition, D a k i n [1], K e r s h e n b a u m and V a n S l y k e [11] have shown that there is more to the implementation of greedy algorithms than previously suspected, and have developed rather ingenious procedures for organizing and updating the information used by a greedy algorithm to improve its efficiency.

Throughout all this flurry of activity, an extremely important relative of the minimum spanning tree problem has surprisingly been neglected: that of determining a minimum weight spanning tree subject to the additional restriction that a given node be constrained to a specified order (i.e., have a fixed number of incident edges). Such a problem is directly relevant in the traveling salesman context, where nodes are constrained to order 2. The problem also arises, with perhaps greater practical immediacy, in a telecommunications setting. Here the objective is to find the minimum cost way of setting up transmission cables to connect users in various cities to a common computer installation. The "order constraint" derives from the requirement that the immediate links to the computer facility must be at least of a certain number, in order to accommodate the fact that too few links will be unable to support the anticipated transmission load. (The requirement that a node be constrained to "at least" or "at most" a certain order can be handled as a simple variant of constraining it to be exactly of that order.)

In view of the foregoing remarks, the purpose of this paper is to address the following problem: $P(K)$ — *Find a minimum weight spanning tree with node 0 constrained to order K.* Here, as customary, we implicitly have reference to an underlying graph of nodes and edges, and the weight of a subgraph (hence a spanning tree) is defined to be the sum of the weights of the edges in that subgraph. Node 0 may of course represent any selected node in the graph, and K is assumed to be a positive number for which a spanning tree with exactly K edges incident to node 0 exists. (Otherwise, the solution of $P(K)$ will determine the nonexistence of such a tree.)

Our principal results for characterizing optimal spanning trees with a constrained order at node 0 consist of a "primal theorem" and a "dual theorem". The former gives a method for constructing an optimal tree beginning with any tree that already satisfies the order requirement at node 0, and the latter gives a method for constructing an optimal tree of order $K + 1$, or $K - 1$ at node 0 (as desired) from an optimal tree with order K at node 0. The dual theorem is in fact a characterization of a "quasi-greedy" algorithm, for it makes the very best move from the category available to it, not by "putting things into a bucket" (in Edmond's terminology) but by trading things between two buckets.

We also provide special labeling procedures that enable the primal and dual methods to be applied by means of "modified pivot steps" analogous to the basis exchange steps employed in specialized linear programming procedures for solving minimum cost flow network problems. The "modified pivot steps", of course, do not involve the use of a specialized linear programming algorithm, since the problem under consideration is combinatorial and has no LP network equivalent; however, the amount of calculation of these modified pivot steps is in fact on the same order as — or somewhat better than — that of an LP basis exchange in a network. Further in the dual case each step immediately gives an optimal spanning tree of the next higher or lower order at node 0, thereby producing an algorithm of considerable efficiency. In the concluding section we discuss how this "quasi-greedy" algorithm can be similarly applied to the constrained minimum one-tree problem enhancing the significance of this method for the traveling salesman problem.

2. NOTATION AND RESULTS

To lay the groundwork for the primal and dual theorems for constructing optimal ordered-constrained trees we introduce the following definitions and notational conventions. T and T' will denote distinct spanning trees, defined on a common graph. We also allow T and T' to represent the sets of edges for these trees, writing for example, $e \in T - T'$ to indicate that e is an edge in T but not in T'.

The unique edge-simple path in T connecting the endpoints of an edge e will be denoted $T(e)$ (and likewise will interchangeably be used to represent the set of edges for this path). For two edges e, e' such that $e \in T$ and $e' \notin T$, we will call the process of adding e' to T and deleting e form T an *admissible exchange* (relative to T) if the result is also a spanning tree. Thus, in particular, such an exchange is admissible if and only if $e \in T(e')$.

Using these definitions, we will first state a theorem of [7] concerning the existence of a special "matching" of edges from T and T' that is particularly useful for establishing the main results of this paper. (Due to its subordinate role in the present setting, we state it as a lemma.)

Lemma 1. *For any two distinct spanning trees T and T', there is a way of pairing the edges of $T - T'$ with those of $T' - T$ (in a one-one matching) so that every pair gives an admissible exchange relative to T.*

The proof of this result in [7] gives a constructive procedure for producing a pairing that satisfies the stated conditions. Such a construction will not concern us here, but we require an additional preliminary (and somewhat nonintuitive) result to complete the foundation for our principal theorems.

Lemma 2. *Assume that e_0, $e \in T$, e'_0, $e' \notin T$ and e_0 and e'_0 are incident to the same node. Further assume that at least one of the pairs*

e, e' and e_0, e_0' does not give an admissible exchange relative to T (by deleting the first member of the pair and adding the second). Then e_0, e' and e, e_0' both yield an admissible exchange relative to T if and only if the addition of e' and e_0' and the deletion of e_0 and e result in a spanning tree (hence, if and only if the pairs e_0, e' and e, e_0' yield successively admissible exchanges, executed in either order).

Proof. For the "only if" part, assume $e_0 \in T(e')$ and $e \in T(e_0')$. Swapping e' and e_0 gives a tree T' in which e_0' and e still give an admissible exchange unless $T'(e_0') \neq T(e_0')$, which occurs only if $e_0 \in$ $\in T(e_0')$, implying e_0 can exchange admissibly with e_0'. By assumption it follows that $e \notin T(e')$ (else e and e' could exchange admissibly). Thus $e \in T(e_0') - T(e')$, and it follows that the edge simple path $T(e') \cup$ $\cup \{e'\} \cup T(e_0') - (T(e') - T(e_0'))$ in fact contains e and is $T'(e_0')$. Thus the second exchange is admissible in T', proving that a tree results. (A similar argument leads to the same conclusion by considering the swaps in reverse order.) For the "if" part of the lemma, assume that $T \cup \{e_0', e'\} -$ $- \{e_0, e\}$ is a tree. By Lemma 1 there is some way of pairing the edges, e_0', e' with the edges e_0, e so that every pair gives an admissible exchange relative to T. If e_0' cannot be paired with e_0 or if e' cannot be paired with e, this leaves the two pairings, e, e_0' and e_0, e' by default. The equivalence of the statement that these two pairings give successively admissible swaps when executed in either order follows immediately from the foregoing.

For the statement of the following "primal" theorem, we call an admissible exchange *improving* if the resulting tree has a smaller weight than the original (hence if the weight of the added edge is less than the weight of the deleted edge). We also follow the convention that an edge is incident to node 0 if and only if it is subscripted with a "0".

Theorem 1 (Primal Approach). *A spanning tree T with order K at node 0 is optimal for problem $P(K)$ if and only if*

(1) *There are no improving admissible exchanges involving a pair e, e', where $e \in T$, $e' \notin T$ (and neither edge is incident to node 0);*

(2) *There are no improving admissible exchanges involving a pair* e_0, e_0', *where* $e_0 \in T$, $e_0' \notin T$ *(and both edges are incident to node* 0*);*

(3) *There are no two exchanges, both admissible relative to* T, *involving a pair* e_0, e' *and a pair* e, e_0', *such that* $e_0, e \in T$, $e_0', e' \notin T$, *which together yield a net improvement — i.e., for which the sum of the weights of* e_0' *and* e' *are less than the sum of the weights of* e_0 *and* e. *(In particular, this says that coupling the "best admissible pair" of the form* e_0, e' *with the best admissible pair" of the form* e_0', e *does not yield a net improvement, disregarding whether the exchanges can actually be carried out in sequence.)*

Proof. First we prove the "only if" part of the theorem. Clearly if there are any improving exchanges of the type indicated in (1) or (2), then T is nonoptimal. If there are no such exchanges but there exists a pair of exchanges such as described in (3), then we may assume that either e_0, e_0' or e, e' cannot give an admissible exchange, else at least one would be improving, contrary to assumption. But then by Lemma 2 the two exchanges of (3) can in fact be carried out sequentially, again establishing that T is nonoptimal. To prove the "if" part of the theorem, suppose that (1), (2) and (3) hold, but that there exists a spanning tree T' which is feasible for $P(K)$ and has a smaller weight than T. By Lemma 1 we can match the edges of $T - T'$ with those of $T' - T$ so that each pair gives an admissible exchange in T. Since node 0 has the same order in both T and T', it follows that these admissible exchanges consist exactly of the types indicated in (1) and (2) together with the two types of exchanges indicated in (3), where the number of each of these two latter types is equal. Since the weight of T' is less than that of T, and since no admissible e, e' and no admissible e_0, e_0' exchanges are improving, it follows that the sum of weights of all the admissible exchanges of the e, e_0' and the e_0, e' type must be negative (adding the weights of the edges in T' and subtracting those of the edges in T). But then the sum of the weights of *some* admissible e, e_0' exchange and *some* admissible e_0, e' exchange (in particular, the "best" of each type) must be negative, contrary to the assumptions of (3). The contradiction establishes the theorem.

By means of the foregoing theorem we can now state and prove the two forms of the "dual" theorem for order-constrained sapnning trees (expressed as Theorem 2 and its corollary), which show how to obtain optimal solutions for $P(K + 1)$ and $P(K - 1)$ from an optimal solution for $P(K)$.

Theorem 2. Dual Approach — increasing order). *Assume T is optimal for $P(K)$ and T' is obtained from T by applying a single admissible exchange involving the edges e_0', e where $e \in T$, $e_0' \notin T$ (e_0 is incident to node 0 and e is not), and the weight of e_0' less the weight of e is minimum over all admissible exchanges of the specified type. Then T' is optimal for $P(K + 1)$.*

Proof. We will show that T' satisfies the optimality conditions of Theorem 1. First, we show that (1) holds. We may restrict attention to admissible exchanges of the form e_1, e_1' in T' that were not available in T. Such an exchange yields a tree $T'' = T \cup \{e_0', e_1'\} - \{e, e_1\}$ and by Lemma 1 e_0', e_1 and e_1', e must both give admissible exchanges in T. But the first of these is no better than e_0', e and the second is a nonimproving move, and hence T'' is not better that T'. Next we establish condition (2). The admissible exchange of the form indicated in (2) applied to T', gives a tree $T'' = T \cup \{e_0', e_0''\} - \{e, e_0\}$ where $e_0 \in T'$ hence $a_0 \in T$ (disregarding $e_0 = e_0'$ which reduces to a tree already known to be no better than T') and $e_0'' \notin T'$ hence $e_0'' \notin T$. By Lemma 1, and the fact that e_0, e_0'' cannot give an admissible exchange in T, both e_0', e_0 and e_0'', e must give admissible exchanges in T. But the first is nonimproving and the second no better than e_0', e, and hence T' again cannot be improved. Finally, we show that (3) holds. A double exchange involving e_0'', e_1 and e_1', e_0^* which yields a net improvement must be capable of being executed in sequence, applying Lemma 2 and the fact that conditions (1) and (2) have been established for T'. Here $e_1, e_0^* \in T'$ hence $\in T$, and $e_1'', e_1' \notin T'$ hence $\notin T$, disregarding $e_0^* = e_0'$ and $e = e_1'$, both of which reduce to earlier cases.

Thus we have a tree $T'' = T \cup \{e_0', e_0'', e_1'\} - \{e, e_1, e_0^*\}$ where the latter set of edges is from T and the former is not. Applying Lemma 1, these two sets of edges may be matched in some way so that all resulting pairs give admissible exchanges in T. We shall examine the relevant "possible" matchings to determine their implications for T''. First the pairing $\{e_0^*, e_1'\}, \{e_1, e_0''\}, \{e_0', e\}$ is not possible, because if the first two pairs had been admissible (i.e., given rise to admissible exchanges) in T they would have implied the nonoptimality of T in the same way we assume they imply the nonoptimality of T'. Similarly $\{e_0^*, e_0''\}, \{e_1, e_1'\}, \{e_0', e\}$ is impossible, because at least one of the first two pairs must be improving by the assumed improvement of T'' over T', and the admissibility of such a pair in T violates its presumed optimality. This leaves the following cases: $\{e_0'', e\}, \{e_1, e_0'\}, \{e_0^*, e_1'\}; \{e_0'', e\}, \{e_1, e_1'\}, \{e_0^*, e_0'\}; \{e_0^*, e_1\}, \{e_1', e\}, \{e_0'', e_0'\}; \{e_0'', e_1\}, \{e_1', e\}, \{e_0^*, e_0'\}$. All of these may be ruled out because in each case the last two pairs are nonimproving (due to the optimality of T) and the first pair gives a tree no better than T'. This contradicts the postulated improvement of T'' over T' and completes the proof.

From this theorem we may infer the following "inverse" result.

Corollary (Dual Approach — decreasing order). *Assume T is optimal for $P(K)$ and T' is obtained from T by applying a single admissible exchange involving the edges e_0, e', where $e_0 \in T$, $e' \notin T$ (e_0 is incident to node 0 and e' is not), and the weight of e' less the weight of e_0 is minimum over all admissible exchanges of the specified type. Then T' is optimal for $P(K - 1)$.*

Proof. The corollary follows by essentially the same reasoning used to establish Theorem 2.

In Theorem 2 and its corollary, the absence of an admissible exchange that increases of decreases the number of edges incident to node 0 of course implies the nonexistence of a spanning tree of the resulting order at this node. (This is a direct consequence of the stated results and the use of "infinite weight" edges to represent those not contained in the graph.)

We now show how to take advantage of these theorems if an efficient manner.

3. LABELING PROCEDURES

The identification of an admissible exchange that is the "best" of all admissible exchanges in its category which is required by both Theorem 2 and its corollary (and also, indirectly by Theorem 1) appears at first glance to involve the computation of "exchange values" over a potentially vast number of partial chains. We will show in this section how to apply labeling procedures (different, but comparably efficient, in each of the three cases) that succeed in generating all such relevant values, with an amount of computation essentially no greater than that of evaluating updated objective function coefficients for nonbasic variables in specialized linear programming approaches to ordinary network problems. (We refer here to "streamlined" basis evaluation procedures such as those of [5], [6], [14],) In addition, we show how to apply the foregoing primal and dual results iteratively by means of correspondingly refined updating steps that impose minimal amounts of recalculation (likewise, comparable in efficiency to the approaches of [5], [6]).

In all of the labeling procedures, it is assumed that the current spanning tree T is recorded as an arborescence with J o h n s o n's "triple label" scheme [10], with the root at node 0. As customary, a node r will be called an *immediate successor* of mode q if there is an edge in T incident on nodes q and r and if the unique path in the arborescence from r to the root contains node q. A node r will be called a *successor* of node q if the unique path from r to the root contains node q.

Labeling rule for the Dual Approach — decreasing order

1. Assign a label $t_q = r$ to each successor q of an immediate successor r of node 0. To each immediate successor node r of node 0 also assign a label of $t_r = r$. Assign node 0 a label of 0.

2. For each edge $(i, j) \notin T$ whose node labels are not the same and for which neither i nor j is node 0, set

$$\theta_{ij} = w_{ij} - \max (w_{0t_i}, w_{0t_j})$$

where w_{ph} denotes the weight on edge (p, h). Set $\theta_{ij} = \infty$ for all other edges.

3. To determine the e_0, e' exchange of the corollary to Theorem 2: let $\theta_{rs} = \min_{(i,j)} \theta_{ij}$. If θ_{rs} is finite, then edge $(r, s) = e'$, and e_0 is the edge associated with $\max (w_{0t_i}, w_{0t_j})$ in step 2. If θ_{rs} is infinite, no spanning tree of the described order exists.

The validity of the foregoing procedure follows from the corollary to Theorem 2 and the fact that e_0, e' gives an admissible exchange if and only if $e_0 \in T(e')$.

The above procedure is clearly quite easy to implement. Additionally, the labels used in the procedure can easily be updated. Specifically, suppose an optimal spanning tree T for $P(K)$ is known and an optimal spanning tree T' for $P(K - R)$ (where $R < K$) is desired. The above procedure can be successively used without completely re-labeling the nodes for each intermediate spanning tree. This is readily accomplished by using the API method [5] to update the rooted tree pointers (predecessor, successor, and brother indexes) and using the following observations to update the node labels.

Deleting edge e_0 splits T into two disjoint trees. One of these trees (say T_0) contains the root (node 0) and the other tree (say T_1) does not. (Note that all the node labels of T_1 are the same.) The addition of edge $e' = (r, s)$ reconnects these trees. When T_1 is re-attached to T_0 via edge (r, s) then all node labels of T_0 are still correct and all node labels of T_1 should bechanged to t_r if $r \in T_0$ or t_s if $s \in T_0$.

Labeling rule for the Dual Approach — increasing order

1. Assign a label $w_r = 0$ to each immediate successor r of node 0, and assign node 0 a label of 0. To each immediate successor r of a node t whose node label has been set, assign a label $w_r = \max (w_t, w_{tr})$, where w_{tr} is the weight on edge (t, r).

2. To determine the e, e_0' exchange of Theorem 2

For each edge $(0, j) \notin T$, set $\theta_{0j} = w_{0j} - w_j$ and let $\theta_{0q} =$
$= \min_{(0,j) \notin T} \theta_{0j}$.

Then edge $(0, q) = e_0'$ and e is the edge in $T(e_0')$ whose weight
is equal to w_q. (If this edge is not unique pick any such edge that is not
incident to node 0).

The validity of this procedure follows directly from Theorem 2. As
in the case of decreasing node order, the procedure is quite easy to implement and the labels can be updated with minimal effort. In particular,
suppose an optimal spanning tree T for $P(K)$ is known and an optimal
spanning tree T' for $P(K + R)$ is desired. Then the node labels can be
easily updated using the observations similar to those made earlier. Deleting
edge e split the minimum spanning tree into two disjoint trees. As before, one of the trees (say T_0) contains the root (node 0) and the other
tree (say T_1) does not. The addition of edge e_0' re-connects these trees.
When T_1 is re-attached to T_0 via edge $e_0' = (0, q)$ then all node labels
of T_0 are still correct and thus only tree node labels of T_1 need to be
updated. The updating of the node labels in T_1 occurs by setting $w_q = 0$
and then assigning a node label w_r to each immediate successor r of
each node $t \in T_1$ (whose node label has been set) equal to $w_r =$
$= \max(w_t, w_{tr})$.

The comments made with respect to implementing the decreasing
node order procedure apply in the present setting. Further the above procedure is even more efficient since only the edges incident to node 0 and
not in T have to be evaluated.

Labeling rules for the Primal Approach

The foregoing labeling procedures can be adapted and integrated to
yield an efficient labeling procedure for Theorem 1. In this approach, two
labels must be kept for each node. One label corresponds to the node label used in the Dual Approach — decreasing order procedure and the other
label corresponds to the node label used in the Dual Approach — increasing
order procedure. These labels are determined as follows.

1. Assign a label $t_r = r$ and label $w_r = 0$ to each immediate successor node r of node 0. Assign node 0 a label $t_0 = 0$ and a label $w_0 = 0$. Then to each immediate successor k of a node r whose node labels have been set, assign a label $t_k = r\,(= t_r)$ and a label $w_k = \max\,(w_r, w_{kr})$, where w_{kr} is the weight on edge (k, r).

2. The procedure to determine if the conditions of Theorem 1 are satisfied is:

   (a) Case 1

   For each edge $(i, j) \notin T$ not incident to node 0, set $\theta_{ij} = w_{ij} - \max\,(w_i, w_j)$ if $t_i \neq t_j$; otherwise, set θ_{ij} equal to w_{ij} less the maximum weight associated with the arcs on the unique path between nodes i and j. If $\min\limits_{(i,j)} \theta_{ij} \geqslant 0$, then condition (1) of Theorem 1 is satisfied.

   (b) Case 2

   For each edge $(0, j) \notin T$, set $\theta_{0j} = w_{0j} - w_{0t_j}$. If $\min\limits_{(0,j)} \theta_{0j} \geqslant 0$, then condition (2) of Theorem 1 is satisfied.

   (c) Case 3

   For the edge $(0, j) \notin T$ not incident to node 0, set $\theta_{ij} = w_{ij} - \max\,(w_{0t_i}, w_{0t_j})$ and let $\theta = \min\limits_{(i,\,j)} \theta_{ij}$. For each edge $(0, j) \notin T$, set $B_{0j} = w_{0j} - w_j$ and let $B = \min\limits_{(0,j)} B_{0j}$. If $\theta + B \geqslant 0$, then condition (3) of Theorem 1 is satisfied.

If any of the cases of Theorem 1 are not satisfied, improving exchanges can be easily determined via the above evaluation. The labels can be updated after any of these exchanges in the manner discussed in the dual approaches.

4. ORDER-CONSTRAINED ONE-TREES AND MATROID EXTENSIONS

By rough analogy to the characterization of a one-tree in [8] we can define an *order-constrained one-tree* to be a subgraph which as a spanning tree with order *at most* k at node 0 when node 1 is deleted, and in which node 1 has exactly two incident edges. For k equal to two the minimum order-constrained one-tree problem (defined in the natural manner) is easily established to be a relaxation of the traveling salesman problem. Also an optimal solution to this problem results simply by solving the ordinary minimum spanning tree problem with node 1 deleted, then solving $P(2)$ utilizing the quasi-greedy algorithm of the corollary to Theorem 2 if node 0 has an order exceeding two, and finally re-introducing node 1 together with its two incident edges of least weight. Thus the results of this paper provide the basis for a new relaxation strategy for solving the traveling salesman problem. Moreover, as might be expected, these results have direct analogs of greater generality in the context of matroids. These considerations are treated in [7a].

REFERENCES

[1] Đ.W. Dijkstra, A note on two problems in connexion with graphs, *Numerische Mathematik,* 1 (1959), 269-271.

[2] J. Edmonds, Optimum branchings, *Journal of Research of the National Bureau of Standards,* 71B (1967), 233-240.

[3] J. Edmonds, Matroids and the greedy algorithm, *Mathematical Programming,* 1 (1971), 127-136.

[4] F. Glover, Maximum matching in a convex bipartite graph, *Naval Research Logistics Quarterly,* 15 (1967), 313-316.

[5] F. Glover – D. Karney – D. Klingman, The augmented predecessor index method for locating stepping stone paths and assigning dual prices in distribution problems, *Transportation Science,* 6 (1972), 171-180.

[6]   F. Glover – D. Karney – D. Klingman – A. Napier,
        A computational study on start procedures, basis change criteria,
        and solution algorithms for transportation problems, *Management
        Science,* 20 (1974), 793-814.

[7]   F. Glover – D. Klingman, *A note on admissible exchanges
        in spanning trees,* MSRS 74-3, University of Colorado, April 1974.

[7a]   F. Glover – D. Klingman, *Minimum order-constrained one-
        trees and the traveling salesman problem,* (to appear).

[8]   M. Held – R.M. Karp, The traveling salesman problem and
        minimum spanning trees, *Operations Research,* 18 (1970), 1138-
        1162.

[9]   M. Held – R.M. Karp, The traveling salesman probleam and
        minimum spanning trees; Part II, *Mathematical Programming,* 1,
        (1971), 6-25.

[10]   E. Johnson, Networks and basic solutions, *Operations Re-
        search,* 14 (1966), 619-623.

[10a]   F.S. Hillier – G.J. Lieberman, *Introduction to opera-
        tions research,* San Francisco, California: Holden-Day, Inc., 1967.

[11]   J. Kershenbaum – R. Van Sluke, Computing minimum
        trees, *Proc. ACM Annual Conference,* 1972, 518.

[12]   J.B. Jr. Kruskal, On the shortest spanning subtree of graph
        and the traveling salesman problem, *Proc. Am. Math. Soc.,* 7
        (1972), 48-50.

[13]   P. Rosenstiehl, L'arbre minimum d'un graphe, *Proc. Int.
        Symposium on the Theory of Graphs in Rome* 1966, Dunod/Gordon-
        Breach, 1967.

[14]   V. Srinivasan – G.L. Thompson, Accelerated algorithms
        for labeling and relabeling of trees with application for distribution
        problems, *Journal of the Association for Computing Machinery* 19
        (1972), 712-726.

[15]   H.M. Wagner, *Principles of operations research*, Prentice-Hall, Englewood Cliffs, N.J., 1969.

Fred Glover
University of Colorado, Boulder Colorado 80302
Darwin Klingman
University of Texas, Austin Texas 78712.

NEW ADVANCES IN THE SOLUTION OF LARGESCALE NETWORK AND NETWORK-RELATED PROBLEMS

F. GLOVER — D. KLINGMAN

ABSTRACT

Networks and network related problems occur with remarkable frequency in practical applications. Surprisingly, however, they often go unrecognized even by relatively seasoned modelers, who resort to more cumbersome formulations that may be virtually impossible to solve — or, if solvable, require excessive amounts of computer time and storage. This paper presents a variety of applications from industry and government that illusrate the scope and usefulness of network related formulations. In addition, we report recent breakthroughs in specialized methods that are capable of solving problems in only a few minutes that require many hours of computing time with commercial LP packages. Finally, we report latest developments in large scale applications. These developments have made it possible to solve a manpower planning problem involving 450,000 variables in 26 minutes of central processing time on the IBM 360-65.

1. INTRODUCTION

A question of central concern to the O.R. practitioner is "what type of mathematical programming problems occur most frequently in the real world? " It is admittedly an elusive sort of question, because it is often possible to "identify" a problem as being of one type, without realizing that the use of alternative formulation techniques or appropriate transformations will permit the problem to be represented in another form. (It often seems true that the easiest form of the problem to identify is the hardest one to solve!) Due to the significance of this question, we have pursued an answer for a number of years, surveying O.R. applications reported in the literature, interviewing members of O.R. teams from a variety of different corporations and government agencies, and swapping gossip with our friends and cohorts. As a result of these efforts, we have been led to the somewhat surprising conclusion that a very substantial proportion, perhaps as great as 70%, of the real world mathematical programming consist of − or can be transformed into − networks and "network related" problems. Specifically, the predominant number of practical O.R. applications appear to involve problems of the following types: assignment problems, transportation problems, transshipment problems, generalized transshipment problems, transshipment problems with extra linear constraints, integer problems whose relaxed problem is one of these, or a problem which is equivalent to one of these by a simple linear transformation.

The pioneers of mathematical programming could have said. "I told you so," because similar conclusions were drawn in the early 50's. In fact, a survey by L.W. Smith, Jr. in 1956 indicated that at least half on the linear programming applications involved network models. Some of the reasons cited for the surprising concentration on problems of this kind, particularly in applications, are:

(1) Answers to "large" network problems can be easily computed by *hand,* which is an impossible task for general linear programming problems of similar dimensions. Also, integer solutions are immediately attainable.

(2) Many linear programs can be approximated by network problems, cf [6].

(3) A number of seemingly unrelated linear programs have been found to be equivalent to network problems.

(4) Computer codes have been developed for solving such problems.

(5) Business executives find network models intuitively more understandable, leading to increased demand for their applications in practical settings.

What is perhaps the most remarkable aspect of all this is that in the 70's these "simple" models have gained rather than lost ground to more sophisticated models in applications. In fact, our investigations indicate that the major reasons for the present usage of network models are the same as those given in the 50's.

As a result we began in 1969 to concentrate our research on the development of new techniques which are either computationally efficient for solving such problems or capable of transforming seemingly general linear or integer programming problems into one of these problems. The purpose of this paper is to summarize and relate our accomplishments in this area to earlier efforts. Since the development of these techniques was motivated by a number of real world problems which we were asked to solve by corporations, government agencies, and non-profit enterprises, another purpose of this paper is to summarize some of these problems.

2. APPLICATIONS

Applications arising in practical settings which we have found to be equivalent either to assignment, transportation, transshipment problems, or integer problems whose relaxed problem is one of these problems are briefly described below. Characteristically, in a number of these cases, the implicit network structures were not immediately visible. The techniques used to transform these applications into problems of the above forms are given in [1], [7], [8], [9], [10], [12], [26], [28], [36], [37], [39], [50], [51].

(1) A car distribution model developed by General Motors whose goal is to determine how to assign car models to plant groups, i.e., to determine which models should be manufactured in which plant and then

additionally to assign the cars from these groups to zones in the United States in order to meet customer demand at least cost. This is a transshipment problem whose size varies from 300 nodes and 1200 arcs to 1100 nodes and 3700 arcs. General Motors desired to solve such problems on a routine basis using a small computer with only 32K of central memory. A transshipment problem with 1100 nodes and 3700 arcs is a very large problem to solve in a reasonable time on such a computer since this is an LP with 1100 constraints and 3700 variables. Using our codes [19], [33], we were able to solve this problem in 37 seconds compared with 45 minutes using the G.M. transshipment code on the same computer.

(2) A cash flow model currently being developed by a large corporation to handle their cash flow transactions. This model will identify the most economical way to mange receivables and payables, and is also relevant to the banking industry, aiding in the planning of loans, purchases and sales of securities, etc. This is a transportation problem with extra linear constraints; however using the procedures in [9], [28], [37], [50] it is transformable into a transportation problem. The size of the problem is immense, involving 1000 origins, 1000 destinations, an 500,000 cells (arcs). Using our code [33], this problem can be solved in 30 minutes on an IBM 360/65. Allowing an optimistic estimate a good commerical LP code such as the CDC OPHELIE code would require somewhat more than a 40 hour week of central processing time to solve this problem.

(3) A multi-objective "multi-attribute" planning problem model for personnel assignment is being used by the *Office of Civilian Manpower Management of the Navy* to study personnel allocation to jobs. The original formulation of this problem is a quadratic assignment problem. Using the procedure in [7], the problem can be transformed into an ordinary assignment problem.

(4) A moel used by *Nabisco, Inc.* for scheduling production and distribution of their "cookies" from production plants to regional warehouses, and from warehouses to local distribution facilities. The final formulation is a transportation problem.

(5) A model used by the *Texas Water Resource Management Development Board* for scheduling dam reservoir levels in order to satisfy the peak seasonal demands of each region. This model is solved several thousand times each month in order to simulate all future contingencies over a 36-month planning horizon. There are two basic types of models for this problem. One is a transshipment problem and the other is a generalized transshipment problem. A generalized transshipment problem [3], [23], [29], [31], [42] is one where the flow on an arc may be increased or decreased as the flow traverses the arc (e.g., in this application, evaporation may cause the flow do decrease).

(6) A manufacturing model used by *Farah Manufacturing, Inc.,* which involves a two-stage transshipment model. The first stage involves the acquistion of cloth inventories from textile manufacturers. Once this inventory is ascertained it becomes the supply of the second phase which determines which pants are to be produced and which sew lines (production lines) are to cut these pants. The final formulation is a transportation problem having 150 origins, 1200 destinations, and 20,000 cells.

(7) A model designed by the *Federal Government* to discretize a city into node areas and assign the people in these node areas to bomb shelters.

(8) Problems similar to the preceding for assigning people to parking spaces in a large city.

(9) The disposal waste problem — that is, figuring out where to locate dump areas, etc., in large cities. The formulation of this problem is a plant location whose relaxed subproblems are transshipment problems.

(10) The *Weyerhouser Lumber Company* problem which uses a distriubtion) production model for scheduling logs to plants — to finished products — to local market. The initial formulation is a chance-constrained linear programming problem whose deterministic equivalent can be transformed into a transportation problem using the procedure in [8], [9], [10], [45].

(11) A model used by the *New Mexico Department of Agriculture* for determining the time-phased planting, picking, storing, and distribution

of cotton to ginds. The "natural" formulation of this problem yields a mixed integer transportation problem with extra linear constraints. The transportation part of this formulation involves 2000 origins, 2300 destinations, and 2,460,000 cells. By exploiting the topological characteristics of the problem, the paper [36] showed that this problem can also be formulated as a plant location transshipment problem consisting of 3,441 nodes, 61,640 arcs, and twenty 0-1 variables. Coupling our code [33] with an efficient branch and bound procedure, we have been able to solve this problem in less than 1/2 hour of central processing time on a CDC-6600.

(12) A rotation model used by the *Navy Personnel Research and Development Center* at San Diego for assigning enlisted personnel to sea and shore duty. This model gives rise to transportation problems that vary in size from 10 origins, 12 destinations, and 60 cells, to 1200 origins, 1800 destinations, and 750,000 cells. Using our code [33], we were able to solve a problem with 1093 origins, 1201 destinations, and 450,000 cells on an IBM 360/65 in 26 minutes of central processing time.

(13) A model used by the *Soviet Union* for off-shore oil well drilling. The model selects locations for platforms and assigns wells to platforms. The model [2] is a plant-location problem whose subproblems are transportation problems.

Other applications we have encountered include an ingredient distribution model by Ralston — Purina, an aircraft allocation model, a student-professor-classroom assignment model, a tanker scheduling model, a telecommunication model for the *Texas State Department of Public Welfare,* and an anti-freeze distribution model by *Continental Oil Company.*

3. COMPUTER CODE DEVELOPMENT AND COMPUTATIONAL TESTING

The early historical development of network algorithms involves a number of notable figures in mathematical programming, and offers a variety of interesting contrasts with present day developments.

The first generally satisfactory method for solving the general class of transportation models was due to G.B. Dantzig in 1949. This method is sometimes called the *Row-Column Sum Method* [6], or the MODI method [12]. Charnes and Cooper (1954) later wrote an explanation (dubbed the *Stepping-Stone Method*) of the simplex steps involved in the *Row-Column Sum Method*. With the advent of a method for solving the transportation problem came numerous methods for securing starting bases. Two of the methods commonly referenced are the *Northwest-Corner Rule* [12] and the *Vogel Approximation Method* [46] (often referred to as VAM). Of all the start methods developed, VAM become the one most used for hand calculations due to the excellent start it provides. Thus in the folklore VAM came to be considered the best procedure for both computer and hand calculations.

Subsequent to the development of the simplex based *Row-Column Sum Method,* Ford and Fulkerson (1955), developed a primal-dual method for solving transportation problems. Somewhat earlier Gleyzal [30] developed a method similar to the primal-dual method.

The first computer code for solving transportation problems was based on the *Row-Column Sum Method* and in terms of current jargon is called a primal transportation code. About 1952 such a code was developed by the *George Washington University Logistics Research Project* in conjunction with the *Computation Laboratory of the National Bureau of Standards* [49]. This code, which was designed for use on the *Bureau of Standards Eastern Automatic Computer,* was further improved by the *NBS Computation Laboratory*. The code was capable of solving problems with at most 600 nodes with a pivot time of 3 plus minutes per pivot. Current pivot times for problems of this size are 6-10 milliseconds on the CDC 6600, UNIVAC 1108, and IBM 360/65 computers.

The in-core-out-of-core primal code by Dennis (1958) is one of the first codes to be described in detail in the literature. Dennis' paper is also one of the first to study different criteria for selecting pivot elements. Unfortunately, his study principally involved only one problem of size 30 origins by 260 destinations. The best solution time was 9.6 minutes on the Whirlwind computer.

Another primal code was developed in the late fifties by Glickman, Johnson and Eselson (1959). This code was developed for the UNIVAC I for solving "thin rectangular" problems and was also an in-core-out-of-core code. The code solved a 15 origin by 488 destination problem in 24 minutes. This is approximately 200 times slower than current in-core codes.

Also, during the late fifties a number of transportation codes were developed using *Kuhn's Hungarian Method,* implemented primarily on IBM computers. These codes include the one due to Flood (1961) using his proof of the *König – Egerváry Theorem.* Codes based on Ford and Fulkerson's primal-dual algorithm were also beginning to be implemented, such as the IB-TFL code (1958). The code of Flood and the IB-TFL code were compared on a problem with 29 origins and 116 destinations on an IBM 704. Their times were 3.03 and 3.17 minutes, respectively. Current solution time would probably be 1 second.

Following these developments, there was a hiatus of half a dozen years during which little was visibly accomplished in the development of improved solution methods or computer implementations. From an algorithmic standpoint, it was widely believed that no significant refinements remained to be discovered. In retrospect, this attitude seems surprising, particularly in view of the paucity of experimentation to determine the computational strengths and weaknesses of alternative approaches. Then, in the later sixties and more particularly in the early seventies, a new surge of interest in network methods and applications came about, leading to a number of surprises for those steeped in the notions of a decade earlier.

At this point our narrative shifts from that of an outside observer to that of an active participant for as indicated previously, this was the period in which the remarkable importance of network applications strongly impressed itself upon us, and triggered the series of investigations which we now describe.

In early 1970, we began jointly working with systems analysts in order to develop new techniques which are computationally efficient for solving assignment, transportation, transshipment, and generalized transshipment problems. Our first step in this direction was to elaborate on Johnson's "triple-label method" [32] by providing a method for characterizing successive basis trees with minimal relabeling. This procedure, which is called the augmented predecessor index (API) method, additionally indicates the most efficient way to co-ordinate the activities of finding the representation of the come-in arc (basis equivalent path), pricing-out the basis, and updating basis labels. The API method has been a major contributor to the improvements in the computational efficiency of solution algorithms. Its use was a major factor underlying the efficiency attained by the special purpose primal simplex transportation code of G l o v e r, K a r n e y, and K l i n g m a n [21]. In addition, the procedure was incorporated into the S r i n i v a s a n — T h o m p s o n accelerated primal transportation code [48] and succeeded in cutting the solution times of that algorithm by more than half.

Using the API method, we undertook the development and computational testing (1970-72) of a primal transportation code. This code was expressly designed for computational efficiency but not at the expense of computer memory. The code was further designed for solving both capacitated and uncapacitated problems with non-dense cost matrices (i.e., transportation problems where some cells may not be allowable). After spending 50 hours of central processing time on refining the algorithmic rules of the code, we found that the most efficient solution procedure arises by coupling the primal transportation algorithm with a version of the Row Minimum start rule and a modified row first negative evaluation rule. The G l o v e r, K a r n e y, K l i n g m a n, and N a p i e r study [21] revealed that this primal code was at least eight times faster than the *SHARE out-of-kilter code* [11], [44], and 150 times fater than OPHELIE/LP. Thus the old folklore about the superiority of out-of-kilter methods, and a new folklore among computer service divisions about equivalence of general purpose and special purpose solution codes for transportation and transshipment problems were upended. Additionally, the study showed that this code requires much less memory that any other transportation code.

The largest problems solved in the study of [21] were 1000 origin by 1000 destination problems with an average solution time of 17 seconds.

This study also tested the primal code on four computers, IBM 360/65, UNIVAC 1108, CDC 6400, and CDC 6600 in order to provide insights into conclusions based on comparing times on different machines and compilers. It was discovered that standard guidelines concerning the relative efficiencies of different computers were completely misleading, since the primal code ran only 10%-12% faster on the CDC 6600 than on the UNIVAC 1108 and IBM 360/65, differing substantially from the estimates one would obtain by comparing instruction execution times specified for the machines.

Next we conducted extensive tests [34] on the effect of rectangularity (i.e., the proportionality of the number of origins and destinations), numer of cells (variables), and objective function coefficient distribution, in order to provide users of the code and model builders with solution time estimators and other solution statistics related to structural characteristics of transportation problems. The studies showed that problem structure has an appreciable effect on the computational efficiency of the primal simplex transportation algorithm. The algorithm is sensitive not only to the total number of constraints but also to the relative numbers of origin and destination constraints. In general, rectangular problems can be solved faster than square problems with the same number of constraints and variables. The row oriented start procedure and basis change criterion which yield the best results for square problems become even more efficient for rectangular problems. Additionally, the studies indicate that a change in the number of constraints affects total solution time to a greater extent than a change in the number of variables. Total solution time increases as the number of variables increases and as the variance in the cost coefficients increases.

Motivated by the fact that out-of-kilter codes were found to be substantially slower than the special primal code, B a r r, G l o v e r, and K l i n g m a n [4] developed and coded an improved version of the out-of-kilter method. This code was compared against Clasen's SHARE code, Boeing's code, and the Texas Water Development Board code and found to be at least six times faster than the best of these (which differed from problem to problem). The study also examined a total of 215 capacitated and uncapacitated transshipment problems demonstrating the superiority of the improved version of the out-of-kilter code over the other out-of-kilter codes in all cases. The largest problems solved were 1500 node transshipment problems. The mean solution time was 34 seconds.

Still more recently, G l o v e r, K a r n e y, and K l i n g m a n [19] have developed a general primal transshipment code. Computational comparison of this code with the out-of-kilter code by B a r r, G l o v e r, and K l i n g m a n reveals that the primal code is 50% faster on transshipment problems. This is rather startling since the code of [4] is probably the fastest existing out-of-kilter code and conventional wisdom has it than labeling techniques are inherently more efficient than simplex techniques. The primal transshipment code was also tested against a non-simplex code due to B e n n i n g t o n [5] and found to be eight times faster. This computational study also shows the superiority of the new primal transshipment code in terms of central memory requirements for storing network data. Specifically, the out-of-kilter codes require from 1 1/2 to 3 times the central memory requirements for storing network data as the primal transshipment code. The substantially increased problem size that can be accommodated in-core by the new primal code is illustrated in the study [19] by the solution of an 8000 node problem.

Concurrent with the development of the primal transshipment code [19], G l o v e r, K l i n g m a n, and S t u t z [23] developed a new list structure (called the *Augmented Threaded Index Method*) for recording and updating the basis tree in adjacent extreme point network algorithms. The augmented threaded index (ATI) method provides improvements in both network solution codes and computer sciences list structures for storing and traversing spanning trees. The ATI list structure is the first computer sciences list structure which uses only two pointers per node while providing the user the ability to search a spanning tree both upward and downward. All previously proposed structures require at least three pointers per node. Additionally, computational testing of the ATI method shows that it improves the efficiency of our transshipment code [19] by at least 10% while requiring less computer memory.

All of this computational testing and research has culminated in the development of a large scale in-core out-of-core special purpose primal transshipment code [33] by K a r n e y and K l i n g m a n which is capable of solving transshipment problems of almost unlimited size. This code has solved a problem for the *Navy Personnel Research and Development Center* in San Diego with 2400 nodes and 450,000 arcs on the IBM 360/65 and CDC 6600 using 26 minutes and 23 minutes of central processing time, respectively. Both machines used 40 minutes pf peripheral processing time.

Recently G r a v e s and M c B r i d e [43] have developed an in-core transshipment code using a factorization technique. Their in-core code appears to be roughly comparable in efficiency to our in-core code, running on the average about 30% slower than the method of [19]. To attain this efficiency with their factorization approach however, the Graves and McBride code encounters a serious drawback in requiring an unusually large amount of central memory. In particular, their code requires fourteen node length and two arc length arrays as compared with the five node length and two arc length arrays required by the in-core code of [19]. Thus the Graves – McBridge code requires fully twice as much central memory to solve a problem with 6000 nodes and 18,000 arcs.

Due to the special significance of network-related problems (as opposed to "pure" network problems) in applications, we have broadened our initial investigations to additional areas, correspondingly extending the techniques underlying our previous efforts to provide comparable gains in efficiency for these more difficult problems.

Other classes of problems which we have developed computer codes to solve include the generalized transshipment problems [1], [6], [12], [23], [25], [26], [27], [29], [31], [42]. These generalized problems may be viewed as similar to the classical transportation and transshipment problems except that flow on an arc (i, j) from node i to node j is subject to amplification (or attenuation) by a factor p_{ij} (i.e., the amount flowing into node j along arc (i, j) is p_{ij} times the amount that leaves node i along arc (i, j)). A variety of practical economic problems, which in fact have nothing in common with "transportation," may be stated as such a problem (e.g., cash flow and budget models, electrical circuit models, plastic-limit analysis and design of structures problems, machine loading models, the classical cutting stock problem, blending models, allocation of aircraft types to service routes, etc.). As shown in references [1], [6], [12], [42] this seemingly slight generalization of the classical problems has a drastic effect upon the basis structure. However, by carefully analyzing and specializing the steps of the simplex method, we show in [23], [25] that the augmented predecessor indexing method (which we utilized in solving the pure problems) could be easily extended to handle the generalized problems. We have recently developed a code [29] based on this extension of the API method which, like the pure codes, is expressly designed for computational efficiency. Surprisingly, the generalized code requires very little computer memory beyond that required by the pure codes. Thirty hours of central processing time have been devoted to refining the algorithmic rules of the code, and it is able to solve generalized transshipment problems with 2000 nodes and 15,000 arcs in 50-60 seconds. This is approximately 100 times faster than state-of-the-art LP codes can solve these problems. Additionally, the generalized code is less than twice as slow on pure problems as our pure codes. Thus, our generalized code is able to solve pure problems faster than the widely used codes for solving pure problems (except our own), and at the same time is able to solve more general problems.

Generalized transshipment codes have also recently been developed by Landley [41] and Mauras [42a]. The code by Mauras [42a] is extremely well organized, and appears to be nearly comparable in solution efficiency to our code. However, the price of attaining such efficiency with an alternative approach again appears to involve rather severe demands on central memory. Both the codes of [41], [42a] require at least double the central memory required by the code of [29].

4. CURRENT CODE DEVELOPMENT

Presently our computational research efforts are devoted to imbedding our network codes into more general algorithms for solving plant location problems, fixed charge transportation and transshipment problems, generalized transportation and transshipment problems with integer variables [40], transportation and transshipment problems with arbitrary extra linear constraints [38], and multicommodity transshipment problems. Since the efficient solution of all of these problems rests primarily on efficient procedures for solving transportation, transshipment generalized transportation, and generalized transshipment problems, we firmly believe that highly efficient codes can be developed for each of these problem classes.

Recently the *Office of Tax Analysis* (OTA) has developed excellent models [49a], [49b] for compacting, matching and merging data sets. In particular, the problem of primary interest to OTA is the merging of the Current Population Survey (CPS) and OTA Tax Model files into a more informationally effective composite file to be analyzed by the *Transfer Income Model* (TRIM). The process developed by Turner and Robbins [49b] for matching the compacted data sets involves the solution of extremely large transportation problems which are two orders of magnitude larger than the largest transportation problem solved to date. Consequently, we are currently developing an extended transportation system for OTA which will be capable of solving transportation problems with 50,000 nodes and 62 million arcs on a UNIVAC 1108.

REFERENCES

[1] G.M. Appa, The transportation problem and its variants, *Operations Research Quarterly,* 24 (1973), 79-97.

[2] D. Babyev, *Mathematical model for optimal location of oil platforms and assignment of directed wells.*

[3] E. Balas — P.L. Ivanescu (Hammer), On the generalized transportation problem, *Management Science,* 11 (1964), 188-202.

[4] R.S. Barr — F. Glover — D. Klingman, An improved version of the out-of-kilter method and a comparative study of computer codes, to appear in *Mathematical Programming.*

[5]   G.E. Bennington, *An efficient minimal cost flow algorithm, O.R., Report* 75, Nort Carolina State University, Raleigh, North Carolina, (June 1972).

[6]   A. Charnes – W.W. Cooper, *Management models and industrial applications of linear programming,* Vol. I-II, New York, John Wiley and Sons, Inc., 1961.

[7]   A. Charnes – W.W. Cooper – D. Klingman – A. Niehaus, Static and dynamic biased quadratic multi-attribute assignment models: Solutions and Equivalents, *CS* 115, *Center for Cybernetic Stuedies,* University of Texas, Austin, Texas.

[8]   A. Charnes – F. Glover – D. Klingman, The lower bounded and partial upper bounded distribution model, *Naval Research Logistic Quarterly,* 18 (1971), 277-278.

[9]   A. Charnes – F. Glover – D. Klingman, A note on a distribution problem, *Operations Research,* 18, 6 (1970), 1213-1216.

[10] A. Charnes – D. Klingman, The distribution problem with upper and lower bounds on the node requirements, *Management Science,* 16, 9 (1970), 638-642.

[11] R.J. Clasen, The numerical solution of network problems using the out-of-kilter algorithm, *RAND Corporation Memorandum* RM-5456-PR, Santa Monica, California, (March, 1968),

[12] G. Dantzig, *Linear programming and extensions,* Princeton, New Jersey: University Press, 1963.

[13] G. Dantzig, Chapter XXIII, *Activity analysis of production and allocation,* Edited by T.C. Koopmans, John Wiley and Sons, 1951.

[14] J.B. Dennis, A high-speed computer technique for the transportation problem, *Journal of Association for Computation Machinery,* 8 (1958), 132-153.

[15]   M.M. Flood, A transportation algorithm and code, *Naval Research Logistics Quarterly,* 8 (1961), 257-276.

[16]   L.R. Ford – D. Fulkerson, A primal-dual algorithm for the capacitated Hitchcock problem, *Naval Research Logistics Quarterly,* 4, 1 (1957), 47-54.

[17]   D.R. Fulkerson, An out-of-kilter method for solving minimal cost flow problems, *J. Soc. Indust. Appl. Math.,* 9 (1961), 18-27.

[18]   S. Glickman – L. Johnson – L. Eselson, Coding the transportation problem, *Naval Research Logistics Quarterly,* 7 (1960), 169-183.

[19]   F. Glover – D. Karney – D. Klingman, Implementation and computational study on start procedures and basis change criteria for a primal network code, *Networks,* 20 (1974), 191-212.

[20]   F. Glover – D. Karney – D. Klingman, The augmented precedessor index method for locating stepping stone paths and assigning dual prices in distribution problems, *Transportation Science,* 6 (1972), 171-180.

[21]   F. Glover – D. Karney – D. Klingman – A. Napier, A computational study on start procedures, basis change criteria, and solution algorithms for transportation problems, *Management Science,* 20, 5 (1974), 793-814.

[22]   F. Glover,– D. Karney – D. Klingman, Double-pricing dual and feasible start algorithms for the capacitated transportation (distribution) problem, University of Texas at Austin (1970).

[23]   F. Glover – D. Klingman – J. Stutz, Extensions of the augmented predecessor index method to generalized network problems, *Transportation Science,* 7, 4 (1973), 377-384.

[24]   F. Glover – D. Klingman, Finding minimum spanning trees with a fixed number of links on a node, Presented at 45th National ORSA/TIMS meeting, Boston, April 22-24, 1974.

[25] F. Glover – D. Klingman, A note on computational simplification in solving generalized transportation problems, *Transportation Science,* 7 (1973), 351-361.

[26] F. Glover – D. Klingman, On the equivalence of some generalized network problems to pure network problems, *Mathematical Programming,* 4, 3 (1973), 369-378.

[27] F. Glover – D. Klingman – A. Napier, Basic dual feasible solutions for a class of generalized networks, *Operations Research,* 20, 1 (1972), 126-137.

[28] F. Glover – D. Klingman – G.T. Ross, Finding equivalent transportation formulations for constrained transportation problems, *Naval Research Logistics Quarterly,* 21, 2 (1974), 247-253.

[29] F. Glover – D. Klingman – J. Stutz, Implementation and computational study of a generalized network code, Presented at 44th National Meeting of ORSA, San Diego, California, Nov. 12-14, 1973.

[30] A.N. Gleyzal, An algorithm for solving the transportation problem, *Journal of Research of the National Bureau of Standards,* 54, 4 (1955), 213-216.

[31] W.S. Jewell, Optimal flow through network with gains, *Operations Research,* 10 (1962), 476-499.

[32] E. Johnson, Networks and basic solutions, *Operations Research,* 14, 4 (1966), 619-623.

[33] D. Karney – D. Klingman, Implementation and computational study on an in-core out-of-core primal network code, *CS* 158, *Center for Cybernetic Studies,* University of Texas, Austin.

[34]   D. Klingman – A. Napier – G.T. Ross, A computational study on the effects of problem dimensions on solution time for transportation problems, Research Report *CS* 135, *Center for Cybernetic Studies,* University of Texas, Austin, Texas, (1973). To appear in JACM.

[35]   D. Klingman – A. Napier – J. Stutz, NETGEN – A program for generating large scale (un) capacitated assignment, transportation and minimum cost flow network problems, *Management Science,* 20, 5 (1974), 814-822.

[36]   D. Klingman – P. Randolph – S. Fuller, A cotton-pickin cotton ginning problem, Presented at 44th National Meeting of the *Operations Research Society of America,* San Diego, California, Nov. 10-12, 1973.

[37]   D. Klingman – G.T. Ross, Finding equivalent network for formulations for constrained network problems, *CS* 108, *Center for Cybernetic Studies,* University of Texas, Austin, Texas.

[38]   D. Klingman – R. Russell, On solving constrained transportation problems, to appear in *Operations Research.*

[39]   D. Klingman – R. Russell, The transportation problem with mixed constraints, *Operational Research Quarterly,.* 3, 4 (1974).

[40]   D. Klingman – J. Stutz, Computational testing in integer generalized network code, Presented at 45th National ORSA/TIMS meeting, Boston, April 22-24, 1974.

[41]   R.W. Langley, *Continuous and integer generalized flow problems,* Ph. D. Dissertation, Georgia Tech. June, 1973.

[42]   J. Louris, Topology and computation of the generalized flow problems, *Management Science,* 11 (1964), 177-187.

[42a] J.F. Maurras, Optimization of the flow through networks with gains, *Mathematical Programming,* 4, 2 (1972), 135-144.

[43] R.D. McBride, Factorization in large-scale linear programming, *Working Paper* No. 220, *Western Management Science Institute*, University of California, Los Angeles, June, 1973.

[44] Out-of-kilter network routine, *SHARE distribution* 3536, *SHARE distribution agency*, Hawthorne, New York, (1967).

[45] R.M. Reese, *The marketing of a forest product; A chance-constrained transportation model*, Bureau of Business Research, Graduate School of Business, The University of Texas at Austin, 1974.

[46] N.V. Reinfeld – W.R. Vogel, *Mathematical programming*, (Englewood Cliffs, N.J.: Prentice-Hall, Inc., 1958).

[47] Jr. L.W. Smith, Current status of the industrial use of linear programming, *Management Science*, 2 (1956), 156-158.

[48] F. Srinivasan – G.L. Thompson, Benefit-cost analysis of coding techniques for the primal transportation algorithm, *JACM*, 20 (1973), 194-213.

[49] E.D. Stanley – L. Gainen, Linear programming in bid evaluation, *Naval Research Logistics Quarterly*, 1 (1954), 48-54.

[49a] J.S. Turner, A profile analysis method to reduce the size of microdata files, *Office of Tax Analysis, Dept. of the Treasury*, Washington, D.C.

[49b] J.S. Turner – Gary A. Robbins, Microdata set merging using network models, *Office of Tax Analysis, Dept. of Treasury*, Washington, D.C.

[50] H. Wagner, The lower bounded and partial upper bounded distribution model, *Naval Research Logistics Quarterly*, (1974).

[51] H. Wagner, *Principles of operations research with application to managerial decision*, (Englewood Cliffs, N.J., Trentice-Hall, Inc., 1969).

Fred Glover

University of Colorado, Boulder Colorado 80302

Darwin Klingman

University of Texas, Austin, Texas 78712.

A PENALTY FUNCTION METHOD FOR MINIMAX PROBLEMS

V.A. GORELIK

The general problem of determining the sequential maximin with connected constraints is

$$(1) \qquad W = \sup_{x_1 \in A_1} \inf_{y_1 \in B_1} \ldots \sup_{x_n \in A_n} \inf_{y_n \in B_n} F(x^n, y^n),$$

where

$$A_i = A_i(x^{i-1}, y^{i-1}) = \{x_i \in X_i : g_i(x^i, y^{i-1}) \geqslant 0\},$$

$$B_i = B_i(x^i, y^{i-1}) = \{y_i \in Y_i : h_i(x^i, y^i) \geqslant 0\},$$

$$x^i = (x_1, x_2, \ldots, x_i), \quad y^i = (y_1, y_2, \ldots, y_i), \quad i = 1, 2, \ldots, n,$$

x^0, y^0 are the symbols of the argument's absence.

The fact that there is only one constraint of the inequality type in the definition of the sets A_i, B_i doesn't mean a loss of generality, since any finite number of constraints — equality or inequality — may be summed up into one, and if the cardinality of the constraints is continuum, then — in a rather general case — they may be integrated into one constraint.

Many problems of operation research and game theory may be reduced to the problems of type (1) or their specific cases [1]-[3].

Let's introduce the continuous penalty functionals $\Phi_i(x^i, y^{i-1})$ and $\Psi_i(x^i, y^i)$ such that $\Phi_i(x^i, y^{i-1}) = 0$, if $x_i \in A_i(x^{i-1}, y^{i-1})$, and $\Phi_i(x^i, y^{i-1}) < 0$ in the opposite case, $\Psi_i(x^i, y^i) = 0$, if $y_i \in B_i(x^i, y^{i-1})$, and $\Psi_i(x^i, y^i) > 0$ in the opposite case.

Theorem 1. *Let us suppose, that*

(a) X_i, Y_i *are compact sets in arbitrary metric spaces,*

(b) *the functionals* $F(x^n, y^n)$, $g_i(x^i, y^{i-1})$, $h_i(x^i, y^i)$ *are continuous in every variable;*

(c) $A_i \neq \phi$, $\forall(x^i, y^{i-1})$, $B_i \neq \phi$, $\forall(x^{-i}, y^{-i})$, *maps* A_i, B_i $(i = 1, \ldots, n)$ *are continuous in the Hausdorff metric in all variables, then*

$$W = \lim_{\substack{t_i \to \infty \\ i = 1, 2, \ldots, 2_n}} \max_{x_1 \in X_1} \min_{y_1 \in Y_1} \ldots \max_{x_n \in X_n} \min_{y_n \in Y_n} \left\{ F(x^n, y^n) + \right.$$

$$\left. + \sum_{i=1}^{n} [t_i \Phi_i(x^i, y^{i-1}) + t_{n+i} \Psi_i(x^i, y^i)] \right\}.$$

and any limit point x_1^0 *of the set of the optimal strategies* $x_1^0(t_1, t_2, \ldots$ $\ldots, t_{2_n})$ *of the corresponding problems without constraints is optimal for the problem* (1).

The continuity condition of the point-set maps A_i, B_i is essential; it's not difficult to construct an example showing that the Theorem 1 is false without this condition. It follows from Theorem 1 that the problem of determining the sequential maximin with connected constraints (and, of course, the problem with disconnected constraints as its special case) can be reduced to solving the sequential maximin without any constraints. The latter may be reduced with the help of penalties to the extremal problem without any constraints [4]-[6]. So the following theorem is correct for the problem of determining the simple maximin with connected constraints [4].

Theorem 2. *Let* $F(x, y)$ *and* $\Phi(x, y)$ *be continuous on* $X \times Y$ *and satisfy the Lipschitz condition for* y, $\Phi(x, y) \geqslant 0$ *on* $X \times Y$,

$$Y(x) = \{y \in Y: \Phi(x, y) = 0\} \neq \phi$$

$\forall x \in X$, *Y-parallelepiped in* R^m, σ *is the Lebesgue measure in* R^m, $\beta > 0$, *then*

$$\sup_{x \in X} \min_{y \in Y(x)} F(x, y) =$$

(2)
$$= \lim_{C \to \infty} \max_{(x, u) \in X \times [a, b]} \left\{ U - C^{m + \beta} \int_Y [\min(0, F(x, y) + \right.$$

$$\left. + C\Phi(x, y) - U)]^2 \sigma(dy) \right\}$$

and $\forall C > 0 \; \exists C_0$ *so, that* $\forall C \geqslant C_0$ *the realization of the maximum in* (2) $x_{max}(C)$ *and* $u_{max}(C)$ *are, accordingly,* ϵ*-optimal guaranteeing strategy and* ϵ*-approach to the maximal guaranteed result*

$$\sup_{x \in X} \min_{y \in Y(x)} F(x, y).$$

If Y *is a set consisting of a finite number of points* $y_1, y_2, \ldots, y_N$, *then*

$$\sup_{x \in X} \min_{y \in Y(x)} F(x, y) =$$

$$= \lim_{\substack{C \to \infty \\ K \to \infty}} \max_{(x, u) \in X \times [a, b]} \left\{ U - K \sum_{i=1}^N [\min(0, F(x, y_i) + \right.$$

$$\left. + C\Phi(x, y_i) - u)]^2 \right\}.$$

The penalty functions method may also be applied to the minimax problem of the optimal control where the equation of movement and the functional contain indefinite parameters.

All the following results are obtained with V. V. Fjodorov.

Consider the following problem

(3) $$I_0 = \min_{u(t)} \max_{1 \leqslant i \leqslant N} \int_0^T g_i(t, x^i(t), u(t)) \, dt$$

with constraints

(4) $$\dot{x}^i(t) = f_i(t, x^i(t), u(t)), \quad x^i(0) = x_0^i, \quad i = 1, 2, \ldots, N,$$

(5) $$u(t) \in G \quad \forall t \in [0, T].$$

Let us consider the C-problem corresponding to (3)-(5).

$$h(C) = \min_{x(t),\, U(t)} \max_{1 \leqslant i \leqslant N} \left\{ C \int_0^T |\dot{x}^i(t) - f_i(t, x^i(t), u(t))|^2 \, dt + \right.$$

$$\left. + \int_0^T g_i(t, x^i(t), u(t)) \, dt \right\}, \quad x(t) = (x^1(t), \ldots, x^N(t)),$$

where C is positive and the minimum is taken over the set of all those absolutely continuous vector-functions $x^i(t)$, defined on $[0, T]$, which satisfy: the derivative, $\dot{x}^i(t)$ belongs to $L_2(0, T)$, $x^i(0) = x_0^i$; and over those vector-functions $u(t)$ from $L_2(0, T)$, which are defined on $[0, T]$ and take on values from G.

Theorem 3. *Let's assume that the existence and uniqueness conditions hold for the decision of equations (4), further let us assume that*

Filippov's condition is satisfied;

there exists a decision for the C-problem $x_0(t, C), u_0(t, C)$;

G is convex and compact;

the decision of equation (4) under the condition $u(t) = u_0(t, C)$ is $\hat{x}^i(t, C)$;

then

$$I_0 = \lim_{C \to \infty} h(C) = \lim_{C \to \infty} \max_{1 \leqslant i \leqslant N} \int_0^T g_i(t, \hat{x}^i(t, C), U_0(t, C)) \, dt.$$

Then, using Theorem 2 the problem (3)-(5) may be reduced to the variation problem

$$h(C, K) = \min_{x(t), u(t), V} \left\{ V + K \sum_{i=1}^{N} [\max (0, C \int_0^T |\dot{x}^i(t) - \right.$$

(6)

$$\left. - f_i(t, x^i(t), u(t))|^2 \, dt + \int_0^T g_i(t, x^i(t), u(t)) \, dt - V)]^2 \right\}.$$

Theorem 4. *Let all the conditions of Theorem 3 be satisfied, let* $x_0(t, C, K), U_0(t, C, K), V_0(C, K)$ *be the decision of the* (C, K)-*problem* (6), $\hat{x}^i(t, C, K)$ *be the decision of the equation (4) under* $u(t) = U_0(t, C, K),$ *then*

$$I_0 = \lim_{\substack{C \to \infty \\ K \to \infty}} h(C, K) = \lim_{\substack{C \to \infty \\ K \to \infty}} V_0(C, K) =$$

$$= \lim_{\substack{C \to \infty \\ K \to \infty}} \max_{1 \leqslant i \leqslant N} \int_0^T g_i(t, \hat{x}^i(t, C, K), U_0(t, C, K)) \, dt \, .$$

The above theorems give the basis for developing simple numerical methods for solving the minimax problems.

REFERENCES

[1] Jn.B. Germeier, *Introduction to the theory of operations research*, Moscow, "Nauka" (1972).

[2] Jn.B. Germeier – N.N. Moiseev, *On some problems of the hierarchy systems theory, The problems of applied mathematics and mechanics*, Moscow, "Nauka", 1971, 30-43.

[3] V.A. Gorelik, The guaranteed result principle in non-antagonistic two-person games with information exchange; *Operations Research*, 2, Computational Centre Acad. Sci. USSR, Moscow, 1971, 102-118.

[4] V.A. Gorelik, Approximate determining of maximin with connected constraints, *The Journal of Computational Mathematics and Mathematical Physics*, 2 (1972), 510-517.

[5] V.V. Fjodorov, On the problem of determining the consequent maximin, *ibid*, (1972), 897-908.

[6] Jn.B. Germeier, The approximate reducing of the problem of determining minimax to the problem of maximum determining, *ibid*, (1969), 730-731.

V.A. Gorelik

Moscow 117 806, V-279 Profsojuznaja 81, USSR.

STOCHASTIC SERVICE SYSTEMS WITH TWO INPUT PROCESSES AND REPEATED CALLS
(TRAFFIC ENGINEERING OF TELEX STATIONS)

G. GOSZTONY

INTRODUCTION

Although telex networks handle large amounts of traffic and the growth rate of telex traffic in some countries exceeds 40% per year [1], there are almost no publications of the field of telex traffic engineering. The obvious reasons are the following:

(a) the characteristics of telex traffic differ from those of telephone traffic and

(b) traffic handling is strongly influenced by the repeated call phenomenon.

The nature of telex traffic was the topic of the investigations of B a d r a n [2], [3], who found, that the input process of calls is not Poissonian, but has a peaked character and the distribution of holding times may be interpreted as a mixture of two exponential distributions with short and long mean values, respectively. Recently H a t t o r i and Y a m a d a [4] published some similar results.

Experience shows, that the probability of successful reaching the called station is rather low, frequently less then 0.5. This unhappy situation is responsible for the numerous repeated call attempts thus for the heavy overloads both on common control devices and on connecting networks.

Because of practical reasons the traffic engineering of telex stations, exchanges or networks was up to now mainly based on well proved "telephone" methods. At present no such method exists for repeated call attempts.

The effect of repeated call attempts appears in telephony too, numerous traffic measurements and theoretical investigations were made on this field (See [5], [6], [7] and the bibliography attached to them), but for the time being no specific method is generally accepted.

Measuraments show, that several time periods related to the repeated call phenomenon are not exponentially distributed. Therefore theories using B i r t h & D e a t h *equations,* although powerful in themselves [8], [9], [10] are not true descriptions of reality. Other methods (e.g. [11]) make use of other assumptions but the measurement data available are not yet sufficient to check theories of any kind.

To our best knowledge there are no published extensive measurement results of repeated call attempts on the telex field either. It may be supposed that there will be a lack of appropriate data for some time, because efficient measurements of this type need computer like equipment and rather long time for observations and evaluations.

Telex traffic engineering problems of today must therefore be solved by some approximative method.

To make use of a well developed theoretical method in the following we assume Poisson inputs, exponentially distributed time periods and we use B & D equations.

These assumptions are not fully justified, but the use of them may serve as detailed first approximation. For the time being no better theoretical solution of the complex problem can be performed. In lack of appropriate empirical data computer simulation doesn't give more information either.

Existing difficulties in defining the traffic capacity in the presence of repeated call attempts is also a burden on traffic engineering; there are no congestion standards for this case etc. So a clear, however not quite exact picture may serve as a valuable tool for the people being responsible for traffic engineering of telex stations.

In the first section we give a description of traffic handling features of telex stations. The next section is devoted to mathematical models and the relevant state spaces. In the third section one can find the state equation systems followed by the system characteristics given in the fourth section. Last some numerical examples are given and the motivation of the selected method is summarized.

1. TRAFFIC HANDLING FEATURES OF TELEX STATIONS

The telex stations investigated consist of a group of T both-way telex devices. In the forward direction each call occupies a free device for the setup time. If the attempt is successful the device remains occupied for the message time too. Otherwise, if all devices of the group are busy or the call attempt is unsuccessful for any reason the call shall join the group of messages waiting for repetition. An incoming call attempt occupies a free device for the message time or changes-over to repetition state if all devices of the group are busy.

Incoming messages being in repetition state make new attempts at a random. Outgoing messages may be served in two ways:

(a) If everybody sends his own messages himself the repeated call attempts from the sender side arrive at a random too. The situation is: several outgoing messages can be in repetition state, free telex devices can exist at the same time.

(b) If each device is handled by an operator, the messages in the repetition state form a single queue and looking from the sender side, we have a waiting system. It is assumed that operators can help each other in the operation. No free device can exist if there is any outgoing message waiting for the system. Messages are sent in order of their arrival, unsuccessful messages, if any, are repeated continuously one after the other. There is no strict regulation how to make repetitions (e.g. more attempts of the same message continuously or only one attempt per message, etc.)

The difference between (a) and (b) is that in the second case the operators "see" the busy-idle state of the devices and in the first one they don't.

Messages in repetition state may leave the system and make no further repetitions. This is possible for messages of the queue of service mode (b) too.

The traffic capacity of the system with T devices in a group may be characterised e.g. by the following average values:

(i)   number of call attempts per original message,

(ii)   length of the waiting queue,

(iii) number of messages being in repetition state,

(iv)   amount of messages leaving the system without being served, etc.

As we already mentioned, up to now there is no agreement on the characteristics to be used in this respect.

2. METHEMATICAL MODELS AND STATE SPACES

2.1. *Assumptions*

The systems investigated (Fig. 1) consist of a group of T servers which serve the demands of two input processes. These input processes, No. 1 and No. 2, are the call attempts of the sender and receiver sides.

Each input process has a Poissonian primary part (the original messages) with intensities: λ_1 and λ_2 and a secondary part (the repeated

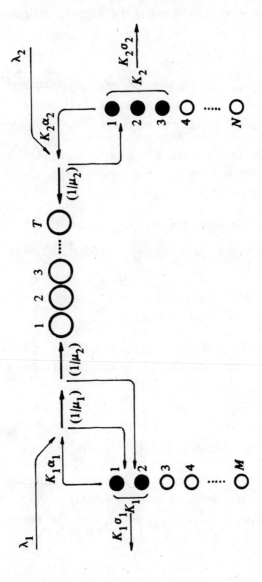

Fig. 1. The model of the system

call attempts). If all T servers of the group are busy the arriving demand enters a repetition position (incoming messages or outgoing messages with service mode (a)) or joins a queue (outgoing messages with service mode (b)).

The repetition intensities are: α_1 and α_2; demands in the queue make repetitions in order of their arrival (FIFO). The number of repetition positions and/or queue places can be finite (M, N) or infinite.

It may occur, that a demand in a repetition position or on a queue place leaves the system without being served, departure intensities for this case are: σ_1 and σ_2.

An outgoing demand of the input process No. 1 first seizes a free server for the setup time (average: $\frac{1}{\mu_1}$, and after this it may be rejected with a probability s or it is served with a probability $(1 - s)$. Rejected demand enter a repetitition position or join the queue according to service modes (a) or (b), respectively.

An incoming demand of the input process No. 2 immediately seizes a free server for service. The average service time (holding time of a message) is $\frac{1}{\mu_2}$ for both types of demands.

All time periods are assumed to be exponentially distributed, thus the behaviour of the system may be described by a B & D process.

The investigations were made in statistical equilibrium. From the state equations the time independent state probabilities may be determined. The solution of the equation system is reduced to the treatment of a linear equation system completed with a normalising condition.

In the following three different mathematical models, TA, TB and TC, are presented according to the already mentioned service modes.

2.2. Model TA, "blind repetition"

The state of the system is designated by the quadruple (j, k, m, n).
Here

$j = 0, 1, 2, \ldots$	is the number of servers being in "call setup" state
$k = 0, 1, 2, \ldots$	is the number of servers being in "message" state
$m = 0, 1, 2, \ldots, M$	is the number of demands in repetition state at the sender side
$n = 0, 1, 2, \ldots, N$	is the number of demands in repetition state at the receiver side.

Obviously $j + k \leqslant T$, and the numbers of repetition positions, M and N, can be unlimited.

Model TA corresponds to service mode (a) in which No. 1 demands in repetition state may exist even if there are free servers in the group.

The TA state space (Fig. 2) may be divided into several planes, the possible transitions beetween states are not indicated. The case $T = 2$ is represented.

2.3. Model TB, "waiting repetition"

Designations are the same as in the Paragraph 2.2. Model TB corresponds to service mode (b) in which No. 1 demands are waiting only if all servers are busy. Fig. 3 shows the TB state space.

2.4. Model TC, "corrected intensity"

The state of the system is designated by the triple (k, m, n). Here

$$k = 0, 1, 2, \ldots, T$$

is the number of busy servers.

All other designations are the same as before. In this approximation of model TB the "call setup" state and the "message" state are not distinguished. To provide the same load on the servers the intensity of the primary input process of No. 1 demands has been corrected properly, i.e. λ_1

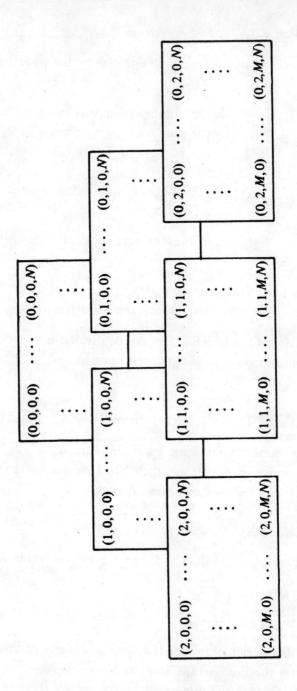

Fig. 2. State space of Model TA

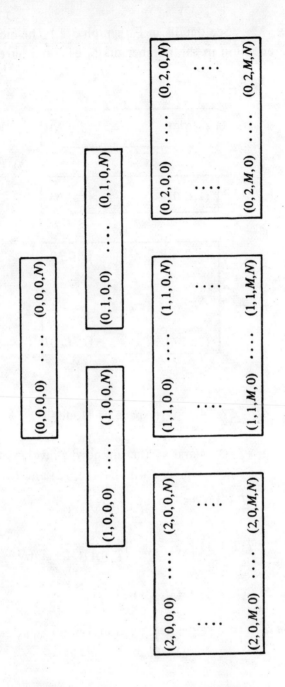

Fig. 3. State space of Model TB

is replaced by λ_1^*. (See details in Paragraph 3.2.) The model was used because drastic reduction in the number of states could have been achieved, see Fig. 4.

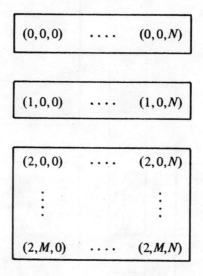

Fig. 4. State space of Model TC

The number of states and so the unknowns involved for the models mentioned may be calculated by formulae (1), (2) and (3) below.

(1) $$U_{TA} = \frac{(T+1)(T+2)}{2}(M+1)(N+1)$$

(2) $$U_{TB} = \frac{T(T+1)}{2}(N+1) + (T+1)(M+1)(N+1)$$

(3) $$U_{TC} = T(N+1) + (M+1)(N+1)$$

Some characterstic values are given in Table I.

	M		
	3	5	7
TA	96	216	384
TB	60	124	216
TC	24	48	80

Table I. The number of states in the models, $T = 2$, $M = N$

3. EQUATIONS OF STATE

In Figures 2, 3 and 4 it was not possible to indicate the permitted transitions beetween the states of the system, the figures would have become too sophisticated.

To illustrate the situation we give the detailed description of model TB including transition possibilities and the equation system. The corresponding items for TA and TC may be concluded from these considerations without any difficulty.

To facilitate this we summarize the differences in the set of input parameters in Table II for the three models (See Section 2).

Parameter	Model		
	TA	TB	TC
Repetition intensity for No. 1 demands	α	∞	
Probability of service after successful dialling	$1 - s$		1

Table II. Differences of the input parameters

It's to be noted that an infinite repetition intensity, i.e. no time interval between consecutive repetitions, means that it is a service on delay basis. On the other hand in Model TC every demand is successful which has previously seized a free server.

3.1. *Model* TB

From the transition point of view, the states of the system should be split up into three groups. These are

(i) $j + k < T, \quad m = 0$,

(ii) $j + k = T, \quad m = 0$,

(iii) $j + k = T, \quad m > 0$.

The transition patterns and the equations are different for these three groups. Only the general case will be dealt with, specialities valid for the edges of the state space are not mentioned. The reader is supposed to be familiar with the methods of deriving equation systems of this type. As a general rule, transitions to or from not existing states are not allowed, so the corresponding transition coefficients are zero.

For the group (i) the permitted transitions are shown in Table III.

If the probability of being in state (j, k, m, n) is designated by $P(j, k, m, n)$ the state equations for group $i.$, read as follows

$$[\lambda_1 + \lambda_2 + j\mu_1(1 - s) + k\mu_2 + n(\alpha_2 + \sigma_2)] P(j, k, 0, n) =$$

$$= \lambda_1 P(j - 1, k, 0, n) + \lambda_2 P(j, k - 1, 0, n) +$$

(4)

$$+ (j + 1)\mu_1(1 - s) P(j + 1, k - 1, 0, n) +$$

$$+ (k + 1)\mu_2 P(j, k + 1, 0, n) +$$

$$+ (n + 1)\alpha_2 P(j, k - 1, 0, n + 1) +$$

$$+ (n + 1)\sigma_2 P(j, k, 0, n + 1).$$

In a similar way the permitted transitions for groups (ii) and (iii) are shown in Tables IV. and V.

From	Transition coeff. →	To/From	Transition coeff. →	To
$(j-1, k, 0, n)$	λ_1		λ_1	$(j+1, k, 0, n)$
$(j, k-1, 0, n)$	λ_2		λ_2	$(j, k+1, 0, n)$
$(j+1, k-1, 0, n)$	$(j+1)\mu_1(1-s)$	$(j, k, 0, n)$	$j\mu_1(1-s)$	$(j-1, k+1, 0, n)$
$(j, k+1, 0, n)$	$(k+1)\mu_2$		$k\mu_2$	$(j, k-1, 0, n)$
$(j, k-1, 0, n+1)$	$(n+1)\alpha_2$		$n\alpha_2$	$(j, k+1, 0, n-1)$
$(j, k, 0, n+1)$	$(n+1)\sigma_2$		$n\sigma_2$	$(j, k, 0, n-1)$

Table III. Transitions from/to state $(j, k, 0, n)$ if $j + k < T$

From	Transition coeff. →	To/From	Transition coeff. →	To
$(j-1, k, 0, n)$	λ_1		λ_1	$(j, k, 1, n)$
$(j, k, 0, n-1)$	λ_2		λ_2	$(j, k, 0, n+1)$
$(j, k-1, 0, n)$	λ_2		$j\mu_1(1-s)$	$(j-1, k+1, 0, n)$
$(j+1, k-1, 0, n)$	$(j+1)\mu_1(1-s)$	$(j, k, 0, n)$	$k\mu_2$	$(j, k-1, 0, n)$
$(j-1, k+1, 1, n)$	$(k+1)\mu_2$		$n\sigma_2$	$(j, k, 0, n-1)$
$(j, k-1, 0, n+1)$	$(n+1)\alpha_2$			
$(j, k, 1, n)$	σ_1			
$(j, k, 0, n+1)$	$(n+1)\sigma_2$			

Table IV. Transitions from/to state $(j, k, 0, n)$, if $j + k = T$

From	Transition coeff. →	To/From	Transition coeff. →	To
$(j, k, m-1, n)$	λ_1		λ_1	$(j, k, m+1, n)$
$(j, k, m, n-1)$	λ_2		λ_2	$(j, k, m, n+1)$
$(j+1, k-1, m, n)$	$(j+1)\mu_1(1-s)$	(j, k, m, n)	$j\mu_1(1-s)$	$(j-1, k+1, m, n)$
$(j-1, k+1, m+1, n)$	$(k+1)\mu_2$		$k\mu_2$	$(j+1, k-1, m-1, n)$
$(j, k, m+1, n)$	$(m+1)\sigma_1$		$m\sigma_1$	$(j, k, m-1, n)$
$(j, k, m, n+1)$	$(n+1)\sigma_2$		$n\sigma_2$	$(j, k, m, n-1)$

Table V. Transitions from/to state (j, k, m, n), if $j + k = T$ and $m > 0$.

The state equations according to the latter two groups may easily be achieved from the relevant Tables IV and V. It must be emphasized, that for the model TB the transition from state (j, k, m, n) to state $(j-1, k, m+1, n)$ with a transition coefficient of $j\mu_1 s$ doesn't exist. This follows from the service mode (b) i.e. if there is a free server there are no waiting demands.

With other words, returning to telex designations, if there are outgoing messages in service mode (b) the operator always tries her message to put through. If she fails in setting up the connection to the called station, she either makes an attempt with the next message (putting back the former message to the end of the queue), or she tries to put through the same message with continuous reattempts. For this time period the telex device is blocked for incoming messages.

3.2. *Intensity correction in Model* TC

The purpose of the correction is to achieve the same load originated by No. 1 demands on the servers, without distinguishing "call set up" and "message" states. The average service time should remain the same i.e. $\dfrac{1}{\mu_2}$. If total perseverance is assumed $(\sigma_1 = 0)$ no No. 1 demand gives up before having got service, so all demands have to make $\dfrac{1}{1-s}$ attempts, as an average. The last one of these attempts will be successful. In this case the corrected intensity of primary demands will obviously be

(5) $$\lambda_1^* = \lambda_1 \left(\frac{\mu_2}{\mu_1(1-s)} + 1 \right).$$

This relation was proved by I o n i n and S e d o l for a single one-way server with "blind repetition" and total perseverance. With some additions this idea could be used also for server groups [12].

Comparing Model TB with Model TC, the corrected intensity approximation proved to be a very good one also for the both-way servers of our investigations. Some numerical results will be given in Section 4.

3.3. *The solution of the equation system*

The rather complicated system of state equations has no closed solution. To solve this type of equation systems the successive overrelaxation method may be advantageously used. Optimum speed of this iterative procedure can be achieved by proper selection of the overrelaxation factor ω involved.

The existence of this optimum ω is exactly proven for many cases (see e.g. Young [13]), but to use it e.g. the spectral radius of a matrix derived from the matrix of the equation system should also be determined. Since the curve of the number of iterations is often flat in the neighbourhood of the optimum, a nearly best empirical ω will satisfy the needs in many cases. It's almost impossible to determine beforehand the best procedure, i.e. whether to calculate e.g. the spectral radius with an other iterative method or to use the empirically best ω in order to have minimum calculation time.

As regards the number of waiting and repetition positions there is no mathematical restriction, M and N may be finite or infinite. But if $\sigma_1 = 0$ or/and $\sigma_2 = 0$ and $\left(\dfrac{\lambda_1}{\mu_1} + \dfrac{\lambda_1 + \lambda_2}{\mu_2} \right) \geqslant T$, than only finite M and N are permitted system has no solution, the steady state probabilities do not exist. In practice one deals always with finite N and M, for the infinite case M and N should be choosen large enough. Up to now the approximate Model TC has not been tested for finite M and N.

4. SYSTEM CHARACTERISTICS

From the state probabilities already determined the characteristics of the system may be calculated. As an example the formulae of some characteristic values for Model TB are given below. The indices refer to No. 1 and No. 2 demands, respectively.

(a) Offered traffics

$$(6) \qquad A_1 = \lambda_1 \left(\frac{1}{\mu_1} + \frac{1}{\mu_2} \right)$$

(7) $\quad A_2 = \lambda_2 \dfrac{1}{\mu_2} \, .$

(b) Average number of demands at waiting and repetition positions

(8) $\quad K_1 = \displaystyle\sum_{j=0}^{T} \sum_{n=0}^{N} \sum_{m=0}^{M} mP(j, T-j, m, n)$

(9)
$$K_2 = \sum_{t=0}^{T-1} \sum_{j=0}^{t} \sum_{n=0}^{N} nP(j, t-j, 0, n) +$$
$$+ \sum_{j=0}^{T} \sum_{m=0}^{M} \sum_{n=0}^{N} nP(j, T-j, m, n) \, .$$

(c) Probability of departure (loss)

(10) $\quad B_1 = \dfrac{K_1 \sigma_1}{\lambda_1} + \displaystyle\sum_{j=0}^{T} \sum_{n=0}^{N} P(j, T-j, M, n)$

(11) $\quad B_2 = \dfrac{K_2 \sigma_2}{\lambda_2} + \displaystyle\sum_{j=0}^{T} \sum_{m=0}^{M} P(j, T-j, m, N) \, .$

(d) Carried traffics (load)

total traffic

(12)
$$Y = \sum_{t=0}^{T-1} \sum_{j=0}^{t} \sum_{n=0}^{N} tP(j, t-j, 0, n) +$$
$$+ \sum_{j=0}^{T} \sum_{m=0}^{M} \sum_{n=0}^{N} TP(j, T-j, m, n)$$

call set up traffic

(13)
$$Y_s = \sum_{t=0}^{T-1} \sum_{j=0}^{t} \sum_{n=0}^{N} jP(j, t-j, 0, n) +$$
$$+ \sum_{j=0}^{T} \sum_{m=0}^{M} \sum_{n=0}^{N} jP(j, T-j, m, n)$$

message traffic

(14) $\quad Y_m = Y - Y_s$

repetition traffic

(15) $\qquad Y_R = Y_s - \dfrac{\lambda_1}{\mu_1} (1 - B_1) .$

(e) Repetition factor (average number of call attempts per message)

(16) $\qquad \beta_1 = \dfrac{Y_R \mu_1}{\lambda_1} + 1 = \dfrac{Y_s \mu_1}{\lambda_1}$

(17) $\qquad \beta_2 = \dfrac{K_2 \alpha_2}{\lambda_2} + 1 .$

(f) Average waiting time (per time units, for all messages)

(18) $\qquad t_{w1} = \dfrac{K_1}{\lambda_2}$

(19) $\qquad t_{w2} = \dfrac{K_2}{\lambda_2} .$

For Model TA the formulae are somewhat different because of the different state space. For this model there is "blind repetition" on the sender side and so the repetition factor for No. 1 demands will have the form

(20) $\qquad \beta_1 = \dfrac{K_1 \alpha_1}{\lambda_1} + 1 .$

For Model TC the calculations were carried out with the corrected intensity.

Formulae similar to those of (6)-(19) may be derived in this case too, taking into account, that the state space has only three dimensions. Only the total traffic, Y, can be calculated directly making use of state probabilities, other traffic quantities should be interpreted as follows

$$ Y_M^* = \lambda_1 \dfrac{1}{\mu_2} (1 - B_1^*) + \lambda_2 \dfrac{1}{\mu_2} (1 - B_2^*) $$

(Quantities with an asterisk are related to Model TC.)

It was found, that there is a very good coincidence between the TB and TC characteristic values except for the average number of waiting No. 1 demands. The matching of TC and TB was made on an "identical load" basis but the holding time distribution of No. 1 demands had been changed. So it is obvious, that the average queue length can't be the same for both cases. The following modified value should be used

(21) $\qquad K_{1M}^* = K_1^* \dfrac{\lambda_1}{\lambda_1^*}$.

In Table VI some comparisons are given between exact and approximate data.

	$\lambda_1 = \lambda_2 = 0.1$		$\lambda_1 = \lambda_2 = 0.3$	
	exact	approximate	exact	approximate
K_1	$1{,}142 \ 10^{-3}$	$1{,}105 \ 10^{-3}$	$0{,}02730$	$0{,}02655$
K_2	$1{,}186 \ 10^{-2}$	$1{,}185 \ 10^{-2}$	$0{,}28280$	$0{,}28313$
B_1	$5{,}74 \ 10^{-4}$	$5{,}56 \ 10^{-4}$	$4{,}609 \ 10^{-3}$	$4{,}425 \ 10^{-3}$
B_2	$5{,}94 \ 10^{-3}$	$5{,}93 \ 10^{-3}$	$4{,}718 \ 10^{-2}$	$4{,}719 \ 10^{-2}$
Y	$0{,}22158$	$0{,}22158$	$0{,}65088$	$0{,}65098$
Y_s	$0{,}02221$	$0{,}02223$	$0{,}06636$	$0{,}06647$
Y_M	$0{,}19937$	$0{,}19935$	$0{,}58452$	$0{,}58452$
Y_R	$0{,}00889$	$0{,}00891$	$0{,}02655$	$0{,}02664$
β_1	$1{,}66646$	$1{,}66725$	$1{,}66367$	$1{,}66160$
β_2	$1{,}01779$	$1{,}01777$	$1{,}14140$	$1{,}14157$
t_{w1}	$0{,}01143$	$0{,}01105$	$0{,}09100$	$0{,}08849$
t_{w2}	$0{,}11860$	$0{,}11849$	$0{,}94268$	$0{,}94377$

Table VI. Comparison of TB and TC results

Other parameters of the system of Table VI are

$$\mu_1 = 7.5 \qquad s = 0.4 \qquad \sigma_1 = 0.05 \qquad T = 2$$

$$\mu_2 = 1 \qquad \alpha_2 = 0.15 \qquad \sigma_2 = 0.05.$$

The following conclusions may be drawn

(i) The approximation is very good for carried traffic, for it's parts and for the receiving side characteristics.

(ii) For sender side the approximation is also good, the deviation from exact values is less then 5%, for practical purposes the corrections used are quite satisfactory.

(iii) The deviation slightly increases with the increase of s.

5. NUMERICAL EXAMPLES

With the mathematical models described some calculations were made for a traffic engineering project. Here are some results given to illustrate the capabilities of the method.

In Fig. 5 the average queue length K_1, is shown as a function of the offered No. 1 message traffic: $\dfrac{\lambda_1}{\mu_2}$.

Parameters are the number of devices T and the offered No. 2 message traffic: $\dfrac{\lambda_2}{\mu_2}$.

The probability of departure (loss) B_2 is given in Fig. 6. On the horizontal axis one may find the offered message traffic, the parameters are the same as in the previous case. For the same offered load per device a slight decrease in B_2 may be experienced with increasing number of devices.

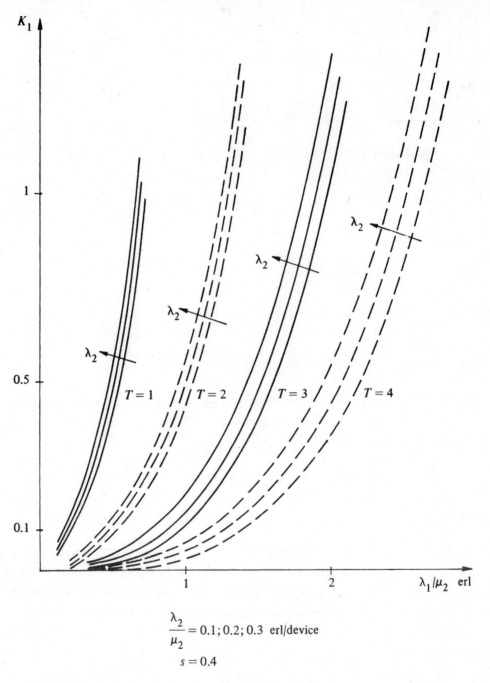

$$\frac{\lambda_2}{\mu_2} = 0.1; 0.2; 0.3 \ \text{erl/device}$$

$$s = 0.4$$

Fig. 5. Average queue length as a function of offered message traffic

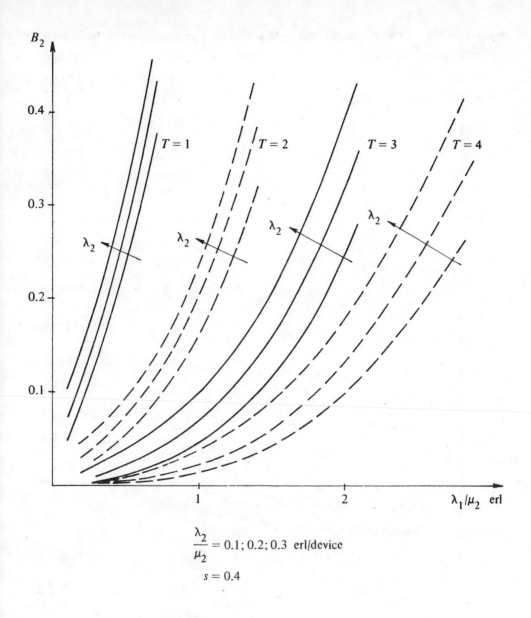

$$\frac{\lambda_2}{\mu_2} = 0.1; 0.2; 0.3 \text{ erl/device}$$

$$s = 0.4$$

Fig. 6. Probability of loss for incoming calls as a function of offered
message traffic

In Fig. 7 the effect of increasing rejection probability, s, is shown. There is practically no difference between B_1, values for $s = 0$ and $s = 0.4$, respectively, but approaching $s = 1$ the increase in B_1 loss is significant.

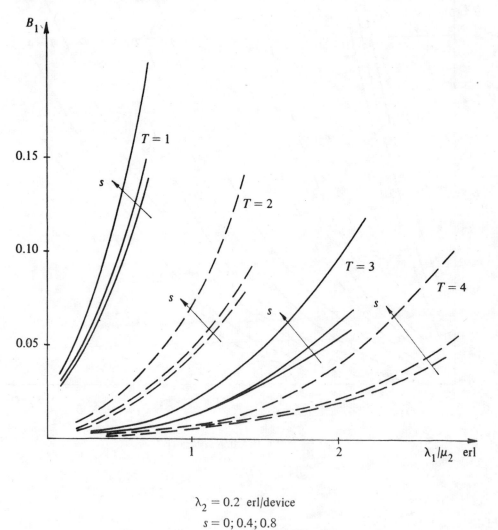

$$\lambda_2 = 0.2 \text{ erl/device}$$
$$s = 0; 0.4; 0.8$$

Fig. 7. Probability of loss for outgoing calls as a function of offered outgoing message traffic and of the probability of being unsuccessful for any reason

6. CONCLUSIONS

The traffic engineering method presented here suffers from some obvious weaknesses, as it has already been mentioned. The basic assumptions of the properties of telex traffic can not be regarded accurate.

On the other hand no proper information exists up to now on these telex traffic characteristics either. Thus, at present neither exact theoretical calculations nor substancial computer simulations can be performed.

Considering this our approach seems to be justified, and has a lot of advantages. (a) A widely used mathematical model could be adapted for a very complex problem. (b) Almost all special features of the problem could be incorporated in to this model. (c) All necessary information about the traffic performance of the systems investigated could be calculated. (d) For the time there is no better method at disposal to solve the probelms raised.

ACKNOWLEDGEMENTS

The work was supported by the *Central Telegraph Department of the Hungarian PTT.* Mr. I. Feczkó Deputy Manager, and Mr. J. Szeidler from the Development Section paid high interest to the project and gave valuable help during the investigations.

Thanks are due to Dr. P. Molnár, Head of Develpoment Department of BHG who gave the possibility to carry out the work. The author is very indebted to his colleagues, especially to Miss M. Ágostházi and Mrs. K. Szentirmai for their assistance.

REFERENCES

[1] R. Chapuis, Common carrier telecommunications in the world economy, *Telecom.,J.,* 39 (1972), 601-620.

[2] F.M. Badran, Verteilungsfunktionen des Verkehrs in Fernschreib-Wählanlagen, *Frequenz,* 17 (1963), 184-188.

[3]   F.M. Badran, Verlustberechnung für volkommene Schaltglieder-gruppen in Fernschreib-Wählanlagen, *Frequenz,* 17 (1963), 217-226.

[4]   N. Hattori – K. Yamada, Traffic characteristics of the international telex calls, 7. ITC 1973, Stockholm, Prebook, 443/1-8.

[5]   P. Henneberg, Die Wiederholung von Anrufversuchen als besondere Form der Wechselwirkung zwischen Fernsprechteilnehmern und Fernmeldenetz, *Fernmelde Ing.,* 28, 7 (1974), 1-38.

[6]   M. Ágostházi – G. Gosztony, Characteristics of repeated telephone calls, (in Hungarian), *Hiradástechnika,* 26 (1975), 109-119.

[7]   P. Le Gall, Sur l'utilisation et l'observation du taux d'efficacité du trafic téléphonique, 7. ITC 1973, Stockholm, Prebook, 443/1-8.

[8]   J.W. Cohen, Basic problems of telephone traffic theory and the influence of repeated calls, *Philips Tel. Rev.,* 18 (1957), 49-100.

[9]   A. Elldin, Approach to the theoretical description of repeated call attempts, *Ericsson Techn.,* 23 (1967), 345-407.

[10] G.L. Ionin – J.J. Sedol, Telephone systems with repeated calls, 6. ITC, 1970, Munich, Prebook, 435/1-5.

[11] P. Le Gall, Sur l'influence des répétitions d'appels dans l'écoulement du trafic téléphonique, *Ann. des Télécom.,* 25 (1970, 339-348.

[12] G.L. Ionin – J.J. Sedol, Fully-availability groups with repeated calls and time of advanced service, 7. ITC 1973, Stockholm, Prebook, 137/1-4.

[13] D.M. Young, *Iterative solution of large linear systems,* Academic Press, New York – London, 1971, 570.

Géza Gosztony

Beloiannisz Telecommunication Works, 1509 Budapest, Pf. 2., Hungary.

COLLOQUIA MATHEMATICA SOCIETATIS JÁNOS BOLYAI

12. PROGRESS IN OPERATIONS RESEARCH, EGER (HUNGARY), 1974.

ON A STOCHASTIC PROGRAMMING PROBLEM WITH RANDOM COEFFICIENTS

SYLVIA HALÁSZ

In his paper [1] A. Prékopa considered the following problem in §5:

What is the probability that the solution to the following system of equations is positive

(1)
$$a_{11}x_1 + \ldots + a_{1m}x_m = b_1$$
$$a_{m1}x_1 + \ldots + a_{mm}x_m = b_m$$

if the a_{ij}'s are independent non-negative random variables of the same continuous distribution and $b_i = 1$ for all i.

Note. the matrix A of the system (1) is non-singular with probability 1, therefore there will be a unique solution with probability 1. We call a solution positive, if each of its components is positive.

This problem can be transformed by introducing the vectors $s_j =$

$$= \frac{a_j}{\sum\limits_{i=1}^{m} a_{ij}}, \quad \text{which will have the property that} \quad \sum\limits_{i=1}^{m} s_{ij} = 1, \quad \text{where}$$

$s_{1j}, \ldots, s_{mj}$ are the components of the vector s_j. This means that the s_j are points of the $m-1$ dimensional simplex

$$S = \left\{ z \mid \sum_{i=1}^{m} z_i = 1, \; z_i > 0 \right\}.$$

Thus we can reformulate the problem in the following manner: choose m independent, identically distributed random points in the simplex S, what is the probability that the convex hull of these points contains the center of gravity of S?

The above question arises in connection with the problem of the statistical behaviour of the number of vertices of random convex polyhedra. Here we shall consider a question which, in a sense, is a generalization of this, and at the same time it is a stochastic programming problem in its own right.

Our problem is the following: given system (1), for what b_i's is the probability of the positivity of the solution maximal, if the a_{ij}'s are exponentially distributed with parameter 1? (It is easy to show that the result holds if we only assume that the parameter of the a_{ij}'s is the same within each row.)

Transforming system (1), as earlier, by introducing the vectors s_j, denoting the new matrix of the system by T and using the fact that the probability of the positivity of the solution remains the same if we multiply the vector b by a positive constant, we can write this problem in the following way:

$$\max P\{T^{-1}b > 0\}$$

$$(2) \qquad b_1 + \ldots + b_m = 1$$

$$b_i \geq 0, \quad i = 1, \ldots, m.$$

This problem has a geometric interpretation. Using the well-known result that the s_j vectors represent points, which are uniformly distributed in the simplex S, the problem can be reformulated the following way: choose m independent, uniformly distributed random points in the simplex S, and consider their convex hull C, which point of S will be contained in C with maximal probability?

In connection with this problem A. P r é k o p a conjectures: this probability will be maximal for the center of gravity of S.

This means that the optimum in (2) is achieved for $b_i = \dfrac{1}{m}$, which in turn implies that the optimum in (1) is attained when every component of the right hand side vector is the expected value of the distribution of the a_{ij}'s. (In case of different parameters of the exponential distribution in each row, the optimum is attained when each component of the right hand side is equal to the expected value of the distribution of the a_{ij}'s in that row).

In a joint paper with D.J. Kleitman we worked out the probability

$$P\{T^{-1}b > 0\}$$

(3) $\qquad b_1 + b_2 + b_3 = 1$

$\qquad b_i > 0, \quad i = 1, 2, 3$

in the form of an integral, and showed this integral to have its unique maximum at the center of gravity, which proves A. Prékopa's conjecture for $m = 3$.

But if we only want to prove that the center of gravity gives the optimum in (3), then it is possible to give a simpler proof, using geometric rather than analytic arguments. Here we give the geometric interpretation of the result and an outline of this simpler proof. The proofs of some propositions are not given here. These can be found in [2].

Theorem. *Fix a point P in a given triangle T. Take three independent random points from the uniform distribution over T, denote the random triangle formed by them by Δ. Let P_0 denote the center of gravity of T. Then*

$$\max_{P \in T} \Pr\{P \in \Delta \mid P \in T\} = \Pr\{P_0 \in \Delta\}$$

i.e. the probability of being covered by Δ *will be maximal for the center of gravity of the triangle.*

Proof. Obviously it is sufficient to prove the result for equilateral triangles, from that it follows for arbitrary ones.

Let us introduce the following notations:

$A_T =$ area of the given triangle T

$A(P, R) =$ area of triangle cut out from T by line PR

$$A(P) = \frac{1}{A_T^2} E_R\{A(P, R)(A_T - A(P, R))\}$$

$\rho(P) = \Pr\{P \in \Delta\}.$

Proposition 1. $\rho(P) = 3A(P) - \frac{1}{2}.$

Proof. Let X_1, X_2, X_3 be the random points.

$\Pr\{\text{line } PX_i \text{ separates the other two random points } |P \in \Delta\} = 1$

$\Pr\{\text{line } PX_i \text{ separates the other two random points } |P \notin \Delta\} = \frac{1}{3}.$

Since $2A(P) = P\{\text{line } Px_i \text{ separates other two random points}\}.$
Therefore $2A(P) = 1 \cdot P\{P \in \Delta\} + \frac{1}{3} P\{P \notin \Delta\} = \rho(P) + \frac{1}{3}(1 - \rho(P))$

$$2A(P) = \frac{1}{3} + \frac{2}{3}\rho(P)$$

hence $\rho(P) = 3A(P) - \frac{1}{2}.$

Definition 1. Let the vertices of T be denoted by A, B and C. Let λ_A be equal to the distance of P from the line BC divided by the distance of A from BC.

Remark. With the above notation $P = \lambda_A A + \lambda_B B + \lambda_C C$ and P can be described by the parameters $\lambda_A, \lambda_B, \lambda_C$. (The center of gravity of T will be characterized by $\lambda_A = \lambda_B = \lambda_C = \frac{1}{3}$.) Obviously $\lambda_i \geqslant 0$, $\lambda_A + \lambda_B + \lambda_C = 1.$

Proposition 2. *If for a point* P *at least one of the* λ's *is less than* $\frac{1}{4}$, *there is only one line through* P *splitting the area of* T *in half.*

Proposition 3. *If there is only one line through* P *splitting the area of* T *in half, then moving* P *along this line toward the center will increase* $\rho(P)$.

Proposition 4. *If for a point* P *all* λ's *are at least* $\frac{1}{4}$, *then moving* P *along a line* FG *parallel to one of the sides of* T, *toward one of the center-vertex lines of* T, *into a point* P', $\rho(P)$ *will incrase.*

Proof. When moving P to P', contributions to the difference between $\rho(P)$ and $\rho(P')$ come from random triangles, two of whose vertices lie on a line separating P from P'.

We show that $\dfrac{dA(P)}{dx} > 0.$

The contribution from a line through P in a given direction to $\dfrac{dA(P)}{dx}$ will contain the following 3 factors:

(1) A factor measuring the number of lines in the given direction encountered in moving a distance dx along FG.

(2) A factor measuring the probability of one vertex of the random triangle lying on either side of FG on a line in the given direction.

(3) A factor measuring the difference between the probabilities that closing the random triangle, two vertices of which lie on our line, it will include P or P'. This will be proportional to the difference in area on the two sides of the line considered. So those lines will favour P' which have more area on the side containing the center.

The proof proceeds by combining the lines favouring P by their reflection about FG, and showing that the net contribution will still favour P'.

Proposition 5. *If* P *is on one of the center-vertex lines of* T, *then moving it on this line toward the center,* $\rho(P)$ *will increase.*

Conclusions. It follows from the above propositions that starting from any point P of the triangle T we keep increasing $\rho(P)$ by performing the following steps:

(1) If all λ's are less than $\frac{1}{4}$, then move P along the only line splitting the area of T in half toward the center by dx. Repeat this until at least one λ will achieve $\frac{1}{4}$.

(2) If at least one of the λ's (say λ_c) is at least $\frac{1}{4}$, move P along a line parallel to side AB toward a center-vertex line by a distance dx. Repeat this until P hits a center-vertex line of T.

(3) Move P along the center-vertex line it is on, toward the center by a distance dx. Repeat it until P reaches the center.

This means that the center of gravity of T gives the unique maximum for $\rho(P)$.

REFERENCES

[1] A. Prékopa, On the number of vertices of random convex polyhedra, *Periodica Math. Hung.*, 2 (1972), 259-282.

[2] S. Halász – D.J. Kleitman, A note on random triangles *Studies in Applied Math.*, Vol. LIII, No. 3, September 1974.

Sylvia Halász

Institute for Building Economy and Organization, Budapest.